The Risen Crucified Christ in Galatians

Robert A. Bryant

Society of Biblical Literature
Atlanta

THE RISEN CRUCIFIED
CHRIST IN GALATIANS

Robert A. Bryant
Ph.D., Union Theological Seminary and
Presbyterian School of Christian Education, 2000
Paul J. Achtemeier, Dissertation Advisor

Library of Congress Cataloging-in-Publication Data

Bryant, Robert A. 1958–
    The risen crucified Christ in Galatians / Robert A. Bryant.
        p. cm. — (Dissertation series / Society of Biblical Literature ; no. 185)
    Includes bibliographical references.
    ISBN 1-58983-021-0 (alk. paper)
        1. Bible. N.T. Galatians—Criticism, interpretation, etc. 2. Bible. N.T.
    Galatians—Language, style. I. Title. II. Dissertation series (Society of
    Biblical Literature); no. 185.

    BS2685.52.B79   2001
    227'406—dc21   2001049627

07 06 05 04 03 02 01   5 4 3 2 1

Printed in the United States of America
on acid-free paper

THE RISEN CRUCIFIED
CHRIST IN GALATIANS

SBL
Dissertation Series

Saul M. Olyan,
Old Testament Editor

Mark Allan Powell,
New Testament Editor

Number 185
The Risen Crucified
Christ in Galatians

Robert A. Bryant

TABLE OF CONTENTS

ACKNOWLEDGEMENTS

Dissertations are never produced in isolation, despite all outward appearances. Such works are ultimately a culmination of efforts by a community of scholars, colleagues, friends, and family members. It is appropriate, therefore, to acknowledge from the beginning my deep appreciation for this larger community and to give special thanks to particular members of it.

First, it is a pleasure to acknowledge the contribution of those scholars who helped equip me for this study, especially William P. Brown, Ray C. Jones, Peter Lampe, James L. Mays, S. Dean McBride, Mathias Rissi, W. Sibley Towner, and Steven S. Tuell. I am especially appreciative of my advisor, Paul J. Achtemeier, and my dissertation committee members, John T. Carroll and Jack D. Kingsbury, for they have not only helped prepare me for such a study but have also read and commented on this work as it took shape. For their counsel and encouragement, I am especially grateful. I thank all of these Christian servant scholars, though none of them should be held accountable for the views presented here or the errors that remain in it. Naturally, I am also appreciative of all the scholars whom I cite in this study, and I hope that I have represented their works fairly

Secondly, I am indebted to my colleagues who, by sharing themselves, have invigorated my study and research, especially Naoto Kamano, Ming-Chin Lin, Jeff Riddle, and Craig Vondergeest. I am also grateful to Michael Barram, Peter Chang, Andrew Das, Jay Dozier, Johann Kim, Bill Malas, Jim Miller, and Michael Vines.

Of course, every work of this type depends upon the support of institutions that provide the necessary support and resources for research and publication. I am indebted to Union Theological Seminary and Presbyterian School of Christian Education for its assistance and to the entire library staff for its help in gathering resources for this project. Special thanks are due to Patsy Verreault for her tireless efforts in securing interlibrary loan materials and to Robert Benedetto for his guidance in matters of formatting and style. I am indebted also to Presbyterian College and my colleagues there for their support and helpfulness. Much appreciation is also directed toward the Society of Biblical Literature for publishing this work and to Leigh Andersen for her gracious editorial assistance.

Finally, I want to express my thanks to my family and friends. Were it not for their encouragement and support over these many years, the difficulties of this work would have been compounded and the joys greatly diminished. I am grateful to my friends at Cross Roads Presbyterian Church in Mebane, North Carolina, for the enduring joy of their faithful fellowship. I am thankful, also, for my brothers and sisters—by birth and by marriage—for their encouragement and care; for my parents, Joe and Anne Bryant, whose love and encouragement throughout my life helped make this journey possible; and for my parents-in-law, Bennie and Libby Shumate, who have been most generous in their constant support. Most of all, I thank my wife, Leigh Ann, whose sacrificial love and care of me and our children is an abiding testimony of Christ's own love for us all. To our children, Stephen and Susannah, I am also indebted for they have helped me keep this work in perspective.

CHAPTER ONE

GALATIANS AND THE PROBLEM OF GENRE

Galatians has long been celebrated as Paul's maverick epistle. Hailed as "the offspring of passion, a fiery utterance of chastisement and defense"[1] and "a lion turned loose in the arena of Christians,"[2] it is polemical and confrontational to the core. It does not sit easily with Paul's predominately good-natured epistles. Here the fervor of Paul's self-expression leaves no doubt that he viewed the issues at stake between himself and his opponents in Galatia as a matter of life and death. But what prompted this heated response? And why did Paul express himself as he did?

For different reasons, Paul's letter to the Galatians has attracted close attention throughout the centuries,[3] but these two questions especially have caused scholars to scrutinize it today. One line of scholarly research has centered on the historical matters of the letter's addressees,[4] date,[5] situation, and

---

[1]Adolf Deissmann, *Light From the Ancient East: The New Testament Illustrated by Recently Discovered Texts of the Graeco-Roman World*, trans. Lionel R. M. Strachan (New York: Hodder and Stoughton, 1910), 229.

[2]Richard N. Longenecker, *Galatians*, Word Biblical Commentary, vol. 41 (Dallas: Word Books, 1990), lvii.

[3]For a detailed treatment of the impact of Galatians in the history of Christian thought, see R. N. Longenecker, *Galatians*, xlii–cxix. For a brief overview, see Charles B. Cousar, *Galatians*, Interpretation: A Bible Commentary for Teaching and Preaching (Atlanta: John Knox Press, 1982), 1–11.

[4]At issue here is whether the recipients were in the southern area of the newly expanded Roman province of Galatia (the "South Galatian theory" or "province hypothesis") or in the original Galatian territory of central Asia Minor (the "North Galatian theory" or "territory hypothesis"). A decision either way does not affect significantly the interpretation of the letter's contents, but it does impact one's assessment of Paul's chronology and the dating of the letter. See the following and related references there: Hans Dieter Betz, *Galatians: A Commentary on Paul's Letter to the Churches in Galatia*, Hermeneia (Philadelphia: Fortress Press, 1979), 1–5; F. F. Bruce, *The Epistle to the Galatians: A Commentary on the Greek Text* (Grand Rapids: William B. Eerdmans Publishing Co., 1982), 3–18; E. deW. Burton, *A Critical and Exegetical Commentary on the Epistle to the Galatians*, International Critical Commentary (New York: Charles Scribner's Sons, 1920), xvii–xliv; J. A. Fitzmyer, "The Letter to the Galatians," in *The Jerome Biblical Commentary*, eds., R. E. Brown, et al., vol. 2 (Englewood, N.J.: Prentice Hall, 1968), 236–46; R. N. Longenecker, *Galatians*, lxi–lxxii; James Moffatt, *An Introduction to the Literature of the*

1

the identification of Paul's opponents.[6] The other line of research concerns the letter's relation to its Greco-Roman epistolary and rhetorical environment. Both lines have proved fruitful, and both have contributed much to our understanding of Paul and the early church.

This study joins those works that have focused on the literary and rhetorical nature of Galatians in order to understand better the meaning and significance of its contents. It asks about the form and function of Paul's argument. For instance, why does Paul argue in this letter as he does? What is the purpose of the letter? How does it reflect Greco-Roman literary conventions? Is it to be viewed primarily as literature or rhetoric, as a type of letter or a type of speech? And is the central concern of the letter a defense of the gospel, a matter of Paul's apostleship, a promotion of justification by faith, a description of life in the Spirit, a case for including Gentiles into the church, or something else? In short, how is Galatians to be interpreted?

New Testament, 3d (Edinburgh: T & T Clark, 1949), 83–107; Franz Mussner, *Der Galaterbrief*, Herders theologischer Kommentar zum Neuen Testament (Freiburg: Herder, 1974), 3–9. Of these interpreters, Bruce, Burton, and Longenecker favor the "South theory" while Betz, Fitzmyer, Moffatt, and Mussner support the "North theory."

[5]This issue is inseparably related to the question of the letter's destination, and for lack of evidence only approximate dates are possible. Galatians is typically considered either early (A.D. 50–55 according to many who uphold the "South theory") or late (A.D. 53–58 for many who uphold the "North theory;" but see Betz [*Galatians*, 9–12] who posits an early date for this letter directed to the north). See R. Jewett, *A Chronology of Paul's Life* (Philadelphia: Fortress Press, 1979), 103, and P. Vielhauer, *Geschichte der urchristlichen Literatur* (Berlin: de Gruyter, 1975), 79–81, 110–11. For a workable compromise, see F. J. Matera, *Galatians*, Sacra Pagina Series, vol. 9 (Collegeville, Minn.: The Liturgical Press, 1992), 19–26. On the difficult problem of relating Acts to Galatians, see P. J. Achtemeier, *The Quest for Unity in the New Testament Church: A Study in Paul and Acts* (Philadelphia: Fortress Press, 1987).

[6]Investigations into the opponents and situation behind the letter are of great importance and have attracted considerable attention. Advances have been made, but there is no firm consensus. See J. M. G. Barclay, "Mirror–Reading a Polemical Letter: Galatians as a Test Case," *JSNT* 31 (1987): 73–93; B. H. Brinsmead, *Galatians—Dialogical Response to Opponents*, SBLDS 65 (Chico, Calif.: Scholars Press, 1982) and a review by D. E. Aune, *CBQ* 46 (1984): 145–47; J. Eckert, *Die urchristliche Verkuendigung im Streit zwischen Paulus und seinen Gegnern nach dem Galaterbrief*, Biblische Untersuchungen 6 (Regensburg: Pustet, 1971); T. David Gordon, "The Problem at Galatia," *Int* 41 (1987): 32–43; G. Howard, *Paul: Crisis in Galatia*, SNTSMS 35 (Cambridge: Cambridge University Press, 1979); R. Jewett, "The Agitators and the Galatian Congregation," *NTS* 17 (1970–71): 198–212; G. Lüdemann, *Opposition to Paul in Jewish Christianity*, trans. M. E. Boring (Minneapolis: Fortress Press, 1989), 1–32, 97–103 [trans. with additions of *Paulus der Heidenapostel*, vol. 2: *Antipaulinismus im fruehen Christentum*, FRLANT 130 (Göttingen: Vandenhoeck & Ruprecht, 1983)]; W. Lütgert, *Gesetz und Geist: Eine Untersuchung zur Vorgeschichte des Galaterbriefs* (Gütersloh: Bertelsmann, 1919); J. Louis Martyn, "A Law–Observant Mission to Gentiles: The Background of Galatians," *SJT* 38 (1985): 307–24; W. Schmithals, "Judaisten in Galatien?" *ZNW* 74 (1983): 27–58; idem, *Paul and the Gnostics*, trans. J. E. Steely (Nashville: Abingdon Press, 1972).

Even as scholars are strongly divided over historical matters of the letter's background, so, too, is there no consensus on the letter's form, function, and compositional relation to its rhetorical and literary environments. Modern interpreters of Galatians present a bewildering maze of genre classifications and textual divisions for the letter—an immediate indication of confusion about Paul's purpose and the logical order of his argument. Yet research into the epistolary and rhetorical character of Galatians continues because New Testament scholarship recognizes the important relation between the form and purpose of biblical texts.[7] How a message is expressed can be as important to the meaning of the communication as the content of the message itself. Similarly, modern biblical scholarship understands the importance of examining the larger social contexts out of which biblical texts come.[8] The early Christian community and its scriptures did not emerge ex nihilo.

In this chapter, then, we will build upon the contributions of scholars who have shown that the form and character of a composition like Galatians are helpful for understanding it as a whole. In particular, we will summarize contributions of epistolary and rhetorical research that have aided our understanding of Paul's letters and then investigate a variety of attempts to

---

[7]The pioneering methodologies presented in the works of Martin Dibelius (*Die Formgeschichte des Evangeliums* [1919; Eng.: *From [Oral] Tradition to Gospel* [London: Ivor Nicholson and Watson, Ltd., 1934; reprint James Clarke, 1971; New York: Charles Scribner's Sons, 1935]), Hermann Gunkel ("Fundamental Problems of Hebrew Literary History," in *What Remains of the Old Testament* [London: George Allen & Unwin, 1928]), and Rudolf Bultmann (*The History of the Synoptic Tradition* [Ger. 1921; Eng.: New York: Harper and Row, 1963; Oxford: Basil Blackwell, 1963]) have continued to influence and advance biblical scholarship, though not without challenge and modification. Rhetorical criticism, epistolary criticism, structural linguistics, et al, have demonstrated the complexity of analyzing matters of genre, setting, and function which earlier form critics did not yet understand.

[8]Sociological interpretation seeks to understand biblical texts through sociological theory and methodology. Of the many contributions for NT studies, see especially: Adolf Deissmann, *Paul: A Study in Social and Religious History* (London: Hodder and Stoughton, 1912); Robert M. Grant, *Early Christianity and Society* (New York: Harper and Row, 1977); Martin Hengel, *Judaism and Hellenism* (Philadelphia: Fortress Press, 1969); Leander Keck, *The New Testament Experience of Faith* (St. Louis: Bethany Press, 1976); Abraham Malherbe, *Social Aspects of Early Christianity* (Baton Rouge, La.: Louisiana State University Press, 1977); Wayne A. Meeks, *The First Urban Christians: The Social World of the Apostle Paul* (New Haven, Conn.: Yale University Press, 1983); John E. Stambaugh and David L. Balch, *The New Testament in Its Social Environment* (Philadelphia: The Westminster Press, 1986); Stanley K. Stowers, "The Social Sciences and the Study of Early Christianity" in *Approaches to Ancient Judaism*, vol. 5, ed. W. S. Green (Missoula, Mont.: Scholars Press, 1978); Gerd Theissen, *Sociology of Early Palestinian Christianity* (Philadelphia: Fortress Press, 1978).

render a satisfactory account of the genre,[9] structure, and meaning of Galatians. Throughout this review of scholarship we will seek to discern the strengths and weaknesses of the different proposals. We will also consider apparent relationships between these assessments of the letter's form and subsequent interpretations of the letter's meaning. Then, in light of all this we will set forth the proposal of this study which will be developed in the succeeding chapters. It will become evident that Paul's path of reasoning in Galatians is not so tortured as some have supposed.[10]

I. PAUL AND GRECO-ROMAN LETTERS

The literary landscape of the New Testament is dominated by letters. Of the twenty-seven writings of the NT, twenty are letters.[11] Of these, thirteen are attributed to Paul, and—in a rare show of scholarly consensus—seven are indisputably so.[12] Galatians is undeniably a communication from Paul himself.[13] Paul was a letter-writer, and he freely adopted and adapted the epistolary conventions of his day as he proclaimed the good news of Jesus Christ to the Gentiles of the first century A.D. Greco-Roman world. Let us then review some important aspects of the relationship between Paul's letters and his literary

---

[9]Throughout this study I will use the term "genre" in reference to distinguishable types of written and oral communication that are categorized by their shared features of similar form (including structure and style), content, and function. See David E. Aune, *The New Testament in Its Literary Environment*, Library of Early Christianity, ed. W. A. Meeks, vol. 8 (Philadelphia: Westminster Press, 1987), 13.

[10]Cf. Burton L. Mack, *Rhetoric and the New Testament*, Guides to Biblical Scholarship (Minneapolis: Fortress Press, 1990), 67.

[11]Here I am using the term "letter" loosely to include those NT writings that resemble letters but may not have actually been so. Excluded from the letter genre are the Gospels, Acts, Hebrews, and Revelation, though there are encapsulated letters in Acts 15:23–29; 23:26–30; and Rev 2–3.

[12]References to Paul's letters throughout this study will be of the seven undisputed letters: Romans, 1 & 2 Corinthians, Galatians, Philippians, 1 Thessalonians, and Philemon.

[13]Arguments for glosses and interpolations are not convincing. See for instance J. C. O'Neill, *The Recovery of Paul's Letter to the Galatians* (London: SPCK, 1972), who contends that "the Galatians we possess is not entirely Paul's" (8). O'Neill's proposal is a revival of similar failed efforts by Marcion, Spinoza, Locke, B. Bauer, and C. H. Weisse. See also J. Smit, "The Letter of Paul to the Galatians: A Deliberative Speech," *NTS* 35 (1989): 1–26, who argues that Gal 5:13–6:10 "contains a rounded off fragment of Paul added to the letter at a somewhat later time" (25), and J. Bligh, *Galatians in Greek: A Structural Analysis of St. Paul's Epistle to the Galatians with Notes on the Greek* (Detroit: University of Detroit Press, 1966), who conjectures that "the archetype from which the whole manuscript tradition derives was neither St. Paul's autograph nor a transcript of it, but a copy reproduced from memory" (2). The majority of scholars, however, accept Galatians as a single unified composition of Paul's.

environment in order to understand better the problem of genre in Paul's letter to the Galatians.

The Place of Letters in the Greco-Roman World

Throughout the Greco-Roman world, letters were used in a variety of ways. The Greek term ἐπιστολή ("epistle" or "letter"), which originally referred to an oral message sent by a messenger, was applied broadly to nearly any written document sent from one party to another. The earliest Hellenistic letters were primarily military reports and commands, but the practice of letter-writing spread widely and served other ends as writing materials became more available and the custom became more established. Letters were also used for conducting business, carrying out governmental functions, reporting legal and political matters, and expressing a host of personal concerns.[14]

Letters were typically a replacement for a personal visit. And many people, such as the great Greek orator Isocrates (ca. 436–388 B.C.), viewed the letter as inferior to a personal encounter because letters lacked the power and persuasiveness of personal oral delivery and the sender had no way of ensuring that the message was fully and properly understood.[15] Seneca (ca. 5 B.C.–A.D. 65) also regarded the letter as a less desirable substitute for a personal visit. To a friend he wrote:

> I never receive a letter from you without being in your company forthwith. If the pictures of our absent friends are pleasing to us, though they only refresh the

---

[14]See especially W. G. Doty, *Letters in Primitive Christianity*, Guides to Biblical Scholarship (Philadelphia: Fortress Press, 1973), 1–19. See also D. E. Aune, *The New Testament in Its Literary Environment*, 158–82; M. Luther Stirewalt, *Studies in Ancient Greek Epistolography*, SBL Resources for Biblical Study 27 (Atlanta: Scholars Press, 1993), 1–25, 67–87; S. K. Stowers, *Letter Writing in Greco-Roman Antiquity*, Library of Early Christianity, ed. W. A. Meeks, vol. 5 (Philadelphia: The Westminster Press, 1986), 27–47; J. L. White, *Light From Ancient Letters* (Philadelphia: Fortress Press, 1986), 191–93.

[15]Isocrates, *Isocrates*, 3 vols., trans. George Norlin, LCL (London and New York: William Heinemann Ltd. and G. P. Putnam's Sons, 1928–29), vol. 1, "To Philip," 25–26: "I do not fail to realize what a great difference there is in persuasiveness between discourses which are spoken and those which are to be read, and that all men have assumed that the former are delivered on subjects which are important and urgent, while the latter are composed for display and personal gain. And this is a natural conclusion; for when a discourse is robbed of the prestige of the speaker, the tones of his voice, the variations which are made in the delivery, and, besides, of the advantages of timeliness and keen interest in the subject matter; when it has not a single accessory to support its contentions and enforce its plea, but is deserted and stripped of all the aids which I have mentioned; and when someone reads it aloud without persuasiveness and without putting any personal feeling into it, but as though he were repeating a table of figures,—in these circumstances it is natural, I think, that it should make an indifferent impression upon its hearers." See also "To Dionysius," 1.2.

memory and lighten our longing by a solace that is unreal and unsubstantial, how much more pleasant is a letter, which brings us real traces, real evidences, of an absent friend! For that which is sweetest when we meet face to face is afforded by the impress of a friend's hand upon his letter—recognition.[16]

Paul was a letter-writer, and he no doubt shared some of these sentiments about the inferiority of letters to a personal visit and direct interpersonal communication.[17] But it does not necessarily follow, as some modern interpreters have supposed, that Paul *always* considered the letter a poor substitute for a personal visit.[18]

As Paul likely understood, there are unique advantages to committing an argument to writing. The great orator Quintilian (c. A.D. 35–95) himself conceded that "it is the pen which brings at once the most labor and the most profit."[19] That is because letter-writing, like other types of writing, made possible the preservation of speech, ideas, and events. Moreover, it allowed for more carefully constructed and detailed arguments than spontaneous speech might permit, although Cicero (106–43 B.C.) acknowledged that good speakers are those "who have been well trained, who have had extensive practice in writing, and who, even if they speak extemporaneously, will produce something which resembles a speech written down beforehand."[20]

Letters enabled persons to maintain relationships and to express their ideas, concerns, or commands with precision across even vast distances when their own physical presence and speech were impossible or imprudent. Letters were also quite useful in communicating important messages between estranged parties, especially in matters where the outcome of a personal visit was

---

[16]Seneca, *Ad Lucilium epistulae morales*, trans. R. M. Gummere, LCL (Cambridge, Mass.: Harvard University Press, 1953), Ep. 40:1; cited in Abraham J. Malherbe, *Ancient Epistolary Theorists* (Atlanta: Scholars Press, 1988), 29, S. K. Stowers, *Letter Writing in Greco-Roman Antiquity*, 29 and Jerome Murphy-O'Conner, *Paul the Letter-Writer: His World, His Options, His Skills* (Collegeville, Minn.: The Liturgical Press, 1995), 45.

[17]Cf. Rom 1:10; 1 Cor 16:5; Phil 1:7–14; 1 Thess 2:17f; Phlm 9–10. See also Col 4:10, 18 and Eph 3:1. On the priority of speaking over writing, see also Cicero *Orator*, trans. H. M. Hubbell, LCL (Cambridge, Mass.: Harvard University Press, 1942), 141 and Quintilian *Institutio Oratoria*, trans. H. E. Butler, LCL (Cambridge, Mass.: Harvard University Press, 1995), 10.1.2–3.

[18]Cf. R. Funk, *Language, Hermeneutic, and Word of God: The Problem of Language in the New Testament and Contemporary Theology* (New York: Harper & Row, 1966), who argues that Paul always emphasized the priority of the spoken word over the written word. Funk insists that "Paul resists the written word" (249) and "wrote reluctantly" for he viewed "the letter as a poor substitute" for the spoken word and a personal visit (269). See also W. G. Doty, *Letters in Primitive Christianity*, 76, who writes that "in the Pauline letters we are confronted with a writer who at best wrote unwillingly, and whose 'natural' preference was to speak directly with those to whom circumstances forced him to address letters."

[19]Quintilian *Institutio Oratoria* 10.3.1.

[20]Cicero *Orator* 200.

uncertain or might result in greater conflict or harm. Consider an anonymous letter from a penitent son:

> I know that I err in treating you badly. Wherefore, having repented, I beg pardon for the error. But for the Lord's sake do not delay to forgive me. For it is just to pardon friends who stumble, and especially when they desire to obtain pardon. . . . I entreat you, mother, be reconciled to me.[21]

Or again in a letter of a son to his father. The son, Terentianus, sought his father's consent in order to bring a woman home with him whom he planned to marry. Terentianus, however, expected strong opposition, perhaps even rejection from his father and so he wrote to persuade his father to be favorably inclined toward the woman.

> Already two years ago I wanted to take a woman into my house, but I did not allow myself nor am I now permitting myself to take someone apart from your approval . . . If it is the case somehow that the woman I bring down should be one who, for my sake, would be more kindly disposed to you and to have more consideration for you than for me, it works out that I do you a favor rather than that I am a cause of blame by you. . . [and if (?)] you remain immovable for the rest of your life I will renounce (the right to) my woman. If not, whatever woman you approve is the one that I also want.[22]

When emperor Claudius was at odds with the Alexandrians, he expressed himself forcefully in a letter when he wrote "if you do not lay to rest this destructive and obstinate hostility against one another, I shall be forced to show what a benevolent ruler can become when turned to (inflict) a justified wrath."[23] Paul himself wrote to the Corinthian Christians warning, "Shall I come to you with a stick?" (1 Cor 4:21). Obviously, letters could be preferred over the sender's personal presence by both sender and recipient alike, especially in difficult circumstances. Written correspondences could prepare the way for either a favorable resolution to a problem or a peaceful visit.

Of course, letters—like speech—could be disputed by the recipients. Letters were considered an effective extension of the sender's "voice" that "ought to be written in the same manner as a dialogue, . . . as one of the two sides of a dialogue."[24] And as with any dialogue, a disturbing correspondence

---

[21]SelPap I 120=BGU III 846 in J. L. White, *Light From Ancient Letters*, 181. See also the letter from a prodigal son, Antonis Longus, to his mother, Nilus (2d cent. A.D.) in Deissmann, *Light from the Ancient East* (1910), 176–80.

[22]PMich VIII 476 in J. L. White, *Light From Ancient Letters*, 173–74.

[23]CPJud II 153 (=PLond VI 1912) in J. L. White, *Light from Ancient Letters*, 136.

[24]Demetrius quoting Artemon, the editor of Aristotle's *Letters*, in *De Elocutione*, trans. W. Rhys Roberts, LCL, in Aristotle *The Poetics* (Cambridge, Mass.: Harvard University Press, 1927), 4.223. See also S. K. Stowers on the influence of rhetorical theory and practice upon letters. There are limitations, of course, but the close relationship between them is unmistakable. See, for instance, S. K. Stowers, *Letter Writing in Greco-Roman Antiquity*, 51–57. Also Abraham J. Malherbe, *Ancient Epistolary Theorists*, 2–11; G. A.

could evoke a swift oral rebuttal and reproof among the listening assembly.
Controversies over the contents of letters were a well-known occurrence in the
ancient Greco-Roman world. So in his lengthy discussion of handling
controversies over written documents, Cicero advised that:

> If the writer is alleged to have meant one thing and written another, the advocate
> who follows the letter will say, 'It is not right for us to argue about the intent of
> one who left us a clear indication of his intent in order that we might not be able to
> dispute it.'[25]

In this way, then, the letter could be advantageous to the sender by limiting the
boundaries of the discussion and controlling the basic terminology, content, and
agenda for any subsequent correspondence or discourse. Simply put, letter-
writing was not without its peculiar advantages. Letters were not always poor
replacements for a personal visit.

The recipients could also benefit from letters because the substance of the
message or any part of it could be analyzed and reviewed in ways not possible
in spontaneous oral communication.[26] Moreover, because letters retained the
precise content of a particular message, the recipients could, if the message was
well-written and expressed the writer's views exactly, know more certainly the
writer's meaning and intent. Again, though, letters could be misunderstood and
there was often no opportunity for immediate clarification from the sender,
except perhaps through an advocate who accompanied the letter and could
speak on the sender's behalf.[27] Similarly, just because something was written
did not guarantee coherency and accuracy of thought or expression.[28]

Kennedy, *New Testament Interpretation through Rhetorical Criticism*, Studies in Religion
(Chapel Hill: University of North Carolina Press, 1984), 31; and J. L. White, *Light From
Ancient Letters*, 189–93.

[25]Cicero *De Inventione*, trans. H. M. Hubbell, LCL (Cambridge, Mass.: Harvard
University Press, 1949), 2.116–143; quote is from 2.128.

[26]Cf. Quintilian *Institutio Oratoria* 10.1.19, where he writes, "Reading, however, is
free, and does not hurry past us with the speed of oral delivery; we can reread a passage
again and again if we are in doubt about it or wish to fix it in the memory."

[27]It was possible, of course, for letter bearers to provide some clarification of the
writer's intentions or meanings and even to add supplementary points to the letter in its
delivery. See J. L. White, *Light From Ancient Letters*, 214–17. See also Doty, *Letters in
Primitive Christianity*, 45–46. It is not clear how Paul sent his letter to the Galatians, either
by an unknown carrier or trusted messenger, and whether or not additional communication—
written or oral—accompanied it. The Greek word "epistle" (ἐπιστολή), however, referred to
oral communications entrusted to messengers (Cf. D. E. Aune, *The New Testament in Its
Literary Environment*, 158, who cites Herodotus 4.10.1 and Thucydides 7.11.1). Doty
contends that Paul likely used trusted messengers who were among his "co-workers." Doty
also points to the Deutero-Pauline witnesses of the practice in Eph 6:21–22 and Col 4:7–8.

[28]Cicero observed long ago that poor communication could "contain so many dark
and obscure sentences as to be scarcely intelligible" (*Orator* 9.30).

Nevertheless, the written communication provided the recipients a tangible record of a communication which they could keep, read again, analyze, and answer with reciprocating care.

In short, letters had particular advantages for both senders and recipients and so written correspondences were widely employed throughout the Greco-Roman world of late Western antiquity. Paul certainly used letters advantageously in his mission to the Gentiles, and he himself bears witness to this point through his preservation of a criticism aimed against him. Paul wrote, "they say, 'His letters are weighty and strong, but his bodily appearance is weak, and his speech is of no account'" (2 Cor 10:10). That Paul's opponents understood his correspondences as powerful communications that were "weighty and strong" runs counter to the views of many ancient rhetoricians and modern commentators who have viewed the letter as always second-best to personal presence and oration. Here, however, Paul's opponents attribute greater prestige and power to his written rhetorical letters.[29]

Paul utilized the epistolary medium of his culture effectively for communicating the gospel of Jesus Christ. But Paul was not the only Christian who used letters. Some of his letters are responses to letters that he received, and there are other letters of the NT that are not attributed to Paul. The early church certainly found the letter form to be useful in spreading the gospel. The letter genre also came to dominate the literary works of the early church fathers, and letters are still influential in the church today as pastoral letters and encyclicals.[30] It may seem natural, then, that the literary forms of letters in the NT should have always drawn the church's attention. This has not been the case, however, for, while it is true that the letters of the NT have been imitated and repeatedly probed for their theological content with both fascination and frustration, it is predominately a modern phenomenon that the letters have been examined methodically for their literary characteristics and relations to their Greco-Roman environment.

The Rise of Epistolary Criticism of the New Testament

Adolf Deissmann is widely credited with launching the debate over the literary character of Paul's letters, and the subsequent discussion has

---

[29]Frank W. Hughes, *Early Christian Rhetoric and 2 Thessalonians*, JSNTSup 30 (Sheffield: Sheffield Academic Press, 1989), 19. It is also worth noting that criticizing an opponent's physical appearance was a standard rhetorical practice. Cf. Cicero *De Inventione* 1.35; Quintilian *Institutio Oratoria* 5.10.23–31; *Rhetorica ad Herennium*, trans. Harry Caplan, LCL (Cambridge, Mass.: Harvard University Press, 1954), 3.7.14. See also Acts 4:13 where Peter and John are called ἀγράμματοί καὶ ἰδιῶται.

[30]For a discussion of the early and persistent prominence of the epistolary genre in the church, see Doty, *Letters in Primitive Christianity*, 65–81.

precipitated an increased understanding of Paul and his literary environment.[31] Deissmann's primary contribution to biblical criticism—following his extensive study of newly discovered Greek papyri, inscriptions, and other Greco-Roman literature—was the identification of Biblical Greek with common Koine Greek of the first century A.D.[32] But Deissmann's study of the broader Greco-Roman social and literary contexts to which the New Testament belongs also led him to draw a distinction between "real letters" (letters) and "non-real letters" (epistles). Deissmann concluded that Paul's correspondences resemble "real" Greek letters written to particular persons in response to specific situations. He contended that these personal letters lack any concern for literary conventions of form and style. They are warm, private, and spontaneous. Epistles, on the other hand, are not really letters but are carefully constructed works of literature that adhere to common forms. Cold and impersonal, they are written for larger audiences regarding general matters for the present and the future. The only common bonds between letters and epistles that Deissmann acknowledged were their beginnings, thanksgivings, and closings. As for Galatians, Deissmann saluted its keen letter-like spontaneity as "genius flashing like summer lightning."[33]

Developments in the Epistolary Analysis of Paul's Letters

Since Deissmann's distinctions between "letter" and "epistle" at the beginning of the 20th century, scholars have widely accepted his position regarding the occasional nature of Paul's correspondences. Deissmann's conclusions, however, that Paul's letters are spontaneous works without formal structure or style which belonged exclusively to the Hellenistic private letter genre are no longer tenable. Throughout the remainder of the 20th century, scholars have made important refinements and necessary corrections of Deissmann's thesis. As a result, Paul's correspondences are now viewed as far more carefully composed and more intricately related to a larger literary

---

[31]See, for instance, Stanley K. Stowers, *Letter Writing in Greco-Roman Antiquity*, 17–26. See also Adolf Deissmann, *Light From the Ancient East*, 224–246; idem, *Bible Studies. Contributions Chiefly from Papyri and Inscriptions to the History of the Language, the Literature, and the Religion of Hellenistic Judaism and Primitive Christianity*, trans. A. Grieve (Edinburgh: T & T Clark, 1901), 3–59.

[32]Prior to Deissmann's work, Biblical scholars were bewildered by much of the grammar and syntax of NT Greek. There were evidences of literary Greek and Semitic influences, but NT Greek is neither classical Greek nor Hellenized Hebrew. With Deissmann's discoveries, however, the study and understanding of NT Greek expanded exponentially.

[33]Deissmann, *Light from the Ancient East* (2d, 1927), 237. See also William G. Doty, "The Classification of Epistolary Literature," *CBQ* 31 (1969): 185–89; and Stowers, *Letter Writing in Greco-Roman Antiquity*, 18. For Deissmann's own summaries, see *Light from the Ancient East* (1910), 224–46, 230–32.

environment than Deissmann understood.[34] An overview of these developments is helpful for understanding the problem of genre in Galatians.

A Broad Field of Literary Relationships. To begin with, Paul's letters fuse a variety of characteristics from a broad range of Greco-Roman[35] literary traditions. There are, for instance, many Hellenistic letter types and, while none of Paul's letters perfectly match existent letter forms or any of the theoretical examples in the epistolary handbooks,[36] a closer inspection of their purposes, styles, and organization provides the basis for some scholars to align Paul's letters with particular types of Hellenistic letters. Thus Philemon has been classified as a letter of recommendation, Philippians as a letter of thanksgiving, Romans as an ambassadorial letter, 1 Corinthians as a letter of response and instruction, and Galatians as a letter of rebuke and request.[37] There are also

---

[34]Apart from the evident epistolary conventions in the salutation, thanksgiving, and closing, Deissmann viewed Paul's letters as chaotic compositions driven by the situation and the whim of the author (*Bible Studies*, 3–59). This assessment, however, is wrong. See W. G. Doty, *Letters in Primitive Christianity*, 21–47; J. Sykutris, "Epistolographie" in *Paulys Realencyclopädie der klassischen Altertumswissenschaft: Supplementband 5*, ed. August Friedrich von Pauly, 218–219; P. Wendland, *Die urchristlichen Literaturformen*, 3d ed., Handbuch zum Neuen Testament, band 1 (Tübingen: Mohr, 1912), 344. See also J. L. White, *Light From Ancient Letters*; S. K. Stowers, *Letter Writing in Greco-Roman Antiquity*; and D. E. Aune, *The New Testament in Its Literary Environment*. For a demonstration of how Deissmann's presuppositions shaped his conclusions, see Doty, "The Classification of Epistolary Literature," 185.

[35]It is important to recognize that Greco-Roman includes not only Greek and Latin but also Hebrew and Aramaic.

[36]Two epistolary handbooks especially give evidence of the wide variety of letter types. The *Typoi Epistolikoi* (300 B.C.–A.D. 300), which are incorrectly attributed to Demetrius of Phalerum (Pseudo Demetrius), presents 21 epistolary types and seems aimed for intermediate instruction regarding epistolary style, though it may also be that they are not intended for instruction but rather were used by professional letter writers (so Malherbe, *Ancient Epistolary Theorists*, 7–9, 14–16). The *Epistolimaioi Characteres* (4th–6th c. A.D.) is attributed to Libanius in one manuscript and to Proclus (Pseudo Libanius) in another. It is more expansive in its enumeration of 41 letter types, and it was likely used by professionals, too (Malherbe). See J. L. White, *Light From Ancient Letters*, 189–90. See also S. K. Stowers, *Letter Writing in Greco-Roman Antiquity*, 51–57; D. E. Aune, *The New Testament in Its Literary Environment*, 161–62. See also R. N. Longenecker, "On the Form, Function, and Authority of the New Testament Letters," in *Scripture and Truth* (Grand Rapids, Mich.: Zondervan, 1983), 101–14. There are many types of letters including letters of friendship, family letters, letters of praise and blame, apologetic letters, and letters of exhortation, advice and mediation. Some letter types also possess narrower groups which share common characteristics. Stowers (*Letter Writing in Greco-Roman Antiquity,* 91–152), for instance, distinguishes within the category of "exhortation and advice" narrower categories of paraenetic, advice, protreptic, admonition, rebuke, reproach, and consolation.

[37]Cf. R. Jewett, "Romans as an Ambassadorial Letter," *Int* 36 (1982): 5–20; G. W. Hansen, *Abraham in Galatians: Epistolary and Rhetorical Contexts*, JSNTSup 29 (Sheffield:

many affinities between Paul's letters and those of Epicurus who, although predating Paul by four centuries and presenting a radically different message, also wrote to encourage, exhort, advise, teach, settle disputes, and maintain relationships.[38] Moreover, there are close parallels between Paul's use of the Greek language and that of Epictetus, a Stoic philosopher and near contemporary of Paul.[39]

The Greco-Roman letter tradition, however, is not the only link between Paul's letters and his literary environment. Other literary traditions apparent in Paul's letters include chiastic structures,[40] midrashic exegetical and interpretive techniques,[41] early Christian confessions and hymns,[42] and fixed ethical traditions.[43] Relationships have also been observed between Paul's letters and

---

Sheffield University Press, 1989), 25; and R. N. Longenecker, *Galatians*, ciii. We will examine their epistolary assessments of Galatians below.

[38]Stowers, *Letter Writing in Greco-Roman Antiquity*, 39–40; Doty, *Letters in Primitive Christianity*, 23.

[39]Cf. Adolf Bonhöffer, *Epiktet und das Neue Testament*, Religionsgeschichtliche Versuche und Vorarbeiten, x. bd. (Giessen: A. Töpelmann [vormals J. Ricker], 1911), and D. S. Sharp, *Epictetus and the New Testament* (London: Charles L. Kelly, 1914). See also C. Thomas Rhyne, *Faith Establishes the Law*, SBLDS 55 (Chico, Calif.: Scholars Press, 1981) on Epictetus' and Paul's similar uses of rhetorical questions followed by μὴ γένοιτο and the significance of this understanding for interpreting Paul.

[40]See especially Ian H. Thomson, *Chiasmus in the Pauline Letters*, JSNTSup 111 (Sheffield: Sheffield Academic Press, 1995) for an extensive treatment of this topic and an exhaustive bibliography. See also J. W. Welch, ed., *Chiasmus in Antiquity: Structures, Analyses, Exegesis* (Hildesheim: Gerstenberg, 1981), Joachim Jeremias, "Chiasmus in den Paulusbriefen," *ZNW* 49 (1958): 145–56, and N. W. Lund, *Chiasmus in the New Testament: A Study in Formgeschichte* (Chapel Hill, N.C.: University of North Carolina Press, 1942).

[41]Cf. Richard Lemmer, "Why Should the Possibility of Rabbinic Rhetorical Elements in Pauline Writings (eg. Galatians) Be Reconsidered?" in *Rhetoric, Scripture and Theology*, eds. Stanley E. Porter and Thomas H. Olbricht (Sheffield: Sheffield Academic Press, 1996), 161–79. See also Joseph Bonsirven, *Exégèse rabbinique et exégèse paulienne* (Paris: Beauchesne, 1939); David Daube, "Rabbinic Methods of Interpretation and Hellenistic Rhetoric," *HUCA* 22 (1949): 239–64; Joachim Jeremias, "Paulus als Hillelit," in *Neotestamentica et Semitica: Studies in Honour of Principal Matthew Black*, ed. E. E. Ellis and M. Wilcox (Edinburgh: T. & T. Clark, 1969), 88–94. For an opposing view regarding the relation between Greco-Roman rhetoric and Hillel's rules, see Jacob Neusner, "The Use of the Later Rabbinic Evidence for the Study of First–Century Pharisaism," in *Approaches to Ancient Judaism: Theory and Practice*, ed. W. S. Green (Missoula, Mont.: Scholars Press, 1978), 215–25.

[42]Cf. R. P. Martin, *Carmen Christi: Philippians 2:5–11 in Recent Interpretation and in the Setting of Early Christian Worship*, SNTSMS 4 (Cambridge: Cambridge University Press, 1967); K. Wengst, *Christologische Formeln und Leider des Urchristentums*, 2d, Studien zum Neuen Testament, Band 7 (Gütersloh: Gütersloh Verlagshaus, 1972).

[43]Cf. D. E. Aune, *The New Testament in its Literary Environment*, 194–97. See also Stowers, *Letter Writing in Greco-Roman Antiquity*, 91–152; and Doty, *Letters in Primitive Christianity*, 37–39, 68.

Jewish pastoral letters.[44] Of course, Old Testament (LXX) quotations and allusions figure most prominently in Paul's writing.[45]

In short, a closer inspection of literary and non-literary writings of the Greco-Roman world in relation to Paul's letters has revealed that Paul's writings are far more eclectic than Deissmann realized and are not solely related to real, private, non-literary Hellenistic letters. Paul freely adopted and adapted various elements from different literary traditions common in his day. Thus Deissmann's distinction between "real letter" and literary "epistle" is still valid for comparing writings such as Cicero's informal "personal letters" addressed to Atticus with the "moral epistles" of Seneca or Pliny. In this way the designation of "real letters" and "apparent letters" is still an important genre distinction.[46] But Paul's rich conflation of characteristics from these literary types and others renders the distinction obsolete for Paul. The terms "letter" and "epistle" are now used synonymously for Paul, and most scholars recognize that his writings stand between the two extremes and share characteristics of both.[47]

Public Occasional Letters. Closer scrutiny of Paul's works also reveals they are not as "private" as Deissmann's terminology suggested. Deissmann distinguished between "private" personal letters and "public" literary essays or official letters. Certainly Paul's undisputed letters show no indications of being written for the whole church everywhere as timeless pieces of literature. But

---

[44]Cf. R. N. Longenecker, "On the Form, Function, and Authority of the New Testament Letters," 102–04, who recognizes the difficulty of documenting this point because of the scarcity of examples but accepts it on the evidences of Acts 28:21 and the Talmud's frequent mention of pastoral letters. See also Longenecker's reference to J. Neusner, *A Life of Yohanan ben Zakkai, Ca. 1–80 C. E.*, 2d, (Leiden: Brill, 1970), 238–41. W. G. Doty, *Letters in Primitive Christianity*, 22–23, on the other hand, contends that while such letters could have been common, "It is difficult if not impossible to establish any direct lines of borrowing by Paul from Jewish epistolary materials in terms of their form and structure . . . Jewish epistolary materials primarily reflect official letter traditions rather than personal letter traditions; the possible continuity between Jewish letters and primitive Christian letters is difficult to establish, and seems less important (because of its restricted compass and lack of formal continuity) than the contacts with Hellenistic correspondence."

[45]See especially Richard B. Hays, *Echoes of Scripture in the Letters of Paul* (New Haven, Conn.: Yale University Press, 1989), and idem, *The Faith of Jesus Christ: An Investigation of the Narrative Substructure of Galatians 3:1–4:11*, SBLDS 56 (Chico, Calif.: Scholars Press, 1983).

[46]Stowers, *Letter Writing in Greco-Roman Antiquity*, 18.

[47]Ibid., p. 25. Stowers writes, "There is considerable variation among New Testament letters. But taken as a whole, they resemble neither the common papyri from the very lowest levels of culture and education nor the works of those with the highest levels of rhetorical training. They fall somewhere in between and have the cast of a Jewish subculture." See also Doty, *Letters in Primitive Christianity*, 45; and J. Murphy-O'Conner, *Paul the Letter-Writer*, 44.

neither are they strictly private correspondences. Paul's letters were to be read aloud to congregations and were often shared among churches.[48] Moreover, Paul often identifies colleagues as fellow senders of his letters and calls attention to others by his greetings—another sure indication of the letters' public character.[49] There are also many public issues which Paul addresses— matters such as his apostleship, living the Christian life together, and carrying out the mission of the church.

In these ways, Paul's letters are public communications. But because Paul's letters are occasional—that is, written not to society at large or even to whole communities but to specific groups of Christians with whom he is related—most epistolary critics follow the lead of Sykutris and Wendland and assert that the best designation of Paul's letters is "more private" than public.[50] The point is simply that Paul's letters are not "personal" and "private" in the usual sense of these terms today. Rather, they are occasional letters from an apostle who sees his task as proclaiming the gospel to particular Christian communities regarding their shared life in Christ. With this refinement, then, Deissmann's conclusion still stands that Galatians is a real letter of Paul written to a specific people in response to a particular situation.

Structured Correspondences. Another correction to Deissmann's thesis has been the widespread rejection of the view that Paul's letters are primarily spontaneous, unstructured communications.[51] Recognition of the broader literary relations between Paul's letters and other writings in his environment has spawned extensive studies of their unique and common structural characteristics. Consequently, it is now understood that Paul's letters utilize many conventional letter forms and devices common to the Hellenistic period. To begin with, closer examination of the structure of Paul's letters and Greco-Roman letters has revealed Paul's remarkable consistency in following the overall pattern of Greco-Roman correspondences. Since Paul and his contemporaries often used letters to address persons or communities they were unable or reluctant to visit personally, the letter logically reflects the principal

---

[48]See especially 1 Thess 5:27. See also Rom 1:7; 1 Cor 2:2; 2 Cor 1:1; Gal 1:2; Phil 1:1; 1 Thess 1:1; and Phlm 2.

[49]Cf. Rom 16:1–23; 1 Cor 1:1; 16:19–20; 2 Cor 1:1; etc. Even Paul's personal letter to Philemon includes in the address Apphia, Archippus, "and the church in your house."

[50]Cf. J. Sykutris, "Epistolographie," 187; P. Wendland, *Die urchristlichen Literatur– formen*, 345; G. W. Hansen, *Abraham in Galatians*, 22–23; W. G. Doty, *Letters in Primitive Christianity*, 25.

[51]Deissmann asserted that Paul "wrote with absolute abandon" and "never calculated for systematic presentment" (*Light from the Ancient East*, 1910 ed., 233–37). Although Deissmann recognized the recurrent conventions of greetings, thanksgivings, and closings in Paul's letters, he did not observe common patterns or bonds in the bodies of Paul's letters.

pattern of personal engagement and communication. It has three principal parts: the greeting, the body of the communication, and the farewell. All of Paul's letters follow this common Hellenistic letter pattern, though some scholars distinguish the parts further as opening, thanksgiving or blessing, letter body, paraenesis, and closing.[52]

Studies have also located Hellenistic epistolary formulas within the letter forms of Paul's openings,[53] thanksgivings,[54] and closings.[55] Some scholars have even sought to locate and interpret Hellenistic literary formulas which occur in the letter-body of Paul's correspondences. J. L. White contends that every letter-body is "composed of a formal opening, connective and transitional formulas, concluding 'eschatological climax' and apostolic *parousia* . . . [and] paraenesis."[56] T. Y. Mullins has argued further that certain formulas in the body tend to be clustered at strategic points that mark transitions from one section of the letter's body to the next.[57] Most epistolary critics, however, have focused more narrowly on certain formulaic aspects in different portions of the letter-body.[58] The result is nothing short of an avalanche of studies on Hellenistic epistolary forms and formulas in Paul's letters. Studies have been made of the presence and function of travelogues,[59] request formulas,[60] benedictions,[61]

---

[52]W. G. Doty, *Letters*, 27–42; Calvin J. Roetzel, *The Letters of Paul: Conversations in Context*, 3d (Louisville: Westminster/John Knox Press, 1991), 59–71.

[53]Cf. P. Wendland, *Die urchristlichen Literaturformen*; F.X.J. Exler, *The Form of the Ancient Greek Letter: A Study in Greek Epistolography* (Washington: Catholic University, 1923); Otto Roller, *Das Formular der paulinischen Briefe* (Stuttgart: Kohlhammer, 1933); and Franz Schnider and Werner Stenger, *Studien zum Neutestamentlichen Briefformular*, New Testament Tools and Studies, vol. 11 (Leiden: E. J. Brill, 1987), 3–68.

[54]Cf. Paul Schubert, *Form and Function of the Pauline Thanksgivings*, BZNW 20 (Berlin: Töpelmann, 1939); J. T. Sanders, "The Transition from Opening Epistolary Thanksgiving to Body in the Letters of the Pauline Corpus," *JBL* 81 (1962): 348–62; Terence Y. Mullins, "Disclosure, a Literary Form in the New Testament," *NovT* 7 (1964): 44–50; and Peter T. O'Brien, *Introductory Thanksgivings in the Letters of Paul*, Supplements to Novum Testamentum (Leiden: E. J. Brill, 1977).

[55]Cf. Gordon Bahr, "The Subscriptions in the Pauline Letters," *JBL* 89 (1969): 27–41. See also, Jeffrey A. D. Weima, *Neglected Endings: The Significance of the Pauline Letter Closings*, JSNTSup 101 (Sheffield: Sheffield Academic Press, 1994); and F. Schnider and W. Stenger, *Studien zum Neutestamentlichen Briefformular*, 108–81.

[56]J. L. White, *The Form and Function of the Body of the Greek Letter: A Study of the Letter-Body in the Non-Literary Papyri and in Paul the Apostle* (Missoula, Mont.: The Society of Biblical Literature, 1972), 71. See also Longenecker, *Galatians*, cii–cix.

[57]See especially T. Y. Mullins, "Formulas in New Testament Epistles," *JBL* 91 (1972): 387. See also Longenecker, *Galatians*, cvi, and G. W. Hansen, *Abraham in Galatians*, 27–31, who base their structural analysis of Galatians on the presence and clustering of epistolary formulas.

[58]For a comprehensive overview, see especially F. Schnider and W. Stenger, *Studien zum Neutestamentlichen Briefformular*.

[59]R. W. Funk, "The Apostolic Parousia: Form and Function," in *Christian History and Interpretation: Studies Presented to John Knox*, ed. W. R. Farmer, et al., 249–68

introductory formulas,[62] disclosure formulas,[63] confidence formulas,[64] autobiographical statements,[65] transitional practices,[66] self-praise and irony,[67] and rhetorical questions.[68]

Not surprisingly, these formulaic and structural similarities between Paul's letters and Hellenistic private letters have led some scholars to join J. L. White in asserting that "the common letter tradition, though certainly not the only tradition on which Paul depends, is the primary literary *Gattung* to which Paul's letters belong."[69] There are other views, of course, as we will see below. Some scholars interpret the genre of Paul's letters primarily in terms of classical rhetorical categories, especially in the case of Galatians. Nevertheless, nearly all would agree that Paul's letters have recognizable structural features and so are not the unstructured and chaotic correspondences Deissmann proposed. Deissmann's distinction between structured literary epistles and unstructured non-literary letters is no longer persuasive regarding Paul.

(Cambridge: Cambridge University Press, 1967), and T. Y. Mullins, "Visit Talk in New Testment Letters," CBQ 35 (1973): 350–58.

[60]C. J. Bjerkelund, *Parakalo: Form, Funktion und Sinn der Parakalo-Sätze in den paulinischen Briefen*, Bibliotheca Theologica Norvegica 1 (Oslo: Universitetsforlaget, 1967).

[61]R. Jewett, "The Form and Function of the Homiletic Benediction," *ATR* 51 (1969): 18–34; T. Y. Mullins, "Benediction as a New Testament Form," *AUSS* 15 (1977): 59–64.

[62]J. L. White, "Introductory Formulae in the Body of the Pauline Letter," *JBL* 90 (1971): 91–97.

[63]T. Y. Mullins, "Disclosure as a Literary Form in the New Testament," *NovT* 7 (1964): 44–50; idem, "Formulas in New Testament Epistles," *JBL* 91 (1972): 380–90.

[64]S. Olsen, "Epistolary Uses of Expressions of Self-Confidence," *JBL* 103 (1984): 585–97; idem, "Pauline Expressions of Confidence in His Addressees," *CBQ* 47 (1985): 282–95.

[65]G. Lyons, *Pauline Autobiography: Towards a New Understanding*, SBLDS 73 (Atlanta: Scholars Press, 1985).

[66]J. H. Roberts, "Pauline Transitions to the Letter Body," in *L'apôtre Paul: Personnalité, Style et Conception du Ministère*, BETL 73, ed. A. Vanhoye (Leuven: Leuven University Press, 1986), 93–99.

[67]C. Forbes, "Comparison, Self-Praise, and Irony: Paul's Boasting and the Conventions of Hellenistic Rhetoric," *NTS* 32 (1986): 1–30.

[68]W. H. Wuellner, "Paul as Pastor. The Function of Rhetorical Questions in First Corinthians," in *L'apôtre Paul: Personnalité, Style et Conception du Ministère*, BETL 73, ed. A. Vanhoye (Leuven: Leuven University Press, 1986), 49–77; Duane F. Watson, "1 Corinthians 10:23–11:1 in the Light of Greco-Roman Rhetoric: The Role of Rhetorical Questions," *JBL* 108 (1989): 301–18.

[69]J. L. White, *The Form and Function of the Body of the Greek Letter*, 3. White basis this conclusion on the genre characteristics of form and function. Matters of style, content, and length are not included. White is followed by W. G. Doty (*Letters in Primitive Christianity*, 23), G. W. Hansen (*Abraham in Galatians*, 24) and R. N. Longenecker (*Galatians*, ciii.). But B. H. Brinsmead (*Galatians—Dialogical Response*, 39), expressing the opposing view, concluded that the "papyri give us no help in understanding the overall structure of Paul's letters."

Here again, however, it is crucial to note that Paul was not constrained by epistolary structural conventions. He freely expanded epistolary forms and formulas to Christianize them, or he modified them in some other way to suit his purposes. Moreover, as the absence of a customary εὐχαριστῶ thanksgiving in Galatians shows, Paul was also quite capable of deleting an entire epistolary section or radically changing it. Thus, as White himself cautions, anyone relating Paul's letters to other letters of the period ought to be "wary of assuming simple congruence; we may anticipate that Paul will have modified the common letter tradition at various points."[70] More to the point, still, is Longenecker's plain observation that "none of Paul's letters corresponds exactly to the types described in the handbooks or as exemplified in the papyri."[71] Paul's letters undoubtedly share some of the formal characteristics of Greco-Roman letters, but Paul's letters are also quite unique in the sphere of Paul's literary environment.

Thanksgiving Periods and Epistolary Themes. Although Deissmann located the common "epistolary" and "letter" forms of openings, thanksgivings, and closings in the letters he studied, he attributed their presence in Paul's letters to mere adherence to secular custom.[72] Several generations later, however, Paul Schubert's *Form and Function of the Pauline Thanksgivings* (1939) challenged and overturned this assumption and stimulated many of the works cited above. Schubert's thesis has been refined over the years, but his essential point still stands: the thanksgiving periods[73] which usually follow the salutation and precede the letter-body are not banal social conventions but are in fact personalized religious expressions that highlight the writer's central concerns and correspond to major themes developed in the letter.[74]

The significance of this insight for interpreting Paul's letters is apparent, but Pauline scholars have since noted—nearly without exception—that Paul's letter to the Galatians has no thanksgiving. Paul evidently found nothing about the Galatians for which to be thankful, and so scholars must look elsewhere for

---

[70]J. L. White, *Light from Ancient Letters*, 74.

[71]R. N. Longenecker, *Galatians*, ciii.

[72]Cf. A. Deissmann, *Light from the Ancient East* (1910 ed), 168–69. On the use of εὐχαριστῶ, Deissmann writes, "This is a thoroughly 'Pauline' way of beginning a letter, occurring elsewhere in papyrus letters. . . St. Paul was therefore adhering to a beautiful secular custom when he so frequently began his letters with thanks to God."

[73]Aristotle used the term "period" in his discussion of rhetoric as "a form of expression which has a beginning and an end." Demetrius applied the term similarly to epistolary conventions to mean "a collection of members or phrases, arranged dexterously to fit the thought to be expressed." The Greco-Roman thanksgiving period is a rounded unit of thought in both oral and written communication. See Demetrius *De Elocutione* 10.

[74]P. Schubert, *Form and Function of the Pauline Thanksgivings*. See especially 179–85.

early signs of the letter's major topics. But here an important point needs to be made. Following his careful analysis of thanksgiving periods, Schubert himself was unwilling to concede the total absence of a thanksgiving in Galatians. Rather, recognizing Paul's remarkable freedom in adapting epistolary conventions, Schubert wrote:

> [I]t is not altogether correct to say that in Galatians the thanksgiving is entirely omitted. There is at the very end of the opening formula (1:5b) the singular clause ᾧ (sc. τῷ θεῷ) ἡ δόξα εἰς τοὺς αἰῶνας τῶν αἰώνων ἀμήν. It may very well be that Paul 'intended' this brief benediction as a substitute for his normal epistolary introduction—the thanksgiving. At all events, it is clear that the regular εὐχαριστῶ thanksgiving is omitted, because the specific epistolary situation did not permit it.[75]

We will examine this issue more thoroughly below, but the point here is simply that scholars now widely recognize the importance of Paul's letter openings for identifying important themes that are developed in the remainder of his letters.

Clearly, all of these studies on the epistolary character of Paul's letters have contributed much to our understanding of Paul's writings and their relationships with the larger Greco-Roman literary environment. Paul's letters are not only related to Hellenistic private papyri letters but show numerous connections to other writings in his social environment. Moreover, Paul's letters are understood to be "public" occasional letters that are purposefully structured. Of course, it is impossible to know for certain the extent of Paul's literary training, but there can be no doubt that he was quite familiar with the letter-writing conventions common in his day and that he used them effectively as he freely adopted and adapted them in proclaiming Christ among the Gentiles. Let us then turn to another important dimension of Paul's letters which New Testament scholars have sought to understand—the relation between Paul's letters and the oral environment in which Paul lived.

II. PAUL'S LETTERS AND GRECO-ROMAN RHETORIC

Paul was a letter writer, but he was also a public speaker. If the quest to understand the epistolary nature of Paul's letters is supported in part by the criticism that his letters were "weighty and strong" and his speech was "of no account" (2 Cor 10:10), then the quest for discerning the rhetorical aspects of Paul's letters is demanded in part by Paul himself who, responding to this very criticism, answered, "Let such people understand that what we say by letter when absent, we do when present" (2 Cor 10:11). Here Paul relates his speech and actions when he is bodily present with his "speech" and bearing when

---

[75]Ibid., 162.

"present" only by letter. That Paul's critics in Corinth disliked his oratory probably refers more to Paul's manner of speaking than to the substance and consequence of his oral messages, for Paul himself acknowledged his rhetorical ability prior to citing their complaint (2 Cor 10:1–6). And when Paul conceded the merit of their charge regarding his own unpolished oratorical delivery, he added, "Even if I am unskilled in speaking, I am not in knowledge" (2 Cor 11:6). That is, he may not be a professional orator (ἰδιώτης τῷ λόγῳ), but he does have knowledge (γνῶσις) of rhetoric and more importantly of God.[76]

In short, Paul's preaching evidently did not fit the popular oratorical ideal of "eloquence or superior wisdom" (1 Cor 2:1; ὑπεροχὴν λόγου ἢ σοφίας).[77] He did not preach the gospel with "words of wisdom, lest the cross of Christ be emptied of its power" (1 Cor 1:17). Rather, Paul understood his preaching to be a God-given task (Gal 1:15–16; Rom 1:1) to proclaim the word given to him through Christ and it was this word which effected "signs and wonders" (cf., Rom 15:18–19). For this reason, Paul typically credited God for the weight and strength of his message—written or spoken—and accepted personal responsibility for whatever was "of no account."[78] Nevertheless, he was

---

[76]W. A. Meeks, *The First Urban Christians*, 72. Note also that in Acts 4:13, Peter and John are called ἀγράμματοι καὶ ἰδιῶται. See also the interesting article by Edwin A. Judge in which he considers whether or not Paul was a "layman in rhetoric" ("Paul's Boasting in Relation to Contemporary Professional Practice," *AusBR* 16 [1968]: 37–50). Judge concluded that Paul deliberately wanted to distance himself from professional "sophistry" and so accepted the charge that he was not a professional orator. By his demonstration of oratorical ability, however, Paul uses the charge to his own persuasive advantage. These points were made earlier by A. T. Robertson in *A Greek Grammar of the Greek New Testament in the Light of Historical Research*, 3d ed. (New York: George H. Doran Company, 1919), 129.

[77]According to Cicero, eloquence was popularly measured by one's ability to "adapt his speech to fit all conceivable circumstances" (*Orator* 123). Superior wisdom was primarily a matter of content so that "no word should fall from the orator's lips that is not impressive and precise" (*Orator* 125). Also, Tacitus' definition of a true orator reflects the commonly held view that "Only he is an orator who can speak on any topic with beauty and elegance and in a manner that carries conviction, in keeping with the importance of the subject, appropriately to the circumstances, with pleasure to the audience" (Tacitus *Dialogus de Oratoribus*, trans. W. Peterson, LCL [Cambridge: Cambridge University Press, 1932], 30).

[78]Paul's referral to his rhetorical weaknesses may not only reflect his humility and repeated emphasis that faith must be based on God rather than on persuasive proofs or human wisdom, but it may also reflect his effort to establish a favorable ethos between himself and the recipients of his letters. Rhetoric had been viewed in a pejorative way at least as early as Plato's criticism of it in *Georgias* 450, 457, 463, but by Paul's day its common misuse was axiomatic. See, for instance, Tacitus (*Dialogus de Oratoribus* 30–32). Paul would certainly not have wanted his oratory to be misconstrued as manipulative and unrelated to truth and reality. It is also important to observe that Paul and his critics have in mind an "ideal orator" with which they are comparing him. Whatever their standards were, neither Paul nor his Corinthian critics rank him highly as a professional orator. Luke in Acts,

undoubtedly a knowledgeable and effective speaker who succeeded in drawing many Gentiles to Christ.[79] The Corinthians' critique of Paul's "unprofessional" rhetorical style does not mean that Paul was unskilled or impotent of persuasive speech.

Paul was a preacher, and in his letters he repeatedly calls attention to his principal apostolic task of *proclaiming* the good news of the gospel of Jesus Christ crucified and risen.[80] It should come as no surprise, then, that Paul's letters have oral qualities. Indeed, as we have already observed, Paul's letters were public correspondences that were written to be spoken aloud to assemblies (ἐκκλησίαις). This means the letters were written with the understanding that they would be heard as they were read or performed. Furthermore, the process of letter writing itself was largely an oral-aural transaction, and Paul typically followed the customary practice in his day of dictating to secretaries or amaneuenses.[81] The oratorical nature of Paul's letters is supported further by the visual appearance of the writings themselves. The original letter to the Galatians, like its earliest existent copies and other written documents of the period, would have lacked the visual clues of punctuation, sentence and paragraph divisions, and spacing between words. The result would have been a solid-text style of writing with random divisions of words that created sizable difficulties for readers, especially for those unfamiliar with the text.[82] The longer the text, the greater the obstacle, and Paul's letters are much larger than the common private Greco-Roman letter.[83] The appearance of the letter, then, emphasizes the predominately oral-aural environment of which Galatians is a

---

however, preserves an entirely different tradition of Paul's oratorical prowess. As John Knox put it, "No one would have been likely to say about the orator of Mars' Hill or before Agrippa, "As a speaker he amounts to nothing." (*Chapters in a Life of Paul* [Nashville: Abingdon Press, 1950], 92).

[79]Cf. Gal 3:1–2; 4:13f; 1 Cor 1:12, 17; 3:10; 2 Cor 1:19–22; 1 Thess 2:10–12; etc.

[80]Cf. Gal 1:16; Rom 1:5–17; 15:14–21; 1 Cor 1:17; 2:2; 9:16; 15:1; 2 Cor 1:8–10, etc.

[81]On the difficult problem of assessing the extent to which Paul used secretaries, see W. G. Doty, *Letters in Primitive Christianity*, 41. See also Rom 16:22; 1 Cor 16:21; Gal 6:11; Quintilian *Institutio Oratoria* 10.3.19–21. On scribes and messengers in general, see J. L. White, *Light From Ancient Letters*, 215–16.

[82]Paul J. Achtemeier, "Omne Verbum Sonat: The New Testament and the Oral Environment of Late Western Antiquity," *JBL* 109 (1990): 3–27.

[83]Ibid., 22. Achtemeier observed that Cicero's average letter length was 295 words and Seneca averaged 955 words. But Paul's average letter is 2,500 words long. Aune (*The New Testament in Its Literary Environment*, 205) catalogs the length of Paul's unusually long letters as follows: Romans has 7,094 words (920 stichoi); 1 Corinthians has 6,807 words (870 stichoi); 2 Corinthians has 4,448 words (590 stichoi); Galatians has 2,220 words (293 stichoi); Philippians has 1,624 words (208 stichoi); 1 Thessalonians has 1,472 words (193 stichoi); and Philemon has 328 words (38 stichoi). Regarding Paul's longer letters like Galatians, his listeners would be lost in a sea of wordiness apart from clear oral/aural clues in Paul's letters and a clear progression of thought.

part.[84] Of course, it also calls attention to the question of how the letter was presented to the churches of Galatia. We cannot know for certain how Paul used letter carriers or how the circulation of this letter—or any other—was conducted. It may be that Paul used trusted messengers who "preached" the letter, possibly with more bodily presence and rhetorical force than Paul presented. In Galatia it could have been one of the brothers who were with him (Gal 1:2). Or it may be that copies were made and distributed with or without any oversight from any of Paul's supporters. In any event, Paul "wrote" with an ear for how his letters might be heard as they were presented or read aloud.

Paul's letters reveal that he was not only a skilled letter-writer but was also knowledgeable of rhetorical techniques. Numerous studies on the oral character of Paul's letters have shown that Paul adopted and adapted many rhetorical conventions common in the Hellenistic world and this awareness has increased our understanding of Paul, of his relationship to his social environment, and of his letters. Galatians has been at the center of much of this scholarly activity since many rhetorical qualities are so evident in it. Let us then review some salient points regarding rhetoric in the Hellenistic culture of late Western antiquity in order to address Paul's apparent rhetorical skills in Galatians. This, too, will help us clarify the problem of genre in Galatians.

The Place of Rhetoric in the Greco-Roman World

Paul lived in a predominately oral-aural environment[85] where oratory was esteemed as "the mistress of all the arts."[86] With the rise of large democratic juries in the Greek society during the 5th century B.C., the art of rhetoric ascended to a position of chief importance in the Hellenistic world.[87] Its continued prominence is stated precisely by Cicero who asked rhetorically four centuries later, "Will anyone ever doubt that in peaceful civil life eloquence has always held the chief place in our state?"[88] In the ancient Greco-Roman world, public speaking was critically relevant to every aspect of life—from government, business, and industry to education, family matters, and courtship. Success in public life depended in large measure then—as in republics today—

---

[84]P. J. Achtemeier, "Omne Verbum Sonat," 10–11. Achtemeier shows conclusively the fundamental oral/aural nature of the NT texts and their relation to the oral environment out of which they emerged. See also Walter Ong, *Orality and Literacy: The Technologizing of the Word* (London: Methuen, 1982).

[85]P. J. Achtemeier, "Omne Verbum Sonat," 3–27.

[86]Tacitus *Dialogus de Oratoribus* 30–32. So also Quintilian, quoting Pacuvius, called oratory "the queen of all the world" (*Institutio Oratoria* 1.12.18).

[87]G. A. Kennedy, *The Art of Rhetoric in the Roman World: 300 B.C.–A.D. 300* (Princeton: Princeton University Press, 1972), 8.

[88]Cicero *Orator* 41.141.

on one's ability to speak well.[89] This was no less true for Paul who regarded his
principal task to be the work of announcing the gospel of Jesus Christ to the
Gentiles.

The study and practice of effective oral communication was a natural and
early development. Quintilian wrote that it came about as persons "observed
that some things were useful and some useless in speaking, and noted them for
imitation or avoidance."[90] These observations were codified into rhetorical
handbooks as early as the 5th century B.C.,[91] and a variety of handbooks spread
far and wide throughout the culture. These handbooks represented different
rhetorical traditions but each sought to classify, describe, order, and prescribe
the essential characteristics of persuasive speaking. As rhetoric permeated
public discourse and became the subject of books, so also it became a core
subject in Greco-Roman schools.[92] Courses were taught in Greek and Latin
literature, philosophy, rhetoric, and other areas of the liberal arts, but the focus

---

[89]Jerome Murphy-O'Conner, *Paul the Letter-Writer*, 65. See also Tacitus' *Dialogus
de Oratoribus* 36–40: "the more influence a man could wield by his powers of speech, the
more readily did he attain to high office . . . moreover, it was a conviction that without
eleoquence it was impossible for anyone either to attain to a position of distinction and
prominence in the community or to maintain it . . ."

[90]Quintilian *Institutio Oratoria* 3.2.3.

[91]Aristotle's *Art of Rhetoric* drew from earlier texts and became a prominent
handbook in the classical world from the 4th century B.C. on. Other standards include: the
anonymous *Rhetorica ad Alexandrum* which has been incorrectly attributed to Aristotle;
Cicero's *De Oratore, Oratoriae Partitiones, De Optimo Genere Oratorum, De Claris
Oratoribus, Topica,* and *De Inventione* (which Cicero discounted as a weak presentation of
his school notes; on this, Quintilian agrees [*Institutio Oratoria* 3.6.59]); the anonymous
Rhetorica ad Herennium (ca. 85 B.C.) which has been credited to Cicero (This is the earliest
complete Latin handbook and is clearly dependent on the Greek rhetorical tradition); and
Quintilian's *Institutio Oratoria*. See also G. A. Kennedy, "The Earliest Rhetorical
Handbooks," *AJP* 80 (1959): 169–78; idem, *The Art of Persuasion in Greece* (Princeton:
Princeton University Press, 1963); idem, *The Art of Rhetoric in the Roman World* (Princeton:
Princeton University Press, 1972); W. Kroll, "Rhetorik," *PW Sup.* 8 (1940): 1039–1138, esp.
1096–98; J. Martin, *Antike Rhetorik: Technik und Methode*, HAW II, 3 (Munich: Beck,
1974).

[92]Donald L. Clark, *Rhetoric in Greco-Roman Education* (New York: Columbia
University Press, 1967), 3–23. See also G. A. Kennedy, *A New History of Classical Rhetoric*
(Princeton: Princeton University Press, 1994), 28, 43–46, 81–84, 174–78, 242–56, and
William Barclay, *Educational Ideals in the Ancient World* (Grand Rapids: Baker Book
House, 1959), 157, 169–91. See also Cicero, *Brutus*, 89–91; Plutarch, *Marcus Cato*, in
Plutarch's Lives, vol. 2, trans. B. Perrin, LCL (Cambridge, Mass.: Harvard University Press,
1914; reprint 1985), 20.3–8; and Tacitus *Dialogus de Oratoribus* 34. In the ancient Greco-
Roman world, home was largely the center of education. Tutelage was provided by the
paterfamilias and the matrona. By the 3rd and 2nd centuries B.C., education became
increasingly institutionalized. Wealthy families used Greek slaves and freedmen as
paidagogoi who oversaw their charge's continued instruction outside of school. All subject
matter was largely utilitarian.

was oratorical training. Rhetoric was applied to a variety of disciplines because the advantages of clear and orderly speech were fundamental to them all. Greco-Roman rhetoric was also incorporated into the educational system of Palestinian Judaism,[93] and some scholars have even found correspondences between Greco-Roman rhetoric and Hillel's rules.[94] Rhetoric was an important part of all public life in the Hellenistic world. As Kennedy put it, persons "would, indeed, have been hard put to escape an awareness of rhetoric as practiced in the culture around them, for the rhetorical theory of the schools found its immediate application in almost every form of oral and written communication."[95]

There were numerous opportunities in the Greco-Roman world for productive oratory. Unfortunately, rhetoric was not always used constructively, and its misuse for manipulative and untruthful ends was criticized as early as the time of Plato and Aristotle.[96] Around the end of the first century A.D., such abuses were so common that Tacitus (ca. A.D. 56–ca. A.D. 120) expressed the view of many when he wrote that,

> eloquence, banished, so to say, from her proper realm, is dragged down by them into utter poverty of thought and constrained periods. Thus she who, once mistress of all the arts, held sway with a glorious retinue over our souls, now clipped and shorn, without state, without honour, I had almost said without her freedom, is studied as one of the meanest handicrafts.[97]

Positively and negatively, rhetoric played a crucial role in the Greco-Roman world. Rhetoric was a popular and powerful tool, a social convention that pervaded public life in Hellenistic culture. Still, what exactly is rhetoric?

Rhetoric and Rhetorical Types. Aristotle defined rhetoric simply as "the faculty of discovering the possible means of persuasion in reference to any subject whatever."[98] According to the rhetorical handbook *Rhetorica ad Herennium*, "The task of the public speaker is to discuss capably those matters which law and custom have fixed for the uses of citizenship and to secure as far

---

[93]M. Hengel, *Judaism and Hellenism*, 81–83. See also M. Dibelius, *Paul*, ed. W. G. Kümmel, trans. F. Clark (London: Longmans, 1953), 31.

[94]Cf. D. Daube, "Rabbinic Methods of Interpretation;" E. Norden, *Die Antike Kunstprosa vom VI. Jahrhundert vor Christus bis in die Zeit der Renaissance*, 9th ed. (Stuttgart: B. G. Teubner, 1983), 476, n. 1. Hillel's seven rules for interpreting scripture became the basis for additional rules and had an important influence on the shape of Pharisaic and Talmudic Judaism.

[95]G. A. Kennedy, *New Testament Interpretation*, 10.

[96]See G. A. Kennedy, *The Art of Persuasion in Greece*, 61–68.

[97]Tacitus *Dialogus de Oratoribus* 32.

[98]Aristotle *The Art of Rhetoric*, trans. J. H. Freese, LCL (Cambridge, Mass.: Harvard University Press, 1926), 1.2.1.

as possible the agreement of his hearers."[99] Or as Quintilian put it, "the aim of rhetoric is to think and speak rightly."[100] In a word, rhetoric is the art of persuasion. It is a studied approach and practice for influencing others to recognize and accept one's own point of view.

Rhetoric was commonly classified into three main sub-genres by both the Greeks and the Romans. There were, of course, a variety of opinions on typologies and their respective methodologies from the 5th century B.C. on, as Quintilian observed in his discussion of the matter,[101] but this three-part organization was predominate since Aristotle's *Art of Rhetoric* in the 4th century B.C.[102] These principal rhetorical types of civic discourse are forensic, deliberative, and epideictic. Each deals with particular kinds of issues in measured ways for certain ends.[103]

Forensic rhetoric (judicial or iudicialis; δικανικόν) is aimed at expounding the truth of a past occurrence and ensuring the execution of justice. It may be offensive or defensive in its approach, but it calls for a decision about a past action. The common speech of law courts, it is the type of argumentation by which defendants and plaintiffs appeal to the judge and jury for favorable decisions regarding a past event. The central concern is the fairness of a settlement.

Deliberative rhetoric (deliberativus; δημηγορικόν, συμβουλευτικόν) has as its goal the adoption or rejection of a future course of action, and it is more intentionally persuasive or dissuasive in its approach than forensic rhetoric. This type of speaking was characteristically used in public assemblies in order to influence the public's decisions regarding upcoming actions. Here the underlying issue is the expediency of a course to be taken.

Epideictic rhetoric (demonstrativus; ἐπιδεικτικόν, πανηγυρικόν), which is also commonly called "display" oratory, has for its aim the celebration and elevation of a person deemed honorable or the shaming and blaming of one deemed dishonorable. The language praises or chastises, but it does not call for a decision. It focuses, rather, on the values of the community in the present, and its underlying issue is the worthiness of the subject.

---

[99]*Rhetorica ad Herennium* 1.2.1. See also Cicero *De Inventione* 1.6.

[100]Quintilian *Institutio Oratoria* 2.15.37.

[101]Ibid., 3.4.1–16.

[102]Aristotle *Rhetoric* 1.3.1–9.

[103]Cf. G. A. Kennedy, *Art of Persuasion in Greece*, 87; idem, *A New History*, 72; idem, *New Testament Interpretation*, 19; Jerome Murphy-O'Conner, *Paul the Letter-Writer*, 66–68; G. W. Hansen, *Abraham in Galatians*, 57; B. Mack, *Rhetoric and the New Testament*, 34. Among the ancient sources, see especially Quintilian *Institutio Oratoria* 3.4.12–15, 3.8.6, 3:9.1; Aristotle *Rhetoric* 1:2.3; 1358b; Cicero *De Inventione* 1.7; and *Rhetorica ad Herennium* 1.1.2.

These three rhetorical typologies, as Quintilian observed, were originally descriptive in their conception, organization and analysis, but they became increasingly prescriptive in that once formalized into written handbooks they were employed as guides for constructing these types of arguments. The problem was that the elaboration and the completion of these full-blown rhetorical types drew more upon theory than upon actual speeches. That is, they achieved their clearly distinguished theoretical forms and purposes *a priori* and not *a posteriori*.[104] This is a crucial point to keep in mind when comparing these descriptions of rhetorical types with actual speeches or rhetorical letters. Far too often, attempts have been made to align Paul's letters with one single type of rhetoric on the assumption that there should be an exact correspondence throughout. But these typologies do not cover every type of speech, and the unlikeliness of such precise relations was noted at least as early as Quintilian who recognized the numerous species of oratory and asked rhetorically:

> On what kind of oratory are we to consider ourselves to be employed, when we complain, console, pacify, excite, terrify, encourage, instruct, explain obscurities, narrate, plead for mercy, thank, congratulate, reproach, abuse, describe, command, retract, express our desires and opinions, to mention no other of the many possibilities? As an adherent of the older view I must ask for indulgence and must enquire what was the reason that led earlier writers to restrict a subject of such variety to such narrow bounds.[105]

Rhetoric could parallel the precise scheme of a single kind of oratory, but it could also—and often did—mix the different types of speech. Aristotle made this same point centuries earlier when discussing the interrelatedness of these three kinds of discourse. He wrote, "It is not uncommon, however, for epideictic speakers to avail themselves of other times, of the past by way of recalling it, or of the future by way of anticipating it."[106] The same applies for the other two types or rhetoric. Thus in addressing a judge and jury, for instance, a speaker might not only render an account of a past action but might also flatter the court and plead for a particular verdict. Or in the case of a deliberative speech, a speaker might emphasize some praiseworthy values

---

[104]On the recognition of the divergence between theory and practice by ancient writers, see J. Murphy-O'Conner, *Paul the Letter-Writer*, 68; Stowers, *Letter Writing in Greco-Roman Antiquity*, 32–35; and J. L. White, *Light from Ancient Letters*, 190. See also Quintilian *Institutio Oratoria* 2.17.5–9 and Cicero *De Oratore*, trans. E. W. Sutton, LCL (Cambridge, Mass.: Harvard University Press, 1942; reprint 1996), 1.32.146. Cicero reminds his readers that "eloquence is not born of the theoretical system; rather, the system is born of eloquence."

[105]Quintilian *Institutio Oratoria* 3.4.3 in J. Murphy-O'Conner, *Paul the Letter-Writer*, 68. For Quntilian's lengthy discussion on this disputed matter, see *Institutio Oratoria* 3.4.1–16.

[106]Aristotle *Rhetoric* 1.3.4.

shared between speaker and hearers and render an account of past events all in order to attract support and establish a favorable ethos.[107] The point is simply that these rhetorical types are theoretical and life is often considerably different from *a priori* theory.

Parts of Rhetorical Discourses. Every rhetorical discourse was comprised of particular parts. The earliest classification comes from Aristotle who asserted that, in its simplest form, "a speech has two parts. You must state your case, and you must prove it."[108] For those who insisted on more intricate divisions, Aristotle allowed that "[t]hese divisions are appropriate to every speech, and at most the parts are four in number, *exordium, statement, proof,* and *epilogue.*"[109] To these four Aristotle added the *narrative* which he viewed as particularly relevant to forensic discourse but usually unnecessary for deliberative or epideictic rhetoric.[110] These five divisions, of course, were not the only classifications used by Greek and Latin rhetoricians. Cicero, Quintilian, and the *Rhetorica ad Herennium* each identified five to six parts of a discourse, though with some distinctive and nuanced terminology.[111] Still, there was remarkable consensus throughout the handbooks that the categories first distinguished and described by Aristotle represent the major divisions of any kind of discourse. A brief overview of these parts will be helpful for analyzing Paul's letters, then, but in the following description of these fundamental parts we will use the Latin terminology rather than Aristotle's Greek because the Latin terms are used most often by scholars today and a common terminology

---

[107]Cf. Cicero *De Inventione* 2.32.100 where Cicero advocates mixing rhetorical genres when warranted by the situation. His example mixes forensic and deliberative speech. See also *Rhetorica ad Herennium* 3.8.15, where the point is made again that "if epideictic is only seldom employed by itself independently, still in judicial and deliberative causes extensive sections are often devoted to praise or censure."

[108]Aristotle *Rhetoric* 3.13.1.

[109]Ibid., 3.13.4. Aristotle's terms are προοίμιον, πρόθεσις, πίστις and ἐπίλογος.

[110]Ibid., 3.13.3.

[111]For a summary of views that range from 2 to 7 parts, see especially the tables in Heinrich Lausberg, *Handbuch der literarischen Rhetorik: Eine Grundlegung der Literaturwissenschaft* (München: Max Hueber Verlag, 1973), 148–49. For a helpful discussion of this matter, see also F. W. Hughes, *Early Christian Rhetoric*, 32–34. Cicero actually presents two schemes. In his early publication of his school notes on rhetoric in *De Inventione* (1.19), Cicero identifies six parts as exordium, narratio, partitio, confirmatio, reprehensio, and conclusio. From a later and more seasoned perspective in *De Partitione Oratoria* (trans. H. Rackham, LCL [Cambridge, Mass.: Harvard University Press, 1942; reprint 1997], 27), Cicero simplifies the essential parts to four: exordium, narratio, confirmatio together with reprehensio, and peroratio. In his *Institutio Oratoria*, Quintilian describes the principal parts as prooemium, narratio, probatio, refutatio, and peroratio (3.9.1; 4.1.1). The *Rhetorica ad Herennium* (1.4) sets forth the parts as exordium, narratio, divisio, confirmatio, confutatio, and conclusio.

will simplify the forthcoming comparison of the different views regarding the structural arrangement and genre classification of Galatians.

The exordium (προοίμιον) is the introduction to the discourse. It is especially important because it is the basis upon which first impressions would be formed and listeners either encouraged or discouraged from listening to what follows. One of its purposes, then, in addition to introducing the speaker, is to get the audience's attention and secure its goodwill.[112] Another function of the well-formed exordium is to set forth a sample of the key issues that will be addressed. As Aristotle describes it, the exordium is, "a paving the way for what follows" and "a sample of the subject, in order that the hearers may know beforehand what it is about." Moreover, "the most essential and special function of the exordium is to make clear what is the end or purpose of the speech."[113] Exordiums were also appropriate places for modest boasting—if the speaker believed it necessary to establish the right to speak. Here, too, the speaker should praise the hearers—if it might help the audience become well disposed toward the speaker. The opening could also include criticism of any common opponents or make startling comments aimed at arousing the hearers' indignation.[114]

The narratio (διήγησις) is usually the second part of a speech. Although Aristotle viewed the narratio as belonging more integrally to forensic rhetoric since it pertains to past time, it could be included in deliberative and epideictic speech.[115] As noted above, however, recounting past facts may be useful for eliciting emotional support and for establishing the moral qualities of the speaker and any adversaries.[116] Simply put, the aim of the narratio is to set forth the facts regarding a past event or issue. Ideally, the narratio should be stated clearly and concisely and convey only the essential elements of the issue. The speaker is not obligated, however, to dwell upon those points which may be unfavorable to his cause. On the other hand, whatever is advantageous can and should be stated as strongly as possible. Everything in the narratio must be

---

[112]Aristotle *Rhetoric* 3.14–19. Cf. Cicero *De Inventione* 1.15–26; Quintilian *Institutio Oratoria* 4.1.5, 3.8.59.

[113]Aristotle *Rhetoric* 3.14.1–2. See also Quintilian *Institutio Oratoria* 4.1.1–5, 23 and 3.8.6–10, 59; and Cicero *De Inventione* 1.20 ("An exordium is a passage which brings the mind of the auditor into a proper condition to receive the rest of the speech.").

[114]Aristotle *Rhetoric* 3.14.7. See also *Rhetorica ad Herennium* 1.6–8.

[115]Quintilian, however, insisted that the narratio always immediately follow the exordium, unless there were solid grounds for abandoning it. Cf. *Institutio Oratoria* 4.2.25–60.

[116]Aristotle *Rhetoric* 3.16.10–11. Aristotle wrote that narration does not often appear in deliberative rhetoric "because no one can narrate things to come; but if there is a narrative, it will be of things past, in order that, being reminded of them, the hearers may take better counsel about the future."

plausible,[117] but not everything must be related strictly to the case. The narratio may also include a digressio which is not essential to the discourse but could be used to draw support from the hearers by giving them an entertaining rest between periods of concentration on the narratio and the main body of the discourse (the argumentatio).[118]

The propositio (partitio, divisio; πρόθεσις, προκατασκευή) is the thesis statement for the entire discourse; it is the point which the speaker wants to establish. Here Cicero's rule of "brevity, completeness, and conciseness" aptly expresses the consensus that the propositio ought to use no unnecessary words, present all the main points of the whole discourse, and be free of redundancy.[119] Ideally, the propositio should aid the hearers by defining the argument's boundaries and its major points in a striking way so that the hearers receive a framework for understanding the following discourse and will know when the argument is completed. If the propositio is complicated, it could be divided into separate headings which identify the parts and the order of their treatment (partitio or divisio).[120]

The main body of the discourse is called the probatio but is also variously called the argumentatio, confirmatio, and refutatio (πίστις, ἔλεγχος, ἀπόδειξις, λύσις, κατασκευή, ἀνασκευή). This portion of the discourse is the main body of the argument, and it is here that the speaker develops and "proves" the propositio. In forensic rhetoric, the aim of the probatio is to establish the truth of the speaker's claims. For deliberative rhetoric, the focus is on determining the preferable course of action and persuading the hearers to pursue it. In epideictic rhetoric, the goal is to prove the worthiness or unworthiness of the subject. In every kind of speech, the probatio forms the basis of persuasiveness. If the proof does not stand, the argument collapses. This explains the considerable attention given in the handbooks to the probatio and the possible ways of constructing persuasive proofs.[121] The probatio may utilize proofs that support the speaker's case (confirmatio) or weaken an opponent's argument (refutatio). The confirmatio and refutatio may be used separately or together. The proofs themselves are to be rooted in the character of the speaker (ethos), the disposition of the audience (pathos), or the content of the speech itself (logos). The degree to which they are persuasive depends on

---

[117]Cicero *De Inventione* 1.27–30; Aristotle *Rhetoric* 3.16.1–10; *Rhetorica ad Herennium* 1.12–16.

[118]Cicero *De Inventione* 1.27.

[119]Ibid., 1.31–33. Cf. Quintilian *Institutio Oratoria* 4.4–5; *Rhetorica ad Herrenium* 1.17.

[120]Quintilian *Institutio Oratoria* 4.5.22–27.

[121]Nearly all of Quintilian's fifth book of the *Institutio Oratoria* addresses the topic of proofs. Cf. Aristotle *Rhetoric* 3.17.3–18.7; Cicero *De Inventione* 1.34f; *Rhetorica ad Herennium* 1.18.

the logical use of examples and enthymemes. Examples prove a point inductively by relating similar cases to a particular proposition. Enthymemes demonstrate the fact through a deductive development leading up to the proposition.[122]

The closing of the discourse is the peroratio or conclusio (ἐπίλογος). If the exordium is important for determining the purpose and goal of the discourse, the end is important for ensuring that the goal is unmistakably reached. The aim of the peroratio, then, is to close the speech by recapitulating the speaker's main point, drawing the listener's support, and, if necessary, attempting once more to turn the listener away from any opponent.[123]

The handbooks specify many techniques related to each of these parts of oratory, but the exordium, narratio, propositio, probatio, and peroratio are the principal parts of fully developed rhetorical discourse. It was not enough, though, for speakers to be knowledgeable of the parts of speech and their general order. Speakers also had to give careful attention to the way in which these rhetorical parts where related to one another and to the work as a whole. Persuasive oratory depended much upon the orator's skills of "invention, arrangement, style, memory and delivery."[124] By "invention" (inventio; εὕρεσις) the rhetoricians meant the identification of the speaker's goal in speaking, the appropriateness of the argument to the occasion, and the choice of subject matter. The "arrangement" (dispositio; τάξις) referred to the selection of the type or types of rhetoric that would provide the basic order of the argument for achieving the speaker's goal. The "expression" or "style" (elocutio; λέξις, ἑρμηνεία) of the argument referred to the speaker's use of words that were appropriate to the situation. The ideal speaker then memorized the discourse (memoria; μνήμη) and delivered it in a fitting way (pronuntiatio; ὑπόκρισις). Eloquence was measured by the speaker's command of these five skills, and the common denominator for them all was propriety (decorum; πρέπον). As Cicero aptly put it, "the foundation of eloquence, as of everything else, is wisdom. . . . propriety will always be the chief aim."[125]

---

[122]Aristotle *Rhetoric* 1.2. See also B. Mack, *Rhetoric and the New Testament*, 38–41.

[123]Aristotle *Rhetoric* 3.19; *Rhetorica ad Herennium* 2.47–50; Cicero *De Inventione* 1.98–1.109; Quintilian *Institutio Oratoria* 6.1.1–11.

[124]*Retorica ad Herennium* 1.3; Quintilian *Institutio Oratoria* 3.3.1; Cicero *De oratore* 1.31.142. In *De Inventione* 1.9, Cicero writes: "The parts of it, as most authorities have stated, are Invention, Arrangement, Expression, Memory, Delivery. Invention is the discovery of valid or seemingly valid arguments to render one's cause plausible. Arrangement is the distribution of arguments thus discovered in the proper order. Expression is the fitting of the proper language to the invented matter. Memory is the firm mental grasp of matter and words. Delivery is the control of voice and body in a manner suitable to the dignity of the subject matter and the style."

[125]Cicero *Orator* 70–71, 79. For a thorough examination of this matter, see D. L. Clark, *Rhetoric in Greco-Roman Education*, 67–143.

This extremely simplified summary of the types of rhetorical speech and the main components common to Greco-Roman oratory is sufficient to remind us that rhetoric was a highly developed and specialized discipline by the first century A.D. Beyond the few important terms used here, there are hundreds more in the handbooks that are used to classify and describe numerous rhetorical techniques.[126] In short, rhetoric was indeed the "mistress of all the arts" and its influence was felt in nearly every quarter of Greco-Roman society. And while it is impossible to know the extent of Paul's knowledge of these skills or training in their use, there can now be no doubt that Paul understood the fundamentals of rhetoric and possessed a remarkable facility in their use.

The Rise of Modern Rhetorical Criticism of the New Testament

Given the predominately oral-aural culture of Paul's day and some of the evidences in Paul's letters of their own rhetorical nature, it should come as no surprise that the rhetorical aspects of Paul's letters have attracted the church's critical attention. To some extent, this has always been the case, although interest in the matter has waxed and waned at various times. Historically, the rhetorical dimensions of Paul's correspondences have received more notice than the letters' epistolary characteristics. But the modern surge of attention on the rhetorical aspects of Paul's letters follows a time when the topic was nearly forgotten despite a long and rich history of development.

Many of the early church fathers who were trained in rhetoric recognized, examined, and commented on some of the rhetorical features of Paul's letters.[127] Augustine (A.D. 354–430), for instance, a teacher of rhetoric, wrote of Paul's oratorical prowess in 2 Corinthians 11:16–30: "Those who are awake will see how much wisdom lies in these words. With what a river of eloquence they flow even he who snores must notice."[128] Augustine observed

---

[126]See especially H. Lausberg, *Handbuch der literarischen Rhetorik*. Also, Werner Eisenhut, *Einführung in die Antike Rhetorik und Ihre Geschichte* (Darmstadt: Wissenschaftliche Buchgesellschaft, 1974); Hildebrecht Hommel, "Rhetorik," in *Der Kleine Pauly*, eds. Konrat Ziegler und Walther Sontheimer (München: Alfred Druckenmüller, 1972), 1396–1414 [from *PW*, 2611–27].

[127]G. A. Kennedy, *Classical Rhetoric and Its Christian and Secular Tradition from Ancient to Modern Times* (Chapel Hill: University of North Carolina Press, 1980), 132–60; idem, *A New History of Classical Rhetoric* (Princeton: Princeton University Press, 1994), 257–70; E. Norden, *Die Antike Kunstprosa*, 512–13; H. D. Betz, "The Problem of Rhetoric and Theology According to the Apostle Paul," in *L'Apôtre Paul: Personalité, Style et Conception du Ministère*, ed. A. Vanhoye, BETL 73 (Leuven: Leuven University Press, 1986), 16–48.

[128]Augustine, *De doctrina Christiana* 4.7.12 in E. A. Judge, "Paul's Boasting," 48. See also Peter Prestel, *Die Rezeption der ciceronischen Rhetorik durch Augustinus in de doctrina Christiana*, Studien zur klassischen Philologie 69 (Frankfurt: Peter Lang, 1992), and G. A. Kennedy, *Classical Rhetoric*, 170–82.

further that Paul used rhetorical techniques which are "intermixed with a pleasing variety." They "lend all that fair appearance to the diction, its good looks as it were, by which even the uneducated are delighted and moved to action." John Chrysostom (A.D. 347–407) also admired the power of Paul's speech, but did not regard Paul as an expert rhetorician by classical standards.[129] Gregory of Nyssa (ca. A.D. 331–395) noticed that Paul preferred the plain style of rhetoric and shunned ornamental speech so that the truth of the gospel would not be obscured,[130] and Jerome (ca. A.D. 348–420) related this rhetorical simplicity and directness to Paul's missionary success.[131]

Many of the Greek and Latin Fathers up to the mid-sixth century, who had been schooled in the discipline of classical rhetoric and had used it effectively in spreading the gospel and building Christian communities, also found rhetorical qualities in Paul's letters. Still they offered little in the way of critical commentary on Paul's use of rhetoric.[132] Similarly, ties between classical rhetoric and Paul's letters continued to be observed—however slightly—by some biblical interpreters through the Middle Ages. But all this changed dramatically when interest surged during the Renaissance.[133] Desiderius Erasmus (1469–1536), Jacques Lefèvre d'Etaples (Jacobus Faber, ca. 1455–1536) and other Christian humanists did much to revive and expand the study and use of classical rhetoric.[134] The Reformers Martin Luther (1483–1546), Ulrich Zwingli (1484–1531), Philipp Melanchthon (1497–1560), John Calvin (1509–1564), and Heinrich Bullinger (1504–1575) all employed rhetorical techniques in their works and in their interpretation of scripture.[135]

---

[129]John Chrysostom, *de Sacerdotio*, 4.5 in E. A. Judge, "Paul's Boasting," 41. See also E. Norden, *Die Antike Kunstprosa*, 501–02, and Reinhart Staats, "Chrysostomus uber die Rhetorik des Apostels Paulus: Makarianische Kontexte zu De Sacerdotio IV, 5–6," *Vigiliae Christianae* 46 (1992): 225–40.

[130]Gregory of Nyssa *adv. Eunomium I* 253b in E. A. Judge, "Paul's Boasting," 41.

[131]Jerome *comm. Ephes.* III.5 in E. A. Judge, "Paul's Boasting," 42.

[132]G. A. Kennedy, *A New History*, 133–60.

[133]See especially R. Meynet, "Histoire de 'l'analyse rhétorique' en exégèse biblique," *Rhetorica* 8 (1990): 291–320. See also, C. J. Classen, "St. Paul's Epistles and Ancient Greek and Roman Rhetoric," in *Rhetoric and the New Testament*, eds. S. E. Porter and T. H. Olbricht (Sheffield: Sheffield Academic Press, 1993), 265–91; and J. H. Bentley, *Humanists and Holy Writ: New Testament Scholarship in the Renaissance* (Princeton: Princeton University Press, 1983).

[134]Cf. Jerry H. Bently, *Humanists and Holy Writ*. See also Erasmus's works on letter writing, *De Conscribendis Epistulis*, and preaching, *Ecclesiastes sive de Ratione Concionandi*, which plainly show his understanding and use of classical rhetoric in biblical interpretation.

[135]On Erasmus' attraction and aversion to rhetoric, see especially his biting critique of the rhetorical fundamentalism of the Ciceronians in "The Ciceronian: A Dialogue on the Ideal Latin Style / Dialogus Ciceronianus," trans. B. I. Knott, *Collected Works of Erasmus*, vol. 28, ed. A. H. T. Levi (Toronto: University of Toronto Press, 1986). On Martin Luther, see especially Kenneth Hagen, *Luther's Approach to Scripture as seen in his*

They used the language of rhetoric and dialectic to describe Paul's logic and use of language. Melanchthon, for instance, exemplifies how vigorously some Reformers applied classical rhetorical terms and techniques both as a course of study in its own right and as a tool for biblical interpretation. Between 1519 and 1547, Melanchthon wrote three rhetorical handbooks and three works on dialectic.[136] In his work *De Rhetorica,* he frequently used scriptural passages as examples of good rhetoric. Moreover, he praised Galatians and Romans as examples of rhetorical excellence. Regarding his analysis of Galatians, Melanchthon first classified the rhetorical genre of the letter, but because Galatians did not fit neatly within the standard classical categories of forensic, deliberative, or epideictic, Melanchthon used his own rhetorical category for the letter which he termed "genus didacticum." He justified this innovation on the basis of the flexible rhetorical tradition he received. Then following his designation of the letter's genus, Melanchthon identified and interpreted the letter's opening (1:1–5; ἐπιγράφη and salutatio), its exordium or proposition (1:6–2:21), its argumentation (3:1–6:10; occupatio and paraenesis), and its epilogue (5:1f).[137]

Classical rhetoric and the rhetorical character of Paul's letters drew considerable attention from many Reformers, but, as an interpretive approach to scripture, the enthusiasm for rhetoric did not long endure. Interest in the relation between rhetoric and the New Testament waned following the Renaissance and Reformation, but the topic was never fully forgotten. Within a couple of centuries, however, from the late eighteenth century on, biblical

---

"Commentaries" on Galatians: 1519–1538 (Tübingen: J. C. B. Mohr [Paul Siebeck], 1993), ix, 101, 107–10, 126–37, 127 n.332, 149–57; Knut Alfsvag, "Language and Reality: Luther's relation to classical rhetoric in Rationis Lattomianae confutatio (1521)," *StTh* 41 (1987): 85–126. Luther often urged his public to pay attention to the biblical text's distinctive use of language, grammar, rhetoric and example. Luther also considered Paul to be one of the world's most brilliant rhetoricians. On John Calvin's debt to the rhetorical tradition, see Benoit Girardin, *Rhétorique et Théologique: Calvin, le commentaire de l'Épître aux Romains,* Théologie Historique 54 (Paris: Editions Beauchesne, 1979). On Melanchthon, see E. Bizer, ed. *Texte aus der Anfangszeit Melanchthons* (Neukirchen–Vluyn: Neukirchener Verlag, 1966), and Heinz Scheible, *Melanchthon und die Reformation: Forchungsbeiträge* (Mainz: Verlag Philipp von Zabern, 1996). For an overview, see C. Joachim Classen, "Paulus und die antike Rhetorik," *ZNW* 82 (1991): 1–33; especially 24–25, n. 83; and R. Meynet, "Histoire de 'l'analyse rhetorique'" 291–320.
    [136]C. J. Classen, "St. Paul's Epistles," 271–78. Classen identifies Melanchthon's rhetorical works as follows: the handbooks are *De Rhetorica libri tres* (Wittenberg, 1519), *Institutiones Rhetoricae* (Hagenau, 1521), and *Elementa rhetorices libri duo* (Wittenberg, 1531); the dialectic works are *Compendiaria Dialectices* (Leipzig, 1520), *Dialectices libri quatuor* (Hagenau, 1528), and *Erotemata dialectices* (Wittenberg, 1547).
    [137]C. J. Classen, "St. Paul's Epistles," 272–75. See also E. Bizer, *Texte aus der Anfangszeit Melanchthons,* 34, and John R. Schneider, *Philip Melanchthon's Rhetorical Construal of Biblical Authority: Oratio Sacra* (Lewiston, N.Y.: Edwin Mellen Press, 1990), 97–109.

scholars began addressing once more the relation between the New Testament and rhetoric. Karl Ludwig Bauer examined Paul's method of argumentation (1774) and use of rhetorical techniques (1782).[138] Christian Gottlob Wilke then investigated the rhetorical forms and aspects of the New Testament letters (1843).[139] Carl Heinrici used rhetorical parallels to interpret 2 Corinthians (1887) and then Johannes Weiss's essay "Beiträge zur Paulinischen Rhetorik" emphasized once more Paul's "sure rhetorical movement"[140] (1897). Weiss exhorted scholars to study Paul's "outstanding rhetorical properties,"[141] and a response came the next year (1898) from Eduard Norden[142] who found Paul's rhetorical style to be "strange" and "unhellenic." Heinrici then countered Norden's assessment of Paul with an appendix to a later edition of his commentary on 2 Corinthians which stressed Paul's debt to Hellenistic rhetoric (1900).[143] The negative assessment of Paul's use of Greco-Roman rhetoric was countered more decisively in 1910, however, by J. Weiss's student Rudolf Bultmann who demonstrated the close relation between certain features of the Cynic-Stoic diatribe and the Pauline letters.[144]

Remarkably, very few advances were made in the rhetorical analysis of Paul's letters in the decades immediately following Bultmann's dissertation. Instead, many other concerns emerged in the early twentieth century that drew biblical scholarship in other directions. Nevertheless, the topic of rhetoric did not die but began to re-emerge in the 1960's as scholars with literary critical leanings such as Wayne Booth,[145] Amos Wilder,[146] and Kenneth Burke[147]

---

[138]*Logica Paullina* (Halae: Impensis Orphanotrophei, 1974) and *Rhetorica Paullina*, 2 vols. (Halae: Impensis Orphanotrophei, 1982) in B. Mack, *Rhetoric in the New Testament*, 11.

[139]C. G. Wilke, *Die neutestamentliche Rhetorik: Ein Seitenstuck zur Grammatik des neutestamentlichen Sprachidioms* (Dresden and Leipzig: Arnold, 1843).

[140]J. Weiss, *Beiträge zur Paulinischen Rhetorik* (Göttingen: Vandenhoeck & Ruprecht, 1897), 5. Weiss described Paul's rhetorical letters as weak in *Kunstprosa* (artistic prose) but there was nevertheless "eine gewisse rhetorische Bewegung." Weiss viewed Paul's real rhetorical strengths as "symmetry (Symmetrie), rhythm (Rhythmus), force (Schwung), and full–tone (Vollklang)." That is, Weiss recognized Paul's rhetorical strengths largely in terms of aural characteristics.

[141]Ibid., 3.

[142]E. Norden, *Die antike Kunstprosa*, 21.

[143]C. F. G. Heinrici, *Der zweite Brief an die Korinther, mit einem Anhang: Zum Hellenismus des Paulus*, MeyerK 6, 8th edn. (Göttingen: Vandenhoeck & Ruprecht, 1900), 436–58.

[144]R. Bultmann, *Der Stil der paulinischen Predigt und die kynisch-stoische Diatribe*, FRLANT 13 (Göttingen: Vandenhoeck & Ruprecht, 1910; reprint 1984).

[145]Wayne C. Booth, *The Rhetoric of Fiction* (Chicago: University of Chicago Press, 1961; 2d ed., 1982).

[146]Amos N. Wilder, *Early Christian Rhetoric: The Language of the Gospel* (New York: Harper & Row, 1964; reprint, Cambridge: Harvard University Press, 1971).

applied rhetoric to literary and biblical studies. Then in 1968, James Muilenburg gave his presidential address to the Society of Biblical Literature: "Form Criticism and Beyond." Muilenburg focused on issues pertaining to Old Testament studies, but he pointed to rhetorical criticism as a way "to venture beyond the confines of form criticism into an inquiry into other literary features which are all too frequently ignored today."[148] By this, Muilenburg meant that attention ought to focus on "discerning the many and various devices by which the predications are formulated and ordered into a unified whole."[149] Almost simultaneously, Chaim Perelman and L. Olbrecht–Tyteca's book *The New Rhetoric: A Treatise on Argumentation* was published in English and received a ready welcome by scholars wanting to apply rhetorical rules in literary criticism.[150] This work is also significant in that it defined rhetoric in terms of its classical definition—as types of argumentation—and not simply as style or ornamentation. At the same time, Edwin A. Judge re-focused attention on Paul's use of rhetoric by raising the question of Paul's relation to professional Greco-Roman sophists.[151] Thus by the close of the 1960's, important groundwork was laid for taking a fresh approach to rhetorical criticism of biblical texts.

Finally, the new era of rhetorical criticism erupted fully in 1974 with Hans Dieter Betz's lecture on "The Literary Composition and Function of Paul's Letter to the Galatians." The lecture was published the next year[152] and was soon followed by the full development of his thesis in his commentary on Galatians (1979).[153] Betz's work not only set rhetorical criticism among the leading concerns of biblical scholars but it also signaled a shift in the typical use of rhetorical criticism for interpreting biblical texts. For the most part, earlier uses of rhetorical techniques for understanding the letters of the New Testament, especially Paul's, were focused on smaller units of text and their relation to particular rhetorical styles, figures, and the structure of periods and other small units. There were a few earlier attempts to describe the overall genre of Galatians, such as Melanchthon's classification of Galatians as belonging to the "genus didacticum," but most rhetorical studies of the New

---

[147]Kenneth Burke, *A Rhetoric of Motives* (Berkeley: University of California Press, 1970).

[148]James Muilenburg, "Form Criticism and Beyond," *JBL* 88 (1969): 4.

[149]Ibid., 8.

[150]Chaim Perelman and L. Olbrecht–Tyteca, *The New Rhetoric: A Treatise on Argumentation*, trans. John Wilkinson and Purcell Weaver (Notre Dame: University of Notre Dame Press, 1969).

[151]E. A. Judge, "Paul's Boasting," 37–50. Judge takes his point of departure from 2 Cor 11:6.

[152]H. D. Betz, "The Literary Composition and Function of Paul's Letter to the Galatians," *NTS* 21 (1975): 353–79.

[153]H. D. Betz, *Galatians*.

Testament did not attempt interpretations of whole documents as types of oratorical discourses. H. D. Betz's analysis of Galatians, however, did just that. Betz analyzed Galatians as an apologetic letter that followed the formal characteristics of forensic rhetoric as set forth in the rhetorical handbooks. Other works that were similar to Betz's in their rhetorical approaches to whole documents of the NT soon appeared, and a new arena of biblical interpretation was established as scholars worked to understand the relationships between classical rhetorical discourse and Paul's letters.

Developments in the Analyses of the Rhetorical Genre of Paul's Letters.
Since the 1970's, many NT scholars, especially in the United States, have sought to interpret whole New Testament texts through the application of rhetorical categories. The result is nothing short of a deluge of literature and discussion on the matter.[154] Not surprisingly, there is a wide range of opinions on the rhetorical classifications of Paul's letters. Regarding Romans, for instance, Wilhelm Wuellner (1976) and George A. Kennedy (1984) aligned it primarily with Greco-Roman epideictic rhetorical forms.[155] Robert Jewett (1982) extended the epideictic genre classification of Romans to include the epistolary categories of ambassadorial letter, paraenetic letter, hortatory letter, and philosophical diatribe.[156] David E. Aune (1987), however, contends that Romans functions on two rhetorical levels. The present character of Romans may be epideictic but the letter's prior setting was deliberative because its persuasive purpose was to prepare the way for Paul's arrival by demonstrating the truth of the gospel and promoting their acceptance of it.[157] Jean-Noël Aletti views Romans as a deliberative letter because of its unequivocal future

---

[154]For extensive bibliographies on the subject, see especially D. F. Watson, "The New Testament and Greco-Roman Rhetoric: A Bibliography," *JETS* 31 (1988): 465–72; idem, "The New Testament and Greco-Roman Rhetoric: A Bibliographical Update," *JETS* 33 (1990): 513–24; B. Mack, *Rhetoric and the New Testament*; and G. A. Kennedy, *New Testament Interpretation*.

[155]W. Wuellner, "Paul's Rhetoric of Argumentation in Romans: An Alternative to the Donfried-Karris Debate over Romans," *CBQ* 38 (1976): 330–51 (reprinted in *The Romans Debate*, ed. K. P. Donfried [Minneapolis: Augsburg Publishing House, 1977], 152–74); idem, "Greek Rhetoric and Pauline Argumentation," in *Early Christian Literature and the Classical Intellectual Tradition: In honorem Robert M. Grant*, ed. W. R. Schoedel and R. L. Wilken, Théologie historique 53 (Paris: Éditions Beauchesne, 1979), 177–88; G. A. Kennedy, *New Testament Interpretation*, 152; David E. Aune, *The New Testament in Its Literary Environment*, 219.

[156]R. Jewett, "Romans as an Ambassadorial Letter."

[157]D. E. Aune, *The New Testament in Its Literary Environment*, 219. Aune uses the term "protreptic" ("persuasive") here for "deliberative."

orientation and Paul's persuasive argument for the letter's recipients to acknowledge God's divine justice.[158]

Assessments of the rhetorical genre of 1 Corinthians are similarly diverse. G. A. Kennedy (1984) and Margaret Mitchell (1991) classify the letter as deliberative.[159] In their view, Paul is seeking to persuade the Corinthians to be reconciled with one another and with himself. Paul wants them to be united in their present and future life together. Wuellner (1987), however, views the situation and response differently. For Wuellner, 1 Corinthians is epideictic because Paul's overriding concern is not so much about changing their beliefs and lifestyles as it is teaching them how to continue growing in their faith and practice.[160]

Agreement on the rhetorical genre classification for 2 Corinthians fares no better. Kennedy identifies the letter as belonging largely to forensic rhetoric in chapters 1–7 and 10–13 and to deliberative rhetoric in chapters 8–9. He views Paul's principal purpose as a defense of his apostleship (1984).[161] Murphy-O'Conner, on the other hand, sees the aim of chapters 1–7 more as a persuasive appeal for the Corinthians to reject the gospel of Paul's opponents and to embrace Paul's message instead (1986).[162] The letter, then, is interpreted primarily as deliberative rhetoric. In Betz's detailed analysis of 2 Corinthians 8 and 9 (1985), he also views this portion of the letter as deliberative but he interprets the entire letter as a redacted compilation of several letters exhibiting forensic and deliberative rhetoric at a variety of places in the letter.[163]

---

[158]Jean Noël Aletti, *Comment Dieu est-il juste? Clefs pour interpréter l'épître aux Romains* (Paris: Editions du Seuil, 1991), 31–32; idem, "La présence d'un modèle rhétorique en Romains: Son rôle et son importance," Biblica 71 (1990): 1–24. Aletti recognizes the rhetorical characteristics of the letter but does not insist on fitting Romans into a standard dispositio.

[159]G. A. Kennedy, *New Testament Interpretation*, 87; Margaret M. Mitchell, *Paul and the Rhetoric of Reconciliation: An Exegetical Investigation of the Language and Composition of 1 Corinthians*, First American edition (Louisville, Ky.: Westminster/John Knox Press, 1991).

[160]W. Wuellner, "Where is Rhetorical Criticism Taking Us," *CBQ* 49 (1987): 460.

[161]G. A. Kennedy, *New Testament Interpretation*, pp. 86f.

[162]J. Murphy-O'Conner, "Pneumatikoi and Judaizers in 2 Cor 2:14–4:6," *AusBR* 34 (1986): 42–58.

[163]H. D. Betz, *2 Corinthians 8 and 9: A Commentary on Two Administrative Letters of the Apostle Paul* (Philadelphia: Fortress Press, 1985). See especially pp. 141–44 in which Betz discusses the relationship of chapters 8 and 9 to the remainder of the letter. Simply put, Betz argues for the original independence of these chapters as separate letters because they can be construed as separate letters. Regarding the justification of Betz's conclusion, however, S. K. Stowers quipped, "The only good answer is that Betz is determined to describe chapter 8 as an autonomous discourse" ("Review of 2 Corinthians 8 and 9: A Commentary on Two Administrative Letters of the Apostle Paul by H. D. Betz," *JBL* 106 [1987]: 730.)

Paul's other undisputed letters are subjected similarly to a range of rhetorical interpretations. Kennedy regards 1 Thessalonians as an example of the deliberative rhetorical form. Paul's main purpose is to exhort the Thessalonians to stand fast in the Lord and to give instructions on the Christian life.[164] But because Paul praises the Thessalonians so clearly and persistently in the letter, R. Jewett aligns 1 Thessalonians with epideictic rhetoric. Paul is writing foremost to support and encourage them in the faith and values they share.[165] Aune also views the letter as paraenetic discourse through which Paul aims to remind the Thessalonians of what they already know.[166] Philippians is regarded as a mixture of epideictic (1:3–3:1; 4:2–9) and deliberative (3:2–4:1) rhetoric by Kennedy who interprets the purpose of the letter primarily as an exhortation to remain faithful in the Lord and as advice for Christian discipleship in the days to come.[167] D. F. Watson (1988) classifies Philippians as deliberative because he interprets Paul's main intention to be persuading and dissuading the Philippian Christians regarding particular courses of action.[168] Philemon—Paul's shortest letter, however, is viewed solely as a deliberative address. Since F. F. Church's (1978) conclusion that Paul uses rhetorical conventions in the letter to persuade an entire Christian community to apply the principle of Christian love with one another,[169] little has been added or changed beyond D. E. Aune's (1987) refinement on the letter's structural parts.[170] Galatians, on the other hand, stands at the other end of the spectrum from Philemon both because of the numerous studies of its rhetorical structure and the greatest range of interpretations for any of Paul's letters. Let us look more closely, then, at the variety of rhetorical and epistolary classifications assigned to Galatians and the different conclusions drawn about the letter's main purpose.

III. PAUL'S LETTER–SPEECH TO THE GALATIANS

Galatians is without doubt one of the most vigorous and expressive of Paul's letters; his language is everywhere strong and vivid. Little wonder it has attracted great rhetorical and epistolographical interest from biblical scholars, especially since Betz's commentary a few years ago. But what exactly have the

---

[164]G. A. Kennedy, *New Testament Interpretation*, 142–44.

[165]R. Jewett, *The Thessalonian Correspondence: Pauline Rhetoric and Millenarian Piety, Foundations & Facets* (Philadelphia: Fortress Press, 1986), 71–72.

[166]D. E. Aune, *The New Testament in Its Literary Environment*, 206.

[167]G. A. Kennedy, *New Testament Interpretation*, 142–44.

[168]D. F. Watson, "A Rhetorical Analysis of Philippians," *NovT* 30 (1988): 59–60.

[169]F. F. Church, "Rhetorical Structure and Design in Paul's Letter to Philemon," *HTR* 71 (1978): 17–33.

[170]D. E. Aune, *The New Testament in Its Literary Environment*, 211–12.

various studies of Galatians revealed about the epistolary and rhetorical genre and structure of the letter? And what are the relationships between these classifications and interpretations of the letter's aim?

Epistolary Analyses of Galatians.

As evident in many of the studies noted above, Galatians has been at the center of much rigorous epistolary analysis through the last century. Yet most interpreters have restricted their investigations to particular epistolary conventions in the letter itself and have not attempted to align Galatians with any specific epistolographical form.[171] Some scholars, however, have related the whole letter of Galatians to particular epistolary genres.

An Apologetic and Magical Letter. In his pioneering commentary on Galatians, Betz classified the letter's compositional structure and function as an "apologetic letter" which operates in conjunction with Greco-Roman rhetorical categories of forensic speech.[172] In support of this claim, Betz cited Plato's pseudo-autobiography of Socrates and its apologetic autobiographical offspring of Isocrates' *Antidosis*. He also identified the examples of Plato's *Epistle* 7, Demosthenes' *De corona*, Cicero's *Brutus*, and Libanius' *Oratio* 1. Betz was not without some reservation regarding these assertions of literary precedents for identifying the genre of Galatians, "since most of the pertinent literature did not survive."[173] Nevertheless, Betz appealed to these Greco-Roman writings along with the work of Momigliano on the apologetic letter genre and classified Galatians as an apologetic letter.[174] In this, Betz was joined by others such as B. H. Brinsmead[175] and G. Howard,[176] yet because Betz also noticed the conditional curse (1:8–9) and blessing (6:16) which bracket the letter he also described Galatians as a "magical letter" related to the *Zauberpapyri*.[177] By "magical letter," however, Betz was not expanding or altering his designation of the letter's apologetic nature. Rather, he was seeking to account for the evidences in the text that Paul viewed his letter to the Galatians to be the watershed between their being blessed or cursed—depending on their verdict over the gospel he proclaimed to them.

With these literary precedents, Betz supported his epistolographical classification of Galatians as an apologetic letter. But for Betz, "the apologetic

---

[171]W. G. Doty, *Letters in Primitive Christianity*, 27–47.
[172]H. D. Betz, *Galatians*, 14.
[173]Ibid., 15.
[174]Ibid., 14–15, 23–25.
[175]B. H. Brinsmead, *Galatians—Dialogical Response*, 42–43.
[176]G. Howard, *Paul: Crisis in Galatia*, 48f.
[177]H. D. Betz, *Galatians*, 25.

letter is by definition a part of rhetoric."[178] Not surprisingly, then, Betz analyzed the structure of the letter primarily as a forensic self-apology, that is, as judicial rhetoric in written form. According to Betz, Galatians "presupposes the real or fictitious situation of the court of law, with jury, accuser, and defendant. . . . the addressees are identical with the jury, with Paul being the defendant, and his opponents the accusers."[179]

Betz found the chief epistolary conventions of the letter in the prescript (1:1–5) and the postscript (6:11–18). These he viewed as an "epistolary framework" or "a kind of external bracket" for the body of the letter which he described using categories of classical forensic rhetoric.[180] He did not consider them to be insignificant appendages, however. Rather, while the prescript was largely an epistolary convention, the postscript was related integrally to the whole composition and functioned rhetorically as the "peroratio" or "conclusio." Still, Betz described and analyzed the entire letter predominately as a speech in written form whose oral characteristics reigned from 1:6 to 6:10.

Betz's commentary on Galatians is a landmark study and turning point in NT scholarship, particularly for its role in launching fresh studies in Paul's epistolary and rhetorical practices and its demonstration that Paul's argument in Galatians is carefully structured from beginning to end. Consequently, all subsequent discussions of the genre and structure of Galatians must take into account Betz's analysis of the letter. But, as with other pioneering works, Betz's commentary is not without its difficulties and critics. Many of its strengths and weaknesses are well documented,[181] but a few salient points regarding his epistolographical criticism of Galatians are in order here. We will return later to Betz's rhetorical analysis and interpretation of the letter's purpose.

Perhaps the heaviest criticism of Betz's analysis of Galatians was set against his epistolographical designation of the letter's genre as "apologetic letter." R. B. Hays, for instance, noted that Betz's principal source for the designation of an "apologetic genre," A. Momigliano, did not view the genre as firmly established in the Greco-Roman world as Betz supposed.[182] Meeks

---

[178]Ibid., 24.

[179]Ibid.

[180]Ibid., 14–25.

[181]See for instance the reviews by W. D. Davies, P. W. Meyer, and D. E. Aune, *Religious Studies Review* 7 (1981): 304–18; C. K. Barrett, *Int* 34 (1980): 414–17; W. A. Meeks, *JBL* 100 (1981): 304–07; J. N. Aletti, *Recherches de Science Religieuse* 69 (1981): 601–02; M. Silva, "Betz and Bruce on Galatians," *WTJ* 45 (1983): 371–85; H. Hübner, *Theologische Literaturzeitung* 109 (1984): 241–50; E. A. Russell, "Convincing or Merely Curious? A Look at Some Recent Writings on Galatians," *IBS* 6 (1984): 157–61; and G. A. Kennedy, *New Testament Interpretation*, 144–52.

[182]R. B. Hays, *The Faith of Jesus Christ*, 243, n. 92.

observed further that Betz's classification of the genre is based "almost exclusively [on] rhetorical and epistolary *theory* rather than [on] specific examples of real apologies and real letters from antiquity."[183] Others, such as G. W. Hansen[184] and R. N. Longenecker,[185] concurred that the basic problem with Betz's apologetic letter theory is that the apologetic letters he cited were not *real* letters but were apologetic essays embedded within autobiographies. Galatians, however, was a *real* letter. The absence of examples of apologetic letters significantly weakened Betz's position on the epistolary genre of Galatians. As for Betz's suggestion of a functional relationship of Galatians to Hellenistic "magical letters," W. A. Meeks expressed the judgment of many when he asked, "Will anyone who has actually read the *Zauberpapyri* to which Betz refers, and then read Galatians, really imagine that he is reading the same kind of literature?"[186] Or as Longenecker put it, Betz's work simply "push[ed] a good thesis too hard and too far."[187] Longenecker's main contentions are that Betz's "classification of Galatians as an apologetic letter has more to do with the style of the letter's argument than with its epistolary structure . . . [and that] rhetorical analysis must not be confused with or replace attempts to describe the letter's structure."[188] We will probe the legitimacy of the latter assertion below, but the former highlights the focus of much subsequent scholarship that has sought to analyze Galatians primarily on epistolary terms in relation to real Greco-Roman letters. Unlike the approach of Betz and others, this branch of scholarship has sought to establish the common Greco-Roman papyrus letter tradition as the most appropriate genre for analyzing and interpreting the structure and meaning of Galatians.

A Rebuke and Request Letter. Over against Betz's classification of Galatians as an apologetic letter, G. W. Hansen[189] and R. N. Longenecker,[190] following the earlier work of N. A. Dahl,[191] have classified the entire letter of Galatians as belonging to the epistolary genre category of a Greco-Roman letter of "rebuke and request." They do not ignore the rhetorical elements of the

---

[183]Meeks, review of *Galatians: A Commentary on Paul's Letter to the Churches in Galatia*, by H. D. Betz, In *JBL* 100 (1981): 306.

[184]G. W. Hansen, *Abraham in Galatians*, 25–27.

[185]R. N. Longenecker, *Galatians*, cxi–cxiii.

[186]W. A. Meeks, review of *Galatians*, 306.

[187]R. N. Longenecker, *Galatians*, cxi.

[188]Ibid., civ.

[189]G. W. Hansen, *Abraham in Galatians*; idem, *Galatians*, The IVP New Testament Commentary Series (Downers Grove, Ill.: InterVarsity Press, 1994), 29–30.

[190]R. N. Longenecker, *Galatians*.

[191]N. A. Dahl, "Paul's Letter to the Galatians: Epistolary Genre, Content, and Structure" (unpuplished paper for the SBL Paul Seminar, 1973), which both Hansen and Longenecker cite.

letter, but, on the basis of common Hellenistic epistolary formulas, they do insist that Galatians be regarded foremost as a literary composition whose structural precedent is found primarily in the common Hellenistic papyrus letter tradition.

Of central importance to Longenecker's and Hansen's analysis of Galatians is the presence and position of epistolary formulas. Similar to other studies of Galatians, they acknowledge the textual boundaries of the letter's opening and closing pericopes with their respective formulas[192] and so, like Betz, separate the letter's salutation (1:1–5) and subscription (6:11–18) from the letter-body (1:6–6:10). Unlike Betz, however, they agree with T. Y. Mullins that:

> The opening is a sort of warm-up for the main issue and provides a convenient clustering place for matters less important than the main issue (but not necessarily introductory to it). The closing constitutes the final communication and is a natural clustering place for matters of minor importance which the writer wants to add before breaking off.[193]

To be sure, this may be true for the Greco-Roman common letter tradition, but, as we will see, it does not reflect accurately Paul's use of the letter opening and closing in Galatians.

The focus of Longenecker's and Hansen's structural analyses, however, is the letter-body. Here they draw from J. L. White's study of the body of Greek letters[194] and have identified 16 and 18 nonliterary papyrus formulas (respectively) which have parallels in Galatians.[195] They also recognize certain repetitions of words. From this they have concluded that 31 phrases in Galatians should be regarded as conventional epistolary formulas.[196] Next, they examined the relationships between these formulas in Galatians observing T. Y.

---

[192]For instance, the opening formula of Greco-Roman letters identifies the sender and the recipient and bestows greetings. It is most commonly expressed as "A to B, Greetings!" but sometimes as "To B from A, Greetings!" Paul follows this practice in all of his letters, though not without modification to suit his own purposes. And while Paul's letter closings lack entirely the common Greco-Roman closing formula which employs the perfect passive imperative singular or plural form of ῥώννυμι (i.e., "Be made strong!"), Paul is consistent in using his own adapted letter closing pattern of hortatory remarks, peace wish, closing greetings, and a benediction. See especially H. Gamble, *The Textual History of the Letter to the Romans: A Study in Textual and Literary Criticism*, SD 42 (Grand Rapids: Eerdmans, 1977), 83.

[193]"Formulas in New Testament Epistles," *JBL* 91 (1972): 387.

[194]*The Form and Function of the Body of the Greek Letter.*

[195]R. N. Longenecker identifies 16 formulas in Galatians (*Galatians*, cv–cviii). Hansen finds 18 formulas (*Abraham in Galatians*, 27–32).

[196]Their terminology differs on a few formulas, but they are unanimous in their identifications of them. See Longenecker, *Galatians*, cvii–cviii; and Hansen, *Abraham in Galatians*, 30–31.

Mullins's proposal that *"one form tends to precipitate the use of others with it"* and *"they almost always punctuate a break in the writer's thought."*[197] Then, on the basis of clustered formulas, they divided the letter-body into two parts: 1:6–4:11 and 4:12–6:10.

Longenecker and Hansen contend that this major break in Galatians is justified not only by the "transitional" clustering of epistolary formulas that they classify in 4:12–20 but also because of existent two-part nonliterary Greco-Roman θαυμάζω letters which, they contend, correspond structurally to Galatians. This assertion is based on Hansen's analysis of at least twelve examples of these letters which highlight their two-part "rebuke" and "request" structure.[198] It is worth noting that Hansen's model parallels the two-part εὐχαριστῶ-παρακαλῶ structure proposed earlier for Paul's letters by C. J. Bjerkelund,[199] but Hansen's and Longenecker's structure has a different purpose marked by the key formulas θαυμάζω and δέομαι ὑμῶν.

According to their proposal, the rebuke section begins with the Pauline hapax θαυμάζω at 1:6 and continues through 4:11. The purpose of this rebuke section is to provide the necessary background for the request section which begins at 4:12 with δέομαι ὑμῶν and concludes with 6:10. Their overall structure of the letter, then, is: Salutation (1:1–5), Rebuke Section (1:6–4:11), Request Section (4:12–6:10), and Subscription (6:11–18).[200]

Given this division of the letter, Longenecker and Hansen appeal to categories of classical rhetoric and relate the rebuke and request portions of the letter-body to different types of speech. The rebuke section is linked to forensic rhetoric, for in this portion Paul defends his apostleship and past actions (1:11–2:14) and refutes the teachings of the Judaizers against legalism (3:1–18) and nomism (3:19–4:7). Within this section lies the interpretive key or *propositio* of the entire letter—2:15–21. Here they agree with Betz and others that this is the central affirmation of the letter in which Paul summarizes his preceding argument and establishes the issues for the remainder of the letter.[201] Hansen and Longenecker then correlate the request portion of the letter (4:12–6:10) with deliberative rhetoric because Paul exhorts the Galatians to withstand the

---

[197]T. Y. Mullins, "Formulas in New Testament Epistles," 387; italics his.

[198]See G. W. Hansen, *Abraham in Galatians*, 34–42. He cites: BGU 850.1–6; P. Baden 35.1–11; P. Mich. 209.1–13, 26; P. Merton 80.1–15; P. Oxy 113.19–24, 3063.11–16, 2728.1–10, 123.1–9, 1223.1–22, 33–37; P. Ryl 235.6–14; P. Cornell 52.1–12; and P. Herm 11.1–19. The BGU and P. Baden letters are dated A.D. 76 and 87 respectively. The other letters are dated from A.D. 2–4.

[199]C. J. Bjerkelund, *Parakalo: Form, Funktion und Sinn der parakalo-Satz in den paulinischen Briefen*, Bibliotheca Theologica Norvegica 1 (Oslo: Universitetsforlaget, 1967).

[200]R. N. Longenecker, *Galatians*, cix; Hansen, *Abraham in Galatians*, 53–54.

[201]R. N. Longenecker, *Galatians*, 83; Betz, *Galatians*, 114. It is important to observe that other interpreters of Galatians have reached similar conclusions about the importance of this passage apart from epistolographical and rhetorical approaches.

threats from the Judaizers (4:12–5:12) and their own libertine tendencies (5:13–6:10). This, they contend, is Paul's main purpose in writing the letter.

Longenecker and Hansen offer important contributions to the study of Galatians, not the least of which is their synchronic rhetorical approach to the letter through which they recognize the combination of forensic and deliberative rhetoric in the text. Thus, whereas Betz's forensic structure lacks a satisfactory category for integrating the exhortations in chapters 5 and 6, Longenecker and Hansen propose an epistolary basis for understanding this portion of the text in deliberative terms. But it is precisely at this critical point of their epistolary analysis that they are also susceptible to the same criticism they leveled against Betz and others who interpret Galatians primarily on the basis of rhetorical structures and features. That is, it is not clear that their epistolary analysis is less diachronic than Betz's rhetorical analysis. Longenecker, for instance, asserts that Betz pushed his thesis too far because he failed to notice the epistolary evidences that signal transitions in the letter. He attributes this to Betz's diachronic approach by which Betz "lays emphasis on the rhetorical forms in their historical context and seeks to trace out lines of genetic relations with other writings of the time."[202] But the same charge can be made against Hansen and Longenecker for their own emphasis on epistolary formulas and forms in the historical context of nonliterary papyrus letters from which they claim to establish genetic relations between Galatians and θαυμάζω letters. They have also pushed a good thesis too far by overemphasizing the foundational epistolary significance of θαυμάζω (1:6) and δέομαι ὑμῶν (4:12) over the letter's rhetorical features.

As constructive as their works are, Hansen's and Longenecker's structural and interpretive critique of Galatians is not without difficulties. As G. N. Stanton has observed,[203] their overall analysis of Galatians depends heavily on their assertion that Galatians belongs to the genre of private nonliterary Hellenistic rebuke and request letters. Of the forty-three existent papyrus θαυμάζω letters, ranging in dates from the mid-third century B.C. to the fourth century A.D., Hansen presents twelve examples in which the θαυμάζω formula is *almost* always followed by some sort of request. And because Galatians uses the "formula" θαυμάζω (1:6) and a request eventually follows (4:12), all of Galatians is classified as a "rebuke-request" letter. These papyrus letters, however, are quite different from Galatians in several important respects. First of all, the θαυμάζω letters are all extremely short. Second, they are personal

---

[202]R. N. Longenecker, *Galatians*, cix.

[203]Graham N. Stanton, "Review of Abraham in Galatians: Epistolary and Rhetorical Contexts," In *JTS* 43 (1992): 614–15. See also the insightful article by D. F. Watson, "Rhetorical Criticism of the Pauline Epistles Since 1975," *Currents in Research: Biblical Studies* 3 (1995): 234.

letters written or sent by individuals that are addressed to individuals, many of whom are clearly members of the sender's family. As Stanton puts it, "In such a social context a request follows an expression of surprise or mild rebuke almost as surely as day follows night."[204] It ought to be noted further that where θαυμάζω does appear in the ancient epistolary literature, it is a *mild* reproof of some inappropriate or foolish action which is evidently out of character for the recipients. Third, the letters' content, tone, and style are radically different. Echoing Meeks' rhetorical question regarding Betz's association of Galatians with the *Zauberpapyri*, Stanton challenges the "rebuke-request" proposal asking, "Will anyone who reads these twelve papyri and then reads Galatians, really imagine that he is reading the same kind of literature?"

Attempts to align Galatians with particular epistolary sub-genres, such as the "apologetic and magical letter" or "rebuke and request letter," no matter how cogently argued, are burdened with significant problems. This is because Galatians, like Paul's other letters, does not correspond exactly to any other existent letters. Points of convergence between them, then, must be sought by relating isolated aspects of parts of the letters to each other rather than relating the letters to one another as whole correspondences with related parts and similar content. This means that the basis of comparison for establishing relationships of genre is necessarily restricted to disjointed matters of structure, function, setting, mood, length and/or style. Since Paul's letters do not match other writings in these respects, genre comparisons of Paul's letters with other existent letters cannot be exact; they can only be approximate at best. In the end, then, the extent to which connections are found depends on the criteria chosen for defining the term "genre" and the number of exemplars required to establish a genre class. Obviously, interpretive results will vary widely if "epistolary genre" is defined by aspects of form and function alone (e.g., Hansen, Longenecker) or along with form and function includes aspects of content, style, and length (e.g., Betz, Aune). Clearly, as with other dimensions in life, where one begins has a strong influence on where one ends. A similar problem is apparent in studies on the rhetorical nature of Galatians.

Rhetorical Analyses of Galatians

Most studies on the structure of Galatians have focused on the rhetorical traits of the letter rather than the epistolary characteristics, and this is due in no small measure to the abundant rhetorical aspects of the letter. Scholars have used different rhetorical terms for classifying the divisions of the letter, but in

---

[204]Regarding the larger social context of Galatians, it is also relevant to note Quintilian's remark that moving one's hearers to respond is one of "three aims which the orator must always have in view" (*Institutio Oratoria* 3.5.2). See also Cicero *De Optimo Genere Oratorum* 1.3, 5.15.

the following survey we will use a common terminology as described above in order to clarify the relations between these works.

Forensic Rhetoric. As noted above, Betz classified Galatians as an apologetic letter that follows the pattern of forensic rhetoric. Using structural guidelines from classical Greco-Roman rhetoric, he outlined the major parts of the letter as follows: epistolary prescript (1:1–5), exordium (1:6–11), narratio (1:12–2:14), propositio (2:15–21), probatio (3:1–4:31) exhortatio (5:1–6:10), and the epistolary postscript which also functions rhetorically as the conclusio (6:11–18).[205] The purpose of the letter is then described as a defense of Paul's apostleship and a defense of the Spirit.[206] According to Betz's analysis, Paul wrote Galatians as an apology in order to assert the legitimacy of his apostolic authority and the power of God at work in the Spirit through his apostleship.

Betz is not alone in this analysis of Galatians as a forensic letter. G. Howard (1979) compared Galatians to Cicero's *De Inventione* and derived a structural design similar to Betz's: epistolary prescript (1:1–5), exordium (1:6–10), narratio (1:11–2:14), partitio (2:15–21), confirmatio (3:1–4:31), reprehensio (5:1–6:10), and conclusio which also serves as the epistolary postscript (6:11–6:18).[207] Howard assessed the letter's primary purpose, however, as Paul's defense for "the inclusion of uncircumcised Gentiles" in the church.[208] For Howard, this theme is the common thread which binds the parts of the letter together.

B. H. Brinsmead (1979) joined Betz and Howard in proposing that Galatians is best understood in light of forensic rhetoric as an apologetic letter.[209] His structural analysis of the letter closely paralleled Betz's, but Brinsmead joined Howard with a slight modification by concluding the exordium at 1:10. For Brinsmead, though, the purpose of the letter is foremost a "dialogical response to Paul's opponents" and the letter's central issue is Paul's defense of his radical doctrine of justification by faith. This "polemical doctrine," he says ". . . epitomizes Paul's whole answer to the opponents."[210] Certainly justification by faith is an important theme in Galatians, but

---

[205]H. D. Betz, *Galatians*, 16–23.

[206]Ibid., 24–25.

[207]G. Howard, *Paul: Crisis in Galatia*, 48–49. Howard also proposes that the evident epistolary (prescript and postscript) and rhetorical patterns are clear signals that "the letter as a whole is a unit and concentrates on one theme" (49).

[208]Ibid., 82.

[209]B. H. Brinsmead, *Galatians—Dialogical Response*, 187–189. Brinsmead divides the letter as follows: epistolary prescript (1:1–5), prooemium or exordium (1:6–10), narratio (1:11–2:14), propositio (2:15–21), probatio (3:1–4:31 with 3:1–5 functioning as an interrogatio bridging the propositio and probatio), refutatio (5:1–6:10), and epistolary postscript (6:11–18).

[210]Ibid., 200–202.

Brinsmead's assertions about the traditions and theology of Paul's opponents in Galatia are not so conclusive as Brinsmead suggests. J. M. G. Barclay has since demonstrated the problem of "mirror reading" and the weaknesses of Brinsmead's analysis.[211] The point is simply that Brinsmead's study of the letter's genre as forensic rhetoric led him to assume that the position of Paul's opponents could be delineated simply by taking Paul's statements in Galatians as the mirrored response to Paul's opponents.

There have been others, of course, who have accepted or interpreted Galatians as forensic rhetoric. Hans Hübner criticized Betz for pushing the rhetorical analysis too far, but he agreed that Galatians largely fits the judicial type of rhetoric.[212] Similarly, James D. Hester's early work on Galatians[213] followed Betz in classifying the letter as judicial in its rhetorical form and intent. Hester did make some modifications, however, of Betz's structural analysis of the letter's exordium and narratio. His main changes were to hold together 1:11–12 as the stasis (i.e., the basic issue) of the narratio in particular and the letter as a whole and to begin the narratio at 1:15 rather than at 1:12. He thus proposes the following outline for 1:6–2:14: exordium (1:6–10), stasis (1:11–12), transitio (1:13–14), narratio (1:15–2:10), and digressio (2:1–10). Hester has not held his position on the letter's genre in an ironclad way, however; as we will see below. More recently he has interpreted the letter as belonging to the epideictic genre. His forensic reading of Galatians 1:11–2:14, though, emphasizes Paul's struggle with the Galatians as a matter of defining the nature or quality of Paul's apostleship.[214] Hester's study refines and supports Betz's conclusions about the letter's genre and purpose.

In each of these forensic analyses of Galatians, the structural characteristics are largely the same and each interpreter views Paul's central concern in the letter as a defensive response to opponents in Galatia. They diverge from one another on the particular thrust of Paul's apology. The basis for their points of convergence is the letter's internal evidences of a forensic rhetorical structure. The different views on who or what is "on trial" are based on their interpretations of the letter's content. Not everyone has been satisfied with their conclusions, however. Betz himself recognized the problem of fitting 3:1–4:31 into his rhetorical structure. He called this section "extremely difficult to follow" and asserted that evidently "Paul has been very successful—as a skilled rhetorician would be expected to be—in disguising his argumentative

---

[211]J. M. G. Barclay, "Mirror-Reading," 73–93.

[212]Hans Hübner, "Der Galaterbrief und das Verhältnis von antiker Rhetorik und Epistolographie," *TLZ* 109 (1984): 241–50.

[213]James D. Hester, "The Rhetorical Structure of Galatians 1:11–2:14," *JBL* 103 (1984): 223–33.

[214]Cf. J. D. Hester, "Rhetorical Structure of Galatians," 227.

strategy."[215] Perhaps more troubling, though, is relating the paraenetic portion of the letter in chapters 5 and 6 to the forensic genre.[216] Some scholars contend that Betz's difficulties stem from classifying Galatians wrongly as forensic rhetoric.

Deliberative Rhetoric. George A. Kennedy (1984) was among the earliest critics of forensic interpretations of Galatians. He held that such interpretations were misleading and were the result of inadequate methodological procedures. Drawing from David Greenwood's (1970) proposed guidelines for rhetorical criticism,[217] Kennedy developed a more extensive methodology and applied it to writings in the New Testament.[218] When he analyzed the rhetorical nature of Galatians. Kennedy concluded that the letter is unmistakably and wholly deliberative and is comprised of the following parts: amplified salutation (1:1–5), exordium (1:6–10), confirmatio (1:11–5:1), exhortatio (5:2–6:10), and peroratio (6:11–18). Kennedy argued that, as deliberative rhetoric, Galatians is not about judgment of any matters in the past but is, rather, about the immediate future and the particular choice of belief and course of action before the Galatians. Paul's central concern in Galatians is not a self-defense but a persuasive argument aimed at convincing the Galatians that "neither circumcision counts for anything nor uncircumcision, but a new creation" (6:15).[219] Stated another way, the main purpose of the letter is not to defend Paul from his opponents' accusations but to persuade them to hold fast to his gospel and to reject the false gospel of his antagonists.

---

[215]H. D. Betz, *Galatians*, 129.

[216]Ibid., 254. See also critiques of this point in the reviews by Meeks and Aune. See note 181 above.

[217]David Greenwood, "Rhetorical Criticism and Formgeschichte: Some Methodological Considerations," *JBL* 89 (1970): 418. Greenwood wrote, "The first concern of the rhetorical critic is to define the limits of the literary unit, his second is to recognize the structure of a composition and to discern the configuration of its component parts, noting the different rhetorical devices that it contains."

[218]G. A. Kennedy, *New Testament Interpretation*, 33–38. Kennedy's points are: (1) determine the rhetorical unit, (2) assess the rhetorical situation, (3) define the rhetorical problem which is usually evident at the beginning, (4) determine to which of the three types of rhetoric the unit belongs, (5) consider the arrangement and order of the material for persuasive force, and (6) review the process and see how it fits in its context. Margaret Mitchell has contributed further by proposing the following refinement: (1) approach rhetorical criticism as an historical endeavor, (2) consult throughout the investigation actual speeches and letters from antiquity along with the rhetorical handbooks, (3) designate the rhetorical species of the text on the basis of the evidences in the text, (4) demonstrate the appropriateness of genre classification to the content of the text, and (5) examine the rhetorical unit as a compositional unit. See M. Mitchell, *Paul and the Rhetoric of Reconciliation*, 6–19.

[219]G. A. Kennedy, *New Testament Interpretation*, 151.

Kennedy has been joined by others who have aligned Galatians with the deliberative species of the rhetorical genre. Joop Smit (1989) contends that Galatians "contains a speech that exactly corresponds to the model which Hellenistic rhetoric drew up for the genus deliberativum." As for Paul's purpose in Galatians, Smit writes that "The unity of the Christian community twice forms the end and goal of Paul's entire line of thought. In the end the highest ideal he aims at is 'the Israel of God' (6:16). God's purpose with his people has now been realised in Christ as 'the Israel of God' uniting Jews and Gentiles within itself. Paul's eloquence is at the service of that goal."[220] François Vouga (1988) found direct correspondence between Galatians and Demosthenes' speech "Concerning the Peace" (ΠΕΡΙ ΤΗΣ ΕΙΡΗΝΗΣ).[221] What is interesting about Vouga's study is that the rhetorical parts of his deliberative structure of the letter are the same as Betz's forensic structure of the letter. Vouga, however, does not include the prescript (1:1–5) and postscript (6:11–18) of Galatians in his analysis. He evidently saw no rhetorical connection between their obvious epistolary functions and the rhetorical body of the letter.

Benoît Standaert (1985) also interpreted Galatians as deliberative. His structural outline of the letter parallels Betz's and Vouga's rhetorical parts, but for Standaert the principal aim of Galatians is to convince the Galatians to remain firm in the teaching they received from Paul and to dissuade them from accepting circumcision.[222] George Lyons (1985) took a harder line regarding the deliberative force of Galatians to preserve the gospel of freedom. Paul's aim, he argued, "was specifically directed toward securing the Galatians' excommunication of the troublemakers, rejection of their perverted 'gospel,' and renewed allegiance to the gospel of freedom, that they like Paul might abandon Judaism for Christ, that they might turn once again from man to God."[223]

Verena Jegher-Bucher's (1991) deliberative analysis of Galatians presents a different perspective on the organization for the letter. Her structural description runs as follows: epistolary prescript (1:1–5), exordium (1:6–12), argumentatio 1 (1:13–2:16), transitio 1 (2:17–3:5), argumentatio 2 (3:6–4:7), transitio 2 (4:8–20), exhortatio (4:21–6:10), and epistolary postscript (6:11–

---

[220]Joop Smit, "The Letter of Paul to the Galatians," 25.

[221]François Vouga, "Zur rhetorischen Gattung des Galaterbriefs," *ZNW* 79 (1988): 291–292. Vouga's comparison of Demosthenes' ΠΕΡΙ ΤΗΣ ΕΙΡΗΝΗΣ with Galatians is as follows: exordium (lines 1–3 correspond with Gal 1:6–11), narratio (4–12 with 1:12–2:14), propositio (13–14a with 2:15–21), probatio (14b with 3:1–4:31), and exhortatio (24–25 with 5:2–6 :10).

[222]Benoît Standaert, "La rhétorique antique et l'épître aux Galates," *Foi et Vie* 84 (1985): 33–40. Standaert's basic outline of Galatians (36) is: epistolary introduction (1:1–5), propositio (1:6–12), narratio (1:13–2:14), argumentatio (3:1–4:31), exhortation (5:1–6:10), and epilogue (6:11–18).

[223]George Lyons, *Pauline Autobiography*, 175.

18).[224] Jegher-Bucher agrees with others that Paul intends his letter to persuade the Galatians of the truth of his gospel. Robert G. Hall (1987) has also interpreted Galatians as an entirely deliberative letter.[225] He, too, joins those who view Paul's central aim in Galatians to be an attempt to move the Galatian Christians to cleave to his gospel and reject the gospel of his opponents, but Hall offers a further refinement on the letter's beginning. After probing Betz's observation that "[T]he Galatian prescript shows several expansions, notably at the very points where we also find close relationships between the prescript and various other parts of the body of the letter: the title and its definition (1:1), and the christological–soteriological statements (1:4),"[226] Hall was unwilling to classify 1:1–5 as purely an epistolary prescript which set the stage for the beginning of the real rhetoric of the letter at 1:6. Instead, Hall contends that "[b]y anticipating two major lines of argument that he will develop in the letter, Paul has added to his salutation features expected in an exordium."[227] Consequently, Hall develops the rhetorical scheme of Galatians as follows: salutation/exordium (1:1–5), proposition (1:6–9), proof (1:10–6:10), and epilogue (6:11–18). Except for the placement of the exordium in the opening of the letter, Hall's analysis largely parallels Kennedy's.

A Mixture of Forensic and Deliberative. Some scholars are not content to classify Galatians as either forensic or deliberative. For instance, Hansen may view the letter primarily in epistolary terms as a letter of "rebuke and request," but he does not ignore the rhetorical aspects of the letter. As noted above, he views the letter as a mixture of forensic (1:6–4:11) and deliberative (4:12–6:10) oratory. The rebuke section of the letter (1:11–2:14) shows Paul defending his apostleship and past actions. The propositio or interpretive key of the letter follows in 2:15–21 after which comes Paul's refutation of the Judaizers regarding legalism (3:1–18) and nomism (3:19–4:11). The request section of the letter (4:12–6:10) consists of Paul's exhortations for the Galatians to withstand the threats of the Judaizers (4:12–5:12) and their own libertine tendencies (5:13–6:10). As for the purpose of the letter, Hansen concluded that "the overall purpose of the letter is to defend Paul's mission to the Gentiles. To achieve this purpose Paul rebukes his Gentile converts for departing from the

---

[224]Verena Jegher-Bucher, *Der Galaterbrief auf dem Hintergrund antiker Epistolographie und Rhetorik: ein anderes Paulusbild*, AThANT 78 (Zürich: Theologischer Verlag, 1991), 203.
[225]Robert G. Hall, "The Rhetorical Outline for Galatians: A Reconsideration," *JBL* 106 (1987): 277–87.
[226]H. D. Betz, *Galatians*, 37.
[227]R. G. Hall, "Rhetorical Outline for Galatians," 283.

gospel preached beforehand to Abraham and commands them to expel those who have perverted this gospel."[228]

Longenecker also emphasizes the primacy of epistolary characteristics over any rhetorical influences, but his rhetorical analysis is as follows: salutation (1:1–5), exordium (1:6–10), narratio (1:11–2:14), propositio (2:15–21), probatio (3:1–4:11), exhortatio (4:12–6:10), subscription (6:11–18). Again, forensic rhetoric is prominent in 1:6–4:11 and deliberative rhetoric governs 4:12–6:10. As for Paul's central purpose, Longenecker asserts that Galatians is a rebuttal to the message of the Judaizers and a restatement of Paul's "essential message: 'Christ gave himself for our sins' (1:4), 'Christ crucified' (3:1), 'Christ redeemed us from the curse of the law' (3:13), Christians being 'all sons of God through faith in Christ Jesus' (3:26), Christians being 'all one in Christ Jesus' (3:27–28), and Christians having 'the full rights of sons' before God apart from the law (4:4–5)."[229] In all this, Longenecker contends, Paul was drawing from the early church's proclamation.

Wolfgang Harnish (1987) also views Galatians as a mixture of rhetorical species in which forensic rhetoric dominates the first portion of the letter (1:6–4:31) and deliberative rhetoric governs the second portion of the letter (5:1–6:10). But whereas many other rhetorical and epistolary critics of Galatians have found little evidence of Paul's characteristic eschatological perspective in Galatians, Harnish views Paul's main purpose through the mirror of the postscript and asserts that the paraenesis of Galatians—indeed the whole letter—centers precisely on Paul's effort to persuade the Galatians to accept the true gospel's eschatological alternative of "new being."[230]

Epideictic Rhetoric. A fourth perspective on the rhetorical form of Galatians is that of epideictic. Although Hester classified the letter of Galatians earlier as strictly forensic, he has since re-evaluated the rhetorical quality of the letter and aligned it with epideictic rhetoric (1991).[231] The basis for this change is his renewed assessment of the letter's stasis (1:11–12) which led him to the

[228]G. W. Hansen, *Abraham in Galatians*, 159.

[229]Longenecker, *Galatians*, cxix.

[230]Wolfgang Harnisch, "Einübung des neuen Seins: Paulinische Paränese am Beispiel des Galaterbriefs," *ZTK* 84 (1987): 279–96. See especially 286–87. On the eschatological dimension of the paranesis in Galatians, Harnisch writes, "Für die paulinischen Redeakte von Warnung und Empfehlung oder Abraten und Zuraten ist somit gerade nicht die Dimension eines ethischen Komparativs, sondern die einer *eschatologischen Alternative* charakteristisch. . . . Was auf dem Spiel steht, ist ja nichts anderes als das vom Evangelium eröffnete neue Sein" (287).

[231]James D. Hester, "Placing the Blame: The Presence of Epideictic in Galatians 1 and 2," in *Persuasive Artistry: Studies in New Testament Rhetoric in Honor of George A. Kennedy*, ed. D. F. Watson, JSNTSup 50 (Sheffield: Sheffield Academic Press, 1991), 281–307.

conclusion that the "larger issue is the quality of the relationship Paul had with the Galatians and the values that were the foundation of that relationship."[232] Since the stasis of quality is primarily a concern of epideictic rhetoric and Hester views the overall tone of the letter as a reproach, epideictic rhetoric, which emphasizes praise (i.e., of Paul) and/or blame (i.e., of the Galatians), is the most suitable genre class for Galatians. Paul's purpose, according to Hester, is "to remind the Galatians of the character of the gospel that was revealed to him and preached by him to them; he is its model and therefore theirs."[233] Stated another way, Hester sees Paul's overriding concern not as a matter of faith's substance but as a matter of how to live life faithfully. Although Hester's study has the whole letter in view, his structural analysis focuses only on chapters 1 and 2, which he outlines as follows: epistolary prescript (1:1–5), exordium (1:6–10), and an encomium (1:11–2:21) which is comprised of a stasis statement (προοίμιον, 1:11–12), and an encomiastic narrative (1:13–2:14) with a slightly expanded chreia (2:11–14) and an elaboration of the chreia in the epilogue (2:15–21).[234]

Antonio Pitta (1992) has developed a more comprehensive analysis of Galatians as an example of epideictic rhetoric. According to Pitta, Galatians is comprised of an epistolary prescript (1:1–5), an exordium (1:6–10), a propositio (1:11–12), four demonstrations (demonstratio) of the propositio (1:13–2:21; 3:1–4:7; 4:8–5:12; 5:13–6:10), and an epistolary postscript (6:11–18). The demonstrations do not match any epistolographical or rhetorical models, but each demonstration follows the same pattern of apostrophe (1:6–10; 3:1–5; 4:8–11; 5:13–15), protraction (1:13–2:14; 3:6–29; 4:12–5:1; 5:16–6:10), and peroration (2:15–21; 4:1–7; 5:2–12; 6:11–18). In addition to the primary propositio (1:11–12), Pitta identifies two secondary propositios (3:6–7; 5:16) that highlight the essential content of the letter and prepare the way for the synthesis of the propositios in the declaration of "new creation" (6:15), which

---

[232]Ibid., 281.

[233]Ibid., 282.

[234]An encomium is a feature of epideictic rhetoric in which the speaker uses examples that demonstrate a person's virtues and establish the basis for honor. The encomium itself was often a speech. A chreia is a rhetorical term that designates memorable, widely-known sayings. Hester outlines the narrative as follows: γένος, 1:13–14; ἀναστροφή, 1:15–17, πράξεις, 1:18–24; and σύγκρισις, 2:1–14. The γένος is a statement of origin legitimating the basis for praise. The ἀναστροφη is a review of circumstances that indicate the person's character. The πράξεις states those activities or occurrences that demonstrate the person's virtues. The σύγκρισις is a comparison with others that "proves" the person's character. See Hester, 296, 306–307. See also idem, "The Use and Influence of Rhetoric in Galatians 2:11–14," *TZ* 42 (1986): 386–408.

Pitta sees as a summary statement of the whole gospel Paul presents in Galatians.[235]

Pitta contends that Paul's letter to the Galatians is not a matter of self-defense or defense of his gospel; neither is it a rebuke of his opponents nor a persuasive appeal to show the place of circumcision or the law for the Christian life. Rather, Pitta asserts that Paul is responding to a situation in which the gospel is becoming increasingly irrelevant to the Galatians and so his principal aim is to re-evangelize the Galatians on the full implications of the Christian life because they are nearing apostasy. By this he means that Paul's fundamental concern is the quality of relationships between himself and the Galatians. Thus issues of christology, pneumatology, the law, and the opponents are all secondary concerns, for Paul is most concerned with the implications of being "one in Christ" (3:28). This is the new level of existence for both circumcised and uncircumcised Christians.[236]

Galatians and the Problem of Genre

The epistolary and rhetorical character of Galatians has received intense scrutiny from both scholars whose expertise is primarily in the area of biblical literature and those whose specialty is classical literature. Together, they have demonstrated the inescapable truth that Paul's letters are integrally related to the literary and rhetorical environments of the first century A.D. Hellenistic world. They have also shown the strong influence of rhetoric upon epistolary theory and practice as well as the predominately oral character of Paul's rhetorical letters. And while they may differ in their emphases on the epistolary or rhetorical character of Galatians as well as in their assessments of the letter's structure, logic and purpose, nearly all agree that Galatians is a carefully structured argument. But how is it that such careful and skillful scholars can draw such a broad range of conclusions about the letter's genre and central purpose?

The spectrum of interpretive results is especially conspicuous given their common appeals to the same subject matter and the use of rhetorical and epistolary practices to clarify the development and meaning of Paul's argument. One recognizable problem is the evident tendency in some studies to force Galatians into a theoretical epistolary or rhetorical pattern. Yet even in works that demonstrate methodological advances in giving priority to the biblical text over the theoretical descriptions in epistolary and rhetorical handbooks, the remarkably diverse conclusions about the genre and purpose of Galatians

---

[235] Antonio Pitta, *Disposizione e Messaggio della Lettera ai Galati: Analisi retorico letteraria*, AnBib 131 (Rome: Pontifical Biblical Institute, 1992), 211–15.
[236] Ibid., 186.

remain. This is because many scholars have sought to align the letter with a single rhetorical genre and once that decision is made, no matter how carefully, the interpreter's view of the letter's central purpose will be shaped accordingly. Those who identify the compositional structure and tone of Galatians as forensic rhetoric must view Paul's principal aim as accusation or defense. Interpreters who assess the evidence as deliberative must understand Paul's central purpose as a persuasive appeal for moving the Galatians to reject one course of action or to pursue a favorable one. Epideictic assessments must render Paul's purpose as the elevation of a certain quality of a shared relationship or value. Paul's use of an epistolary rebuke and request structure must mean that Paul is most concerned with refuting his opponents and exhorting the Galatians to withstand the threats against them. In short, the first problem with locating the genre of Galatians is that no single rhetorical or epistolary interpretation of the letter is wholly satisfactory. The wide range of conclusions by many capable scholars demonstrates that Paul's letter to the Galatians cannot be constrained within any single rhetorical or epistolary pattern. In this study, then, we will leave the question of genre open even though we will appeal to certain rhetorical and epistolary practices and categories.

Another reason for the divergent interpretations of Galatians' genre and purpose is that these studies have largely failed to take into account the ancient Mediterranean world's emphasis on flexibility and adaptability in its rhetorical and epistolary practices. There were limits, of course, or effective communication would not be possible. But while rhetorical and epistolary critics have given close attention to those points of convergence between Galatians and particular aspects of the literary and oral environment of Paul's world, they have yet to take sufficiently into account the evidence and consequence of Paul's uniqueness or "wise adaptability" in the letter. In chapter two of this study, then, we will examine the place of propriety for effective communication in the ancient Greco-Roman world. Later, we will also see something of Paul's appropriate rhetorical and epistolary flexibility in Galatians.

A third difficulty with these studies is that their concentrated focus on the rhetorical and epistolary type (genus, γένη) and structure (dispositio, τάξις) of Galatians has not adequately addressed other dimensions of the text, such as its invention (inventio, εὕρεσις) or the presence and function of stylistic oral clues within the letter (elocutio; λέξις, ἑρμηνεία) that would help the hearer understand Paul's message and intention regardless of whether or not the listener had any formal oratorical training. Throughout chapter three, then, we will draw from certain parts of the ancient handbooks that have been largely overlooked in discussions of Galatians. In particular, we will seek to be attentive to Greco-Roman resources and principles for arranging and expressing a message persuasively. That is, we will consider the matter of invention—a topic which Cicero called "the most important of all the divisions."[237] We will also consider principles for arrangement and some stylistic matters of Greco-Roman communication that are relevant to this study of Galatians, such as periods, figures of speech, repetition, word selection, oral formulas, and oral themes. In other words, we will be attentive to some of the oral and aural clues that would help the Galatian listeners receive and interpret Paul's message.

A fourth problem with these epistolary and rhetorical approaches to Galatians is their frequent dismissal of the letter's prescript as an expanded epistolary convention that has little bearing on the meaning or direction of the whole letter. But in light of the evidences of Paul's remarkable flexibility in adapting and adopting many rhetorical and epistolary conventions in his day, and recognizing the dominant oral character of Galatians and the aural environment in which it would have been received, does it not seem reasonable to suspect that the strange expansions in the prescript might also express a clear and intentional rhetorical and interpretive function? As we will see below in chapter four, the prescript has not been neglected entirely, but R. B. Hays was certainly correct in his assessment that the prescript "has probably received insufficient attention as an indicator of central themes in the letter."[238] In this study, then, we will not push past the prescript in route to "weightier" theological problems or to the more widely discussed epistolary or rhetorical aspects of the letter. Rather, we will focus intensely on the letter's beginning and then explore its thematic relationships with the remainder of Paul's message to the Galatians. It will become evident by the conclusion of this study that the ancient Greco-Roman practice of putting an argument's strongest points at the beginning and ending of the argument throws new light on the development and emphasis of Paul's letter to the Galatians by highlighting the crucial role of the Risen Crucified Christ for understanding and interpreting the letter.

---

[237]Cicero De Inventione 1.9.
[238]R. B. Hays, "Christology and Ethics in Galatians," CBQ 49 (1987): 277, n. 28.

CHAPTER TWO

SPEECH, LETTER, AND THE GOAL OF PROPRIETY

Epistolary and rhetorical characteristics are inextricably combined in Galatians. On one hand, Paul's communication to the Galatians is written and sent as a letter. It incorporates epistolary structures and formulas that are especially evident in the prescript and postscript. On the other hand, Galatians bears evidences of rhetorical arrangements and techniques, including acknowledgment of an amanuensis (6:11) which signals the letter's oral dictation. Although we cannot know the extent of the scribe's own contribution to the letter, it seems that the problems challenging the churches in Galatia were topics of conversation between Paul and "all the brothers" who were with him—a point which suggests further that the letter was not hastily or carelessly composed.[1] Moreover, the letter would have been read aloud or delivered as a speech to the Galatian congregations, which is to say that the letter would have been heard widely as a speech before it was read at-large and scrutinized as a letter. Simply put, Galatians is more than either a common private letter or a written public speech; it is letter-speech[2] which fuses both epistolary and rhetorical elements in order to address the crisis in Galatia.

The necessity and difficulty of interpreting the epistolary and rhetorical aspects of Paul's letters is not a new concern. Many studies have concentrated on one dimension or the other. More recently, however, scholars have recognized that rhetorical analyses should not be superimposed indiscriminately upon Paul's letters without regard for the correspondences' epistolary characteristics.[3] Similarly, epistolary analyses cannot ignore the letters'

---

[1]On the practice of collaboration, see G. A. Kennedy, *The Art of Rhetoric in the Roman World*, 183. See also Cicero *Brutus* 51.190 and idem, *Orator* 37.130.

[2]Sam K. Williams, *Galatians*, Abingdon New Testament Commentaries (Nashville: Abingdon Press, 1997), 30.

[3]This is precisely M. Mitchell's criticism of R. Jewett's rhetorical analysis of 1 Thessalonians in which "he subsumes the epistolary salutation and thanksgiving formulae under the rhetorical category of exordium without discussion" (Mitchell, *Paul and the Rhetoric of Reconciliation*, 10, n. 33). In her analysis of 1 Corinthians, Mitchell contends that the rhetorical genre "applies to the argument in the body of the letter; it does not replace the letter as the genre of the text," thus when Mitchell identifies 1 Corinthians as a "deliberative

inescapable rhetorical aspects.[4] Thus regardless of whether interpreters now view Paul's letters primarily in terms of rhetorical or epistolary categories, many are aware that both dimensions must be addressed in the interpretation of Paul's compositions.

Still, a problem remains. Even though epistolary and rhetorical forms are often recognized and analyzed according to their respective theories and examples, adequate attention has not been given to the uniqueness of Paul's rhetorical and epistolary forms and their relation as coordinated aspects of single, united communications. Consequently, epistolary characteristics of Paul's letters—such as the prescript and postscript in Galatians—are often separated from the letter's rhetorical dimensions and purposes so that, even when correspondences between the two kinds of forms are recognized, the significance of their integrated relationships for interpreting the letters is often missed.[5] Conversely, rhetorical forms and functions—such as the exordium and

---

letter," she means "a letter which employs deliberative rhetoric in the letter body" (22, n. 5). Mitchell then analyzes 1 Corinthians utilizing both epistolary and rhetorical forms and functions as follows: 1:1–3, epistolary prescript; 1:4–9, epistolary thanksgiving; 1:10–15:58, epistolary body containing a deliberative argument; and 16:1–24, epistolary closing with customary business, travel plans, final admonitions and greetings (184–86). Other scholars have analyzed Paul's letters likewise with similar productive results. For Galatians, see especially Longenecker (*Galatians*), Hansen (*Abraham in Galatians*), and J. Louis Martyn (*Galatians*, The Anchor Bible, v. 33A [New York: Doubleday, 1997]).

[4]See especially Longenecker (*Galatians*, cv–cix) and Hansen (*Abraham in Galatians*, 21–71) who stress the letter's epistolary context but not to the exclusion of the letter's rhetorical context. Their common criticism of Betz is that he did not give adequate attention to the epistolary characteristics of Galatians. Classen ("St. Paul's Epistles," 269) agrees, but he goes further in asserting that "there is no reason why one should restrict oneself to the rhetoric of the ancients in interpreting texts from antiquity, and not avail oneself of the discoveries and achievements of more recent times" (290). Here, Classen has in mind the New Rhetoric reflected in such works as W. Wuellner's, "Where is Rhetorical Criticism Taking Us," *CBQ* 49 (1987): 448–63, and "Greek Rhetoric and Pauline Argumentation." The New Rhetoric was set forth in 1958 by Perelman and Olbrechts-Tyteca who drew from ancient rhetorical conventions but made deliberate alterations as proposed improvements. Mitchell is correct, however, that using 20th century genre classifications and rules to interpret first century texts is a methodological error that "only confuses" and "can skew an analysis." See Mitchell, 7–8, n. 23. For Mitchell's own methodological "mandates," see above, chapter one, n. 218.

[5]Cf. Betz, *Galatians*, 37, where he observes that the curious expansions in Gal 1:1–5 are closely related to important points in the rhetorical argument that he traces through the body of the letter. Mitchell makes a similar observation in her analysis of 1 Cor. She writes, "Already in the epistolary prescript Paul begins to lay the groundwork for his argument for unity . . ." (*Paul and the Rhetoric of Reconciliation*, 193). Neither noticed, however, that Paul is applying a fundamental rhetorical principal in the epistolary prescript that is crucial for understanding and interpreting the letter.

peroratio—are often ignored because of an interpreter's emphasis on epistolary forms.[6]

This is due in part to the current view among some scholars that rhetoric and epistolography were two separate fields in antiquity whose genres and components ought to be classified and analyzed by modern interpreters primarily within the realms of their respective theory and practice.[7] Certainly, of course, there can be no doubt that careful attention to the unique

---

[6]This is especially evident in the widespread designation of Gal 1:1–5 as only "epistolary prescript." See also T. Y. Mullins ("Formulas in New Testament Epistles," 387) who, on the basis of epistolary characteristics of papyri letters, asserts that "the opening is a sort of warm-up for the main issue and provides a convenient clustering place for matters less important than the main issue (but not necessarily introductory to it). The closing constitutes the final communication and is a natural clustering place for matters of minor importance which the writer wants to add before breaking off." Longenecker (*Galatians*, cvi) and Hansen (*Abraham in Galatians*, 29, 33) cite Mullins approvingly regarding Galatians, though primarily for his position that epistolary formulas are clustered at points of transition in the letter. Nevertheless, while openings and closings for non-literary papyri letters may function as Mullins proposes, the role of beginnings and endings is quite different from a rhetorical perspective and from Paul's use of them in Galatians.

[7]Cf. C. Joachim Classen, "St. Paul's Epistles," 288–9. Classen writes, "rhetoric (oratory) and epistolography were regarded as two different fields in antiquity, and it seems advisable, therefore, to stay within the elaboration and presentation of their respective theory." The same point is upheld by Stowers who writes that "the letter-writing tradition was essentially independent of rhetoric" (*Letter Writing*, 52). On the secondary influence of rhetoric on Paul's epistles, see especially Stanley E. Porter, "The Theoretical Justification for Application of Rhetorical Categories to Pauline Epistolary Literature," and Jeffrey T. Reed, "Using Ancient Rhetorical Categories to Interpret Paul's Letters: A Question of Genre," in *Rhetoric and the New Testament: Essays from the 1992 Heidelberg Conference*, eds. S. E. Porter and T. H. Olbricht, JSNTSup 90 (Sheffield: Sheffield Academic Press, 1993), 100–22 and 292–324. On the singular influence of rhetoric, see F. Vouga and J. Smit who ignore entirely the prescript and postscript of Galatians (Vouga, "Zur rhetorischen Gattung des Galaterbriefs," 291–92; Smit, "The Letter of Paul to the Galatians," 1–26). Similarly, D. Hellholm excludes the prescript in his analysis of Romans ("Amplificatio in the Macro–Structure of Romans," in *Rhetoric and the New Testament: Essays from the 1992 Heidelberg Conference*, ed. S. E. Porter and T. Olbricht, JSNTSup 90 [Sheffield: Sheffield Academic Press, 1993], 125–27, 137). But on the primary influence of rhetoric upon epistolography, G. A. Kennedy (*The Cambridge History of Literary Criticism, Volume 1: Classical Criticism* [Cambridge: Cambridge University Press, 1989; repr. 1995], 88–89) notes correctly that "A written text may have implied a gradual privileging of the visual over the aural . . . But it is easy to exaggerate these potentialities. Throughout antiquity, texts continued to be read aloud, rather than silently. Sound remained an integral part of the literary experience." D. E. Aune observed similarly that "one must, of necessity, turn to other genres taken into the letter form (such as those from oratory) in order to understand adequately NT letters" ("Review of Galatians—Dialogical Response to Opponents," *CBQ* 46 (1984): 147). See also Klaus Berger, "Apostelbrief und apostolische Rede: Zum Formular frühchristlicher Briefe," *ZNW* 65 (1974): 190–231; G. A. Kennedy, *New Testament Interpretation*; and D. W. Watson, "A Rhetorical Analysis of Philippians," 57–88.

characteristics of rhetoric and epistolography have expanded our understanding of Paul and the world in which he lived. But were letters and speech delineated so sharply in the Greco-Roman world of the first century A.D.? More particularly, does Galatians maintain such a clear separation between rhetorical and epistolographical forms and functions, particularly in its curious opening and closing? Just what are we to make of the apparent fusion of letter and speech in Paul's message to the Christians in Galatia?

In this chapter, we will explore certain relationships between epistolography and oratory as mediums of communication in the ancient Greco-Roman world. In particular—because of the prominence of rhetoric in Paul's world and the widespread recognition of Galatians' rich rhetorical features, we will begin by reviewing several salient points regarding the goals of oratory and the orator's chief means for reaching them. We will then examine the place of epistolography within the realm of rhetoric. Here, too, we will see the ancient Mediterranean world's emphasis on flexibility and propriety in communication.

In the next chapter, we will look more closely at Greco-Roman principles for communicating persuasively in speech and in writing. It will become apparent that the ancients placed particular emphasis on a communication's beginning, linear progression, and end—regardless of the particular medium of expression. In subsequent chapters, we will consider the significance of this principle for understanding Galatians and the curious fusion of letter and speech in its beginning. Indeed, as J. Classen has noted, we will see that it is "not what conforms to the rules, but what seems at variance with them [that] often proves most instructive for interpretation. Correspondingly, in trying to understand a particular composition, one should always look not primarily for what is in accordance with the rules or with general practice, but for the contrary."[8]

I. RHETORIC AND SPEECH

The aim of rhetoric in the Hellenistic world of late Western antiquity was persuasive communication. The ideal orator was one who possessed an ability to communicate persuasively on any conceivable subject under any circumstance.[9] To accomplish this goal, the ideal orator learned "to think and speak rightly."[10] That is, Greco-Roman rhetoric was not a matter of crafting and

---

[8]J. Classen, "St. Paul's Epistles," 290.

[9]Cf. Plato *Phaedrus* (trans. H. N. Fowler, LCL [Cambridge, Mass.: Harvard University Press, 1990]) 261A; Aristotle *Rhetoric* 1.1.12, 1.2.1, 3.1.5; Cicero *De Inventione* 1.5 and *De Oratore* 1.6.21; Quintilian *Institutio Oratoria* 2.21.4; and Tacitus *Dialogus de Oratoribus* 30, 32.

[10]Quintilian *Institutio Oratoria* 2.15.37. Here Quintilian expresses quite well the view of Cicero who wrote that "eloquence consists of language and thought" (*De Optimo Genere Oratorum* 2.4). Quintilian also defines rhetoric as "the science of speaking well" (2.15.34).

uttering words opportunistically with "the fluency of a cheapjack."[11] Rather, "true oratory" was aimed at persuasive eloquence, that fitting and fine-tuned discourse that delights the ear like a well-played harp and enlightens the mind with truth.[12]

The Goal of Eloquence

Eloquence (εὐγλωσσία, δεινότης, *eloquentia*) held a place of chief importance in the domain of Greco-Roman communication, especially among rhetoricians. Its cultivation was an orator's greatest care, and students of rhetoric worked diligently to meld their personal resources with the rules of the art in order to forge themselves into articulate communicators. Of eloquence, Quintilian wrote that:

> it is on this that teachers of rhetoric concentrate their attention, since it cannot possibly be acquired without the assistance of the rules of art: it is this which is the chief object of our study, the goal of all our exercises and all our efforts at imitation, and it is to this that we devote the energies of a lifetime.[13]

See also Cicero *De Inventione* 1.5.6, 3.1.20; idem, *De Oratore* 1.31.138, 1.2.5; and *Rhetorica ad Herennium* 1.2.1. In this, they are all following Aristotle who began his *Rhetoric* (1.1.1) with the assertion that rhetoric is the corresponding "antistrophe" to the "stophe" called Dialectic. Logic and rhetoric are not the same, yet they constitute a pair. They are alike in terms of their modes of thought and their applicability to all subject matter. They are different in that logic is more abstract and analytic and rhetoric is more concrete and synthetic. Logic focuses on analysis and study; rhetoric concentrates on organizing and presenting communication. Cf. Aristotle *Rhetoric* 1.1.1–6.

[11]Quintilian *Institutio Oratoria* 10.1.8. See also Cicero *Orator* 14.47, where he insists that the true orator is not "a ranter in the forum, but a scholarly and finished speaker."

[12]Quintilian *Institutio Oratoria* Pr. 14–16; 2.8.15; 5.14.30–32. It should be noted at the outset, of course, that there were divergent views about the meaning and place of rhetoric in the ancient Hellenistic world. Some philosophers, from at least the time of Plato, condemned rhetoric for it seemed to have more to do with appearances and manipulation than truth and goodness. Such, indeed, was much of the popular rhetoric in the first centuries B.C. and A.D. See, for instance, Seneca who derides popularized rhetoric for "trying to win the approbation of a throng of hearers" and to "allure the ears of young men" (*Epistulae Morales* 20.1–2). Nevertheless, the influence of Aristotle, Isocrates, Cicero and Quintilian prevailed and rhetoric was widely accepted and taught as an essential valued skill for exercising responsible citizenship in the Greco-Roman world. On the shift in rhetorical training from the art of persuasion to secondary matters of style and embellishment, see G. A. Kennedy, *The Art of Rhetoric in the Roman World.*

[13]Quinitlian *Institutio Oratoria* 8.Pr.16. He also wrote encouragingly, "let those that are young, or rather let all of us whatever our age, since it is never too late to resolve to follow what is right, strive with all our hearts and devote all our efforts to the pursuit of virtue and eloquence; and perchance it will be granted to us to attain the perfection that we seek" (12.1.31). See also Quintilian *Institutio Oratoria* 1.1.6, 2.2.8; 8.Pr.12–33; Cicero *Orator* 13.40–42; *Rhetorica ad Herennium* 4.6.9.

Throughout the Greco-Roman world, the ability to communicate well was critical for citizenship and eloquence was essential for success.[14] Seneca expressed well the view of many when he wrote, "Give your mind to eloquence for from this you can range easily into all the arts."[15] Of course, eloquence, then as now, was not easily defined. Indeed, it was widely acknowledged that "eloquence has more than one face" and that "the types and varieties of eloquence change with the age."[16] Eloquence was often viewed differently according to the situation, the audience, and the speaker's own utilization of his or her own unique gifts.[17] Nevertheless, there were common identifiable principles of communicating well and there were recognizable characteristics of ideal communicators regardless of these changing variables.

From at least the time of Homer, eloquence for both Greeks and Romans was understood primarily in terms of clarity, orderliness and appropriateness of expression.[18] Eloquence was also marked by rhythm, vividness, timeliness, precision and ornamentation.[19] Considered a difficult though worthy prize to achieve, articulate communication was measured by its power to instruct, delight and move an audience. In whatever form it took, either as a type of speech or written composition, eloquence was viewed not only as communicating what was necessary but also as the fluent expression of ideas with words that would accomplish the communicator's aim.[20] Thus communicators sought eloquence or the mastery of language by striving after knowledge and wisdom. To be sure, eloquence was the goal of every true communicator, but its characteristics and appropriate expressions in the oral environment of the Greco-Roman world were especially the concern of orators.

---

[14]Cf. Cicero *Orator* 41.141; Tacitus *Dialogus de Oratoribus* 36–40; Seneca *Controversiae*, trans. M. Winterbottom, LCL (Cambridge, Mass.: Harvard University Press, 1974), 2.Pr.3.

[15]Seneca *Controversiae* 2.Pr.3.

[16]Tacitus *Dialogus de Oratoribus* 18; also Quintilian *Institutio Oratoria* 11.1.4.

[17]Quintilian *Institutio Oratoria* 12.10.64–72.

[18]Homer *Iliad* (trans. A. T. Murray, LCL [Cambridge, Mass.: 1985–88]) 3.214, 3.221–223, 1.249. See also Plato *Phaedrus* 260c, 272d, 269d; Aristotle *Rhetoric* 3.2.1–15, 3.5, 3.6, 3.7, 3.12.1–6, 5.1; Quintilian *Institutio Oratoria* 2.3.8, 3.10.37, 5.14.30–32, 8.Pr.13–15, 8.1.1, 8.2.22–24, 9.4.22, 12.10.64; Cicero *De Partitione Oratorica* 2.31, *Brutus* 72.252–3; *Rhetorica ad Herennium* 1.9.14f, 4.12.17.

[19]Cf. Cicero *Orator* 36.125, 68.229, 71.236; idem *De Oratore* 1.32.144, 3.14.53; Quintilian *Institutio Oratoria* 8.Pr.27–28, 8.3.2–3, 9.2.40, 10.7.28; Aristotle *Rhetoric* 3.8.1f.

[20]Cf. Quintilian *Institutio Oratoria* 1.2.30, 1.8.17, 8.Pr.13–14, 9.4.7, 10.1.109, 10.3.6, 12.5.1, 12.10.69–72; Cicero *Orator* 44.150, 68.229; *De Optimo Genere Oratorum* 5.16; Aristotle *Rhetoric* 3.1.5, 3.2; Tacitus *Dialogus de Oratoribus* 30–32.

The Ideal Orator

Rhetoricians held that the goal of eloquence was achievable principally through an orator's harmonious blend of nature (φύσις, *natura*, *ingenium*, *facultas*), technique or art (τέχνη, παιδεία, ἐπιστήμη, μάθησις, *ars*, *scientia*, *doctrina*), and experience drawn from constant exercise (γυμνασία, ἐμπειρία, ἄσκησις, μελέτη, συνήθεια, declamatio).[21] Some orators included imitation as a means and measure of eloquence, but most included it under art.[22] In order to speak eloquently on any given occasion, though, the ideal orator not only sought excellence in each of these areas but also desired practical wisdom for speaking appropriately.

Natural Ability. By "nature" and its related terms, the rhetoricians meant a speaker's innate qualities and natural dispositions. The ideal speaker ought to be physically attractive and healthy, and he or she should also possess a strong and pleasant voice. The true orator's natural mental capacities would include a good memory, perceptiveness, imagination, and a special facility with language. Special importance lay here because the speaker's natural "genius" was the foundation of the rhetorician's most important faculty—invention.[23] The term "nature" also encompassed the orator's moral character. The ideal orator was a good person who was fair and honest and who could speak wisely and courageously even in dangerous circumstances.[24] Together, the orator's

---

[21]Cf. Plato *Phaedrus* 269; Isocrates *Antidosis* 187–191; *Adv. Soph.* 14–18; Cicero *De Inventione* 1.1.2, *De Oratore* 1.4.14; Tacitus *Dialogus de Oratoribus* 33; and Plutarch *De liberis educ.* 4.

[22]Cf. Quintilian *Institutio Oratoria* 3.5.1: "Oratorical skill is brought to the highest degree of excellence by nature, art, and exercise, to which some add a fourth, imitation, which I include under art." Here, Quintilian is following the earlier position of Plato who, in *Phaedrus*, roots this three-dimensional view of rhetorical excellence in a dialogue of Socrates: "The perfection which is required of the finished orator is, or rather must be, like the perfection of anything else, partly given by nature, but may also be assisted by art. If you have natural power and add to it knowledge and practice, you will be a distinguished speaker. If you fall short of either of these, you will be to that extent defective"(269). See also Quintilian 10.1.20f, 10.2.13f; Cicero *De Oratore* 2.21.89f; Isocrates *Against the Sophists* 14–15; and *Rhetorica ad Herennium* 1.2.3.

[23]"Invention is the devising of matter, true or plausible, that would make the case convincing" (*Rhetorica ad Herennium* 1.2.3). Lausberg describes the connection between "nature" and "invention" precisely when he writes, "Tätigkeit des ingenium ist die inventio" (Lausberg, 550, par. 1152). Quintilian asserted that "the greatest qualities of the orator are beyond all imitation, by which I mean, talent, invention, force, facility and all the qualities which are independent of art" (Quintilian *Institutio Oratoria* 10.2.12). See also Cicero *De Inventione* 1.7.9; and Quintilian *Institutio Oratoria* 10.1.130.

[24]Cf. Quintilian *Institutio Oratoria* 1.Pr.9, where he insists, "The first essential for such an one is that he should be a good man." Again, the orator "should be blameless in point of character" (1.Pr.18). See also 1.2.3; 2.15.28; 2.20.8. Regarding the true orator's courage, see especially Quintilian *Institutio Oratoria* 2.16.7–19 and Seneca *Epistulae Morales* 6.5.

physical, mental, and moral qualities formed the material basis for oratorical success.[25]

Linguistic Skills. By the terms τέχνη and *ars*, along with their synonyms, the rhetoricians meant the whole system of grammatical and rhetorical principles and rules which were developed descriptively and promoted prescriptively for persuasive communication.[26] Rhetorical systems classified and summarized matters pertaining to the speaker's resources (*vis oratoris*), the speech itself (*oratio*), and the particular speech situation (*quaestio infinita* and *quaestio finita*).[27] Again, however, it is important to note that "eloquence is not born of the theoretical system; rather, the system is born of eloquence."[28] That is, the basic rhetorical precepts and skills taught by rhetoricians were written and collected into treatises and handbooks for instruction in persuasive speaking,[29] but the typologies presented there were not intended to be exhaustive of every conceivable type of speech.[30] Rather they were written primarily for students of rhetoric to help them learn the art of communicating persuasively in the civic expressions of forensic, deliberative, and epideictic discourse. Toward this end the manuals and treatises on rhetoric describe in clear, logical order the general principles and specific techniques for effective oral communication. But the faculty of true oratorical prowess, which the Greeks called ἕξις, was also a matter of writing, reading, and acquiring knowledge about a wealth of subjects. So intimately connected are all these elements of the "art of speaking" that Quintilian insisted:

> if one of them be neglected, we shall but waste the labour which we have devoted to the others. For eloquence will never attain to its full development or robust health, unless it acquires strength by frequent practice in writing, while such practice without the models supplied by reading will be like a ship drifting aimlessly without a steersman.[31]

---

[25]There were natural limits for an orator's success, of course, depending on ones natural aptitudes and training. Persons possess different abilities for learning, remembering, and applying their knowledge. Cf. Isocrates *Antidosis* 188–191; Cicero *De Oratore* 1.25. Cicero again through the character of Crassus, adds that one's natural endowment should also include "a passionate inclination, an ardor like that of love, without which no man will ever attain anything great in life" (1.30).

[26]Cf. Quintilian *Institutio Oratoria* 2.14.5, 2.17.41; *Rhetorica ad Herennium* 1.2.3; Cicero *Brutus* 29.111.

[27]Rhetors used the terms *quaestio infinita* for general theses and *quaestio finita* for the specific genres of forensic, deliberative, and epideictic discourse.

[28]Cicero *De Oratore* 1.32.146. See also Quintilian *Institutio Oratoria* 9.4.14.

[29]For a list and brief discussion of the handbooks, see chapter one, note 91.

[30]Cf. Quintilian *Institutio Oratoria* 3.4.3, 11.1.47.

[31]Quintilian *Institutio Oratoria* 10.1.1–2. For Quintilian true oratory was attainable only "by reading and listening to the best writers and orators, since we shall thus learn not

Cicero also maintained that "no man can be an orator possessed of every praiseworthy accomplishment unless he has attained the knowledge of all liberal arts."[32]

Greco-Roman rhetoric was a popular systematic approach for acquiring eloquent persuasive speech for civic oratory. Yet the ordered "technique" for achieving this end was largely the training of the mind in the art of clear, precise thinking and expression through listening, reading, writing, and speaking. Through this holistic approach to thinking and to appropriate, powerful self-expression in words, the ideal orator became equipped for communicating well in any circumstance with "the weapons of his eloquence ready for battle and prepared to deal with every emergency."[33] But how does one prepare to communicate readily in organized fluency and maximize one's natural talents? Through persistent practice.

Ample Experience. The third critical area of development for the ideal orator is experience drawn from constant exercise in communicating. Proficiency in utilizing grammatical and rhetorical skills along with one's natural abilities required extensive experience and ongoing maintenance. Continuous drill was deemed absolutely necessary for approaching the goal of ideal oratory. Thus Isocrates compared the training of the rhetorician's mind for eloquent communication to the training of a gymnast's body for athletic events,[34] and Cicero likened rhetorical practice to preparing for sport and battle.[35] Quintilian insisted that "the art of speaking can only be attained by hard work and assiduity of study, by a variety of exercises and repeated trial."[36]

Practice was essential for approaching and achieving the goal of eloquence. It involved repeated exercises and healthy criticism in each aspect of the art. Throughout their education, then, students were evaluated by teachers and fellow classmates as they worked to develop their faculties of invention, arrangement, style, memory and delivery through a rigorous blend of reading,

---

merely the words by which things are to be called, but when each particular word is most appropriate" (10.1.8).

[32]Cicero *De Oratore* 1.6. See also Cicero *De Oratore* 2.20.90–92 and Isocrates *Antidosis* 267. Opinions differed between the Greeks and Romans regarding the necessity of a liberal arts education for acquiring eloquent speech, but the Greek program of instruction became widely employed in the Greco-Roman world by the first century B.C. and rhetoric was a fundamental part of a larger curriculum that also included logic, music and athletics.

[33]Quintilian *Institutio Oratoria* 10.1.2. On the relation between language and logic, or thinking and speaking well, Quintilian is reflecting the tradition of Aristotle who began his *Art of Rhetoric* by emphasizing the relation between rhetoric and dialectic.

[34]Isocrates *Antidosis* 178–214.

[35]Cicero *De Oratore* 1.32.

[36]Quintilian *Institutio Oratoria* 2.13.15. See also Plato *Phaedrus* 269; *Rhetorica ad Herennium* 1.1f.

writing, and speaking.[37] Paraphrasing, translating, and imitating were also core elements of their study and practice.[38] Of course, the guidance of a skillful teacher was essential for a student's mastery of grammar and rhetorical precepts and rules, but achievement was finally the responsibility of the student.[39] A student's degree of success, no doubt, was strongly influenced by the student's natural aptitudes for learning, remembering, and applying knowledge and language skills. Still, the ancients understood well that a hard working student of modest natural ability could often outperform more gifted students who lacked the discipline to practice.[40]

Rhetoric was a widespread, rigorous, and—for the most part—holistic discipline in the Greco-Roman world, and one misses a crucial aspect of the art if it is conceptualized and interpreted only as technical skills for particular forms of oral civic discourse.[41] Rhetoricians were concerned fundamentally with eloquent, persuasive communication that was pleasing to the mind's ear and fitting for any given situation. In order to be eloquent and persuasive, they sought to become proficient in expressing themselves appropriately in content,

---

[37]Cf. Quintilian *Institutio Oratoria* 2.5.6f. See also 1.8.1 and 9.4.114 ("assiduous practice in writing will be sufficient to enable us to produce similar rhythmical effects when speaking extempore").

[38]Cf. Quintilian *Institutio Oratoria* 1.9.2.

[39]Quintilian writes, "Neither the precepts nor textbooks are of any value . . . they are of no profit in themselves without a skilfull teacher, persistent study, and continued exercise in writing, reading, and speaking" (Proem 26–27). Also, ". . . to possess this gift, our orator will require all the resources of nature, learning and industrious study. Therefore let no man hope that he can acquire eloquence merely by the labour of others. He must burn the midnight oil, persevere to the end and grow pale with study: he must form his own powers, his own experience, his own methods: he must not require to hunt for his weapons, but must have them ready for immediate use, as though they were born with him and not derived from the instruction of others. The road may be pointed out, but our speed must be our own. Art has done enough in publishing the resources of eloquence, it is for us to know how to use them" (7.10.14–15). See also Cicero *De Oratore* 2.20.90–92.

[40]Cf. Isocrates *Antidosis* 188–91 and Plutarch *De Liberis Educandis* 2C.

[41]This, in fact, was a major factor in the decline of oratory under the Empire. Oratory became subordinate to technical skills in rhetoric with the result that the orator became the servant of rhetoric rather than rhetorical skills the servant of the orator. The effect was the limitation of rhetoric's scope. But the domain of rhetoric "is composed of everything that may be placed before it as a subject for speech" (Quintilian *Institutio Oratoria* 2.21.4). Moreover, Quintilian quotes Cicero (*De Oratore* 3.14.54) to emphasize that "it is the duty of the true orator to seek out, hear, read, discuss, handle and ponder everything that befalls in the life of man, since it is with this that the orator is concerned and this that forms the material which he has to deal" (2.21.6). Quintilian also reflects the common view that the task of oratory included the writing of speeches and historical narratives (2.18.5). Similarly, it cannot be insignificant that one of the great Greek "orators," Isocrates was a *writer* of speeches. His reputation was built upon the publication of his written speeches and his popularity as a teacher. Note also Quintilian's broad view of rhetoric beyond forensic, deliberative, and epideictic expressions (*Institutio Oratoria* 3.4.3).

arrangement, and style. And since they lived in a predominately oral and aural environment, the spoken word was the dominant medium of their communication. Moreover, since the responsibilities of citizenship often necessitated participation in the main arenas of civic discourse (forensic, deliberative, epideictic), extensive rhetorical training in these areas was useful for all citizens. Nevertheless, the art of rhetoric was concerned with the whole domain of language and self-expression as it related to persuasive eloquence, and so its practice included rigorous exercises in reading, writing, listening, learning, reasoning, and speaking clearly and powerfully in any situation.[42]

In sum, then, the ideal orator sought to develop his or her natural abilities, become knowledgeable of many topics through a liberal arts education, and master the skills for persuasive communication, all through industrious practice.[43] Yet there is another important characteristic of the ideal orator, and it is crucial because its absence renders the other traits ineffectual.

Wise Adaptability. The combination of the communicator's natural endowments, the control of the principles and techniques of persuasive communication, and the mastery of the art itself through rigorous practice were all crucial for achieving oratorical prowess. But the ideal orator also possessed flexibility. Quintilian referred to it as *praecipua consilium* or "wise adaptability," and he writes that:

> If the whole of rhetoric could be thus embodied in one compact code, it would be an easy task of little compass: but most rules are liable to be altered by the nature of the case, circumstances of time and place, and by hard necessity itself. Consequently the all-important gift for an orator is wise-adaptability since he is called upon to meet the most varied emergencies.[44]

---

[42]Practical exercises of composition and delivery were called "declamation" and were enormously popular in the first centuries B.C. and A.D. Cf. Stanley F. Bonner, *Roman Declamation in the Late Republic and Early Empire* (Berkeley: University of California Press, 1949); G. A. Kennedy, *The Art of Rhetoric in the Roman World*, 91–96, 312–22.

[43]Cf. Quintilian *Institutio Oratoria* 2.19.1, who writes, "I know there is a question whether nature or education contributes more to eloquence. But this problem has no concern with my work, for the perfect orator can be formed only with the aid of both." See also Dionysius of Halicarnassus, *De Compositione Verbum* (In *Dionysius of Halicarnassus: The Critical Essays*, vol. 2, trans. S. Usher, LCL [Cambridge, Mass.: Harvard University Press, 1974–1985]), who plainly has oral and written communication in mind when discussing the common ground for all kinds of discourse as subject matter and appropriate expression in words. He writes that "all those who aim to become good orators pay close attention to both these aspects of discourse equally" (1).

[44]Quintilian *Institutio Oratoria* 2.13.2. In 5.13.13, he notes, "We shall therefore adapt our method of refutation to the exigencies of our case." See also 9.4.117, 130–131; 11.1.46.

For Cicero, also, the eloquent communicator is one "who can adapt his speech to fit all conceivable circumstances."[45] The ideal orator could accommodate his speech to the situation as readily and surely as a seasoned pilot could adjust his ship's course to fit the weather and the sea.[46]

Undoubtedly there were orators who, for deficiencies of nature, technique, and practice, adhered rigidly to set rhetorical arrangements. Some used the handbooks as blueprints that must be followed explicitly in every situation. And it was not uncommon for some orators to use a repertoire of rehearsed speeches that were so general that they could be applied equally inappropriately to a host of circumstances.[47] But the true orator recognized that "rules are helpful all the same so long as they indicate the direct road and do not restrict us absolutely to the ruts made by others."[48] Indeed, Cicero held that variety was an essential aspect of communicating well for "in everything monotony is the mother of boredom."[49] Likewise the historian Tacitus

---

[45]Cicero *De Orator* 123. For Cicero the closest example of the ideal orator is Demosthenes who could adapt immediately to any situation and change at will his style and type of argument in a single discourse in an appropriate way. See also *Brutus* 35, 141–142; idem, *De Optimo Genere Oratorum* 2.6, 4.10, 6.17. It is also noteworthy that Cicero praised the written speeches of Isocrates but did not include Isocrates in his classification of "supreme orator" because "his oratory does not take part in the battle nor use steel, but plays with a wooden sword" (*De Optimo Genere Oratorum* 6.17). That is, Isocrates seldom spoke in the arena of the public courts. He wrote his speeches to be read.

[46]Quintilian *Institutio Oratoria* 10.7.3. Quintilian also refers to this characteristic as "sagacity" (*consilium*) for it "involves both invention and judgment"(6.5.3). Moreover, "It is sagacity again that teaches us to adapt our speech to circumstances of time and place and to persons with whom we are concerned"(6.5.11).

[47]Cf. Quintilian *Institutio Oratoria* 1.Pr.13–14; 2.4.27–29; 2.20.2–3. Interestingly, on the problem of rigid conformity to the handbooks, Quintilian (1.Pr.24) assigns some of the responsibility for this to the rhetorical handbooks themselves, "For as a rule the result of the dry textbooks on the art of rhetoric is that by straining after excessive subtlety they impair and cripple all the nobler elements of style, exhaust the lifeblood of the imagination and leave but the bare bones, which, while it is right and necessary that they should exist and be bound each to each by their respective ligaments, require a covering of flesh as well".

[48]Quintilian *Institutio Oratoria* 2.13.15. Again, "it is generally expedient to conform to such rules . . . but if our friend expediency suggests some other course to us, why, we shall disregard the authority of the professors and follow her"(2.13.7).

[49]Cicero *De Inventione* 1.41.76. See also Demetrius *De Elocutione* 15, who criticizes orators who are so transparent in their use of rhetorical structures and conventions that the audience can even "audibly anticipate the conclusions of the orator's periods and declaim them in advance." The same emphasis on variety applies to literary compositions. In his work *De Compositione Verbum* (περὶ συνθεσέως ὀνομάτων), Dionysius of Halicarnassus insists that "we should relieve monotony by the tasteful introduction of variation, since variety is a source of pleasure in everything we do" (12, p. 89). See also pp. 149 and 153 along with Aristotle *Rhetoric* 1.11.20; 3.12.3; Isocrates *Against the Sophists* 16, *Antidosis* 47, *Philippus* 27; Cicero *De Oratore* 2.41.77; 3.25.96–100, *Orator* 57.195; *Rhetorica ad Herennium* 4.13.18.

recognized there are times when "eloquence must resort to new and skillfully chosen paths, in order that the orator may avoid offence to the fastidious ear."[50]

So thoroughgoing was the ancient appreciation and insistence on maintaining flexibility in oratory that not even the proven arrangements of the three major kinds of civic discourse were unalterable. True, forensic rhetoric maintained the strictest order while deliberative and epideictic were far more pliable. Yet there are many situations, wrote Quintilian, when "it is often expedient and occasionally becoming to make some modification in the time-honoured order" in any type of rhetoric.[51] Thus the standard parts of a speech could be dropped[52] and types of speech mixed.[53] The rule of flexibility was also applied to the orator's style of speaking—a point which Cicero summarized precisely when he wrote that "it is certainly obvious that totally different styles must be used, not only in the different parts of the speech, but also that whole speeches must be now in one style, now in another."[54]

The ancient rhetorical emphasis on wise adaptability was forged by the clear understanding that life's situations are seldom, if ever, the same. Quintilian, for instance, compared oratory to generalship in war. He wrote:

> The skilled commander will know how to distribute his forces for battle, what troops he should keep back to garrison forts or guard cities, to secure supplies, or guard communications, and what dispositions to make by land and by sea.[55]

---

[50]Tacitus *Dialogus de Oratoribus* 19. Here, Tacitus writes that of "Cassius Severus who was the first, they assert, to deviate from the old and plain path of the speaker, I maintain that it was not from poverty of genius or ignorance of letters that he adopted his well known style, but from preference and intellectual conviction. He saw, in fact, that, as I was just now saying, the character and type of oratory must change with the circumstances." Again on the necessary adaptability of the orator, Tacitus writes that, "An orator practised in such arts and exercises, whether he has to address the angry, the biased, the envious, the sorrowful, or the trembling, will understand different mental conditions, apply his skill, adapt his style, and have every instrument of his craft in readiness, or in reserve for every occasion" (31).

[51]Quintilian *Institutio Oratoria* 2.13.8. Here, in order to emphasize this point, Quintilian appeals to the authority of Virgil *Aeneid* 3.436. See also Cicero *Orator* 70; and *Rhetorica ad Herennium* 3.9.16–17.

[52]*Rhetorica ad Herennium* 2.19.30.

[53]Again, on the theoretical basis for mixing genres in a single speech, see, for instance, Aristotle *Rhetoric*, 1.3.4 and *Rhetorica ad Herennium* 3.8.15. See also Cicero's example for mixing causes in *De Inventione* 2.32.98–100 in which he sets out the events of the case in a forensic pattern and then shows the advantage of shifting to "adopt the arguments of a deliberative speech."

[54]Cicero *Orator* 21.74. This same point is made by Quintilian *Institutio Oratoria* 11.1.4, 12.10.66–68. See also Cicero *De Oratore* 3.55.210.

[55]Quintilian *Institutio Oratoria* 7.10.13. See also 12.10.66–68 where he compares the flexibility of oratory to the changing winds.

But, Quintilian asks,

> What if you should instruct a general, as often as he marshals his troops for battle, to draw up his front line, advance his wings to left and right, and station his cavalry to protect his flank? This will perhaps be the best plan, if circumstances allow. But it may have to be modified owing to the nature of the ground, if, for instance, he is confronted by a mountain, if a river bars his advance, or his movements are hampered by hills, woods or broken country. Or again it may be modified by the character of the enemy or the nature of the crisis by which he is faced. On one occasion he will fight in line, on another in column, on one he will use his auxiliary troops, on another his legionaries; while occasionally a feint of flight may win the day. So, too, with the rules of oratory.[56]

To be sure, the rules of oratory have their necessary place as the ancient writers testify and modern studies show. It is unlikely that a person could become an effective orator without mastering the basic skills, either through direct or indirect instruction. But oratory is more than a science or technical skill; it is also an art. And so the rules of rhetoric were viewed best as guidelines—tested resources for describing and constructing eloquent and persuasive communication, especially in the arena of civic discourse.

In sum, then, the hallmarks of the ideal orator were the orator's nature—particularly an ability for inventiveness, the mastery of rhetoric and the liberal arts, a seasoned expertise in applying knowledge, and a sagacity for using the appropriate words and forms of expression when addressing any audience and situation. These were the essential characteristics of the true orator. Yet among these, Quintilian expressed well the common view of the Greco-Roman world that "the all-important gift for an orator is a wise adaptability." That is, the ideal orator wisely determines the precise message that is appropriate for the occasion and expresses it persuasively.[57] But how were messages conveyed?

---

[56]Quintilian *Institutio Oratoria* 2.13.3–5. The same point is made regarding literary compositions by Dionysius of Halicarnassus who holds that writing well "is something like what clever tacticians do when they are marshalling their armies: they mask the weak parts with the strong, and so no part of their force proves useless" (*De Compositione Verbum* 12).

[57]Cicero contends that the ideal orator is one who possesses "rare judgment and great endowment; for he will decide what is needed at any point, and will be able to speak in any way which the case requires. For after all the foundation of eloquence, as of everything else, is wisdom. In an oration, as in life, nothing is harder than to determine what is appropriate. The Greeks call it πρέπον; let us call it decorum or 'propriety'" (Cicero *Orator* 70). On this point also, Quintilian praises Menander for his superior skill and "consummate appropriateness" (*Institutio Oratoria* 10.1.69–71).

II. RHETORIC AND EPISTOLOGRAPHY

Rhetoric was indeed the "mistress of all the arts" throughout the Hellenistic world of late Western antiquity. Its influence was felt everywhere. By the middle of the second century B.C., rhetoric had secured a place of prominence in the Greco-Roman educational program, and its precepts and principles were studied and practiced throughout the empire.[58] So broad and deep was the influence of rhetoric by the first century A.D. that Quintilian could direct his students to study carefully not only the speeches and letters of orators[59] but also the works of certain philosophers, poets, comedians, tragedians, and historians, because these authors also showed excellence and adaptability in using rhetorical rules and techniques.[60] Examples of oratorical excellence were not restricted to rhetorical handbooks and written speeches. Neither was the "art" of rhetoric limited to oral discourse.[61]

---

[58]Cf. Stanley F. Bonner, *Roman Declamation in the Late Republic and Early Empire* (Berkeley: University of California Press, 1949), D. L. Clark, *Rhetoric in Greco-Roman Education*, 60–61; G. A. Kennedy, *The Art of Rhetoric in the Roman World*, 318–21, 489; idem, *A New History of Classical Rhetoric*, 201–29; Henri–Irenée Marrou, *A History of Education in Antiquity*, trans. George Lamb (New York: Sheed and Ward, 1956); D. A. Russell, *Greek Declamation* (Cambridge: Cambridge University Press, 1983).

[59]Quintilian *Institutio Oratoria* 10.1.105f. It is especially significant that Quintilian refers to both the discourses and letters of Cicero and Demosthenes as objects of study for rhetoricians. Letters are here treated as literary texts to be analyzed for their use of language and the art of rhetoric. See also G. Kennedy, *Cambridge History of Literary Criticism*, 290.

[60]See especially Quintilian *Institutio Oratoria* 10.1.46–131. Of the philosophers, Quintilian gives special recognition to Plato, Aristotle, and Theophrastus. Demosthenes holds first place among Greek orators. Favorite historians include Thucydides, Herodotus, and Theopompus. Among the epicists and poets, Quintilian gives special praise to Homer, for his works are so rich in rhetorical elements that "the majority of writers on the principles of rhetoric have gone to his works for examples of all these things" (10.1.49). Again, Homer's excellence in the use of language is "a model and an inspiration for every department of eloquence" (10.1.46) and he has "outdistanced all that have come after him in every department of eloquence, above all, he has outstripped all other writers of epic"(10.1.51). Latin authors of special note include Virgil, Ovid, Lucilius, Horace, Accius, Pacuvius, Sallust, and—most importantly—Cicero who "succeeded in reproducing the force of Demosthenes" (10.1.108). See also Dionysius of Halicarnassus who wrote, "the summit on which everyone's gaze should be fixed may rightly be named as Homer" (24; also 16).

[61]At least since Aristotle, rhetoric was viewed in terms of speech and writing. He writes, "we must not lose sight of the fact that a different style is suitable to each kind of Rhetoric. That of written compositions is not the same as that of debate; nor, in the latter, is that of public speaking the same as that of the law courts. But it is necessary to be acquainted with both; for the one requires a knowledge of good Greek, while the other prevents the necessity of keeping silent when we wish to communicate something to others, which happens to those who do not know how to write. The style of written compositions is most precise, that of debate is most suitable for delivery" (*Rhetoric* 3.12.1–2). Isocrates also views the field of rhetoric as encompassing both written and spoken forms. In *On the Peace* (Περι

Rhetoric and Writing

The rhetorical handbooks emphasize speaking persuasively in the three main arenas of civic discourse, but they do not lose sight of the whole communication process—including the medium of writing—and the goal of communicating powerfully, which is the ideal orator's central concern. Thus reading the best authors aloud, for instance, was of central importance in rhetorical training at every stage, for in this way students amassed the resources of eloquence.[62] Writing was also an essential practice, for through it students imitated and utilized these resources.[63] The pursuit and the achievement of articulate, powerful self-expression involved both writing and speaking. Indeed, the relation between them was considered inseparable for "the art of writing is combined with that of speaking"[64] and "there is absolutely no difference between writing well and speaking well."[65]

Not surprisingly, then, on the question of whether an orator was "always to speak as he writes," Quintilian answered, "If possible, always."[66] Indeed, writing was so important to the art of rhetoric that Quintilian began his massive treatise on the teaching of rhetoric with the affirmation that "Writing is of the utmost importance in the study which we have under consideration and by its means alone can true and deeply rooted proficiency be obtained."[67] Again, "It is in writing that eloquence has its roots and foundations, it is writing that provides the holy of holies where the wealth of oratory is stored, and whence it is produced to meet the demands of sudden emergencies."[68]

Speaking and writing were held together because they provide "mutual profit." That is, "writing will give us greater precision of speech, while speaking will make us write with greater facility. We must write, therefore, whenever possible."[69] And when Quintilian stresses the "continuous and conscientious practice in writing, so that even our improvisations may

---

Ειρηνης) 145, for instance, he writes, "I urge and exhort those who are younger and more vigorous than I to speak and write the kind of discourses by which they will turn the greatest states—those which have been wont to oppress the rest—into the paths of virtue and justice."

[62]Quintilian writes that the way to achieve eloquence is through "reading and listening to the best writers and orators, since we shall thus learn not merely the words by which things are to be called, but when each particular word is most appropriate" (*Institutio Oratoria* 10.1.8). See also 10.1.20–24 where Quintilian encourages students to read and re-read the best authors carefully as though they were transcribing what they read.

[63]Ibid., 10.1.3.

[64]Ibid., 1.4.3.

[65]Ibid., 12.10.51.

[66]Ibid., 12.10.55.

[67]Ibid., 1.1.28; see also Cicero *De Inventione* 1.41.76 where he stresses "writing rhetorical exercises."

[68]Quintilian *Institutio Oratoria* 10.3.3.

[69]Ibid., 10.7.29.

reproduce the tone of our writing,"[70] he is emphasizing the Greco-Roman ideal of clear, orderly, persuasive expression.

The ancients esteemed oral communication, but their emphasis on eloquence involved more than speech alone. To be sure, the development of a systematic "art" or "technique" of rhetoric was for training in powerful, appropriate, persuasive civil speech. In this way, the ancient descriptions of the rhetorical "art" do not dissolve the differences between oratory and other types of communication, such as poetry and history.[71] But neither do the rhetoricians lose sight of the important common ground shared between them all. As Quintilian reminded his readers:

> Each branch of literature has its own laws and its own appropriate character. Comedy does not seek to increase its height by the bushkin and tragedy does not wear the slipper of comedy. But all forms of eloquence have something in common, and it is to the imitation of this common element that our efforts should be confined.[72]

That common ground, again, is primarily the expression of thought in a manner that is clear, concise, organized, and appropriate. This is the proper and efficient use of language which is "based on reason, antiquity, authority and usage."[73] Consequently, Quintilian urges his students to give special attention to the "rules which must be observed both by speakers and writers."[74] Dionysius of Halicarnassus (d. ca. 8 B.C.) made the same point regarding literary composition when he stressed that the careful "putting-together of words" was the common branch of study for all the ancient poets, historians, philosophers, and orators, for "they considered that neither words, nor clauses, nor periods

---

[70]Ibid., 10.7.7.

[71]That the ancients distinguished between such aspects of communication as rhetoric and poetics is evidenced by the philosopher Aristotle's great works *Rhetoric* and *Poetics*. Poetry, history, and rhetoric, for instance, were not viewed as the same kind of communication. See also Quintilian's contrast of rhetoric and poetry (10.1.90) or Polybius's distinction between history and poetry (2.56). Rhetoric, for instance, designated a form of communication that stressed the clear ordering of thoughts in concrete expression whereas poetry stressed the imaginative and emotional. Nevertheless, the use of language in epic, drama, narrative, poetry, etc., was fundamentally the same regarding the matter of eloquence or well-formed communication.

[72]Quintilian *Institutio Oratoria* 10.2.22. See also Dionysius of Halicarnassus *De Compositione Verbum* 1 (p. 17), who writes that "in virtually all kinds of discourse two things require study: the ideas and the words. We may regard the first of these as concerned chiefly with subject-matter, and the latter with expression; and all those who aim to become good orators pay close attention to both these aspects of discourse equally."

[73]Quintilian *Institutio Oratoria* 1.6.1.

[74]Ibid. See also 9.4.22 where Quintilian writes that "in all artistic structure there are three necessary qualities: order, connexion, and rhythm."

should be put together at random, but they had a definite system of rules which they practiced, and so composed well."[75] Dionysius urged all who would communicate well to give close study to many good poets, historians, philosophers and orators.[76]

Simply put, the common aim of eloquence in speaking and writing persuasively was the expression of organized fluency that succeeded in delighting, instructing and moving an audience.[77] This was achievable largely through the careful orchestration of words and ideas that—spoken or written—resonated powerfully in the mind's ear of the listener and reader. That is to say, there are certain fundamental aspects of effective communication common to both rhetoric and epistolography, and any discussion of the relationship between them ought to include recognition of their theoretical and practical alliance.[78] Thus, before examining more fully some of the common resources and general principles of arrangement for both speaker and writer which are beneficial for interpreting Galatians, it will be helpful to survey the development of epistolography within the field of rhetoric in the Greco-Roman world.

Rhetoric and Epistolary Theory

Given the Greco-Roman preoccupation with orderly thinking and persuasive communication, it should come as no surprise that rhetoric was employed in the composition of letters. Indeed, Aune describes the situation precisely when he writes that "By the first century B.C., rhetoric had come to exert a strong influence on the composition of letters, particularly among the educated."[79] Many ancient letters, of course, were brief correspondences that expressed a particular concern with few evidences of persuasive or literary sophistication. But the letters of Cicero, Seneca, Dio Chrysostom and Paul, for instance, are rich in rhetorical artistry.

Interestingly, there is very little written about letter writing theory and practice in the Greco-Roman world prior to the first century B.C. Early Greeks and Romans wrote treatises on rhetoric and poetics, for instance, but a

---

[75]Dionysius of Halicarnassus *De Compositione Verbum* [περὶ συνθεσέως ὀνομάτων or the "putting–together of words"] 5.

[76]Ibid., 20, 22, 23.

[77]Cf. Quintilian *Institutio Oratoria* 10.3.7–8.

[78]Hermann Peter, *Der Brief in der römischen Literatur: Literargeschichtliche Untersuchungen und Zusammenfassungen* (Abhandlungen der Königlichen Sächsischen Gesellschaft der Wissenschaften, philogisch-historische Classe, 20/3; Leipzig: B. G. Teubner, 1901; reprint, Hildesheim: Georg Olms, 1965), 19.

[79]Aune, *The New Testament in Its Literary Environment,* 160. On the relation between the oral and written word, see also G. A. Kennedy, *Cambridge History of Literary Criticism,* 87–89.

systematic treatment of letters is noticeably absent before this time.[80] The ancients, nevertheless, used epistolary conventions to open and close their letters long before the first century B.C. It is also likely that letter-writing was practiced in Greco-Roman schools as evidenced, in part, by the widespread use of these basic conventions from the 5th century B.C. [81] Still, there is no existent evidence that the ancients had composed systematic treatises of theoretical precepts and formalized rules for the practice of letter-writing as a distinct type of communication before the 1st century B.C. [82]

The earliest extensive discussion of letter-writing theory is found in a manual on rhetorical styles. The treatise *De Elocutione*[83] is wrongly attributed to Demetrius of Phalerum and there is some dispute over the dating of this treatise, but most agree it appears to be a document from the 1st century B.C.[84]

---

[80]Cf. G. A. Kennedy, *Cambridge History of Literary Criticism*, 78, 197, who proposes that writers in the Hellenistic period may well have viewed composing a treatise on letter-writing as beneath their dignity.

[81]Grammarians were also interested in letter-writing, but the existent sources go back only as far as the first century A.D. The grammatical handbooks of Dionysius of Alexandria (1st century A.D.) and Apollonius Dyscolus (2nd century A.D.) show concern for grammatical aspects of letter forms, and may be based on earlier works, but their earlier roots can only be conjectured. See Malherbe, *Ancient Epistolary Theorists*, 6–7.

[82]See especially Malherbe, *Ancient Epistolary Theorists*, 6–7, and Peter L. Schmidt, "Epistolographie," *Der Kleine Pauly*, vol. 2, eds. Konrat Zieler and Walther Sontheimer (Stuttgart: Alfred Druckenmüller, 1967), 324–27. The most elaborate epistolary handbooks come from the 3rd to 6th centuries A.D. The Latin and Greek *Bologna Papyrus* is dated from the 3rd to 4th centuries A.D. and presents eleven sample letters which seem to be a student's epistolary exercises (Malherbe, *Ancient Epistolary Theorists*, 4–5). More substantial is the *Epistolimaioi Characteres* from the 4th to 6th centuries A.D. This handbook lists, defines, and describes stylistic matters for 41 types of letters. Behind the *Epistolimaioi Characteres* are two manuscript traditions rooted in a common source. One manuscript tradition is attributed to Libanius and another to Proclus but, despite their variations and shared heritage, there is no evident connection between these works and the earlier *Typoi Epistolikoi* which is often incorrectly attributed to Demetrius of Phalerum (Malherbe, *Ancient Epistolary Theorists*, 4–5). This earlier epistolary handbook of "Demetrius" identifies and describes stylistic concerns for 21 types of letters and is dated from 200 B.C. to A.D. 300. Most date it from the first century B.C. Its present structure and contents demonstrate both the author's rhetorical interest for classifying types of address and his assumption of the reader's understanding of rhetorical theory and practice (Malherbe, *Ancient Epistolary Theorists*, 4). The *Typoi Epistolikoi* is a stylistic guide for arranging and writing certain kinds of letters. These handbooks present brief descriptions of situations that accompany the name of the letter type and then reflect the appropriate tone of the letter with a short expression that is most often a rhetorical syllogism. Also see Stowers, *Letter Writing*, 51–54.

[83]The Greek title is ΠΕΡΙ ΕΡΜΗΝΕΙΑΣ which means "concerning the expression of thoughts in words."

[84]The range of suggested dates runs from the 3rd century B.C. to the first century A.D. and even later. See Malherbe, *Ancient Epistolary Theorists*, 2. See also G. A. Kennedy, *Cambridge History of Literary Criticism*, 196, who treats it as a work of early Peripatetics regardless of its dating.

In it, Pseudo-Demetrius includes under the topic of the "plain and elegant style" a discussion on the appropriate style for letters (223–35). Citing the authority of Artemon who edited Aristotle's letters, he writes that "a letter ought to be written in the same manner as a dialogue [is written]; for the letter is like one of the two parts of the dialogue."[85] The relation between epistolography and rhetoric is made stronger, though, when Pseudo-Demetrius adds his own improvement to the standard in that the "letter should be a little more formal than the dialogue, since the latter imitates improvised conversation, while the former is written and sent as a kind of gift."[86] Pseudo-Demetrius means that a letter should be more carefully composed in the manner of a prepared speech than in the broken, often disorganized and abrupt manner of spontaneous conversation.[87]

There is further evidence of a growing interest in the rhetorical use of letters in the Greco-Roman world during the first century B.C. Cicero's letters, for instance, indicate some awareness of epistolary classifications, and there were evidently some types of letters—such as the letter of recommendation—that were known by their function.[88] Epistolary conventions were used also for literary works and letters embedded in narrative.[89] But again, in line with the rhetorical emphasis on propriety, it was generally accepted that the style of the letter should be appropriate for the situation and the message's content.[90] This emphasis on appropriate self-expression is maintained in the epistolary handbooks written for students. The *Typoi Epistolikoi* (ca. 200 B.C. to 300 A.D.)

---

[85]Demetrius *De Elocutione* 223. The same point is made by Cicero *Ad Fam.* 12.30.1 and *Ad Att.* 13.18 and Ovid *Ars. Amat.* 1.468. The wording of Demetrius is revealing. He writes, δεῖ ἐν τῷ αὐτῷ τρόπῳ διάλογον τε γράφειν καὶ ἐπιστολάς or "it is necessary in the same way as a dialogue to write *also* a letter." The implication is that a letter is to be written in the same way that a dialogue is to be written. The writing of dialogues was a common rhetorical practice in the exercise of *prosopopoeia*.

[86]Demetrius *De Elocutione* 224. For additional discussion on appropriate styles for letters, see especially Demetrius 226, 228, 229, 232, 234; Cicero *Ad Fam.* 2.4.1; 4.13.1; 9.21.1; 15.21.4; 16.16.2; Seneca *Epistulae Morales* 40.1; 75.1; and Quintilian *Institutio Oratoria* 9.4.19.

[87]Demetrius *De Elocutione* 226. "Yet a series of abrupt sentence breaks such as <. . .> does not suit the letter. Abruptness in writing causes obscurity, and the imitation of conversation is less appropriate to writing than to real debate."

[88]Malherbe (*Ancient Epistolary Theorists*, 2–3) observes that Cicero knows of both *litterae publicae* and *litterae privatae* (*Pro Flacco* 16.37) and is also concerned with epistolary style (Cf. *Ad Fam.* 2.4.1f; 4.13.1; 3.11.2; *Ad Att.* 6.5.4; 8.14.1). See also the important article by H. Koskenniemi, "Cicero über die Briefarten (genera epistularum)," *Arctos* (1954): 97–102; and G. A. Kennedy, *Cambridge History of Literary Criticism*, 197. For a discussion of the advantages and disadvantages of epistolary typologies proposed by Stowers and Aune, see Aune, *The New Testament in Its Literary Environment*, 161–72.

[89]Aune, *The New Testament in Its Literary Environment*, 162.

[90]Demetrius *De Elocutione* 223–35; Quintilian *Institutio Oratoria* 9.4.19–21.

and the *Epistolimaioi Characteres* (ca. A.D. 300–500) do not present sample letters of each letter type. Neither do they address invention, arrangement, or other matters of language and logic. Rather they assume such basic understandings, use rhetorical terms, and focus clearly on appropriate styles of expression for particular situations.[91] The epistolary handbooks are guides for propriety.

Now it is likely that Greco-Roman schools provided some instruction in letter writing as evidenced by Theon's *progymnasmata* (1st century A.D.).[92] The Greco-Roman school system was comprised of three stages: primary, secondary or "grammar," and advanced. Theoretically, the art of oratory was reserved for advanced education in schools of rhetoric and the basic rhetorical exercises or *progymnasmata* began here. It was not uncommon, however, for these elementary rhetorical exercises to begin in the final stages of grammar school.[93] Mentioned as early as the 4th century B.C., these exercises and the help of a grammaticus (teacher) guided the student through the basics of rhetoric in progressive stages. One of the final activities of the *progymnasmata* was called impersonation or προσωποποιία (*prosopopoeia*). The aim of this practice was to express another person's point of view or thoughts on a topic in words that approximate as nearly as possible the actual words that person would use. How did they practice this form of expression? Primarily through the writing of dialogues and letters. Thus Malherbe observes the significance of this exercise precisely when he emphasizes that "the purpose of the exercise was not to learn how to write letters, but to develop facility in adopting various kinds of style."[94] Again, the concern for style was motivated by the deeper concern for propriety.

---

[91]See especially F. W. Hughes, *Early Christian Rhetoric*, 27, where he examines the 21 epistolary types listed in the handbook of Pseudo-Demetrius and finds that the author identified types of letters using technical terms for rhetoric. For instance, Hughes notes that "blaming" (*memptikos*) and "praising" (*epainetikos*) are aspects of epideictic rhetoric (See also Artistotle *Rhetoric*, 1.2.3; 1.3.5–7). The "advising" letter is classified as *symbouleutikon*, the Greek technical term for deliberative rhetoric (i.e., Aristotle *Rhetoric* 1.3.3; etc.). The "apologetkos" letter is related to forensic rhetoric (i.e., Ibid. 1.10.1). So also for *psektikon* (vituperative) and *egkomiastikon* letters which belong to epideictic rhetoric (Cf. *Rhetorica ad Alexandrum* 1421b9). Obviously, the shared terminology suggests a close theoretical relationship between rhetoric and epistolography.

[92]Cf. D. L. Clark, *Rhetoric in Greco-Roman Education*, 59–66 and S. F. Bonner, *Education in Ancient Rome*. The primary school was for students who were usually from the ages of 7 to 11 or 12. The principal subject matter was basic reading and writing. Between the ages of 11 and 15, students were instructed by a grammaticus in more complex matters of literature and language. At about the age of 15, students entered schools of rhetoric to develop their own use of language and broaden their understanding of other disciplines of the liberal arts.

[93]Quintilian *Institutio Oratoria* 2.1.1–13; 9.2.29.

[94]Malherbe, *Ancient Epistolary Theorists*, 7. Also, Dionysius of Halicarnassus (*De Compositione Verbum*) expresses well the ancient ideal of mastering many styles when he

Given the broad and deep interest in communication by so many orators throughout the Greco-Roman world, it is difficult to understand why letter-writing was not addressed more completely.[95] It is possible, of course, that earlier treatises on letter-writing simply did not survive. But it may well be, as Kennedy has suggested, that rhetoricians, philosophers, and grammarians viewed letter-writing as speech in written form and too simple and variable a topic to warrant the attention of an entire treatise.[96] In any event, Malherbe is certainly correct that "epistolary theory in antiquity belonged to the domain of the rhetoricians."[97] In practice, too, rhetoric exerted considerable influence upon letters, especially those written by educated communicators.

Epistolography and rhetoric have their differences, but they are not so separate and distinct in the ancient Greco-Roman world as some have supposed. In theory and in practice, rhetoric exerted considerable influence upon the letters of educated communicators. Thus the prevailing view of letters in the Greco-Roman world was that of speech in a written medium.[98] And—like ideal speech—ideal letters were to be clear, orderly, and perfectly suited to their circumstances, regardless of their particular styles of expression.[99] Here again, then, we find these celebrated aspects of efficient and effective communication, which Quintilian and others hailed as the common ground both for letter and speech. Let us now consider some of the chief resources available to a communicator to achieve these ends and the principles that guide them.

---

praises Homer for possessing "the most voices of all" (16) and insists that communicators of every sort ought to set their sights firmly on Homer for he is "the source whence all the rivers flow and all the seas, and every fountain" (24). The ancient writers and speakers took quite seriously the goal of developing many "voices."

[95]It was not until the 4th century A.D. that a rhetorician addressed the issue of letter-writing as a distinct branch of rhetoric. Julius Victor included two appendices, *de sermocinatione* and *de epistulis*, to his rhetorical handbook. See Malherbe, *Ancient Epistolary Theorists*, 3.

[96]Kennedy, *Cambridge History of Literary Criticism*, 197.

[97]Abraham J. Malherbe, *Ancient Epistolary Theorists*, 2–6. See also F. W. Hughes, *Early Christian Rhetoric*, 19–30.

[98]Cf. Cicero *Ad Fam.* 2.4.1; idem *Ad Att.* 8.14; 9.10.1; 12.53; Seneca *Epistulae Morales* 40.1; 75.1; Demetrius *De Elocutione* 223; Quintilian *Institutio Oratoria* 9.4.19.

[99]Cf. Cicero *Ad Fam.* 2.4.1; 4.13.1; 9.21.1; 12.30.1; 15.21.4; idem, *Ad Att.* 9.4.1; Seneca *Epistulae Morales* 40.1–2; Demetrius *De Elocutione* 226, 228, 229, 234. See also Quintilian *Institutio Oratoria* 9.4.19, who describes the loose style as that which is "found in dialogues and letters, except when they deal with some subject above their natural level, such as philosophy, politics (de re publica) or the like." Demetrius, on the other hand, restricts the term "letter" to those writings that "express friendship briefly, and set out a simple subject in simple terms" (*De Elocutione* 231). It is not clear how Demetrius would classify correspondences that were not friendly personal letters.

CHAPTER THREE

GRECO-ROMAN RESOURCES AND PRINCIPLES FOR PERSUASIVE COMMUNICATION

Speaker and letter-writer alike faced the common challenges of inventing and expressing communications that were appropriate in content, arrangement, and style for particular situations and purposes. The aim of such persuasive self-expression, of course, was in large measure the goal of the Greco-Roman educational system before and during the first century A.D.[1] Rhetoricians, though, were especially concerned with using language effectively in these ways and—not surprisingly—produced most of the existent treatises on the subject up to and through Paul's day. Consequently, we will continue to draw largely from the theory and practice of rhetoricians as we turn now to review some common elements of the communicator's resources along with some fundamental principles for arranging any persuasive communication. Here we will see more clearly the ancient Greco-Roman emphasis upon placing an argument's strongest points at the beginning and ending of a discourse. Then we will look more particularly at the importance of beginnings for effective, persuasive communication.

To begin with, Greco-Roman treatises on rhetoric classify and describe five areas from which communicators may bring their own resources to bear upon any situation. Cicero grouped these aspects together under the heading of *vis oratoris* or the speaker's resources. In *De Oratore*, he asserts that:

> since all the activity and ability of an orator falls into five divisions, I learned that he must first hit upon what to say; then manage and marshal his discoveries, not merely in orderly fashion, but with a discriminating eye for the exact weight as it were of each argument; next go on to array them in the adornments of style; after that keep them guarded in his memory; and in the end deliver them with effect and charm.[2]

---

[1] Cf. Quintilian *Institutio Oratoria* 1.9.2ff, 1.10; Cicero *De Oratore* 1.137–159.
[2] Cicero *De Oratore* 1.31.142.

Quintilian classified these five parts as invention (*inventione*), arrangement (*dispositione*), expression (*elocutione*), memory (*memoria*), and delivery or action (*pronuntiatione sive actione*).[3] Together they comprise the chief resources of orators. Thus before crafting any particular kind of speech to address a given situation, the communicator must first choose what to say, decide how to arrange and express it, set the message firmly in mind, and deliver it. Described especially for orations, these aspects of communication are applicable to most every form of communication, though there will be some differences depending on the medium of expression, especially regarding the selection of an appropriate style, the role of memory, and the means of delivery. For our purposes, we will review only certain aspects of the first three areas.

I. INVENTION

The foundational challenge facing every communicator—writer and speaker—is discerning what to say and how best to say it. The ancient orators called this dimension of communication "invention" (εὕρεσις, *inventio*). It is first in order of position among the five principal resources of the orator (*vis oratoris*) and first in order of importance.[4] It is the basis of every kind of communication. As a process, invention guides the communicator in the effective use of available resources. As a tool, invention is governed by basic principles that are essential for persuasive power.

Resources for Invention
Educated communicators were equipped with resources for discerning their own goal for communicating a message, choosing the relevant subject matter for their communication, and determining the appropriateness of their communication for the occasion. They were trained to identify the stasis for their argument and the relevant topics that would render their communication persuasive.

The Stasis. Before speaking or writing, the ideal orator sought first to investigate the situation and distill the facts regarding it.[5] Once the "situation" was known as fully as possible, the communicator began the process of

---

[3] Quintilian *Institutio Oratoria* 3.1.1 and 3.1.11f. Quintilian, like Cicero before him, reflects the general view presented by Aristotle (*Rhetoric* 3.1). See also Cicero *De Inventione* 1.7.9; *Rhetorica ad Herennium* 1.2.3.

[4] Cicero *De Inventione* 1.7.9 ("*princeps omnium partium*"); idem *Orator* 50; *Rhetorica ad Herennium* 2.1.1.

[5] Cf. Quintilian *Institutio Oratoria* 2.21.14–15 and Cicero *De Oratore* 2.24.99–101. But see also Aristotle *Rhetoric* 1.2 where establishing and presenting the facts are not essential to the orator's art.

discovering the proper response, argument, or presentation for an anticipated audience. This involved determining the main character and the central issues of the situation through a process of rigorous questioning on matters of fact, definition, and quality.[6] That is, rhetoricians sought to determine "whether a thing was done, what was the quality of the act, and what name it should have."[7] The result of this assessment then became the orator's central point to address in the response. Rhetoricians called this the στάσις (stasis) or status of the argument. In this way, the speaker arrived at the heart of the issue and determined what must be said in relation to it.

Only after completing this investigation and determining the fundamental point at issue did the speaker begin the quest for discovering all the possible resources for making a persuasive response. Since at least the time of Aristotle, the means of persuasion or types of proofs were viewed as a triad composed of ethos, pathos, and the speech itself.[8] We will examine these more closely below, but here it is sufficient to note that the persuasiveness of an address depended on the audience's perception of the orator as trustworthy (ethos), the audience's investment of their own emotions (pathos), and the ordered fluency and power of the orator's language (logos). Of course, the "true orator" was a good and moral person in whom trust was rightfully placed, but it was well known—despite Quintilian's insistence otherwise—that speaking well was not always dependent on good character. In any event, rhetoricians gave the matters of ethos, pathos, and logos considerable attention because they understood that a failure in any of the three areas impaired the persuasiveness of their speech.[9] Consequently, these means of persuasion were to be kept in mind when gathering and evaluating possible resources for an address.

Still, once the stasis was identified, how were speakers to invent or discover the appropriate argument necessary for persuading an audience to

---

[6]Cf. Cicero Orator 15 and De Oratore 2.24.26, 2.30.132; Quintilian Institutio Oratoria 3.6.80–82. It is interesting that Aristotle advocates a similar process for poets whose examination of the "situation" focused on plot, character, and thought and was a prerequisite of appropriate expression. See Aristotle Poetics, trans. S. Halliwell, LCL (Cambridge, Mass.: Harvard University Press, 1995),1450b.

[7]Cicero De Oratore 2.30.132.

[8]Aristotle Rhetoric 1.2.4f; Cicero De Oratore 2.27.114–115; 2.28.121; Quintilian Institutio Oratoria 3.5.2. Interestingly, each of these three aspects constitute, in turn, the central themes of each of Aristotle's three books in his Rhetoric: ethos in book one, pathos in book two, and logos in book three.

[9]Aristotle Rhetoric 1.2.7f.

accept the point of view presented and to respond as desired?[10] Here, the orators turned to the "places" of all arguments—the *topoi* or *loci*.[11]

Topics. The topics (*topoi*) or locations (*loci*) are "the secret places where arguments reside, and from which they must be drawn forth."[12] In the same way that certain animals and fish are found in particular habitats, so, also, arguments reside in types of habitats or *topoi* and the orator will find the precise argument needed by looking in the right place. There was widespread agreement that all arguments could be drawn from certain habitats in which they originated.

Topics of argument were found in the specifics of person, place, and event. There were general topics which could be applied to any situation. These were called "common places" (*communes loci*).[13] There were also "special places" (*speciales loci*) which were unique to particular kinds of situations, such as the place of justice for forensic discourse or expediency for deliberative speech or virtue for epideictic oratory. These *topoi* were comprised of ready resources for discussion under certain topics and included such sites as persons, cause and effect, time, quantity, quality, means, manner, definition, relationship of genus and species, similarity, difference, property, order of events, and consequences.[14]

From these *topoi* and others, through rigorous inquiry into the facts of the issue, orators sought to locate the appropriate point or points—if the matter were complex—upon which to build an oration. Thus—in the same way that the basic issue or stasis was discerned by answering the questions of who, what, where, when, how and why—the ideal orator attempted to discover the best "place(s)" from which resources could be drawn for constructing the most appropriate message for the situation and his purposes.[15] The challenge and

---

[10]Cicero *De Oratore* 2.28.121: ". . . three things which alone can carry conviction; I mean the winning over, the instructing and the stirring of men's minds."

[11]Cf. Quintilian *Institutio Oratoria* 2.39.162; Cicero *De Oratore* 2.39.162–2.40.173; Aristotle *Topica*, trans. E. S. Forster, LCL (Cambridge, Mass.: Harvard University Press, 1960; reprint 1989), 2.6–8, 23.87–90.

[12]Quintilian *Institutio Oratoria* 5.10.20.

[13]Cf. Aristotle *Rhetoric* 2.18.2–2.19.27.

[14]Cf. Quintilian *Institutio Oratoria* 5.10.94 where he summarizes his discussion of topoi (5.10.20) which are derived from "persons, causes, place and time (which latter we have divided into preceding, contemporary and subsequent), from resources (under which we include instruments), from manner (that is, how a thing has been done), from definition, genus, species, difference, property, elimination, division, beginnings, increase, consummation, likes, unlikes, contradictions, consequents, efficients, effects, results, and comparison, which is subdivided into several species." See also Aristotle *Rhetoric* 2.22.13f; Cicero *De Oratore* 2.39.162–2.40.173; idem *De Partitione Oratoria* 2.7; idem *De Inventione* 1.24.34f, 2.14.47f.

[15]Quintilian *Institutio Oratoria* 5.10.32.

purpose of invention, then, was foremost a matter of wisely identifying the fundamental stasis and selecting the most advantageous *topos* or *topoi* for addressing it.

Not surprisingly, the abundance of *topoi* complicated the task of identifying the most appropriate topics. But, as with all skills, practice and experience could make the process of analysis less burdensome. Some orators recommended a simplified process of concentrating on the unique aspects of the situation itself since most of the appropriate proofs were found there.[16] Still, the persuasive communicator had to be both accurate in selecting the core *stasis* and judicious in choosing the best topos from which to build an address. If the communication were complicated, then several topoi might be used, but the communicator had to be careful to include only those that rendered the most support and to order them wisely.[17] Propriety, again, was crucial.

Principles for Invention

Clearly, invention is not a matter of saying or writing anything or everything that comes into the communicator's mind on a given subject. Invention, rather, is the selection of particular subject matter and supporting arguments that render the communicator's message most convincing. Invention depends, then, not only upon the communicator's knowledge of the subject but also upon the communicator's shrewdness and prudence. Moreover, in addition to the communicator's proficiency in the practice of invention, an understanding of the message's recipients is also crucial for communicating persuasively.

Of course, without invention a communication will be fragmentary at best and at worst meaningless. Appealing to the resource of invention, though, with the guiding principles of brevity, clarity, and propriety as the measures for discernment, the communicator is able to identify and structure the communication's purpose. Once this is done, the communicator may pass on to the arrangement and style of the subject matter to achieve the communicator's purpose.

In short, then, the persuasiveness of any communication—spoken or written—is rooted in the communicator's investigation, analysis, and mastery of the subject matter. Moreover, effective composers of speeches and literary

---

[16]Of the complexity and difficulty of expanding systems of topoi, Quintilian writes that "the majority of students, finding themselves lost in an inextricable maze, have abandoned all individual effort, including even that which their own wits might have placed within their power, as though they were fettered by certain rigid laws" (5.10.101). Quintilian's remedy is to emphasize the method for questioning the circumstances of each particular case in order to find its unique topoi (5.10.103–104). This, too, though, requires diligent study and extensive practice. See also Cicero *Orator* 200.

[17]Cf. Quintilian *Institutio Oratoria* 3.8.1f, 7.1.10–17; Cicero *De Oratore* 2.76.309.

letters weighed their material judiciously when deciding what to say and when forecasting how to say it. Invention constituted the foundation of persuasive eloquence.

II. ARRANGEMENT

Once the central point of the argument was identified and its source and related topics were thoroughly examined, the orator knew what to say. The next task was to order the content of the argument in the most appropriate way to be convincing.

Resources for Arrangement

The *dispositio*, τάξις, or arrangement of an argument was the communicator's second principal resource. As we saw earlier, there were some differences in how rhetoricians described the parts of a speech for particular kinds of oratory. Aristotle favored and promoted two-part speeches in which the speaker states his position and proves its worth. Others expanded upon this basic order so that the movement of a speech often progressed from *exordium* to *narratio*, *propositio* (possibly with *partitio* or *divisio*), *probatio* (including *confirmatio* and/or *refutatio*) and finally to *peroratio*. Here, for our purposes, it is important to observe more closely how each section served a particular function in moving a speech persuasively from its beginning to its desired end.

The Introduction. Before orators communicated either the facts of a case (*narratio*) or the thesis (*propositio*) to be developed in the discourse, they often first sought to capture the audience's attention with the opening words and to impress upon the hearers' minds central elements of the whole discourse. This was the function of the introduction or *exordium*. The opening was critically important because it was well-known that a speaker's first impressions upon the audience largely determined how closely or even whether or not the hearers would listen to the speech that followed. In part, then, the function of the exordium was to make the hearers well-disposed, attentive and receptive to the speaker.[18] Toward these ends, orators commonly practiced the four main methods for establishing rapport with their hearers. That is, good exordiums

---

[18]The Greek terms in order are προσεκτικός, εὐμαθῆσ, εὔνους. Cf. Aristotle *Rhetoric* 3.14.1f; Cicero *De Inventione* 1.15.20, 1.16.22–23, 1.20f; idem *Orator* 122; *Rhetoric ad Herennium* 1.3.4–5, 1.4.6f, 1.5.8,1.7.11; Quintilian *Institutio Oratoria* 4.1.5. Cicero (*De Oratore* 2.79.323–80.325) reaffirms Aristotle's basic view when he holds that making hearers well-disposed, attentive, and receptive are important elements of the exordium but are no less important anywhere else in the speech. Foremost, though, the opening passage should not appear as an appendage to the message that follows but, rather, should prove integral to it.

often included brief and appropriate words about the orators themselves, their adversaries, their audience, and/or the issue at hand.[19]

The other main role for the exordium was to strike the "keynote" of the whole communication.[20] As Aristotle put it, exordiums were to "provide a sample of the subject, in order that the hearers may know beforehand what it is about, and that the mind may not be kept in suspense, for that which is undefined leads astray; so then he who puts the beginning, so to say, into the hearer's hand enables him, if he holds fast to it, to follow the story."[21] Communicators recognized that they enhanced their persuasiveness by impressing upon the hearers' minds as quickly as possible in the opening words or exordium the very ideas to be developed in the speech.

When opening remarks do not provide a sample of the communication's subject and are not intimately related to the stasis of the discourse, they are considered faulty. Defective openings are general and can apply to other speeches. Moreover, opponents can use them to cast a counter argument or antagonize the speaker himself. Poor exordiums also lead hearers astray by introducing irrelevant points that cause confusion. They may even alienate hearers so that listening ceases with the opening words. Finally, an introduction is faulty if it uses words and a compositional style that are inappropriate for the situation. Simply put, an exordium that lacked an intimate connection with the speaker's main points was inevitably "bald or trifling or hackneyed or undistinctive."[22] Flawed beginnings were to be avoided, for a failure here could cause the recipients of the message to disregard all that follows.

In order to formulate a right beginning, Cicero insisted that "the opening passage in a speech must not be drawn from some outside source but from the very heart of the case."[23] Thus Cicero taught that the discovery of the appropriate opening came only after the stasis and topics were identified, analyzed, developed and arranged. An opening passage that was drawn from matters central to the whole communication proved most advantageous for speaker and hearer because it formed a solid basis out of which the arguments, digressions, and conclusions would naturally come. Moreover, the opening's specific nature made the message easier to follow.

In these matters, Cicero was following Aristotle who directed orators to the opening lines or exordia of Homer's epic poems, the *Iliad* and *Odyssey*, and

---

[19]Cf. *Rhetorica ad Herennium* 1.4.7; Cicero *De Inventione* 1.16.22.

[20]Aristotle *Rhetoric* 3.14.1.

[21]Aristotle *Rhetoric* 3.14.6. Cicero concurs that "the anticipation of the audience should be gratified as quickly as possible, and if it is not satisfied at the start, a great deal more work has to be put in during the remainder of the proceedings" (*De Oratore* 2.7.313).

[22]Cf. Cicero *De Oratore* 2.77.315–2.79.323; idem *De Inventione* 1.18.26; *Rhetoric ad Herennium* 1.7.11.

[23]Cicero *De Oratore* 2.78.318–319, 2.79.324–2.80.325.

to Euripides' tragic poetry as well as to that of Sophocles. Aristotle noted that many writers of history and comedy also recognized the crucial importance of a composition's opening lines for establishing the central course of their communications. For Aristotle, introductions to speeches ought to be composed especially carefully to make the principal subject matter conspicuous. Thus Aristotle concluded "the most essential and special function of the exordium is to make clear what is the end or purpose of the speech."[24]

Quintilian joined Cicero and Aristotle in highlighting model exordiums from various types of communications. Moreover, he, too, gave high praise to Homer's *Iliad* and *Odyssey*. In fact, regarding their opening lines, Quintilian wrote that:

> in the few lines with which he introduces both of his epics, has he not, I will not say observed, but actually established the law which should govern the composition of the exordium? For, by his invocation of the goddesses believed to preside over poetry he wins the goodwill of his audience, by his statement of greatness of his themes he excites their brief attention and renders them receptive by the briefness of his summary.[25]

First, it is noteworthy that this model exordium for speeches is drawn from epic poetry. Second, the exordium is once again characterized by its four-fold function. Exordiums ought to be brief, well-composed statements that make the hearers well-disposed, attentive and receptive to the speaker. Moreover, they should present themes that are central to the following communication. As we will see below, Homer did indeed launch the main themes of the *Iliad* and *Odyssey* in their opening lines, and, since Homer, this practice became quite common to communications throughout the Greco-Roman world, including Paul's letter to the Galatians.

Another characteristic of the well-formed exordium is its practical relevancy. Quintilian stressed the importance of a good exordium because of its special benefit for busy orators who lacked the time to write out their entire speeches before delivering them. Out of a good exordium, an entire speech could be unfurled. According to Quintilian, this was the common practice of the industrious Cicero.[26]

Exordiums were classified as one of two types: the direct opening (προοίμιον or *principium*) or the subtle approach (ἔφοδος or *insinuatio*).[27] The

---

[24]Aristotle *Rhetoric* 3.14.6. See also Quintilian *Institutio Oratoria* 10.3.18.

[25]Quintilian *Institutio Oratoria* 10.1.48.

[26]Quintilian *Institutio Oratoria* 10.7.30.

[27]Cf. *Rhetorica ad Herennium* 1.4.6; 1.6.9–10; Cicero *De Inventione* 1.15.20, 1.17.23–25; Quintilian *Institutio Oratoria* 4.1.42; Aristotle *Rhetoric* 3.14.1f. On the history of *insinuatio*, see especially E. W. Bower, "Epodos and *insinuatio* in Greek and Latin Rhetoric," *CQ* 52 (1958): 224–30.

selection of the most appropriate opening type depended on the orator's assessment of whether the cause of the address was honorable (*honestum*), discreditable (*turpe*), doubtful (*dubium*), or petty (*humile*). The author of the *Rhetorica ad Herennium* recommended that:

> If our cause is of the doubtful kind, we shall build the Direct Opening upon good will, so that the discreditable part of the cause cannot be prejudicial to us. If our cause is of the petty kind, we shall make our hearers attentive. If our cause is of the discreditable kind, unless we have hit upon a means of capturing goodwill by attacking our adversaries, we must use the Subtle Approach, which I will discuss later. And finally, if our cause is of the honourable kind, it will be correct either to use the Direct Opening or not to use it. If we wish to use it, we must show why the cause is honourable, or else briefly announce what matters we are going to discuss. But if we do not wish to use the Direct Opening, we must begin our speech with a law, a written document, or some argument supporting our cause.[28]

The direct opening seeks to establish immediate concord with the hearers and is used on occasions when hearers have an interest in the subject-matter, are supportive of the speaker—or are at least not hostile, and when hearers are rested and are able to listen. In certain agreeable circumstances, exordiums are not needed at all.[29] The subtle approach, on the other hand, strives for the same end less obviously and is reserved for three conflictual situations: when the subject itself alienates the hearers from the speaker, when the hearers are siding with the opposition, or when the hearers are tired from listening to the previous speakers.[30] On occasions such as these, an exordium should make a subtle approach to the cause by the following means:

> the point which our adversaries have regarded as their strongest support we shall promise to discuss first; we shall begin with a statement made by the opponent, and particularly with that which he has made last; and we shall use Indecision, along with an exclamation of astonishment.[31]

We will examine below these aspects of the exordium in relation to the opening of Galatians. The point here is simply that, whether subtle or direct, the exordium was critically important for setting a communication on the right path

---

[28]Cf. *Rhetorica ad Herennium* 1.4.5f. Cicero (*De Inventione* 1.15.20) distinguishes five kinds of cases: honorable (honestum), difficult (admirabile), mean (humile), ambiguous (anceps), and obscure (obscurum).

[29]Cf. Quintilian *Institutio Oratoria* 3.8.6–10. It is also the case, however, that exordiums could be deleted if the degree of controversy was such that hearers might not have the patience to listen to an introduction. In this case, orators were encouraged to proceed immediately into the statement of facts. Cf. *Rhetorica ad Herennium* 3.10.17.

[30]Cf. *Rhetorica ad Herennium* 1.6.9.

[31]*Rhetorica ad Herennium* 1.6.10, 4.29.40. See also Cicero *De Inventione* 1.17.25.

for reaching the speaker's goal. Not only were opening remarks designed to make listeners and readers attentive, receptive, and well-disposed, but the introduction—even, if not especially, the first words—of a written or spoken composition were recognized for their critical importance in establishing the central course and persuasiveness of the entire communication.

The Conclusion. After the speech's inauguration with a good exordium and the subsequent development of the appropriate subject matter in the body of the speech, the ideal speaker brought the communication to a fitting end. The closing of a discourse is called the *peroratio, conclusio* or ἐπίλογος (*epilogos*) and—regardless of the kind of speech—was the communicator's last opportunity to summarize his most important points (ἀνακεφαλαίωσις, *enumeratio, recapitulatio*), amplify his or her own position (*amplificatio*), and appeal to the hearers' pity (ἔλεος, *conquestio*). It was also an appropriate place to praise an ally (*laudatio*) or blame an opponent (δείνωσις, *indignatio*).[32] The peroration's special function, however, was to bring the speech to a memorable and persuasive close.

Whether the conclusion deals primarily with the facts and so functions as a recapitulation or summation of the speaker's message, or whether the conclusion focuses on amplification and so functions as a final appeal for praise, blame, or pity, the chief virtues of the peroration remain the same. The speech's ending ought to be brief and it should strike the central points of the discourse which were signaled first in the exordium.[33] Moreover, the peroration also merited special care for it was the climax of the speech. As Quintilian put it: "our eloquence ought to be pitched higher in this portion of our speech than in any other, since, wherever it fails to add something to what has preceded, it seems even to diminish its previous effect."[34]

Emotional appeals in the peroration were quite popular because of their proven effectiveness in moving an audience. This was especially true for forensic pleading though emotional amplification was equally advantageous in deliberative and epideictic rhetoric. Of course, emotional appeals were not restricted to the peroration but were commonly used throughout a speech.[35] Nevertheless, the end of a discourse was uniquely suited for stirring the

---

[32]Cf. Aristotle *Rhetoric* 3.19.1–6; Cicero *De Inventione* 1.52.98–100; Quintilian *Institutio Oratoria* 3.7.1f, 6.1.1f; *Rhetorica ad Herennium* 2.30.47f and note *a* on pp. 144–145.

[33]Cf. *Rhetorica ad Herennium* 2.30.47, 3.8.15, 4.30.41; Quintilian *Institutio Oratoria* 6.1.1f. In 6.1.9, Quintilian distinguishes the duties of the peroration from those of the exordium in that the former are "freer and wider in scope." See also 4.1.27–28.

[34]Quintilian *Institutio Oratoria* 6.1.29.

[35]Cf. Quintilian *Institutio Oratoria* 6.1.53.

emotions,[36] and the topic drew considerable attention from rhetoricians who distinguished between two types of emotion—*ethos* and *pathos*. Discussions typically describe *pathos* appeals as the more turbulent expression of emotion that commands and disturbs. *Ethos* appeals, on the other hand, are often more calm and subdued—even gentle—and persuade by inducing feelings of goodwill.[37]

The effectiveness of emotional appeals depended in large measure upon the speaker's ability to create vivid images in the hearers' minds. One common practice, especially in law courts, was to actually display persons, actions, and things during the peroration in order to leave a strong and lasting impression upon the judge and audience that would move them to accept the speaker's position. Still, some final oral interpretation or statement was nearly always necessary. For instance, Quintilian wrote of persons using paintings of crimes that "the pleader who prefers a voiceless picture to speak for him in place of his own eloquence must be singularly incompetent."[38] Understandably, though, a powerful imagination that was capable of verbally depicting things and actions in a realistic way (εὐφαντασίωτος) was prized among orators. Their aim, though, was not a lengthy elaboration of an oral picture in the conclusion but rather a clear and brief illumination of a particular image that would stick in the minds of the hearers and make the speaker's fundamental point. Such an ending enhanced the persuasiveness of the whole speech.[39]

Thus, if the exordium is the place from which the speaker's course is begun, the peroration is the goal toward which the course is run. The beginning and ending of a speech were critically important to the effectiveness of the whole communication. If the communicator faltered at the beginning or fizzled at the end, the communicator's main points could be lost in a sea of words. Of course, conclusions could be employed in a speech after a direct opening, at the end of the narratio, and at the end of the discourse's strongest argument,[40] but the peroratio ought to mark the end of the speech clearly and powerfully. Now

---

[36]Cf. Quintilian *Institutio Oratoria* 6.1.51–52.

[37]Cf. Quintilian *Institutio Oratoria* 6.2.8–10. See especially Steven J. Kraftchick, "Ethos and Pathos Appeals in Galatians Five and Six: A Rhetorical Analysis," Emory University Dissertation (Atlanta: Emory University, 1985).

[38]Quintilian *Institutio Oratoria* 6.1.32.

[39]Quintilian *Institutio Oratoria* 6.2.29–32. Earlier (6.1.30–35), Quintilian gives an account of some striking images created by particular *actions* during the peroration which may also effective in moving an audience to pity. Common practices in forensic cases included "bringing accused persons into court wearing squalid and unkempt attire, and of introducing their children and parents, and [showing] . . . blood-stained swords, fragments of bone taken from the wound, and garments spotted with blood . . . wounds stripped of their dressings, and scourged bodies bared to view" (6.1.30).

[40]*Rhetorica ad Herennium* 2.30.47.

let us review some salient points regarding the proven path for persuasive discourse between the speech's beginning and end.

The Speech Body. Between the beginning and the end of the speech stands the body which is usually comprised of a *narratio*, a *propositio*, and an *argumentatio* (*confirmatio* and/or *refutatio*). The *narratio* ordinarily presents an account of past events that pertain to the issue at hand. Ideally, it gives accounts of major events that have a direct bearing on the discourse. The presentation of material ought to be clear, brief, and probable.[41] Too much detail should be avoided. Furthermore, while chronological order was possible, events could also be arranged in whatever way best fit the speaker's purpose. The aim was persuasion rather than a disinterested account of events.[42] The narratio also provided orators an appropriate place to render accounts of conversations. Here, too, they could employ a digressio to sharpen an attack on an opponent or amuse the hearers.[43] Orators knew that a recounting of events in the narratio was often useful in establishing their own ethos or credibility and stirring the emotions or pathos of the audience.[44]

Of course, since the narratio deals with past time, it is usually more integral to forensic pleading than to deliberative and epideictic rhetoric, though it may be incorporated into these forms of civic discourse, too. In each type of speech, for instance, there are occasions when the facts may need to be re-presented or interpreted in a particular way. Still, the narratio may be omitted even from forensic rhetoric when the facts are well-known.[45] Here, as elsewhere, the ideal of flexibility often guarded against the tyranny of rhetorical rules.[46] Statements of fact so characteristic of the narratio might be employed wherever they were useful in the speech.[47] The main purpose of the narratio, though, was to indicate explicitly that which the speaker aimed to prove in the body of the speech or *argumentatio*.[48]

After the narratio—if it was used—the speaker often set forth the *propositio* which is the actual presentation of the main point the speaker plans to make in the discourse. The propositio is the thesis statement of the entire discourse. If the issue was complicated, the speaker might identify specific points of agreement or disagreement between himself and any opponents, or he

---

[41] Aristotle *Rhetoric* 3.16; Cicero *De Inventione* 1.28–29; *Rhetorica ad Herennium* 1.9.14–17.
[42] Quintilian *Institutio Oratoria* 4.2.31.
[43] Cicero *De Inventione* 1.27–30.
[44] Aristotle *Rhetoric* 3.16.10–11.
[45] Quintilian *Institutio Oratoria* 4.2.21; Aristotle *Rhetoric* 3.16.
[46] Quintilian *Institutio Oratoria* 4.2.103.
[47] Aristotle *Rhetoric* 3.16.
[48] Quintilian *Institutio Oratoria* 4.2.79.

could simply list the points he will prove—customarily no more than three. This specification of particular points was called *partitio* or *divisio*.[49]

The main argument of the discourse is often called the *argumentatio* and it is here—following the exordium, narratio, and propositio—that the speaker seeks to prove his thesis (*confirmatio*) or disprove (*refutatio*) the claims of any opponents. In every kind of discourse, the speaker must demonstrate the basis for his position. Since Aristotle, rhetorical proofs were classified under the three main headings of *ethos*, *pathos*, and *logos*. Ethical proofs (*ethos*) sought to establish the moral character of the speaker as trustworthy and authoritative. Emotional proofs (*pathos*) were aimed at the feelings of the hearers or readers and were used for moving the audience to support the speaker. Both ethos and pathos appeals could come anywhere in the speech, though they were especially effective in the opening and closing. The proofs of persuasive reasoning and language (*logos*) deal with logic and ideas. These proofs are especially well suited for concentration in the argumentatio. Together, the rhetorical proofs drawn from the areas of ethos, pathos, and logos cover any rhetorical situation.[50] All three kinds are present in Galatians.[51]

One important dimension of these rhetorical proofs for modern interpreters to observe is that they are not restricted to demonstrable facts but also include the realm of probability. As noted above, orators often incorporated nonrhetorical proofs such as witnesses, contracts, laws and other types of material proofs or evidences.[52] The rhetorical proof, though, is drawn from the more general material of topics regarding persons or actions, thus probability may also form the basis of a proof. As a persuasive argument, then, the rhetorical proof is often presented as an enthymeme or more briefly as a maxim.[53] Argument by example was also a common form of rhetorical proof.

The enthymeme or, as Aristotle called it, the "rhetorical syllogism" was particularly effective in oral discourse.[54] The difference between a syllogism and an enthymeme is that while a syllogism states a major premise, a minor premise, and a conclusion, an enthymeme holds some—or, in the case of a maxim, all—of the premises "in mind" and stresses the conclusion.[55] A maxim

---

[49]Cicero *De Inventione* 1.31–33; *Rhetorica ad Herennium* 1.17; Quintilian *Institutio Oratoria* 4.5.22–27.

[50]Aristotle *Rhetoric* 1.2; Cicero *De Inventione* 1.34–37; Kennedy, *New Testament Interpretation*, 15–16.

[51]Steven J. Kraftchick, *Ethos and Pathos Appeals in Galatians*.

[52]Aristotle *Rhetoric* 1.15; Cicero *De Oratore* 2.28.116; Quintilian, *Institutio Oratoria* 5.1–8; *Rhetorica ad Herennium* 2.6.9.

[53]Cf. Aristotle *Rhetoric* 1.2; Cicero *De Inventione* 1.67. Cicero prefers to use for an *enthymeme* the Latin term *ratiocination*.

[54]Aristotle *Rhetoric* 1.2.

[55]Quintilian *Institutio Oratoria* 5.14.24.

may be simple and may seem true because it states what is commonly held to be true, or it may need the verbal support of reasoned argument, in which case it becomes an enthymeme (major or minor premise stated) or a syllogism (major and minor premise stated). The rhetorical advantage of the enthymeme and maxim is that both involve the hearers in supplying the basis for the conclusion through their own reasoning or assent. Moreover, their brevity make them easier to grasp and remember.[56] Their persuasiveness stems from their probability. The more probable the proof, the more persuasive it is.[57]

Another important rhetorical proof is the example. Since Aristotle, examples were categorized as either actual facts or probable events. The latter category was divided further into the areas of parallel event (*similitudo*) and fable. These were especially useful when facts were disputed, for the speaker could increase the probability of his argument by demonstrating the similarity of his case to another event or story in which the "facts" are known. The principal requirement for examples is that they must be drawn from things that are similar, dissimilar, or contrary. Any example used must be both reasonable and clearly relevant to the argument.[58]

By rhetorical proof and example, the *argumentatio* is the appropriate place in a discourse to confirm a thesis (*confirmatio*). It is also an effective place for mustering a rebuttal (*refutatio*). In a *refutatio*, the speaker aims at countering and overturning an opponent's arguments. This may be accomplished quite well by setting forth opposing enthymemes that draw conclusions contrary to those made by an antagonist. The refutatio is also an appropriate place for attacking and subverting an opponent's premises and conclusions by showing that they are wrong or improbable. A rebuttal is also accomplished if the speaker makes a strong argument that trivializes the opponent's argument.[59]

Principles for Arrangement

This simplified overview of the speech body is sufficient for drawing some basic conclusions about the arrangement of a speech from the *exordium* to the *peroration*. To be sure, the basic movement of a discourse from *exordium* to *narratio*, *propositio*, *argumentatio*, and *peroratio* provides speakers a structure

---

[56]Aristotle *Rhetoric* 2.20–22; Cicero *De Inventione* 1.67. A syllogism may be demonstrated as follows: Every virtue is laudable (major premise). Kindness is a virtue (minor premise). Therefore, kindness is laudable (conclusion). An enthymeme would use only the major or minor premise and the conclusion.

[57]Quintilian *Institutio Oratoria* 5.10.16–19.

[58]Quintilian *Institutio Oratoria* 5.11.6, 25–26; Cicero *De Inventione* 1.30.49; *Rhetorica ad Herennium* 4.69.62.

[59]Aristotle *Rhetoric* 2.25; Cicero *De Inventione* 1.42–90; Quintilian *Institutio Oratoria* 2.4.18.

for addressing topics fully and clearly. That is, the order gives speakers a plan for composing and presenting an argument in a persuasive manner. The arrangement is also advantageous to hearers because it allows them to follow the speaker's argument in an orderly and progressive way so that they may "see" for themselves the speaker's thesis and the proof supporting the speaker's point of view. For instance, before a speaker can be heard regarding the "facts" (*narratio*) or "proofs" (*argumentatio*) supporting the speaker's point of view, he or she must first secure attentive hearers and strike creatively the keynote of the discourse (*exordium*) in order to plant within the hearers' minds—directly or indirectly—issues central to the matter at hand. Then, if facts are to be given, they may be conveyed clearly, concisely, and in an interesting manner so that the listeners are fully prepared to hear the speaker's full thesis or position regarding the issue at hand (*propositio*). If not, then the central issues of the *propositio*, which were sounded in the *exordium* and possibly developed further in the *narratio*, do not surprise but are the natural consequence of the preceding discourse. Once the speaker's thesis is stated, the hearers are prepared to weigh the following evidences or proofs in the *argumentatio* which the speaker presents to support the *propositio*. Then, after the proofs are given, the hearers are aided by a recapitulation that summarizes the argument's main point(s) and vividly depicts the speaker's expectations for the hearers' response (*peroratio*).

Such was the proven order for persuasive communication. Each portion of the speech prepared the way for the subsequent part so that the hearers were more inclined to follow and accept the speaker's successive points and finally give consent to the speaker's argument. The beginning and ending of a discourse should be especially relevant and memorable. The movement of the communication ought to move largely in a linear and progressive fashion. But persuasive communication depended upon more than an orderly arrangement. It was also necessary for the message to be expressed well. Thus, while we will give some attention below to the aspects of arrangement and invention in our study of Galatians, let us first review some important matters regarding the communicator's resource of *elocutio* or "style." Here, too, the importance of beginnings and endings is apparent.

III. EXPRESSION

The third principal resource available to communicators was "style" or what the Greeks called λέξις, ἑρμηνεία, or φράσις and the Romans *lexis* or *elocutio*. As the term *elocutio* makes most apparent, there is a fundamental linguistic bond between "style" and "eloquence." Simply put, *elocutio* is the art of expressing oneself well in words. It involves the study of words and their proper uses (ἐκλογή or *electio*) along with their effective arrangements into sentences for certain ends (σύνθεσις or *compositio*).[60]

Resources for Expression

Since *elocutio* concerns the expression of persuasive eloquence—which is the goal of oratory—the topic drew considerable attention. Indeed, the overwhelming majority of existent rhetorical works address matters pertaining to style.[61] The topic is far too expansive and complex to be addressed fully here; nevertheless, a few salient points on the topic will aid us in our investigation of Galatians.

Classifications of Style. Greek and Latin communicators shared many of the same basic principles regarding eloquent expression. Chief among their common characteristics of eloquent communication—regardless of the particular style and medium—were clarity, orderliness, and appropriateness. Also important were matters of precision or correctness of grammar, rhythm and euphony, vividness, brevity and ornamentation or embellishment. These were commonly referred to as stylistic virtues[62] and formed in varying degrees the basic categories for describing and prescribing the central aspects of the three or four most common types of style which were used by rhetoricians in both written and oral communication.[63]

The plain style (ἰσχνόν, λιτόν, tenue) utilizes the simplest and most current standards of ordinary speech. Its sentence movements are free flowing but not pointless. The expression is clear and well reasoned, but it is not strong or forceful. The plain style reflects concern for diction and composition, but not to the extent required for periodic structures. Wit and humor have their place

---

[60]Cf. Aristotle *Rhetoric* 3.5.1–3.12.6; Cicero *De Oratore* 3.10.37–3.14.55.

[61]D. L. Clark calls attention to this fact by noting that nearly one third of Aristotle's *Rhetoric*, almost half of *Rhetorica ad Herennium*, one third of Cicero's *De Oratore* and all of the *Orator*, Books 8 and 9 of Quintilian's *Institutio Oratoria*, and whole treatises by Pseudo-Demetrius, Dionysius of Halicarnassus, and Pseudo-Longinus all pertain to style. He writes, "No other aspect of rhetoric or poetry in antiquity received so much attention in surviving treatises" (*Rhetoric in Greco-Roman Education*, 83).

[62]Cf. Aristotle *Rhetoric* 3.2–7, who describes the essential virtues as clarity and propriety. Cicero and Quintilian made further distinctions of the fundamental virtues as given here. See, for instance, Cicero *De Oratore* 1.32.144, 3.10.37; and Quintilian, *Institutio Oratoria* 8.Pr.27–9.3. For a thorough summary of Greco-Roman style in antiquity, see especially S. J. Kraftchick, *Ethos and Pathos Appeals in Galatians*,144–208.

[63]On classifications and descriptions of the types of rhetorical styles in Greco-Roman communication, see especially *Rhetorica ad Herennium* 4.8.11–4.11.16; Cicero *De Oratore* 3.45.177–3.52.199, 3.55.212, idem *Orator* 5.20f, 19.62–66, 23.75f; idem *Brutus*, 55.201; Quintilian *Institutio Oratoria* 8.1.1f; Demetrius *De Elocutione* 36; Dionysius of Halicarnassus *De Compositione Verbum* 21–24.

here, but dramatic and stately language would be out of place. This is the arena of common discourse.[64]

The medium or polished style (μέσον, μικτόν, γλαφυρός, medium) uses words and expressions that are neither the lowest, most colloquial nor the highest, most ornate—hence the designation "middle." The choice and arrangement of words is more relaxed than the grand style but is more intentionally crafted for a smoother, more formal expression than that of the simple style. Here there is more concern on the part of the communicator for gaining the sympathy of the audience, thus there is more consideration of the audience's pathos. The principal trait of this style is agreeableness. The speaker or writer of this style is more careful and intentional in both the selection and arrangement of words and subject matter throughout the communication.[65]

The grand style (άδρόν, μεγαλοπρεπές, περιττόν, grande) is by far the most embellished, measured and stately use of the Greek and Latin languages. Of this style, Cicero writes that its characteristic "brilliance and fluency have caused admiring nations to let eloquence attain the highest power in the state."[66] This is not to say that the other styles are not important. They, too, have their places because oratory is about appropriate expression. Moreover, the grand style incorporates aspects from these other styles. The purpose of the grand style, however, is to deal with weighty affairs and it does so by using the most ornate words and the loftiest thoughts.[67]

These three categories constituted the principal ways orators described the typical styles created by particular kinds of choices and arrangements of words and sentences for addressing common, semi-formal, and formal occasions. Demetrius's *De Elocutione*, however, included a fourth style that is called "forceful" (δεινός). More than the other classified kinds, the forceful style emphasizes tight periodic structures and persistent brevity in the presentation of a strong subject matter. Frequent parallelisms and antitheses are avoided. Smoothness in sound and steady cadences also weaken a forceful style. Instead, the aim of this style is vigorous expression that is accomplished primarily through the communication of much meaning through a minimum amount of words.[68]

The ancients stressed stylistic conventions in their quest for persuasive eloquence. But, again, it is important to recall their reciprocal emphasis on

---

[64]Cf. Cicero *Oratore* 23.75–26.90; Demetrius *De Elocutione* 190–235.

[65]Cf. Cicero *Oratore* 26.91–27.96; Demetrius *De Elocutione* 128–89. Dionysius of Halicarnassus, in both *De Compositione Verbum* 21–24 and *On the Style of Demosthenes* 37–41, does not position the middle type of style between the grand and the plain but rather between the middle and the grand.

[66]Cicero *Oratore* 28.97.

[67]Cf. Cicero *Oratore* 28.100–113; Demetrius *De Elocutione* 38–127.

[68]Demetrius *De Elocutione* 240–304.

flexibility. These styles and many of the stylistic techniques could be used alone or they could be mixed in a variety of ways. For instance, Cicero and Quintilian advocated changing from one style to another throughout a discourse as a means of keeping the listener's interest,[69] and Dionysius of Halicarnassus viewed the blended style as the ideal type of expression for its broader appeal.[70] The masterful use of stylistic conventions was a prized attribute among orators. Many pointed to the example of Homer who possessed "the most voices of all"[71] and "outdistanced all that have come after him in every department of eloquence."[72] As noted above, though, not every stylistic device or combination was appropriate for every kind of discourse.[73] The governing rule or virtue for style, again, was propriety.

Compositional Tools. Speakers and writers had at their disposal a wealth of linguistic resources and grammatical tools for constructing clauses and sentences (σύνθεσις) and for expressing them in appropriate ways utilizing figures of diction (σχήματα λέξεως) and figures of thought (σχήματα διανοίας).[74]

Achieving the goal of persuasive eloquence for any situation seldom came by accident. Much grammatical and rhetorical training focused intensely on matters of diction and composition, such as word selection and positioning for euphony, rhythm, and emphasis. Other matters, such as ellipsis, prolepsis, pleonasm, polysyndeton, asyndeton, parenthesis, anacoluthon, synecdoche, and prosopopoeia, also received careful attention.[75] Important stylistic resources

---

[69]Cicero *Orator* 21.74; Quintilian *Institutio Oratoria* 11.1.4, 12.10.66–68.

[70]Dionysius of Halicarnassus *De Compositione Verbum* 16, 21. See also Demetrius *De Elocutione* 15; Quintilian *Institutio Oratoria* 10.1.46–51.

[71]Dionysius of Halicarnassus *De Compositione Verbum* 16, 21.

[72]Quintilian *Institutio Oratoria* 10.1.51.

[73]Cf. Demetrius *De Elocutione* 37, in which the mixing of styles and their parts is permissable except for those that are polar opposites.

[74]Cf. *Rhetorica ad Herennium* 4.13.19.

[75]For these and other rhetorical terms, see especially the very useful works by Richard A. Lanham, *A Handlist of Rhetorical Terms: A Guide for Students of English Literature* (Berkeley: University of California Press, 1968) and H. Lausberg, *Handbuch der Literarischen Rhetorik*. Briefly summarized, though, ellipsis (ἔλλειψις or detractio) is the omission of a word or words implied by the context and used for an economy of expression and the enhancement of forcefulness. Prolepsis (πρόληψις or praesumptio) is a device for increasing the hearer's or reader's anticipation by providing a glimpse of that which is to come. Pleonasm (πλεονασμός or macrologia) refers to excessive speech in which more words are used than are needed. It may be a fault if it results in redundancy, but it may also be used effectively for enhancing the vividness, emphasis and stateliness of a communication. Polysyndeton (πολυσύνδετος) occurs when conjuntions and connecting particles are used in close succession to join words and clauses together to add emphasis to a thought. Asyndeton (ἀσύνδετος) is the opposite of polysyndeton and indicates the

likewise included hyperbole, irony, metaphor, simile, parallelism, vividness, antithesis, repetition, and reasoning by questioning and answering.[76] These stylistic techniques and many others belonged to the common linguistic resources of educated Greco-Roman communicators.

The rhetorical treatises are teeming with discussions on compositional tools for eloquent expression. But while these stylistic aspects of communication received a great amount of attention from orators and others who studied language, again it is important to keep in mind that rhetorical techniques—like grammar itself—are first descriptive. Thus whether persons were formally trained or were simply saturated in the rich use of language, many stylistic devices were broadly applied regardless of the speaker's cognizance or intentionality. Clearly, though, communicators who could purposefully and ably wield these weapons of eloquence throughout a sustained discourse were likely more often convincing.

Sentence Movements. No matter what style(s) or stylistic devices a communicator might employ, there were two basic types of sentence movements common to them all. Sentences were formed and organized in either the running or continuous (εἰρομένη) style or the periodic (ἐν περιόδοις) or compact (κατεστραμμένη) style.[77] These two classifications of sentence movements were often mixed, depending on the communicators' purposes; however, each one had particular uses and advantages. Because of the particular relevancy of periodic sentence movements to exordiums and perorations, we will examine this matter closely.

The running style is common in narrative and historical prose. It has rhythm, but it does not move in measured meters.[78] Clauses, sentences or groups of sentences do not have close attachments or clearly marked endings. Rather, meaning is accomplished only when the syntactical sense is complete. The end is evident only because there is nothing more to say. This older

---

compacting of words, phrases and sentences without connectives in order to add force to an expression. Parenthesis (παρέθεσις or interpositio) is a break in the sentence caused by the insertion of another remark. Anacoluthon (ἀνακόλουθον) is a more decisive break in the sentence. Synecdoche (συνεκδοχή or intellectio) is the use of a word to designate more than its particular designation (such as "bread" in the Lord's Prayer). Prosopopoeia (προσωποποιία or fictio personae or sermocinatio) is impersonation.

[76]See especially Quintilian *Institutio Oratoria* books 8 and 9 for a clear and thorough presentation of stylistic considerations for rhetoric. His three main divisions are tropes—which are essentially figures of similarity such as metaphors (8.6), figures of thought—which pertain to conceptual moves that orators can use for their advantage, such as the rhetorical question (9.1–9.2.107), and figures of speech—which pertain to various patterns of expression, such as repetition and antithesis (9.1.1–45, 9.3.1–102).

[77]Aristotle *Rhetoric* 3.9.1.

[78]Ibid., 3.8.1–2.

running style is often sequential and is useful for adding idea to idea or fact to fact. The rhetoricians generally have little to say about this style. Its characteristics seem well understood.[79]

Periodic sentence movements, on the other hand, attracted a great deal of attention from ancient orators and warrant careful attention still today. This is because periods were used widely throughout the Greco-Roman world in both speech and writing due to their proven effectiveness in advancing the communicator's purposes. Ancient discussions of periods are often elaborate and utilize many examples to demonstrate their logical, grammatical and rhythmical qualities. It is sufficient for our purposes here, however, simply to review significant characteristics of the period and consider some of its important functions.[80]

What exactly is a period? Aristotle wrote, "by period I mean a sentence that has a beginning and end in itself and a magnitude that can be easily grasped."[81] He means that the period is an expression that has an end determined by its structure and the entire length of the period can be heard or seen as a whole entity. Aristotle delineates two major types of periods. The simple period is comprised of one *colon* (κῶλον, membrum) or clause.[82] The compound period is comprised of two *cola* or clauses. The latter has distinct parts, close connections, and—for Aristotle—is utterable in a single breath. Neither the compound nor the simple period should be too long or too short. If the periodic clause or sentence is too short, the hearer stumbles and has insufficient time to grasp the speaker's point. If the periodic clause or sentence is too long, the hearer becomes lost and stops listening. Indeed, periods that are too long take on the character of whole speeches.[83] For Aristotle, then, a *colon*—as the word itself indicates—is a clause or phrase that has some grammatical independence, and a period is comprised of one or two cola. In contrast to the continuous style, these cola are not randomly ordered but are organized and integrated in a purposeful way.

According to Demetrius, "a period is a combination of clauses and phrases which has brought the underlying thought to a conclusion with a neatly

---

[79]Aristotle *Rhetoric* 3.9.2–3f; Demetrius *De Elocutione* 12; Quintilian *Institutio Oratoria* 9.4.19–21. Quintilian observes that this looser style has its own rhythms, which are difficult to analyze, and is more common to "dialogues and letters, except when they deal with some subject above their natural level, such as philosophy, politics or the like" (20).

[80]For a thorough presentation of the Greco-Roman period, see especially H. Lausberg, *Handbuch der Literarischen Rhetorik*, 458–69.

[81]Aristotle *Rhetoric* 3.9.3.

[82]Ibid., 3.9.5. See also Cicero *Orator* 62.211; Quintilian *Institutio Oratoria* 9.4.22, 9.4.122. Cicero and Quintilian identify parts of a *colon* as *commas* or *incisa*.

[83]Aristotle *Rhetoric* 3.9.5–6.

turned ending."[84] That is, like Aristotle, the parts of a period are interdependent and support one another. For Demetrius, though, the period typically moves toward a particular goal. Thus Demetrius wrote:

> the very use of the word 'period' implies that there has been a beginning at one point and will be an ending at another, and that we are hastening towards a definite goal as runners do when they leave the starting-place. For at the very beginning of their race the end of the course should be manifest. Whence the name 'period,' the image being that of paths traversed in a circle. . . . If its circular form is destroyed and the arrangement changed, the subject matter remains the same, but the period will have disappeared.[85]

Demetrius focused more on the period's ending than on the matters of antithesis and assonance that attracted so much of Aristotle's attention. Demetrius also differed from Aristotle regarding the recommended length for periods. Since at least the time of Gorgias and Isocrates, periods quite often were long.[86] Aristotle reacted by promoting shorter periods of one or two cola. Demetrius favored short periods, too, but he rejected Aristotle's limitation of periods to one or two clauses. Instead, Demetrius advocated the use of periods with two to four members.[87]

In essence, periods could be as simple as a clause or as elaborate and complex as a communicator cared to make them.[88] The basic view represented by Aristotle and Demetrius, however, indicates that periods should not be lengthy sentences with boundless subordinate clauses. Good periods, rather, are essentially short sentences or clauses or phrases within a longer sentence that make their own distinct point. Moreover, in periods comprised of more than one member, the last part ought to be longer than the preceding parts. The extension of the last member helps make the concluding point more memorable. The extended length of the last member also adds stateliness to the period—as did the lengthening of the vowels—and makes it more impressive.[89]

Aristotle and Demetrius divided compound periods (cola) and lengthy simple periods into two types: divided and antithetical.[90] The divided period

---

[84]Demetrius *De Elocutione* 10.

[85]Ibid., 11. See also Aristotle *Rhetoric* 3.9.1–6; Quintilian *Institutio Oratoria* 9.4.19, 22, 125; Cicero *Oratore* 61.204; idem *Brutus* 8.34, 44.162.

[86]Cf. Aristotle *Rhetoric* 3.8.6.

[87]Demetrius *De Elocutione* 16, 34. Demetrius seems to be responding to the popular style rooted in Gorgias, Alcidamas, and the Isocrates' School "where period succeeds period no less regularly than the hexameters in the poetry of Homer" (*De Elocutione* 12) and where speeches were comprised entirely of a "string of periods" (15).

[88]Cf. Quintilian *Institutio Oratoria* 9.4.125.

[89]Aristotle *Rhetoric* 3.8.3–6; Demetrius *De Elocutione* 16–18; Cicero *Orator* 53.177, 58.197–202; Quintilian *Insitutio* 9.4.79–80.

[90]Aristotle *Rhetoric* 3.9.7–8; Demetrius *De Elocutione* 22–24.

expresses two aspects of a single thought. Aristotle demonstrates this type with an example from the opening of Isocrates' Panegyricus:

πολλάκις ἐθαύμασα τῶν τὰς πανηγύρεις συναγόντων καὶ
τοὺς γυμνικοὺς ἀγῶνας καταστησάντων
I have often wondered at those who gathered together the general assemblies and instituted the gymnastic contests.[91]

The period indicates the speaker's divided thought regarding two particular characteristics of the men who have attracted the speaker's attention. The other type of period is the antithetical. Here, opposites are thrown against each other, as in the example:

ἀμφοτέρους δ ὤνησαν, καὶ τοὺς ὑπομείναντας καὶ τοὺς ἀκολουθήσαντας·
τοῖς μὲν γὰρ πλείω τῆς οἴκοι προσεκτήσαντο,
τοῖς δὲ ἱκανὴν τὴν οἴκοι κατέλιπον
They were useful to both, both those who stayed and those who followed;
for the latter gained in addition greater possessions than they had at home,
but the former left what was sufficient in their own country.[92]

Aristotle goes on to say of antithetical periods that:

> This kind of style is pleasing, because contraries are easily understood and even more so when placed side by side, and also because antithesis resembles a syllogism; for refutation is a bringing together of contraries.[93]

To be sure, periods may be used in syllogisms or enthymemes, but they are not identical. A period—as we will see more fully below—is primarily a type of sentence structure or movement. Enthymemes and syllogisms are defined by content alone and they function as forms of argumentation.[94]

    Periods were classified further as conversational, historical, or rhetorical. According to Demetrius, the historical period represents the middle ground between the conversational and rhetorical periods. It should not be as relaxed as the conversational nor as polished or pointed as the rhetorical. The rhetorical period is the strongest type of arrangement because of its compactness and its clear indication from the very beginning that "it will not stop on a simple

---

[91]Aristotle *Rhetoric* 3.9.7. Demetrius uses the same example from Isocrates as an example of assonance (*De Elocutione* 25): πολλάκις ἐθαύμασα τῶν τὰς πανηγύρεις συναγαγόντων καὶ τοὺς γυμνικοὺς ἀγῶνας καταστησάντων (i.e., -όντων / -άντων).

[92]Aristotle *Rhetoric* 3.9.7. See also Demetrius *De Elocutione* 22–24.

[93]Aristotle *Rhetoric* 3.9.8.

[94]See, for instance, Aristotle *Rhetoric* 2.22.25; Demetrius *De Elocutione* 30–32; Quintilian *Institutio Oratoria* 5.14.4.

ending."[95] In contrast, the conversational period is so loose that it barely appears as a period at all.[96] Each type of period, though, moves from a definite beginning along a sure path to a clear ending.[97]

Another important aspect of periods is rhythmical arrangement. The period is a unit of thought that is ordered in such a way that the thought and form end together. But the period is also often characterized by its rhythm. Indeed, Aristotle writes that "the period should be broken off by a long syllable and the end should be clearly marked, not by the scribe nor by a punctuation mark, but by the rhythm itself."[98] The rhythm may help signal to the mind's ear the logical completion of the thought.[99] The well-formed period has both logical and rhythmical dimensions.[100]

Now the term "period"—as the word itself indicates from its Greek roots of πέρι (around) and ὁδός (road)—indicates a circular path.[101] Discussions of the period, however, indicate that periods have much to do with balancing and opposing thoughts in a single expression. The significance of Aristotle's descriptive term is more evident, though, when we consider examples of

---

[95]Demetrius *De Elocutione* 20.

[96]See, for instance, the opening period of Plato's *Republic* (327a) which Demetrius cites (*De Elocutione* 21) as an example of the conversational period.

[97]Cf. Demetrius *De Elocutione* 19–21, 45–47. See also especially Aristotle *Rhetoric* 3.9.1f; Quintilian *Institutio Oratoria* 9.4.19–22, 9.4.125; Cicero *Orator* 61.204; idem *Brutus* 8.34, 44.162; Dionysius of Halicarnassus *De Compositione Verbum* 2, 9, 15, 17.

[98]Aristotle *Rhetoric* 3.8.6. Aristotle uses the term παραγραφήν which Freese translates as "punctuation mark." In note *a* on p. 386, Freese writes that scribes often set a dash below the first word of a line to mark clearly the end of the sentence.

[99]See especially Cicero *Orator* 53.177–67.226. Cicero writes, "the ear, or rather the mind which receives the message of the ear, contains in itself a natural capacity for measuring all sounds. Accordingly it distinguishes between long and short, and always looks for what is complete and well proportioned" (177–78).

[100]This subject has drawn considerable discussion. The primary point of contention is whether the ancients understood the period primarily as either a rhythmical or logical formation. It seems to this writer that both views were common and often mixed. See especially the helpful artical by R. A. Fowler, "Aristotle on the Period," *Classical Quarterly* 32 (1982): 89–99, who contends that the period is primarily a logical unit. For a contrary view, that prose-rhythm determines a period, see J. Zehetmeier, "Die Periodenlehre des Aristoteles," *Philologus* 83 (1930): 192–208. For a constructive analysis of these views, see Doreen C. Innes, *Demetrius: De Elocutione*, 2d ed., LCL (Cambridge, Mass.: Harvard University Press, 1995), 316–18.

[101]Cicero also used many different Latin terms for the Greek term *periodus: ambitus, circuitus, comprehensio, continuatio, and circumscriptio* (cf. Ciero *Orator* 55.186–187, 61.204; Quintilian *Institutio Oratoria* 9.4.124). Quintilian also used *circumductum* for *period* (cf. *Institutio Oratoria* 9.4.22).

periods. Demetrius illustrates the properly formed period with the following sentence:[102]

μάλιστα μὲν εἵνεκα τοῦ νομίζειν συμφέρειν τῇ πόλει λελύσθαι τὸν νόμον,
εἶτα καὶ τοῦ παιδὸς εἵνεκα τοῦ Χαβρίου, ὡμολόγησα τούτοις,
ὡς ἂν οἷός τε ὦ, συνερεῖν
Chiefly because I thought it was to the interest of the State that the law should be abrogated, but also for the sake of Chabrias' boy, I have agreed to plead, to the best of my ability, my clients' case.

Demetrius praises this model for it "has a certain bend and concentration at the end." In the Greek above, however, the emphasis on the end of the period is more pronounced than it is in English, for it is not until the very end of the sentence in Greek that the communicator's intended action is fully known. Only with the final word does it become clear that the speaker will be an advocate for his client. This period has a definite beginning and moves in a clear and direct way to its final climactic goal. If the word order were altered, the content would remain the same but the period would be destroyed.[103]

The periodic style was also quite prevalent among Latin communicators. Quintilian turns to Cicero for a premier example of the well-formed period. It reads:[104]

Tu istis faucibus, istis lateribus, ista gladiatoria totius corporis firmitate.
You, with that neck, those lungs, that gladiatorial whole body, make it strong!

Here, too, the unmistakable periodic form has a strong beginning, progresses along a certain path, and arrives at its climax. Of Cicero's periodic brilliance, Quintilian writes that "each phrase is followed by one stronger than the last, whereas, if he had begun by referring to his whole body, he could scarcely have gone on to speak of his lungs and throat without an anticlimax."[105] The whole notion of climax for sentences and entire works is at least as old as Homer's *Iliad* and *Odyssey*, yet here we see in Quintilian's instructions for proper

---

[102]Demetrius *De Elocutione* 10. Demetrius includes this example in his discussion of rhetorical periods. See also the comments of Demetrius on the use of periods for making descriptions impressive (45–47), as in the example from the historian Thucydides (2.102): "The river Achelous, which flows from Mount Pindus through Dolopia and the territory of the Agrianians and Amphilochians and passes inland by the city of Stratus before running into the sea at Oeniadae and surrounding the city with marshes, because of its volume of water makes it impossible to start military operations in winter." This type of drawn out period is best suited for historical accounts and panegyric. It is not the same as the continuous style characteristic of the historian Herodotus. Cf. *De Elocutione* 12.

[103]Demetrius *De Elocutione* 11.

[104]Quintilian *Institutio Oratoria* 9.4.23.

[105]Ibid.

periodic construction a sentence movement celebrated for its memorable and persuasive effect.

The period is very close to the chiasm. The principal difference between them is the position of emphasis. The chiasm sets its most important element in the center of the construction (eg. C – B – A – B' – C') whereas a period moves in a linear fashion and ordinarily sets a strong point at the beginning and the strongest point at the end (eg. B – D – C – A). They are both "rounded" in a sense, only the chiasm more so.[106]

The inflected languages of Greek and Latin are well suited for the emphatic positioning of words and, to a lesser extent, so also is Hebrew. Because word relationships in inflected languages are signaled by word endings and do not depend on their relative position with other words for their meaning, words can be arranged in a variety of ways without altering the meaning of the sentence. What may change is the emphasis on particular words according to their position. Of course, euphony and rhythm could also be influenced to achieve the communicator's purposes through the careful arrangement of syllables and words. Similarly, though, words could be positioned on the basis of sound and meter rather than importance to the communicator's meaning, as in some poetry. This flexibility—which seems most pronounced in Greek—does not mean, however, that anything goes in the arrangement of words in these languages. There were limits and customary patterns for ordering words. Nevertheless, the location of words—particularly the first and last positions in a period—can be quite important for understanding the communicator's focus or intent in a message.[107] Thus, ὁ κύριος φιλεῖ τὸν ἄνθρωπον, ὁ κύριος τὸν ἄνθρωπον φιλεῖ, and φιλεῖ τὸν ἄνθρωπον ὁ κύριος may all be translated into the same English sentence, but they may reflect different emphases in the mind of the Greek communicator.

The periodic style was quite popular in the Greco-Roman world because its movements gave listeners and readers something to grasp and hold clearly in their minds. This was especially true of rhetorical periods in which compact expressions were marked by definite beginnings and endings that could make

---

[106]For chiasms, see especially N. W. Lund, *Chiasmus in the NT* and I. H. Thomson, *Chiasmus in the Pauline Letters.*

[107]Cf. F. M. Wheelock, *Latin: An Introductory Course Based on Ancient Authors* (New York: Barnes & Noble Books, 1963), 4 n. 10, 15–16, 260 n. 22; A. T. Robertson, *A Grammar of the Greek New Testament,* 417–23; K. J. Dover, *Greek Word Order* (Cambridge: Cambridge University Press, 1960); M. E. Davison, "NT Greek Word Order," *Literary and Linguistic Computing* 4 (1989): 19–28. Also note that the periodic style's tendency in Latin to place the verb last reflects something of the status of the last position, because full comprehension of the sentence is suspended until the last word (Cf. Quintilian *Institutio Oratoria* 9.4.26). Variety, however, was still a prerequisite for eloquence. Thus Homer and Demosthenes were frequently praised for having "the most voices of all." Cf. Dionysius of Halicarnassus *De Compositione Verbum* 16, 21; Demetrius *De Elocutione* 15.

the communicator's emphases stronger. It was also true, however, of the looser types of historical and conversational periods. Loose or compact, lengthy or brief, the periodic movement clusters around distinct ideas and images of thought. Not surprisingly, this style was highly favored among oral communicators, and writers, too, because it enabled them to signal their purposes, meaning, and transitions more precisely to their audiences. Similarly, the periodic style helped listeners and readers comprehend better the communicator's intent for there were fewer opportunities to lose the main points. As Aristotle observed:

> What is written in this style is pleasant and easy to learn, pleasant because it is the opposite of that which is unlimited, because the hearer at every moment thinks he is securing something for himself and that some conclusion has been reached; whereas it is unpleasant neither to foresee nor to get to the end of anything. It is easier to learn, because it can be easily retained in the memory.[108]

By the first century A.D., the popularity and abuse of periods had become so pervasive that Quintilian lamented, "our rhetoricians want every passage, even every sentence to strike the ear by an impressive close. In fact, they think it a disgrace, nay, almost a crime, to pause to breathe except at the end of a passage that is designed to call forth applause."[109] Periods were useful, but they could be misused and often were. Long speeches composed only of periods became monotonous, and ending every period with a striking reflection made an address seem more like a collection of disjointed—even irrelevant— epigrams. Worse, it obscured and trivialized the discourse making it nearly impossible to discern the communicator's main points.[110] Thus orators emphasized mixing the periodic and continuous styles in any composition and weighing—not counting—arguments, placing the most important ones—as we will see—at the opening and closing of the communication.[111] Also, while periods could be used anywhere in a composition, the periodic style was noted

---

[108]Aristotle *Rhetoric* 3.9.3.

[109]Quintilian *Institutio Oratoria* 8.5.13–14. Demetrius makes the same point in *De Elocutione* 15, 303.

[110]Quintilian *Institutio Oratoria* 8.5.27f. See also Seneca, *Epistulae Morales* 33.1–4, who, for these reasons, discourages Lucilius from compositions of collected maxims and wise comments from distinguished communicators and thinkers for "a single tree is not remarkable if the whole forest rises to the same height . . . We cannot, I maintain, no matter how we try, pick out anything from so great a multitude of things equally good."

[111]Cf. Demetrius *De Elocutione* 15; Quintilian *Institutio Oratoria* 7.Pr.1f, 7.2.57, 8.5.27f; Cicero *De Oratore* 2.76.309; idem *Orator* 15.50; *Rhetorica ad Herennium* 1.9.14; 3.10.18.

for being especially well-suited for use in a communication's exordium and peroration.[112] As Quintilian put it:

> The full periodic style is well adapted to the *exordium* of important cases, where the theme requires the orator to express anxiety, admiration or pity: the same is true of commonplaces and all kinds of amplification. But it should be severe when we are prosecuting and expansive in panegyric. It is also most effective in the *peroration*.[113]

Periods were especially useful for opening and closing entire communications.[114]

Principles for Expression

This brief overview of sentence movements and the broader arena of *elocutio* points to the great care given to matters of composition in the Greco-Roman world. Issues pertaining to the selection of words and their arrangement into sentences received considerable attention. Rhythm, euphony, balance, grammatical correctness, clarity, embellishment, brevity, figures of diction, figures of thought, and many other stylistic matters all were carefully defined, analyzed and described. Close attention was given to the appropriateness of stylistic techniques for particular kinds of speech situations. The success of a communication depended upon it.

We have now observed that educated communicators were equipped with many common resources for expressing themselves persuasively in organized fluency. Their training included effective methods for inventing appropriate communications, the persuasiveness of which depended fundamentally upon the accurate identification of the stasis and the careful development of the most suitable topics. They learned how to arrange their material in a logical and orderly way so that their views could be understood. They became well versed in the intricacies of expressing themselves in ways that were clear, appropriate, and memorable. In speech and in writing, effective communicators sought to impress their messages upon the mind's ear of their hearer.

The more able a communicator was in utilizing the strategies and resources for persuasive eloquence, the more likely he or she would be in achieving his or her purposes. We have seen something of how the virtues of clarity, correctness, and propriety undergirded matters of invention,

---

[112]Cf. Quintilian *Institutio Oratoria* 9.4.22, 124–125,128; ibid. 11.1.49; Aristotle *Rhetoric* 3.9.3; Cicero *Oratore* 61.204; idem *Brutus* 8.34; *Rhetorica ad Herennium* 4.19.27, 4.32.44; Demetrius *De Elocutione* 32.

[113]Quintilian *Institutio Oratoria* 9.4.128.

[114]For examples and a discussion on the Greco-Roman practice of using periods for opening a communication and establishing central themes, see the appendix below.

arrangement and style. But we have also seen that flexibility was prized among Greco-Roman communicators who desired persuasive eloquence that was appropriate and timely.

Still, a problem remains. How were communicators effectively to relate the static rules of the art to the dynamic situations of life that they sought to address? Are there evidences of basic principles that would aid them in relating the two? The matter warrants more attention than is possible here; nevertheless, one overlapping principle is evident from the foregoing overview of common resources for persuasive communication. In discussions of invention, arrangement, and style, the rhetoricians repeatedly strike upon the importance of beginnings and endings for effective communication. Let us then summarize our findings.

IV. COMPOSING FOR PERSUASION

As we have seen, each part of a speech has a particular function to play in moving an argument through a developmental progression for persuasive ends. But the orator still faced critical decisions about the selection and ordering of his material within each part and in the speech as a whole. That is, given the material selected for the address, which should the orator include and exclude and how could the orator best present and develop the material in a persuasive way? The goal, of course, was to weave the parts of the speech into a seamless argument that ran. from beginning to end without betraying a mechanical reliance on recognizable forms and figures. Failure to do so would undoubtedly bore the audience and weaken or destroy the communication's persuasive power.[115]

Obviously, a communicator's wise adaptability played an important role in the matter of arrangement, especially since the communicator was both to use and disguise the proven order so that hearers would give their attention to the content of the message rather than be distracted by the message's wooden adherence to formal characteristics. The difficulties were somewhat simplified, however, by the orator's recognition that certain general principles were largely applicable to any argument's progression and the placement of its most important points. Rhetoricians delineated effective patterns for communicating persuasively and eloquently in the three primary situations of civic discourse,

---

[115]Cf. Cicero who asserts that if a presentation is too obviously structured, "it robs the audience of their natural sympathy, and utterly destroys the impression of sincerity" (*Orator* 62.209). Again, "however agreeable or important thoughts may be, still if they are expressed in words which are ill arranged, they will offend the ear, which is very fastidious in its judgment" (*Orator* 44.150). Moreover, without careful arrangement, a speech "can possess no force or vigour" (*Orator* 68.229).

but the existent rhetorical treatises also reveal a simpler principle at work regarding the arrangement of one's strongest arguments and those that best support them.

So how could a communicator guide listeners or readers so that they reached the desired conclusion regardless of the type and medium of communication? Where should a communicator place those arguments that offer the strongest support? Here, the rhetorical handbooks and treatises point to the common ground of all effective, persuasive Greek and Latin communication that is based on "reason, antiquity, authority and usage." Simply put, effective communication most often progresses in a tight linear fashion with the strongest arguments coming first and last, the strongest point standing at the end. Remarkably uncomplicated in its assertion, this principle of communication nevertheless requires some further explanation.

Linear Development

To begin with, the Greeks and Romans alike emphasized order and linear development in communication.[116] Order, of course, is a chief ingredient of Greco-Roman eloquence and a central component of the communicator's resources. It was widely understood, then as now, that language which is not carefully arranged lacks clarity and is unlikely to be persuasive.[117] Effective communication, on the other hand, moves forward clearly, swiftly and without encumbrance.[118] In order to achieve this end, though—that is, in order to

---

[116]See, for instance, G. A. Kennedy, *Cambridge History of Literary Criticism*, 88–89. See also Quintilian *Institutio Oratoria* 1.8.17, 7.Pr.1f and 9.4.7–10, where he stresses the crucial value of proper arrangement of periods, parts of a speech and the whole speech. Also, as the title of his treatise makes clear (περὶ συνθεσέως ὀνομάτων), Dionysius of Halicarnassus emphasizes the same critical role of arrangement for all effective communication, whether it be through the mediums of poetry, history, or oratory. Regarding the linear, progressive nature of New Testament Greek, S. E. Porter has shown that it is "best described as a linear language, certainly for word order, but also probably for sentence structure." See S. E. Porter, *Idioms of the Greek New Testament*, Biblical Languages: Greek (Sheffield: Sheffield Academic Press, 1992), 292.

[117]For example, Quintilian wrote that "unless a man speaks in an orderly, ornate and fluent manner, I refuse to dignify his utterance with the name of speech, but consider it the meanest rant" (10.7.12). Of writing, Demetrius warned that anything "which is wholly disjointed and unconnected is entirely lacking in clearness" (*De Elocutione* 192). The *Rhetorica ad Herennium* stressed that "we must see that our language is not confused, involved, or unfamiliar, that we do not shift to another subject, that we do not trace the affair back to its remotest beginning, nor carry it too far forward, and that we do not omit anything pertinent" (1.9.15). In the treatise "On Literary Composition," Dionysius of Halicarnassus repeatedly emphasized both the superiority of arrangement over diction (2–3) and the "compositional" common ground of all communication (5–6, 22).

[118]Quintilian writes, "Just as river-currents are more violent when they run along a sloping bed, that presents no obstacles to check their course, than when their waters are

communicate eloquently—the words and thoughts must be selected with utmost care and ordered with precision to secure the best possible connection between what follows and what precedes.[119] Indeed, ideally, the well-composed speech or writing is so ordered that any change—even the order of particular words—will ruin the whole thing.[120] Consequently, great attention was given not only to the proper ordering of subject matter in a linear, progressive fashion throughout the communication but also to the individual units in each part. Quintilian put it like this:

> It is not enough merely to arrange the various parts: each several part has its own internal economy, according to which one thought will come first, another second, another third, while we must struggle not merely to place these thoughts in their proper order, but to link them together and give them such cohesion that there will be no trace of any suture: they must form a body, not a congeries of limbs. This end will be attained if we note what best suits each position, and take care that the words which we place together are such as will not clash, but will mutually harmonise. Thus different facts will not seem like perfect strangers thrust into uncongenial company from distant places, but will be united with what precedes and follows by an intimate bond of union, with the result that our speech will give the impression not merely of having been put together, but of natural continuity.[121]

With these words, Quintilian summarizes and concludes Book 7 of his *Institutio Oratoria* regarding the topic of arrangement and arrives precisely at the destination marked at this book's beginning.[122] In this way he demonstrates

---

broken and baffled by rocks that obstruct the channel, so a style which flows in a continuous stream with all the full development of its force is better than one which is rough and broken" (9.4.7). Dionysius of Halicarnassus praises Isocrates because his words "are manifestly in a state of motion, being borne onwards in a continuous stream, while the joins which hold the passage together are gentle, soft and flowing"(23). So, too, Dionysius salutes Homer because his words "glide into one another and are carried along together, and they all fit together so closely that they form, in a sense, a single continuum" (20).

[119]Cf. Quintilian *Institutio Oratoria* 9.4.22, 10.3.6, 10.7.5.

[120]Cicero *Orator* 70.232; also 44.140. Quintilian writes similarly that "if we break up and disarrange any sentence that may have struck us as vigorous, charming or elegant, we shall find that all its force, attraction and grace have disappeared" (9.4.14) and, again, "The most important task, however, is to know what word is best fitted to any given place" (9.4.60). See also Dionysius of Halicarnassus *De Compositione Verbum* 2–5.

[121]Quintilian *Institutio Oratoria* 7.10.16.

[122]Quintilian opens his focused discussion on arrangement (*Institutio Oratoria* 7.Pr.1–3) in this way: "But just as it is not sufficient for those who are erecting a building merely to collect stone and timber and other building materials, but skilled masons are required to arrange and place them, so in speaking, however abundant the matter may be, it will merely form a confused heap unless arrangement be employed to reduce it to order and to give it connexion and firmness of structure. Nor is it without good reason that arrangement is treated as the second of the five departments of oratory, since without it the first is useless.

once again what he teaches, this time regarding the principles and techniques of arranging persuasive communication. As a whole message and as individual parts, effective discourse should first gain entrance through the portals of the ears with a statement of the subject, move in a tightly ordered progression that cannot be changed without causing confusion, and stand finished at the end as an harmonious whole.[123]

Thematic Overtures and Conclusions

Beginnings and endings were considered quite important in Greco-Roman life, thought, and communication. Plato, for instance, wrote that "the beginning is the most important part in every work."[124] The context of this statement pertains to the education of a child, but he is drawing upon an ancient and well-known proverb regarding beginnings. The importance of beginnings for Plato and his followers was stressed further by a story preserved about his death. Beside his deathbed were found wax tablets upon which he had been testing words and their various arrangements to perfect the opening sentence of the *Republic*.[125] Plato's student Aristotle also stressed strong beginnings[126] and he was quoting a similar proverb affirmatively when he wrote, "Well begun is half done"[127] and "The beginning is admittedly more than half of the whole, and throws light at once on many questions under investigation."[128]

For the fact that all limbs of a statue have been cast does not make it a statue: they must be put together; and if you were to interchange some one portion of our bodies or of those of other animals with another, although the body would be in possession of all the same members as before, you would none the less have produced a monster. Again even a slight dislocation will deprive a limb of its previous use and vigour, and disorder in the ranks will impede the movements of an army. Nor can I regard as an error the assertion that order is essential to the existence of nature itself, for without order everything would go to wrack and ruin. Similarly if oratory lack this virtue, it cannot fail to be confused, but will be like a ship drifting without a helmsman, will lack cohesion, will fall into countless repetitions and omissions, and, like a traveller who has lost his way in unfamiliar country, will be guided solely by chance without fixed purpose or the least idea either of starting-point or goal."

[123]Cf. Aristotle *Rhetoric* 3.19.4–5; Quintilian *Institutio Oratoria* 10.7.5, 9.4.9–10, 9.4.32; Cicero *De Inventione* 1.33; Demetrius *De Elocutione* 50; Dionysius of Halicarnassus *De Compositione Verbum* 2, 9.

[124]Plato *The Republic*, trans. P. Shorey, LCL (Cambridge, Mass.: Harvard University Press, 1963), 2.377B. See also idem, *Laws*, trans. R. G. Bury, LCL (Cambridge, Mass.: Harvard University Press, 1926; reprint 1984), 753E, 765E.

[125]See Dionysius of Halicarnassus *De Compositione Verbum* 25; Demetrius *De Elocutione* 21; and Quintilian *Institutio Oratoria* 8.6.64.

[126]Cf. Aristotle *Rhetoric* 3.14.1–12.

[127]Aristotle *Politics*, trans. H. Rackham, LCL (Cambridge, Mass.: Harvard University Press, 1932; reprint 1990), 5.4. See also Seneca *Epistulae Morales* 34.3 and Horace *Epistles* 2.1.40, who reiterates the proverb in Latin as "He who has begun has half done." Euripides put this point negatively when he wrote, "A bad beginning makes a bad ending" (*Aeolus*,

In life as in speech, the importance of beginnings was axiomatic in the Greco-Roman world, for it was widely understood that where one began—in nearly any undertaking—largely determined where one ended. But if beginnings are significant for clearly marking the direction of the message's race, the race itself was impossible without a course and a goal.[129] Yet, if the communicator, like a runner, had a good start and ran the course well, the ending was certain to stand as the crowning of the work.

Greco-Roman orators took account of this ancient, authoritative principle drawn from experience as they developed rhetorical theory and practice. Demetrius, for instance, expressed the view succinctly when he wrote that "all of us remember in a special degree, and are stirred by, the words that come first and the words that come last, whereas those that come between them have less effect upon us, as though they were obscured or hidden among the others."[130] Cicero agreed that an argument's strongest points should be set at the beginning and ending of a work, with the weaker points in between.[131] The *Rhetorica ad Herennium* recognized the same fundamental precept and so instructs orators to arrange their topics so that the strongest arguments are placed at the beginning and at the end while supporting arguments of medium or weak force are positioned in the middle. The very strongest argument, though, should be made at the end because "what has been said last is easily committed to memory [and], it is useful, when ceasing to speak, to leave some very strong argument fresh in the hearer's mind."[132] Now on this point, Quintilian takes issue with Celsus because, in Quintilian's view, there are occasions when one is making a defense that the strongest argument should be disposed of first. For instance, when facing hearers who are predisposed to disregard the message and the speaker, the strongest point must come first or the speaker will risk losing a hearing and may forfeit his point altogether. Nevertheless, Quintilian recognized the customary practice and usual advantage of setting the strongest point at the closing.[133]

---

fragment 32, In *Euripides*, trans. A. S. Way, LCL [Cambridge, Mass.: Harvard University Press, 1912–1994]).

[128]Aristotle *Nichomachean Ethics*, trans. H. Rackham, LCL (Cambridge, Mass.: Harvard University Press, 1926–1990), 1.7.23. On this proverb, see especially H. Rackham's note "a" on p. 36.

[129]Cf. Quintilian *Institutio Oratoria* 10.7.5.

[130]Demetrius *De Elocutione* 40.

[131]Cicero *Orator* 50; idem *De Oratore* 77.311. See also Quintilian *Institutio Oratoria* 7.1.10.

[132]*Rhetorica ad Herennium* 3.10.18.

[133]Quintilian *Institutio Oratoria* 7.1.10–17. Celsus argued from the authority of Cicero that in every case "the first place should be given to some strong argument, but that the strongest should be reserved to the end." Quintilian basically agrees with Celsus but

Simply put, unless circumstances called for an intentional rearrangement of the proven practice, a speech's strongest points should come at the beginning and end, but, as Cicero contended, "all the words both at the beginning and in the middle should look to the end."[134] It is this arrangement of topics that, "like the arraying of soldiers in battle, can readily bring victory."[135]

What applied to arguments as a whole, regardless of their type, was also relevant to the arrangement of elements within the speech. Thus regarding the proofs within an argument, here, too, "the strongest should be placed first and last."[136] Even down to the smallest complete compositional unit called a *period*, the beginnings and endings were deemed "most important," although, once again, the greatest care should be given to the conclusion.[137] This does not mean, however, that the middle portions of periods, proofs, or speeches were unimportant. The middle should support the beginning and the end. Thus Quintilian reminds his students that "the feet of a runner, even though they do not linger where they fall, still leave a footprint"[138] and no athlete can run well without a definite beginning aimed toward a certain goal with a clear course between them.[139]

From individual periods to entire speeches, Greco-Roman communicators often placed a strong accent on the beginnings and endings of their communications. There were exceptions, of course, but those who recognized the persuasive influence of beginning and ending well gave the matter considerable attention in designing their exordiums and perorations. Let us now examine the opening of Galatians.

---

resists this ironclad position and makes his point also from the authority of Cicero (*pro Vareno*). See also Cicero *De Oratore* 2.77.311–314.

[134]Cicero *Orator* 59.200.

[135]*Rhetorica ad Herennium* 3.10.18.

[136]Quintilian *Institutio Oratoria* 6.4.22.

[137]Quintilian *Institutio Oratoria* 9.4.61–67. Here Quintilian writes: "Next to the conclusion of the period, it is the beginning which claims the most care: for the audience have their attention fixed on this as well. But the opening of the sentence presents less difficulty, since it is independent and is not the slave of what has preceded. It merely takes what has preceded as a starting point, whereas the conclusion coheres with what has preceded, and however carefully constructed, its elegance will be wasted, if the path which leads up to it be interrupted" (9.4.62–63). See also 9.4.29. In 9.4.23 he writes that "sentences should rise and grow in force." See also Demetrius, *De Elocutione* 11, where he writes, "The very use of the word 'period' implies that there has been a beginning at one point and will be an ending at another, and that we are hastening towards a definite goal as runners do when they leave the starting place. For at the very beginning of their race the end of the course is manifest." Also Demetrius *De Elocutione* 10, 20, 139.

[138]Quintilian *Institutio Oratoria* 9.4.67.

[139]Quintilian *Institutio Oratoria* 10.7.5.

CHAPTER FOUR

A REMARKABLE BEGINNING:
GALATIANS 1:1–10

In few places is Paul's wise adaptability more apparent than in the remarkable beginning of Galatians. Rather than push past the so-called prescript on the way to weightier matters, then, we will now investigate more thoroughly the opening of this letter-speech. Its significance for interpreting the whole communication will become evident. Here Paul sets forth the central points of his argument that he develops in the remainder of the letter.

In this chapter we will first look closely at Galatians 1:1–5 in order to delineate its epistolary characteristics and its variations from customary salutations. We will then examine how letter and speech are fused together in Galatians 1:1–10 as an opening salutation-exordium. Finally, we will propose how 1:1–10 functions as an overture for what follows in Paul's letter-speech to the Galatians. Succeeding chapters will then show how these themes are developed and brought to their memorable climax at the end of this communication.

I. AN UNUSUAL SALUTATION: GALATIANS 1:1–5

We observed in chapter one that the first five verses of Galatians are widely treated as an epistolary prescript. On this basis, some scholars have excluded 1:1–5 entirely from their analyses of this letter.[1] Most interpreters of Paul's letter-speech to the Galatians agree, however, that while the form of 1:1–5 is largely that of epistolary prescript it is not unrelated to the remainder of the letter. Paul has made some curious expansions here. But are they intentional?

---

[1]Cf. F. Vouga, "Zur rhetorischen Gattung des Galaterbriefs," 291–92; J. Smit, "The Letter of Paul to the Galatians," 1–26. See also D. Hellholm, "Amplificatio in the Macro-Structure of Romans," in *Rhetoric and the New Testament: Essays from the 1992 Heidelberg Conference*, eds. S. E. Porter and T. Olbricht, JSNTSup 90 (Sheffield: Sheffield Academic Press, 1993), 125–27, 137, who excludes the prescript of Romans.

Do they serve a particular purpose? Let us review some salient points on the nature of these verses to see how they follow and depart from customary epistolary salutations.

Galatians 1:1–5 as Epistolary Prescript

Greco-Roman letters began with a conventional formula that identified the sender(s) and the recipient(s) and issued a brief salutation.[2] The standard Hellenistic opening was simply "A to B, Greetings!" (cf. Acts 15:23; 23:26; James 1:1) but at times the order of sender and recipient were reversed and read "To B from A." The customary Greek greeting was χαίρειν, which means "rejoice" but was used popularly to express "greetings." The normal Latin salutation was *salus*, and Aramaic letters used a variety of שלמ and ברך formulas to express greetings. Epistolary greetings are prominent in existent letters, but they were not always necessary. The names of the sender(s) and recipient(s), however, were essential elements of the salutation, and sometimes they were written also on the outside of the letter, as one would address an envelope today.[3] In any event, Greco-Roman letter openings or epistolary prescripts were essentially the same and were used throughout the Greco-Roman world in Paul's day.

One of the chief characteristics of the conventional prescript was brevity. Paul, however, nearly always elaborates each part of the customary salutation. He follows the standard form for epistolary openings, but all of his letters show that he is no slave to convention.[4] This is all the more remarkable because Greek and Latin letters from the 4th century B.C. through the 4th century A.D. are so stereotypically bound to these epistolary conventions. Only in the salutation of 1 Thessalonians does Paul follow the conventional letter opening in both form and typical length. Everywhere else he makes elaborations, some of which are quite long, as in the cases of Romans and Galatians.

The prescript of Galatians is similar to Paul's other letter openings in that Paul uses the epistolary salutation form to identify the letter's senders and

---

[2] See F. Schnider and W. Stenger, *Studien zum Neutestamentlichen Briefformular*, 3–41. On Galatians, see especially 8–10, 15–17, 31. See also Doty, *Letters in Primitive Christianity*, 29–30; J. L. White, *Light from Ancient Letters*, 198–202; idem, "The Greek Documentary Letter Tradition Third Century B.C.E. to Third Century C.E.," *Semeia* 22 (1981): 89–106; Joseph A. Fitzmyer, "Some Notes on Aramaic Epistolography," *JBL* 93 (1974): 214–16.

[3] Cf. F. X. J. Exler, *The Form of the Ancient Greek Letter*, 23; J. L. White, *Light from Ancient Letters*, 198.

[4] See Doty, *Letters in Primitive Christianity*, 12–13. As for Paul's own letters, Galatians 1:1–5 is the second most expansive, behind only Rom 1:1–7. 1 Thess 1:1 is Paul's briefest salutation.

recipients and to express his own customary greetings of grace (χάρις) and peace (εἰρήνη). In Galatians, Paul and all the brothers who are with him stand together as the originators of this letter, and they express an opening wish that God's grace and peace be upon the letter's recipients—the churches of Galatia. By these epistolary characteristics, the prescript of Galatians follows the conventional epistolary salutation and resembles all the prescripts of Paul's letters. There are, however, some unique—even startling—differences that separate the opening of Galatians from Paul's other correspondences.

To begin with, Paul's self-identification in 1:1 alerts both hearers and readers that this communication is unlike Paul's ordinary good-natured epistles. The opening's immediate antithetical language is strong and direct. As in some of his other letters, Paul asserts his apostleship[5] but here he affirms his apostolic identity and authority with a sharp denial. He is "an apostle—not from men nor through a man." Rather, he is an apostle "through Jesus Christ and God the Father who raised him from the dead." This unconventional epistolary opening suggests that Paul's apostolic authority was seriously challenged in Galatia—perhaps even rejected by some—and Paul is concerned about it (cf. 1:6–7; 2:4; 4:21f; 5:11–12). Not surprisingly, then, Paul stresses his apostleship and the source of his apostolic authority in the first breath of the letter's utterance. Indeed, Paul has more to say about his apostleship in the first two chapters of Galatians than anywhere else in his letters.[6]

There is more to observe here, however. Attached to this negative assertion regarding the origin of his apostleship, Paul issues a strong adversative ἀλλά and immediately adds a positive affirmation that the origin of his apostleship is διὰ Ἰησοῦ Χριστοῦ καὶ θεοῦ πατρός.[7] That is, Paul identifies Jesus Christ and God the Father as both the agents and the source of his apostleship.[8] Moreover, by this assertion, Paul suggests that he and his

---

[5]Cf. Rom 1:1; 1 Cor 1:1; 2 Cor 1:1. In Rom 1:1, Paul stresses first his identity as δοῦλος Χριστοῦ Ἰησοῦ and then qualifies this as κλητὸς ἀπόστολος ἀφωρισμένος εἰς εὐαγγέλιον θεοῦ. In 1 Cor 1:1, Paul describes himself as κλητὸς ἀπόστολος Χριστοῦ Ἰησοῦ διὰ θελήματος θεοῦ. 2 Cor 1:1 is the same as 1 Cor 1:1 except for the absence of κλητός. See also Eph 1:1; Col 1:1; 1 Tim 1:1; 2 Tim 1:1; Titus 1:1.

[6]For a succinct and helpful discussion of the term "apostle," see especially Longenecker, *Galatians*, 2–4. See also Betz's excursus in *Galatians*, 74–75, and K. H. Rengstorf, "ἀπόστολος," in *TDNT*, vol. 1, 398–447.

[7]Only in Galatians and possibly Romans does Paul use the order "Jesus Christ" in his self-identification in the letter prescript. Everywhere else it is "Christ Jesus." On the textual problem of Rom 1:1, which seems best resolved as "Christ Jesus," see especially Ernst Käsemann, *Commentary on Romans*, trans. G. W. Bromiley (Grand Rapids: Wm. B. Eerdmans Publishing Co., 1980), 5.

[8]Passages such as this made the church's later theological wrestling inevitable. Regarding the genitives' roles, see also Burton, *Galatians*, 3–4; Bruce, *Galatians*, 72–73; and Longenecker, *Galatians*, 4.

opponents agree that the title of apostle belongs to those directly commissioned by Christ. At issue, however, is whether or not Paul's commission to apostleship by the risen Christ is considered legitimate,[9] a problem that is rooted fundamentally in views of the earthly and risen Christ.

The form of the opening verse has attracted attention. Some scholars classify the structure of Gal 1:1 as a chiasm.[10] As such, the phrase οὐκ ἀπ ἀνθρώπων corresponds to (ἀπὸ) θεοῦ πατρός and the phrase οὐδε δι ἀνθρώπου is the counterpart to διὰ Ἰησοῦ Χριστοῦ. According to proponents of this view, Paul intended but omitted the appropriate preposition ἀπό before θεοῦ πατρος. The chiastic structure of this verse is also maintained by separating from θεοῦ πατρος the final clause τοῦ ἐγείραντος αὐτον ἐκ νεκρον. Certainly, ellipsis accounts for the omitted preposition ἀπο, which is the appropriate preposition here. But, as we will see below, there is another way to account for the syntax of this opening declaration, particularly the balancing of antithetical clauses and the amplification of the final clause, which are chief characteristics of periods.

Remarkably, Paul makes specific mention of Christ's resurrection in the salutations only of Galatians and Romans. In Romans 1:4, Paul stresses that he and the Roman Christians are servants of the same risen Lord.[11] In Galatians 1:1, however, the stated emphasis on the resurrection of Jesus comes in the opening breath and is tied directly to Paul's apostolic status. Moreover, Paul's apostolic identity and Jesus' resurrection are linked to the person and work of God the Father. Theologically, it is important to note that Paul views God the Father not only as the Creator God but also—if not especially here—as the God of redemption who has power over death. God the Father has already raised

---

[9]It is noteworthy that, while Luke preserves an early view among Jesus' followers that an "apostle" is a disciple appointed by Jesus (Luke 6:13) or is one chosen by such apostles from among other followers who served with Jesus prior to his crucifixion and resurrection (Acts 1:21–22), the three accounts of Paul's conversion in Acts (9:1–22; 22:6–16; 26:12–23) stress emphatically that Paul's call to faith and ministry were not the results of human choice, reasoning, will, or persuasion. Rather Paul's call was an act of the Lord who personally made his presence and identity known to Paul. See also 1 Cor 9:1–2.

[10]Cf. Bligh, *Galatians in Greek*, 61–62; Betz, *Galatians*, 39; Longenecker, *Galatians*, 5; Gerhard Ebeling, *The Truth of the Gospel: An Exposition of Galatians*, trans. David Green (Philadelphia: Fortress Press, 1985), 13, 266.

[11]In the opening of Romans, Paul encapsulates the "gospel of God" (εὐαγγέλιον θεοῦ) by emphasizing the identity (1:2–4), work (1:5a), and purpose (1:5b–6) of God's Son, Jesus Christ. For the Christians in Rome, Paul makes it clear from the start that Jesus is foretold in Scripture and is the seed of David who has been declared Son of God in power according to the Spirit of holiness by means of resurrection from the dead (ἐξ ἀναστάσεως νεκρῶν). Paul's stately language builds to this point of emphasis regarding the good news of God concerning the risen Jesus Christ their Lord (1:1–4).

Jesus Christ from the dead. In this opening clause, then, Paul establishes an apocalyptic framework for his apostleship and everything else that follows.

The epistolary prescript also identifies Paul's fellow senders as οἱ σὺν ἐμοὶ πάντες ἀδελφοι or all the brothers who are with him (1:2). Ordinarily, Paul identifies particular co-senders by name, for example Timothy (2 Cor 1:1; Phil 1:1; 1 Thess 1:1; Phlm 1), Silvanus (1 Thess 1:1), and Sosthenes (1 Cor 1:1). Only in the prescript of Romans does Paul name himself alone as the sender of the letter, although the letter closing (16:21–23) names others who send greetings and to some extent may stand behind the letter with Paul as co-senders.[12] Here in Galatians, the identification of the sender first suggests that the letter's subject matter was a topic of discussion between Paul and all the brothers who were with him, and thus the letter was not hastily composed. Second, only in Galatians does Paul emphasize co-senders without naming particular individuals. He stresses instead that *all* the brothers who are with him agree on the dimensions of the gospel described in the letter—a not too subtle reminder to the Galatians that Paul is not alone in his understanding and expression of the gospel in the letter. The assertion also emphasizes that he and "all" the brothers are *united* in their view, which is not the case for the Galatian Christians.[13] Moreover, by not naming any particular co-senders, Paul calls attention to his familial type of relationship with all the "brothers"—a well-known Jewish form of address which conveys close family-like ties of equality between him and the fellow missionaries who are with him.[14]

Once Paul identifies himself with this startling expansion and includes his colleagues as fellow senders of the letter, he continues to follow the Greco-Roman epistolary form by designating the letter's recipients. The conventional practice was to identify the recipients briefly. Again, though, Paul takes considerable liberty in modifying the customary form to suit his intentions for the letter. Here, too, a comparison of Paul's letters is revealing for his adaptations convey something more of his relationship with the letters' recipients.

---

[12]Rom 16:21–23. Also see E. Käsemann, *Romans*, 419–21.

[13]Cf. Gal 1:7; 3:1; 4:17; 5:7–12; and 6:12–13. On the agitators in Galatia, see especially R. Jewett, "The Agitators," 198–212; J. L. Martyn, "A Law–Observant Mission," 307–324; W. B. Russell, "Who Were Paul's Opponents in Galatians?," *BSac* 147 (1990): 329–50.

[14]See especially Fitzmyer, "Aramaic Epistolography," 213. "Brother" was a familial address in Aramaic epistolographical prescripts which fathers used regarding their relations to their sons. Similarly, within Judaism men and women of equal standing often addressed one another as "brother" and "sister." On Paul and his co-workers, see E. Earle Ellis, "Paul and His Co-Workers," *NTS* 17 (1971): 437–52; Betz, *Galatians*, 40.

Paul's most frequent term for designating the recipients of his letters is
ἐκκλησία,[15] a term which many Gentiles would have understood as a political
assembly.[16] Among the Jews, though, the term was used widely for
congregational meetings for religious purposes[17] and Christians applied it
similarly.[18] Paul elaborates this term in different ways in his letter openings and
so highlights certain aspects of his message and the churches he addressed. For
instance, in the Corinthian letters, the Christians there are called "the church of
God which is at Corinth" who are both "sanctified in Christ Jesus" and fellow
"saints" with "those who in every place call on the name of our Lord Jesus
Christ." This expansion of ἐκκλησία is an affirmation of the Corinthian
Christians—despite Paul's evident problems with them—and emphasizes the
theme of unity which figures prominently in the message that follows.[19]

In the Galatians prescript, however, Paul identifies his recipients simply
as the "churches" (ταῖς ἐκκλησίαις τῆς Γαλατίας)—his only use of the
plural form of the term in his prescripts. It is not clear how the Galatian
churches were organized, but the letter's recipients were clearly members of
various churches in Galatia. They may have seen themselves as independent
assemblies. Paul addresses the letter to all of them, and it would have circulated
among them. Paul's address, however, makes no elaboration of the recipients
whatsoever. It is possible that the pluralism of the churches and competing
expressions of the Christian faith there made a common description impossible.

Still, Paul's displeasure with the state of the churches in Galatia is
apparent. He indicates neither their relation with God nor any favorable
attributes regarding their common faithfulness. This does not necessarily mean,
though, that Paul denies any religious value to the "assemblies" in Galatia.[20]
First, Paul uses ταῖς ἐκκλησίαις τῆς Γαλατίας also in 1 Cor 16:1 and clearly

---

[15]Cf. 1 Cor 1:2; 2 Cor 1:1; Gal 1:2; 1 Thess 1:1; Phlm 1:2.

[16]For political assembly, see Josephus, *Antiquities of the Jews*, trans. W. Whiston, in
The Works of Josephus (Peabody, Mass.: Hendrickson Publishers, 1987), 12, 164; 19, 332;
Acts 19:39; C. G. Brandis, "Ἐκκλησία," *PW*, vol. 2, '05, 2163–2200. For its use to designate
a communal gathering, see 1 Sam 19:20; Acts 19:32, 40; 1 Macc 3:13; Sir 26:5.

[17]Cf. Deut 4:10, 9:10; 18:16; 31:30; Judg 20:2; 1 Sam 17:47; 1 Kgs 8:14; Acts 7:38;
Heb 2:12; Josephus, *Antiquities* 4,309; Diodorus Siculus 40, 3, 6.

[18]Cf. Matt 18:17; Acts 5:11; Rom 16:1f; 1 Cor 11:18; 14:4f; Phil 4:15.

[19]There is some ambiguity in relating the final clause αὐτῶν καὶ ἡμῶν to either
τόπῳ or τοῦ κυρίου. Regardless of how one resolves the relationship, though, the emphasis
upon unity is clear, and unity is central to the entire message of 1 Corinthians. See M.
Mitchell, *Paul and the Rhetoric of Reconciliation*, 194, n. 43, and the discussion there.

[20]Cf. F. Matera, *Galatians*, 42, who writes "Because they have begun to desert the
one who called them (1:6), Paul makes no mention of their Christian dignity." Also J.
Murphy-O'Conner, *Paul the Letter Writer*, 51, who writes that Paul "is so disappointed in
the Christians there (Gal 1:6) that he is not prepared to qualify ἐκκλησία in such a way as to
give it a religious value."

refers to the Christian community there. Second, Paul everywhere else uses ἐκκλησία with a religious value.[21] Third, Paul refers to other churches with similar brevity and absence of qualification.[22] Fourth, Paul's use of first person plural pronouns in Gal 1:3–4 indicates a common ground of faith between Paul and the Galatians. Finally, he speaks affectionately of them elsewhere in the letter and even concludes the letter by calling them "brothers."[23] There can be no doubt, though, that among Paul's letter openings, the designation of the letter's recipients in Galatia is startling because of its reticence and its stark contrast with Paul's expansive self-identification preceding it. Paul has chosen to minimize his characterization of the churches there, possibly because of his displeasure with them but also possibly because their diversity made any single characterization of all the churches impossible or unfavorable for his case.

In nearly every letter beginning, Paul greets his recipients with the expression "Grace to you and peace from God our Father and the Lord Jesus Christ" (χάρις ὑμῖν καὶ εἰρήνη ἀπὸ θεοῦ πατρὸς ἡμῶν καὶ κυρίου Ἰησοῦ Χριστοῦ). The only variation in this salutation among Paul's undisputed letters is found in 1 Thess 1:1 where Paul simply writes χάρις ὑμῖν καὶ εἰρήνη ("grace to you and peace") as though their source is understood. Paul evidently needed no further introduction with the Christians in Thessalonica. That Paul extends his longer typical greeting to the churches of Galatia—as he does to all the other churches he addresses—suggests again that Paul views the letter's recipients largely as fellow Christians.

Paul's adaptability in the unique fusion of the Hellenistic and Jewish epistolary greetings of χαίρειν and שָׁלוֹם is well noted.[24] Here it is important to observe simply that Paul gives the greeting a strong theological orientation through the addition of the phrase ἀπὸ θεοῦ πατρὸς ἡμῶν καὶ κυρίου Ἰησοῦ Χριστοῦ. Hearers with a Jewish background would have understood that grace is a gift from God.[25] Gentile hearers, though, would have benefited from the

---

[21]It occurs 44 times in his undisputed letters, though 1 Cor 11:18 implies that the Christians there may assemble as a non-church body, probably in line with the Greco-Roman concept of the term.

[22]Cf. Rom 16:1–4; 1 Cor 7:17; 11:18; 14:4, 5, 19; 16:19; 2 Cor 8:1; 11:28; 12:13.

[23]Paul calls the Galatian Christians "brothers" and expresses compassion toward them in 1:11; 3:15; 4:12, 28, 31; 5:11, 13; 6:1, 18. Indeed, the concluding word of the letter before the final "amen" is "brothers."

[24]Cf. R. N. Longenecker, *Galatians*, 6; G. Ebeling, *The Truth of the Gospel*, 26–30. On conventional Aramaic greetings, see Joseph A. Fitzmyer, "Aramaic Epistolography," 214–17.

[25]Cf. Gen 6:8; 32:5; 39:4, 21; Exod 3:21; 33:12; Ps 84:11(83:12); Prov 3:34. See also Philo ("Legum Allegoriae I", 14.47 in *The Works of Philo*, trans. C. D. Yonge [Peabody, Mass.: Hendrickson Publishers, 1993], 30), who understands that grace is something to be admired and sought but that virtue is God's alone to give. See H. Conzelmann, "χάρις," *TDNT*, vol. 9, 387–415; and W. Zimmerli, ibid., 376–87.

expansion Paul gives. Either way, Paul's greeting identifies both the source and
the agents of grace and peace and so stresses the origin and outcome of the
gospel. Moreover, it affirms the lordship of Jesus over them all.

At this point of the prescript (v. 3), Paul has fully satisfied the
requirements of the conventional epistolary salutation and added the noted
expansions. He has identified himself, his recipients, and issued a greeting. In
every other one of his letters, Paul moves immediately from this point into his
customary opening εὐχαριστῶ or thanksgiving period.[26] Rather than
inaugurate his usual thanksgiving period in Galatians, though, Paul adds a
remarkable amplification regarding the work of Jesus Christ (vv. 4–5) and thus
decidedly shifts the customary salutation's focus *away* from both sender and
recipient.

In verse 4, Paul stresses the identity of Jesus Christ and adds that Jesus
gave himself for "our sins." In this, Paul emphasizes Christ's redemptive work
through self-sacrifice.[27] Christ died for our sins. Christ was, in part, our
representative who took upon himself the responsibility and consequence of our
rebelliousness against God.[28] Moreover, Christ gave himself in order that he
might rescue us. This is the purpose of Christ's self-sacrifice. Jesus' self-
offering was for "our behalf" and effects a rescue from the present evil age.

Again, the language and imagery is undoubtedly eschatological and is
rooted in Judaism. With it Paul highlights the current circumstances in which
the present age is tormented by evil but deliverance from it is possible because
of Christ. The implication is that the coming age will be free from sin's power
to corrupt and destroy. This verse, then, divides history into two ages and
announces the eschatological realization of God's deliverance of his people in
accordance with God's will.[29] Together with the affirmation of Jesus Christ's
resurrection from the dead in v. 1—another strong eschatological assertion,
these two verses encapsulate core elements of the gospel that Paul will develop
in the remainder of the letter. They stress both Jesus' identity as the Christ risen
from the dead by God the Father and Jesus' salvific work of rescuing the
faithful from the present evil age.

---

[26]See Rom 1:7f; 1 Cor 1:3f; 2 Cor 1:2f; Phil 1:2f; 1 Thess 1:1f; Phlm 1:3f.

[27]Compare Rom 4:25 and 8:32 where Jesus is "given."

[28]See also 1 Cor 15:3. Cousar (*Galatians*, 17–18) notes perceptively that the language
of the prescript here expresses an atonement theology of expiation (cf. 2:21). Paul's
overwhelming view of Christ's death in Galatians, however, is a matter of self-participation
in Christ's saving death through which alone the new life comes (cf. 2:19–20; 3:23–26; 4:1–
9; 5:1; 6:14). It is also significant to observe in this verse that the existing mss. do not
support overwhelmingly either ὑπερ or περί for the best reading. Longenecker (*Galatians*,
8) is correct, however, that ὑπερ is preferred because of its use in 1 Cor 15:3 and similar role
in Gal 3:13.

[29]Cf. Dan 12:1–3.

Another important aspect of this verse's amplification is the phrase "according to the will of God" (κατὰ τὸ θέλημα θεοῦ). Paul makes this point elsewhere in his prescripts but not always with the same language.[30] In every other case, Paul connects the phrase with his apostleship. In the Galatians prescript alone does it refer specifically to Christ's rescuing work. Here, Paul asserts from the beginning that Christ's self-sacrificial death was not a matter of martyrdom nor did it occur against God's will, as though it were accomplished by the evil powers of this present evil age. Rather, Christ's death and resurrection and its saving effect happened according to God's plan.

This affirmation is then followed by the climactic doxological refrain of verse 5, which is the only doxology in any prescript attributed to Paul.[31] The language here is liturgical and is also rooted in Judaism.[32] The word "glory" (ἡ δόξα; כָּבוֹד) has rich meaning throughout Judaism in reference to God's glory and the praise that is due to God. That this worship of God is to endure forever (εἰς τοὺς αἰῶνας τῶν αἰώνων) is fundamental to Judaism and the early church.[33] The climactic expression ἀμήν is also common and seals the worshipper's assent and praise.[34] In short, praise is the natural consequence for those who see in Jesus the Christ of God who died an expiatory death, was raised again to life, and accomplished the deliverance of God's people. This doxological climax to this lengthy addition to the prescript fastens the attention of both sender and recipient upon their God and Father to whom their praises are to be given because of God's rescuing work effected for them through Christ Jesus their Lord.

Clearly, Paul uses the conventional epistolary form of address in 1:1a, 2–3a. His remarkable expansions in 1:1b, 3b–5 show, however, that he is not constrained by epistolary custom. Still, some questions remain. Are there any other explanations for the forms of expression in these verses? Why would Paul elaborate on these particular points in the letter's salutation? Are his expansions accidental or purposeful? If they are intentional and Paul is adapting the

---

[30]This particular phrase occurs also in 1 Cor 1:1 and 2 Cor 1:1. See also Eph 1:1; Col 1:1; and 2 Tim 1:1. In Rom 1:1–6, Paul does not use this phrase but nevertheless emphasizes the role and purpose of God's will for himself and the Christians in Rome.

[31]Other doxologies in Paul's letters are found in Rom 11:36 and Phil 4:20. See also Eph 3:20–21 and 1 Tim 1:17. Some account of God's saving work precedes each of these cases. All of them end with "amen." See Matera, *Galatians*, 42. The only other letter-opening with a doxology occurs in Rev 1:6.

[32]See Betz, *Galatians*, 43.

[33]See Ps 22:23; 29:2; 50:15; 86:8–12; 96:1–9; 113:1–3; 115:1; Isa 24:15–16; 25:3; 60:7, 13; 66:19; Jer 13:16; Mal 2:2. On the term "glory," see especially Gerhard von Rad and Gerhard Kittel, *TDNT* 2, 238–55.

[34]On the term "amen," see Heinrich Schlier, *TDNT* 1, 335–38.

epistolary salutation form in a unique way for his own purposes, what significance do they have for understanding the letter? Let us turn now to some other formal characteristics evident in these opening verses.

Galatians 1:1–5 as Epistolary Prescript and Early Church Confession

In addition to the prescript's characteristics as an epistolary salutation, some scholars have found evidence that Paul also incorporates into this letter-opening some confessional statements of the early church, particularly in the expansions of vv. 4–5.[35] There are several reasons for this. To begin with, the declaration in v. 4 that Christ died ὑπὲρ τῶν ἁμαρτιῶν ἡμῶν ("on behalf of our sins") is also made in 1 Cor 15:3 where the phrase is clearly part of an earlier confessional formula. In these two places alone does Paul use the plural ἁμαρτιῶν ("sins").

There are also several words and phrases in the prescript that occur nowhere else in Paul. The verb ἐξέληται ("he might rescue") is a hapax legomenon in Paul's letters. Paul most often uses forms of σώζω, ἐλευθερόω, ῥύομαι, and (ἐξ)αγοράζω to express Christ's salvific work, never ἐξαιρεῖσθαι.[36] This verb ἐξαιρέω, though, occurs elsewhere in the NT in Acts 7:10, 34; 12:11; and 26:17. In each of these instances, ἐξαιρέω is used in reference to God's saving acts.[37] The verb is also used in Acts 23:27 in the letter of Claudius Lysias to Felix regarding the Romans' rescue of Paul from the Jews. In the LXX, the verb ἐξαιρέω occurs far more frequently and is most often a translation of נצל ("deliver").[38] It is used occasionally in reference to persons delivering other persons from death,[39] and in one instance it refers to

---

[35]Cf. François Bovon, "Une Formule Prépaulinienne dans L'Épître aux Galates," in *Paganisme, Judaïsme, Christianisme: Influences et affrontements dans le monde antique. Mélanges offerts à Marcel Simon* (Paris: Éditions E. De Boccard, 1978), 91–107; R. N. Longenecker, *Galatians*, 7–10; Martyn, *Galatians*, 84–92; Ebeling, *Truth of the Gospel*, 38.

[36]Bovon, "Une Formule Prépaulinienne," 92.

[37]It is interesting—given Acts' tendency to emphasize Paul over Peter—that, in Acts, God is the subject of the verb in the speeches of Stephen (7:10, 34) and of Paul before Agrippa (26:17). It is an angel of the Lord, however, who is the subject of the verb in Luke's account of Peter's deliverance from prison (12:11).

[38]Cf. Gen 32:11(12); Exod 3:8; 18:4; 18:8–10; Deut 23:14(15); 32:39; Josh 24:10; 1 Sam (LXX = 1 Kings) 7:3; 10:18; 12:10–11, 21; 17:37; 26:24; etc. Further evidence of the rich use of this word in the LXX is indicated by the fact that the translators of the LXX also used this verb to express בחר ("choose," cf. Job 36:21; Isa 48:10), גאל ("redeem," cf. Isa 60:16; Jer 38(31):11), חלץ ("rescue," cf. Lev 14:40, 43; 2 Kgs 22:20; Pss 49[50]:15; 90[91]:15; 114[116]:8; 118[119]:153; 139[140]:1); מלט ("save," cf. 2 Kgs 19:5[6], 9[10]; 3 Kgs 1:12; Eccl 7:27; Ezek 33:5); נצר ("guard," cf. Pss 70[71]:2; 81[82]:4; 139[140]:4; Nah 2:1[2]); פלט ("bring into security," cf. 2 Kgs 22:2; Pss 30[31]:1; 36[37]:40); and שיזב ("deliver," cf. Dan 3:15, 17, [43], [88]; 6:14[15], 15[16], 16[17]).

[39]Cf. Gen 37:21; Num 35:25; Josh 2:13; 9:26; Judg 9:17; 1 Sam (1 Kgs) 14:48; 30:8, 18.

the defense and rescue of the land of Israel.[40] As in Acts, though, it is prominent in passages regarding God's power to save, God's acts of deliverance, and God's promises to rescue the faithful.[41] Its use in conjunction with the Exodus theme is especially common,[42] and it appears in important texts where obedience to God's will is presented as the basis for God's rescue, both in the present and in the day of the Lord's judgment to come.[43] Such uses of the verb in the LXX correlate well with the Jewish Christian legalistic tendencies that draw considerable attention from Paul in Galatians.

Another hapax legomenon for Paul in this text—indeed, for the whole NT—is the expression ὁ αἰὼν ὁ ἐνεστώς ("the present age"). It appears to be an appropriate paraphrase of ὁ αἰὼν οὗτος ("this age") found in the LXX and elsewhere in Paul.[44] A further rarity in this text is Paul's use of πονηρός ("evil").[45] Moreover, nowhere else does Paul use the expression κατὰ τὸ θέλημα ("according to the will").[46] The use of θέλημα in the NT is overwhelmingly in reference to God's will—for Paul and for others.[47] Everywhere else, though, Paul uses the preposition ἐν[48] or διά.[49] In the LXX,

---

[40]In 2 Sam (2 Kgs) 23:12, one of David's men, Shammah, defends and saves a field from the Philistines.

[41]Cf. Exod 3:8; 18:4–10; Deut 23:14; 32:39; 1 Sam (1 Kgs) 4:8(7); 7:3–14; 17:37; 30:8, 18; 2 Sam (2 Kgs) 22:1; 1 Chron 16:35; Jdt 16:3; Job 5:19; 10:7; Pss 30:2; 59(58):1; 143(142):9; 144(143):11; Hos 2:10(12); 5:14; Isa 31:5; 43:13; 44:17, 20; 47:14; 50:2; 57:13; 60:16; Jer 1:8, 19; 15:20; 20:13; Ezek 34:10, 27.

[42]Cf. Exod 3:8; 18:4–10; Josh 24:10; Judg 10:11–15; 1 Sam (1 Kgs) 4:8(7); 10:18; 12:6–25; 2 Kgs (4 Kgs) 17:34–39; Isa 43:1–21; 50:2.

[43]See especially 1 Sam (1 Kgs) 12:10; 26:23–24; 2 Kgs (4 Kgs) 17:37–39; Zeph 1:18; Zech 11:6; Isa 42:22; 60:15–16; Jer 21:12; Ezek 7:19; 33:9, 12.

[44]See Rom 8:38; 12:2; 1 Cor 1:20; 2:6, 8; 3:18, 22; 7:26; 2 Cor 4:4; Bovon, "Une Formule Prépaulinienne," 93; Longenecker, *Galatians*, 7–8. See also 4 Ezra 5:55; 7:12–13, 50; 14:20; and the Freer Logion of Mark 16:14 cited by Longenecker, 8–9. Longenecker also cites Richard B. Hays' discussion in *The Faith of Jesus Christ*, 85f, concerning the likelihood that an early Jesus narrative encapsulating key elements of the early church's confessions is reflected in vv. 4–5 and is integral to Paul's situation and argument in the letter. The rich use of ἐξαιρέω suggests cultic appeal and use.

[45]Rom 12:9; 1Cor 5:13; Gal 1:4; 1Thess 5:22.

[46]Its only other occurrences in the NT are 1 Peter 4:19 and 1 John 5:14.

[47]Emphasizing the will of God are: Matt 6:10; 7:21; 12:50; 18:14; 21:31; 26:42; Mark 3:35; John 4:35; 5:30; John 6:38–40; 7:17; 9:31; Acts 13:22; 21:14; 22:14; Rom 1:10; 2:18; 12:2; 15:32; 1 Cor 1:1; 2 Cor 1:1; 8:5; Gal 1:4; Eph 1:1;1:5; 1:9; 1:11; 5:17; 6:6; Col 1:1; 1:9; 4:12; 1 Thess 4:3; 5:18; 2 Tim 1:1; Heb 10:7, 9, 10; 10:36; 13:21; 1 Pet 2:15; 3:17; 4:2; 4:19; 1 John 2:17; 5:14; Rev 4:11. It is used for human will in: 1 Cor 7:37; 16:12; Eph 2:3; 2 Pet 1:21. Regarding the struggle between human will and God's will, see Luke 12:47; 22:42; 23:25; John 1:13. A single reference to the evil one's will is found in 2 Tim 2:26.

[48]Rom 1:10.

[49]Rom 15:32; 1 Cor 1:1; 2 Cor 1:1; 8:5. See also Col 1:1; 2 Tim 1:1. The only other occurrence is Rev 4:11.

the phrase κατὰ τὸ θέλημα occurs primarily in the apocalyptic book of Daniel. It appears in the Gentile king Nebuchadnezzar's profession of faith in the God of Israel.[50] It is also in Daniel's vision of the ram and the goat that foretells the end of time with its tribulations for God's people and God's ultimate victory over evil.[51]

Further evidence that these opening expansions are drawn in part from an early church confession is the doxological declaration in verse five, which appears to be a refrain with liturgical roots. As noted above, it is the only doxology in any of Paul's prescripts, though Paul uses doxologies elsewhere.[52] Whether or not it belongs with the preceding verse, as the natural complement of the confessional expression of verse 4, or is a separate liturgical closing refrain that was known in the early Christian church and added here is impossible to know. It is clear, however, that the antecedent of ᾧ is τοῦ θεοῦ καὶ πατρὸς ἡμῶν. Thus God our Father is the one to whom praise is due for the salvific deliverance accomplished through Christ Jesus. It is to this God that worship is to endure forever.

In light of these observations, verses 4–5 appear to be elements of an early church confession that Paul has incorporated into the salutation of the letter. The Christological assertion of v. 1 may also be part of an early confession, though it is impossible to know what if any relationship it may have had with vv. 4–5. In light of Paul's letters, though, they are all declarations with which Paul agrees. But why has Paul incorporated these evident confessional fragments with elements of an epistolary prescript in his correspondence to the Galatians?

Bovon has suggested that Paul uses these recognizable statements in a polemical way as an immediate kind of proof to legitimize his own gospel and disprove the so-called gospel of Paul's adversaries.[53] There is, however, no

---

[50]Dan (DanTh) 4:35.

[51]Dan 8:1–25. See especially 8:4 where κατὰ τὸ θέλημα and ἐξαιρούμενος are combined. Here, though, it is in reference to the will and power of the ram—the kings of Media and Persia (v. 20)—from which no human power can rescue. The point of the vision, though, is that in the last days of the goat's or Greeks' rule (v. 21) there will be astounding devastation to the land and to the people of God. Again, no human power can rescue the faithful from the wicked king (v. 23). This time, however, the Prince of princes will destroy the wicked with divine power (v. 25). Elsewhere in Daniel, the phrase refers to the royal will of kings (11:3, 16, 36). In 1 Esdras 8:16 it pertains specifically to the will of God.

[52]See Rom 11:36 and Phil 4:20.

[53]In comparing the evidences of traditional influences in the opening of both Romans and Galatians, Bovon writes: "A cet argument qui remonte l'histoire, il faut ajouter une considération au niveau rédactionnel des textes: dans le début de l'épître aux Romains, Paul allonge de manière inhabituelle le prologue et tient à se référer à la foi traditionnelle de l'Église: d'où la formule de Rom 1,3–4. Pour une raison différente, polémique et non apologétique, l'apôtre agit ici de la même manière. Par son appel à la tradition ecclésiale, il

basis for assuming that these Christological affirmations here are not also held by the Galatian agitators. Indeed, as we will see below, there is good reason to understand Paul's expansions as essential common elements between himself and the agitators. That they should affirm these tenets of the faith and yet promote a gospel that requires adherence to the Jewish Law, however, is a shocking self-contradiction that Paul proves in the letter-body. Thus Paul's amazement finds swift and striking expression in vv. 6–10 and elsewhere in the letter. We will probe this matter further below, but first let us consider another proposal for these opening verses.

Galatians 1:1–5 as Epistolary Prescript and Substitute Thanksgiving Period

Ordinarily after the epistolary prescript, Paul includes in his letter openings a thanksgiving period. Galatians, however, does not have a thanksgiving period. This is significant because, ever since Paul's Schubert's study of the customary thanksgiving periods, scholars have widely recognized that these εὐχαριστῶ periods highlight the writer's central concerns or major themes to be developed in the letter.[54] Schubert's study also called attention to the fact that "the Pauline thanksgivings not only begin with but are structurally characterized by a syntactical period which we have called the εὐχαριστῶ period because εὐχαριστῶ, besides being the principal verb of this period, is also the key-term of every thanksgiving."[55] Schubert observed further that the typical climactic force of Paul's thanksgiving period is eschatological.[56]

Many scholars have accepted Schubert's findings regarding the form and function of Paul's epistolary thanksgivings which Paul uses in Romans, 1 Corinthians, Philippians, 1 Thessalonians, and Philemon (see also Colossians and 2 Thessalonians).[57] Customary εὐχαριστῶ thanksgivings are absent,

---

se situe dans la vérité de l'Évangile reçu et disqualifie ses adversaires d'entrée de jeu" ("Une Formule Prépaulinienne," 93–94).

[54]P. Schubert, *Pauline Thanksgivings*, 27, writes that it is the province of the thanksgiving periods "to indicate the occasion for and the contents of the letters which they introduce." See also pp. 162, 180. J. L. White expresses the view of many others also when he writes, "Schubert . . . rightly proposes, in my opinion, that the thanksgiving contains all the primary information that Paul wished to convey" (*The Form and Function of the Body of the Greek Letter*, 117, n. 63).

[55]Schubert, *Pauline Thanksgivings*, 180. See also 39–46 and Table II on 54–55 where the syntactical units constituting the structure of this period are shown.

[56]Ibid., 4–5, 29. On the close of these periods, see especially Jack T. Sanders, "Transition from Opening Epistolary Thanksgiving," 348–62. See also J. L. White, *The Form and Function of the Body of the Greek Letter*.

[57]Schubert divided Pauline thanksgivings into two types—the simple and the complex (*Pauline Thanksgivings*, 35). Each type, however, "reveals beyond the shadow of doubt their strictly epistolary form and function" (183).

however, from 2 Corinthians and Galatians. Thus scholars must look elsewhere for early signs of the letter's major topics in these letters.[58]

In 2 Corinthians 1:3–11, Paul uses a *berakha* (εὐλογητὸς ὁ θεός) with his salutation rather than a thanksgiving. The *berakha* is essentially a "short christianized form of the Jewish praise-giving or eulogy."[59] Among its distinctive characteristics in 2 Cor 1:11 is that the εὐχαριστῶ clause comes at the conclusion, rather than the opening of the thanksgiving period, and the Corinthians, rather than Paul, are the subject.[60] This subtle subversion was unlikely missed by those Corinthian Christians whose witness was failing and who did not draw from Paul a straightforward εὐχαριστῶ thanksgiving. The *berakha*, however, addresses a different situation but still presents in the opening central themes of the letter.[61] Thus, whereas Paul's thanksgiving periods relate to important issues and needs of the readers here in 2 Cor, it is the apostle's own suffering on behalf of the gospel and the result of God's gracious blessing reaching others that are central.[62]

In Galatians, the customary εὐχαριστῶ thanksgiving period is absent and there is no *berakha* utilizing εὐχαριστῶ in any other way. Therefore, it has been suggested that Paul found nothing about the Christians of Galatia for which to be grateful—a point seemingly supported by the absence of any favorable attributes characterizing the churches in Galatia.[63] Further support is drawn from the startling use of θαυμάζω in 1:6, which Paul uses nowhere else and which has been interpreted as a strong rebuke of the Galatian Christians.[64] We have already observed, however, that Paul's reticence in describing the character of the Galatian churches is not necessarily a condemnation of them all. Moreover, as others have observed, θαυμάζω is used in ancient letters and in the NT—especially in the gospels—to express amazement and astonishment more than rebuke.[65] It is clear that Paul was deeply troubled by the situation in

---

[58]See above, p. 24.

[59]P. T. O'Brien, *Introductory Thanksgivings*, 233. See also the helpful discussion and extensive references on 233–58.

[60]P. Schubert, *Pauline Thanksgivings*, 50.

[61]O'Brien observes, though, that the "tone, language and themes of chap. 1:3–11 do not point forward to chaps 10–13" (*Introductory Thanksgivings*, 256, n. 133).

[62]Ibid., 257. It is also noteworthy that Paul's emphasis on the consolation that God gives to those who suffer for the sake of the gospel stands in stark contrast to the agitators who "sat at home and lived in luxury" (cf. 11:13f).

[63]The Galatians are not described as being called by God or loved by God (e.g. Rom 1:7), made holy or united in Christ (e.g. 1 Cor 1:2; 2 Cor 1:1), in God or in Christ (e.g. 1 Thess 1:1). See Longenecker, *Galatians*, 13; Murphy-O'Conner, *Paul the Letter Writer*, 51, 60–61.

[64]Cf. Mussner, *Der Galaterbrief*, 53, nn. 53–54; T. Y. Mullins, "Formulas," 385.

[65]Cf. Burton, *Galatians*, 18; Betz, *Galatians*, 46–47; Longenecker, *Galatians*, 14; Hansen, *Abraham in Galatians*, 33–34. See also Luther, *Lectures on Galatians* in *Luther's*

Galatia. Indeed, the absence of an opening thanksgiving and the universal curse upon anyone—including himself or an angel from heaven—who preaches a gospel contrary to the one he delivered to them earlier (1:8–9) undoubtedly startled Paul's hearers and pressed upon them the urgency of his case. It does not necessarily follow, however, that Paul's view of the Galatians is entirely negative.

Similarly, some scholars contend that it is not correct to deny the presence of an opening thanksgiving in Galatians. As we have already observed, Paul's prescript moves swiftly to a climactic thanksgiving to God. Moreover, David Cook has called attention to the fact that Schubert himself was unwilling to draw the conclusion that Galatians had no thanksgiving, for:

> There is at the very end of the opening formula (1:5b) the singular clause ᾧ (sc. τῷ θεῷ) ἡ δόξα εἰς τοὺς αἰῶνας τῶν αἰώνων ἀμην. It may very well be that Paul 'intended' this brief benediction as a substitute for his normal epistolary introduction—the thanksgiving. At all events, it is clear that the regular εὐχαριστῶ thanksgiving is omitted, because the specific epistolary situation did not permit it.[66]

Could the epistolary salutation of Galatians function as a "thanksgiving pericope" that identifies the letter's central themes? This is Cook's fundamental question and he answers it affirmatively on the basis that the doxology in v. 5 gives thanks to God and · so performs the purpose of the εὐχαριστῶ thanksgiving. The thanksgiving period's role of identifying the letter's central themes, then, is accomplished by the expansions in vv. 1 and 4. In this, Cook takes his point of departure from the earlier observations of Betz who noted that there are close relations between elements of the prescript and letter-body, especially "the title [of apostle] and its definition (1:1) and the christological-soteriological statements (1:4)."[67]

Other interpreters of Galatians have noted some striking correlations between certain themes introduced in the prescript and their presence

---

Works, vol. 26, Jaroslav Pelikan, ed. (Saint Louis: Concordia Publishing House, 1963), 43, who stressed earlier Paul's wise use of art and skill for "He does not attack them with harsh and stern words; he speaks paternally, not only bearing their fall with patience but even excusing it somewhat. He also shows maternal affection toward them; he speaks gently to them, and yet in such a way that he scolds them, though with words that are very appropriate to the purpose. Toward their betrayers, by contrast, he is extremely violent and indignant . ." Of θαυμάζω itself, there are 43 occurrences of the word in the NT, 35 of which are in the Gospels and Acts.

[66]Schubert, *Pauline Thanksgivings*, 173–74. See also Cook, "The Prescript as Programme in Galatians," *JTS* 43 (1992): 511–12.

[67]Betz, *Galatians*, 37; Cook, "Prescript as Programme," 512.

throughout the body of the letter.[68] Few scholars, though, have joined Cook in viewing 1:1–5 as the program for the entire letter. Moreover, one may correctly question whether it is necessary to recast 1:1–5 as a type of epistolary thanksgiving and on that basis locate the letter's central themes within these opening verses. Similarly, one may rightfully wonder if it is necessary to look beyond 1:1–5 and recast the θαυμάζω, "I am astonished," statement in 1:6 as a substitute for the conventional epistolary thanksgiving that marks the central themes of the letter, as Longenecker and others have proposed.[69]

No satisfactory explanation has yet been given for the relation between the epistolary characteristics of 1:1–5 and the unmistakable thematic clues there, which are characteristic of rhetorical exordiums. Likewise, the apparent uniqueness of this letter-speech's opening which lacks the customary εὐχαριστῶ thanksgiving makes it difficult to understand the basis and purpose of Paul's curious expansions. Is the opening of Galatians, then, best attributed to the whim of an artistic composer, Paul, who in the heat of his passion has abandoned the proven techniques for communicating persuasively in letter and speech? Or is it possible that the location of central themes in the customary opening εὐχαριστῶ thanksgiving periods that follow the prescripts in Paul's other letters has more to do with the position of the thanksgiving at the *beginning* of a letter than with the particular expression of εὐχαριστῶ? That is, are Paul's curious expansions in 1:1–5 understandable in their own right as a common practice of Greco-Roman communication and more particularly as elements of a rhetorical exordium? Let us now consider the rhetorical characteristics of 1:1–5 together with the immediate context of the following verses, 1:6–10, to see how Paul fuses an epistolary salutation with elements of a rhetorical exordium and accomplishes the purposes of both.

II. THE FUSION OF LETTER AND SPEECH IN GALATIANS 1:1–10

Relating the formal characteristics of the epistolary salutation or prescript of Galatians to rhetorical forms and functions is not a new idea. Following Betz, interpreters have observed some of the relations between the prescript and the letter body. By locating the inauguration of some major themes in the

---

[68]Some scholars have noted that Paul's expansions in the epistolary prescript often relate to important issues in the letter-body. See Betz, *Galatians*, 37–43; R. Hall, "Rhetorical Outline for Galatians," 283; Kennedy, *New Testament Interpretation*, 147–48; Longenecker, *Galatians*, 10; Matera, *Galatians*, 43–44. Of those who recognize the significance of the letter-opening as an indicator of central themes in the letter, the general consensus is that here Paul identifies two main issues: the nature of his apostleship and nature of the gospel. But see Martyn (*Galatians*, 92) who adds the human plight and apocalyptic theology and so locates four central themes in 1:1–5.

[69]Longenecker, *Galatians*, 13.

prescript, though, they are attributing to the epistolary salutation essential characteristics of a rhetorical exordium. Still, because of the prominent epistolary characteristics of 1:1–5, some nevertheless conclude that the preface "can be recognized easily and then separated from the letter."[70]

In letters that are influenced by rhetoric, it is ordinarily true that the "speech" as composed by the sender and heard by the recipient follows the brief letter salutation. The two forms of epistolary prescript and rhetorical body are thus appropriately identified and interpreted as distinct elements. Indeed, some rhetorical critics have excluded entirely the prescript and postscript of Galatians from their interpretive analyses. That interpreters largely separate the epistolary and rhetorical forms of Galatians in this way was evident in the preceding survey of various interpretations of the letter's structure.

R. G. Hall has proposed, however, that although the epistolary prescript form is dominant in the letter opening it bears rhetorical characteristics and is better understood as a "salutation/exordium."[71] Hall derives this designation for the following reasons. First, two major lines of argumentation developed in the letter body are clearly present in the salutation/exordium. Following Betz, these are the themes of Paul's apostleship (1:1) and the christological-soteriological significance of Jesus (1:4). Hall observes further that the identification of these themes is a characteristic of exordiums rather than prescripts.[72] Secondly, Hall sees in the salutation/exordium Paul's adherence to the common rhetorical practice of emphasizing those points in an exordium that are most likely to secure a judge's and hearer's favor.[73] Thus Hall's classification of 1:1–5 as a salutation/exordium is intended to call attention to the rhetorical function of the prescript, which he views as both epistolary salutation and rhetorical exordium.[74]

But is the presence of a salutation and these two theme-markers in 1:1–5 sufficient cause for such a designation? Hall is correct that the epistolary prescript of Galatians does incorporate rhetorical aspects of an exordium, as we will see below. The relationship is stronger, however, than in the location of two evident thematic links between 1:1–5 and the letter-body. The boundaries of this salutation/exordium are also broader. Let us now consider the

---

[70]Cf. Betz, *Galatians*, 37.

[71]Hall, "Rhetorical Outline," 282–83.

[72]Ibid., 283. Hall cites Aristotle *Rhetoric* 3:14.6; Quintilian *Institutio* 4.1.23; and *Rhetorica ad Herenium* 4.6–7.

[73]Ibid.

[74]Hall ("Rhetorical Outline," 283) goes on to identify Gal 1:6–9 as the proposition and contends that the point of the letter is to urge the Galatians to reject the false gospel of Paul's opponents and to embrace Paul's true gospel from God.

fundamental rhetorical elements of an exordium that are present throughout
Galatians 1:1–10.

Rhetorical Movements in Galatians 1:1–10

From a rhetorical perspective, Paul utilizes the usual epistolary salutation
form in 1:1–5 but clearly incorporates particular expansions that reshape the
salutation into a rhetorical figure called amplification (*amplificatio*) which rises
to a climax.[75] That is, the words and thoughts of the entire pericope are joined
together as one sentence so that they proceed from one another and reach a
crescendo with the final ἀμήν of praise to "God our Father." The effect of this
amplification is to move the customary salutation emphasis upon sender and
receiver to God the Father who is over them all and to God's work on behalf of
them all through Jesus Christ. Moreover, it stresses that the source and agent of
Paul's apostleship is also the source and agent of grace and peace to the
Galatians. Jesus Christ and God the Father who raised him from the dead have
acted to save all of them from the present evil age.

When we turn to the individual membra of this opening salutation,
several other rhetorical movements are apparent. To begin with, Paul's
expression in verse one is periodic. It is comprised of five membra that increase
in length and suspend the full force of the clause until the final word.[76] The first
membrum is Παῦλος ἀπόστολος; the second is οὐκ ἀπ᾽ ἀνθρώπων; the third
is οὐδὲ δι᾽ ἀνθρώπου; the fourth is ἀλλὰ διὰ Ἰησοῦ Χριστοῦ; the fifth is
καὶ θεοῦ πατρὸς τοῦ ἐγείραντος αὐτὸν ἐκ νεκρῶν. This periodic movement
is antithetical and balanced, which are common characteristics of periods.
Moreover it builds steadily to the lengthier final clause which signals to the
mind's ear a point of emphasis and the logical completion of the thought.
Similarly, the period's rhythm builds to the final clause where the whole
expression ends with a long syllable, which is also a characteristic of periods
and helps mark the completion of the thought for the listeners. Thus, while the
balanced antithetical clauses do reflect a chiastic form, the expression is more
satisfactorily described as a period.

This periodic opening asserts that Paul's apostleship originates and can
be understood only through a living Jesus Christ and a powerful God who
raised Jesus from the dead, a God who is also related to Jesus, Paul and the
Galatians as father. Also, while the antithetical portion of the period emphasizes
the freedom of Paul's apostleship from human origins, the final force of the

---

[75]Quinitlian *Institutio* 8.4.3–21. In discussing the four types of amplificatio
(incrementum, comparatio, ratiocinatio and congeries), Quintilian stresses that each moves
toward a climax. When comparisons are involved, though, as in Gal 1:1, Quintilian observes
that rising from the less to the greater "must necessarily exalt that which is above" (8.4.9).

[76]Cf. Cicero *Brutus* 8.34.

period accentuates not Paul or his apostleship but God the Father and Jesus Christ risen from the dead. God the Father and Jesus Christ are the locus of Paul's utterly apocalyptic apostleship.

At this point, Paul returns to epistolary convention and briefly identifies the co-senders and the letter's recipients (1:2). Then, after issuing the opening greeting (1:3), Paul completes the epistolary custom for salutations and quickly returns to his emphasis on "God our Father and the Lord Jesus Christ (v.3)." Here, though, the source and agents of Paul's apostleship are also identified as the basis and means of grace and peace among the Galatians.

In verses 4–5, which reflect an early church confession, Paul affirms that he and the Galatians have been rescued from their sins by Jesus Christ whose liberating work occurred within the providence of God. On account of this, the people of faith shall praise God forever (1:5). This confessional statement is expressed in a narrative or continuous sentence style. That is, the attributes of Jesus' self-giving are compiled in a consecutive way. Unlike a period, then, each successive clause adds to the meaning of the preceding one, but the sense of the whole is not suspended until the end of either verse four or five. The meaning of the sentence is cumulative and it is brought to a close by the doxological refrain of verse five along with aural and visual punctuation mark of ἀμήν. The end is evident because the syntactical sense is complete. Indeed, it is possible even to rearrange the clauses of this looser sentence movement without destroying the expressed meaning.

In 1:6–7, Paul shifts the style once more and delivers a strong rhetorical period. Here in this compound statement, it is quite clear from the beginning that Paul will not stop on a simple ending. It is only in the utterance of the final clauses εἰς ἕτερον εὐαγγέλιον (v. 6) and, again, τὸ εὐαγγέλιον τοῦ Χριστοῦ (v. 7) that the listener or reader learns the reason for Paul's amazement and the Galatian Christians' abandonment of Christ's grace. The Galatians are now embracing a different gospel which is not the gospel of Christ.

The periodic form of verse 6 is comprised of four membra. The first is θαυμάζω ("I am astonished"). The second is ὅτι οὕτως ταχέως μετατίθεσθε ("that so quickly you are being turned," if μετατίθεσθε is passive, or "that so quickly you are deserting," if the verb is interpreted as middle voice). The third and longest membrum is ἀπὸ τοῦ καλέσαντος ὑμᾶς ἐν χάριτι Χριστοῦ ("from the one who called you by means of Christ's grace").[77] The fourth and final membrum of the period is εἰς ἕτερον εὐαγγέλιον ("for a different gospel").

---

[77] A textual problem exists regarding Χριστοῦ because it is not present in p46 which contains the earliest text of Galatians. See B. M. Metzger, *A Textual Commentary on the Greek New Testament* (Stuttgart: United Bible Societies, 1971), 589.

Only in this last clause is the sense of the whole complete, but the short syllables keep the mouth and the ear from lingering, for more is on the way. It is clear at this point, however, that at the root of Paul's astonishment is this different gospel that is taking hold over the Galatian Christians. Indeed, given Paul's early emphasis on his own role as the one who first called the Galatians to faith in the grace of Jesus Christ, one might expect Paul's amazement to be that they are turning to different apostles.[78] Instead his astonishment is that they are turning to an entirely different gospel, which is a stronger charge against them. More than deserting him, Paul contends that they are abandoning essential tenets of the Christian faith and proclamation.

Anticipating clarification of what he means by εἰς ἕτερον εὐαγγέλιον, Paul swiftly adds a periodic amplification (v. 7) that explains his perspective precisely and reiterates—even sharpens—his point. First, there is no other gospel than the one they are forsaking (ὃ οὐκ ἔστιν ἄλλο). The initial clause of this period asserts with all the forcefulness that brevity brings the singularity of the gospel. Then, as though offering a concession on this matter to possible objections, Paul emphasizes this assertion with a divided period that expresses two consequences of this so-called "different gospel." First, there are some who, because of this gospel are disrupting the Galatian Christians (εἰ μή τινές εἰσιν οἱ ταράσσοντες ὑμᾶς or "nevertheless there are some who are disturbing you"). This non-gospel promotes discord. Second, these disturbers wish to pervert the gospel of Christ (καὶ θέλοντες μεταστρέψαι τὸ εὐαγγέλιον τοῦ Χριστοῦ). Why they desire to do so is not stated. Listeners, however, are subtly compelled to raise their own questions about the motivations of these agitators whose gospel is not the same as that proclaimed by Paul. At the conclusion of this divided period, Paul once again strikes his climactic note upon the gospel.

The gospel of Christ is the only gospel, according to Paul. That anyone would willfully distort this proclamation of good news regarding the Messiah is a damnable offense. In the same way that he stresses the word "gospel" by repetition in vv. 6–7, so also Paul issues a double curse and so emphasizes the gravity of misrepresenting the gospel of Christ. Repetition is a common rhetorical practice that is useful for reinforcing the speaker's point. Ordinarily, the first statement carries the basic informative function (*indicat*) while the duplicated word or phrase adds a reinforcing emotive function (*affirmat*).[79] Repetition is fundamentally a pathos formula,[80] thus communicators must

---

[78]Cf. 1 Cor 1:11–13.

[79]Quintilian *Institutio* 9.3.28–30. Of the three main types of repetition—contact, parenthesis, and intermittent—vv. 6–7 and 8–9 are both intermittent of the closing variety, which means their repeated words come at the endings of their respective clauses.

[80]Cf. *Rhetorica ad Herennium* 4.38; Quintilian *Institutio* 9.3.28–30.

exercise prudence in its use or it will impede the message's reception. Used judiciously, however, repetition may be a powerful tool for setting key points in a listener's mind and for involving the listeners emotionally without overloading them.

The repeated curse of 1:8–9 is aimed carefully at accomplishing both ends. Paul first informs the Galatians that there are serious consequences for any heavenly or earthly creature—including Paul and the brothers—that proclaims a gospel which conflicts with the gospel of Christ which the Galatians first received from Paul and the brothers (ἀλλὰ καὶ ἐὰν ἡμεῖς ἢ ἄγγελος ἐξ οὐρανοῦ εὐαγγελίζηται ὑμῖν παρ᾽ ὃ εὐηγγελισάμεθα ὑμῖν, ἀνάθεμα ἔστω). Such persons will be accursed.[81] Paul then expresses the curse a second time but now incorporates a striking element that sharpens the urgency of the problem and strengthens his emotive appeal to the Galatians (v. 9). The curse Paul issues is immediately relevant to the present situation in Galatia (εἴ τις ὑμᾶς εὐαγγελίζεται παρ᾽ ὃ παρελάβετε, ἀνάθεμα ἔστω). But Paul now throws himself and his own personal relationships against anyone who promotes this perverted gospel (ὡς προειρήκαμεν καὶ ἄρτι πάλιν λέγω). Paul's shift from the first person plural to the first person singular is a consummate pathos appeal. This is because strong emotions can only be produced in listeners and readers who plainly recognize that the speaker himself is strongly and personally seized by those emotions.[82]

Paul also adds persuasive force to these curses by structuring them as periods. Most noticeably, verses 8 and 9 are framed as conditional statements. The protases of each (vv. 8a and 9c) state the conditions that will activate the curse. The apodoses of each (vv. 8b and 9d) state the consequence of the curse in the imperative. The first curse is given as a condition of future possibility (ἐὰν with the subjunctive) while the second curse is formed as a condition of reality (εἰ with the indicative). These conditions, however, did not have to be arranged in their present order or restricted to their particular content to convey their meaning. For instance, Paul could have stated the curses simply as imperatival commands—setting ἀνάθεμα ἔστω at the beginning—or he could have altered the conditional statements in any number of ways. As the curses stand, however, Paul's conditional statements build steadily to their forceful endings of ἀνάθεμα ἔστω. Only in the utterance of the final verb does the meaning of the whole conditional period become apparent. Here the period

---

[81]See especially Betz, *Galatians*, 50–54, for a constructive discussion on these verses and for literature on curses. See also Kjell Arne Morland, *The Rhetoric of Curse in Galatians: Paul Confronts Another Gospel*, Emory Studies in Early Christianity (Atlanta: Scholars Press, 1995).

[82]See especially Quintilian *Institutio* 6.2.27–36. See also 6.2.2–26; 8.3.88; 9.2.104; and Aristotle *Rhetoric* 3.7.11.

arrives at its nicely turned end and reaches its goal. Here the grave seriousness of proclaiming a contrary gospel is emphatically made. Any rearrangement would weaken—even destroy—the strength of these periodic conditional curses.

Paul then raises and answers a pair of rhetorical questions (v. 10) which draw his opening to a close. Raising direct questions is an effective rhetorical device, particularly when a speaker and some listeners view the same topic from opposite points of view.[83] These questions, however, do not necessarily reflect an actual situation.[84] Yet, if there are opponents who have stated that Paul desires popularity among people more than he desires to be faithful to God, or if Paul is anticipating such a challenge, that he is a persuader of people and God,[85] these questions come at an opportune time. In light of the curses given in vv. 8–9, any opponent's insistence that Paul's chief motivation for promoting the gospel is for personal gain now becomes absurd.[86]

Paul stresses this point further by framing the answer to his real or hypothetical questions as a present condition of unreality (εἰ with a past tense in the indicative). Paul makes it clear that he considers the protasis to be untrue. He is not a "man pleaser." He is Christ's slave. With this conditional assertion, Paul also completes a triad of conditional statements that move from general to specific. First, Paul issues a condition of future possibility that is universal in scope (v. 8). The apodosis applies to all humans on earth and even angels in heaven. A curse shall be upon any creature that proclaims a gospel contrary to the gospel which Paul first delivered to the Galatians. Second, Paul uses a condition of reality to narrow the scope of the curse more directly upon any of the Galatians themselves who may promote this distorted gospel (v. 9). Third, after a pair of transitional questions, Paul narrows the scope of his subject matter still further by utilizing a condition of unreality to defend himself from any accusations of being a "man pleaser" (v. 10).

The ordering of these three statements in close succession from general to specific is a common rhetorical move noted for its persuasive force.[87] Also, as with the previous conditions, this last condition is arranged as a strong rhetorical period that ends with a series of long vowels and a verb. Only at the end of this periodic condition is it clear that Paul himself is a slave on behalf of

---

[83]Quintilian *Institutio* 3.11.1.

[84]Cf. Betz, *Galatians*, 56, n. 115. See also Barclay, "Mirror-Reading."

[85]Cf. 1 Thess 2:3–4 and Betz, *Galatians*, 54–55 and notes 103–08. One who persuades a god is a soothsayer. See also my earlier comments regarding the largely negative view of rhetorical persuaders.

[86]Aristotle *Rhetoric* 3.17.18.

[87]Cf. Quintilian *Institutio* 7.1.27; 3.5.15; Aristotle *Rhetoric* 1.2.18; 2.19.27; 2.25.8–10.

Christ. Furthermore, the rhetorical questions in v. 10 stress this point by their parallel arrangement so that each interprets the other.[88] The second question repeats the meaning of the first question in a new way and so amplifies Paul's point that he is foremost a slave of Christ (Χριστοῦ δοῦλος). Remarkably, with this self-designation Paul forms a subtle inclusio and returns to the letter-speech's opening point regarding himself and his title. The title "slave of Christ" is for Paul an amplification of "apostle" (1:1a).

In sum, Galatians 1:1–10 is full of carefully arranged rhetorical movements that are fused together with conventional elements of an epistolary salutation. But, again, how are the elements of speech and letter related here? Is the content of 1:1–10 better understood as two related but independent pericopes—one governed primarily by epistolary rules (1:1–5) and the other by rhetorical standards (1:6–10)? Or are they better interpreted as a single, united textual unit that accomplishes the purposes of both epistolary prescript and rhetorical exordium? Let us now compare 1:1–10 with the characteristics of rhetorical exordiums and explore the relations between them.

Rhetorical Opening and Epistolary Prescript in Galatians 1:1–10

The opening of Galatians contains the standard elements of an epistolary prescript. Less clear is whether or not 1:1–5 may be understood as part of a rhetorical exordium on the basis of any formal characteristics of exordiums beyond the evident thematic overtures regarding Paul's apostleship (v. 1) and the christological-soteriological significance of Jesus (vv. 4–5).[89] Are there any rhetorical categories that can help us understand and interpret the curious expansions in the prescript which epistolographical categories do not explain?

As we noted above, letters were widely viewed as approximations of oral speech. The rules of rhetoric—more than those of epistolography—guided communicators in the creation, organization, and expression of their thoughts. Moreover, letters—especially public letters such as Galatians—would have been read aloud and heard. To begin with, then, speakers and listeners in the Greco-Roman world were largely accustomed to giving and receiving speeches that began with an exordium. These rhetorical openings were not only aimed at introducing the speaker, getting the audience's attention, and securing their good will—all of which are reflected in epistolary salutations. Exordiums also had as a chief function the sounding of a communication's central themes that would be developed in the remainder of the speech. Moreover, rhetorical exordiums were to relate to the communication's peroratio or conclusion where

---

[88]Betz, *Galatians*, 54.

[89]Cf. Betz, *Galatians*, 37; Kennedy, *New Testament Interpretation*, 147–48; Hall, "Rhetorical Outline," 283.

the speech is briefly recapitulated and the speaker's crowning point is made.[90] In order to move a communication to its desired end, trained communicators employed two basic types of exordiums. Is there any evidence that Paul is using a particular one in the opening of Galatians? If so, is the beginning best categorized as a direct opening (principium or prooimion) or a subtle approach (insinuatio or ephodos)?[91] And where does the exordium begin and end? At stake is a clearer understanding of Paul's intentions for his letter to the Galatians. Let us then address these matters, treating the latter issue first.

Textual Boundaries. It is clear from our study of the various rhetorical and epistolary analyses of Galatians in chapter one that many proposals for this letter-speech's arrangement have been made. So, also, there is no consensus on the textual limits of the opening verses of Galatians. To be sure, scholars have largely identified 1:1–5 as an epistolary prescript and so viewed the doxological refrain praising God, with its concluding ἀμήν, as the proper point of separation between an epistolary salutation and the beginning of either the letter-body or the letter's speech in verse 6. Our identification of the rhetorical elements present in 1:1–5 suggests that such a clear division along epistolary and rhetorical lines is not entirely satisfactory. Establishing the limits of the following verses is more difficult and controversial. Both for those who see an integral relation between 1:1–5 and the following verses and those who view them as independent pericopes, various proposals have been made to divide the text of Galatians at verses 9,[92] 10,[93] 11,[94] and 12.[95]

Why so many different views about this appropriate point of transition? To begin with, regardless of any scholar's interpretive approach, much of the problem stems from whether or not v. 10 is more logically and grammatically related to the preceding verses (1:1–9), to the following verses (1:11f), or whether it stands alone. At the center of this controversy lies the particle γάρ,

---

[90]Cf. Quintilian *Institutio* 4.1.5; 6.1.1–2; Cicero *De inventione* 1.52.98; 1.53.100–106.

[91]Cf. *Rhetorica ad Herennium* 1.3.5; 1.4.6; Cicero *De Inventione*, 1.15.20.

[92]Cf. Westcott-Hort Text; Nestle-Aland, *Novum Testamentum Graece*; Hall ("Rhetorical Outline"); H. N. Ridderbos (*The Epistle of Paul to the Churches of Galatia*, trans. H. Zylstra, NICNT [Grand Rapids: Wm. B. Eerdmans Publishing Co.], 9–10); C. J. Roetzel (*Letters of Paul*, 104); Vos, "Paul's Argumentation in Galatians 1–2," *Harvard Theological Review* 87 (1994): 9.

[93]Cf. Tischendorf; Burton (*Galatians*, lxxii–lxxiv); Bruce (*Galatians*, 79–86); Dunn (*Galatians*, 21–22); Kennedy (*New Testament Interpretation*, 148–51); Mack (*Rhetoric*, 69–72); Matera (*Galatians*, 12–13).

[94]Cf. Betz (*Galatians*, 16–23); Vouga ("Zur rhetorischen Gattung," 291).

[95]Jegher-Bucher (*Der Galaterbrief*, 203); J. Smit ("Letter of Paul," 9–11); Bligh (*Galatians in Greek*, 39).

which may function causally, explanatorily, or emphatically.[96] Although some hold that γάρ must be rendered causally in v. 10 and each subsequent time in vv. 11–13,[97] and others contend that γάρ in v. 10 is used to introduce a new topic,[98] γάρ is better translated in v. 10 with explanatory force justifying Paul's declarations in vv. 8–9.[99] This connection is strengthened by Paul's use of ἄρτι in vv. 9 and 10. Some manuscripts reflect this link more emphatically with the insertion of another γάρ in v. 10c (D1, Majority Text, sy) which increases the concluding force of this verse.

There are, however, other important reasons for aligning verse 10 more closely to the preceding verses than the latter. One reason is that Paul characteristically uses γνωρίζω (v. 11) as a disclosure or transition formula signaling the start of a new unit of thought (cf. 1 Cor 12:3, 15:1; Phil 1:12; 1 Thess 2:1). Another reason, from a rhetorical perspective, is that verse 10 is part of a rhetorical argument from general to particular and its content is more closely related to the preceding content than to that which follows, as we have seen. Furthermore, vv. 11–12 form a strong rhetorical period that stands as a thematic overture for the following portion of the letter which pertains to the nature of Paul's apostleship and the reality of the risen Christ. It is a periodic overture for 1:11–2:21, a portion of text which is largely narrative in both form and function until its concluding section.

Still, if the textual boundary for the end of the opening of Galatians is best drawn after 1:10, and the textual unit of 1:1–10 intermingles epistolographical and rhetorical characteristics, how does this opening fulfill the form and role of an exordium?

Exordium Type. Two scholars, especially, have sought answers to this question, and each has drawn the same conclusions regarding the nature and limits of the Galatians exordium.[100] Betz contends that in 1:6–11 Paul mixes two types of exordiums, the direct opening (principium) and the subtle approach (insinuatio). The former is appropriate for attentive and receptive

---

[96]H. E. Dana and Julius R. Mantey, *A Manual Grammar of the Greek New Testament* (New York: Macmillan Publishing Co., 1957), 242–44.

[97]J. S. Vos, "Paul's Argumentation in Galatians 1–2," 9.

[98]H. D. Betz, *Galatians*, 54, n. 100.

[99]Cf. Burton, *Galatians*, 31; Matera, *Galatians*, 47.

[100]Betz, *Galatians*, 44–45. Betz's conclusions about the nature of the exordium, though, are based largely on his extensive knowledge of the letter's rhetorical situation. See also Lüdemann (48–53). A negative assessment on the presence of a mixed type of exordium in Galatians is expressed by rhetorical critic K. A. Morland, who quips, "I find it too farfetched to apply this to Paul as done by H. D. Betz ... and Lüdemann ... especially when they claim that Paul seems to have mixed the two types of *exordia*" (*The Rhetoric of Curse in Galatians*, 128, n. 49).

audiences that are already favorably disposed toward the speaker. The latter is appropriate for audiences that the speaker needs to win over. The present tense of μετατίθεσθε (v. 6) supports Betz's view that both exordium types are fused here, for it is clear that not everyone has abandoned the true gospel, though some have.[101] Such is the situation Paul faces in Galatia. Mixing these two rhetorical forms may seem peculiar to some,[102] but it is not that surprising given the Greco-Roman emphasis on wise adaptability. Lüdemann has also identified the bounds of the exordium as 1:6–10 and interprets it as a mixture of the direct and subtle approaches. Drawing from our earlier investigation of rhetorical principles and exordiums in chapter three, though, we may look more closely at the evidences of a rhetorical opening in all of Galatians 1:1–10.

The author and school of rhetorical training behind the *Rhetorica ad Herennium* counsels communicators to frame the appropriate exordium according to the cause of the address. One principal cause is called *humile* (petty) and refers to situations and issues deemed small, unimportant or insignificant. The speaker's aim, then, is to utilize a direct approach that seizes the listener's attention. Otherwise both speaker and speech will be ignored. Nothing in Galatians suggests that either Paul or the Galatians viewed the cause of his address to be petty.

Another main cause is termed *dubium* (doubtful) and refers to a cause that is partly honorable and partly discreditable. That is, the speaker is unsure of how a group of listeners will respond to the chosen subject matter or point at issue because the subject both attracts and alienates the listeners. The speaker may be judged favorably on certain points and criticized harshly on others. It is incumbent upon the speaker, then, to seize the advantage of a direct opening that will get the audience's attention and swiftly establish goodwill and a positive ethos, usually by praising the audience. Such a beginning is useful for minimizing prejudice against the speaker. Moreover, establishing a common ground between speaker and audience also enhances the speaker's persuasive power for leading others to accept his or her point of view when the controversial matters are addressed later in the speech.

As we saw above, the opening of Galatians is not entirely inimical toward all the Christians there. Paul may not praise the Galatians in his customary fashion, but neither does he condemn all of them outright. The contents of the letter might also suggest that Paul views the cause of the letter-speech as something which both attracts and alienates the recipients of the

---

[101]See also the use of the present tense throughout the letter in Paul's references to the Galatians: 4:9–21; 5:1–13; 6:12–16.

[102]Betz himself comments on the unusual character of a mixed exordium (*Galatians*, 45).

message, particularly regarding Paul's apostleship and the nature of the true gospel. Still, the opening of Galatians is not built straightforwardly upon any common goodwill that exists between Paul and the Galatians. And Paul nowhere tries to minimize prejudice against himself in the opening. Rather he immediately rebuffs any potential criticisms that he is attempting to do so (vv. 8–10). The beginning of Galatians does not suggest that Paul views the cause as doubtful.

The other two principal causes, according to the *Rhetorica ad Herennium*, seem quite similar to one another. They differ primarily in their approaches and their valuations of the cause. The third major cause for choosing and forming an exordium is called *turpe* (discreditable). Here the speaker confronts opponents when something honorable is under attack or when something discreditable is being defended. Careful judgment and invention are necessary if the speaker is to be persuasive. For this reason, the handbook states "unless we have hit upon a means of capturing goodwill by attacking our adversaries, we must use the Subtle Approach."[103] The curses and strong statements in vv. 7–10 leave no doubt that Paul is attacking his adversaries in the manner of a Direct Opening. Whether or not Paul judged this assault to be a means of securing the goodwill of his hearers or accomplished this end is impossible to know. It is possible, however, to understand v. 10 as a rebuttal to rhetorically trained listeners or adversaries who might contend that his opening curses are a rhetorical ploy. In any event, Paul attacks the opponents of the true gospel of Christ in vv. 7–9 and probably saw such an offensive as a way to strengthen—not weaken—his position and thus gain a careful hearing for what follows.

The fourth principal cause is called *honestum* (honorable). Here the perceived cause of the address is either to defend that which the speaker believes all people ought to defend or to attack what all people ought to attack. The speaker's assessment of the topic's value is highest when the cause is honorable. In this case, the speaker may use either the Direct Opening or the Subtle Approach for an effective beginning that will achieve the purposes of the exordium. If the cause is honorable and the speaker elects to use a Direct Opening, the speaker "must show why the cause is honorable, or else briefly announce what matters [he or she is] going to discuss"(1.4.6). As we have seen, all exordiums ought to introduce briefly the topics to be developed in the following discourse. Here, however, the identification of such topics is to be more intentionally blatant. Similarly, an unmistakable statement of the cause's honorable significance should be made.

---

[103]*Rhetorica ad Herennium* 1.4.6.

Paul's opening in his letter-speech to the Galatians meets these criteria in part. For example, his repetition of εὐαγγέλιον and εὐαγγελίζομαι leave no doubt in the minds of attentive listeners that the meaning and significance of the gospel is a central concern in what follows. Similarly, the honorable significance of this matter is expressed forcefully through Paul's double curse (vv. 8–9). As in our consideration of the discreditable cause, then, the opening of Galatians meets several important criteria of a Direct Opening.

There is more, however, concerning exordium strategies of honorable causes. When the cause is honorable, the Subtle Approach is also appropriate because of its proven effectiveness for achieving the purposes of an exordium. According to the *Rhetorica ad Herennium*, "if we do not wish to use the Direct Opening, we must begin our speech with a law, a written document, or some argument supporting our cause"(1.4.6). If in fact Paul is quoting in vv. 1, 4–5 an early church confession that was known by the Galatians and likely written, then 1:1–5 is not only fulfilling the requirements for an epistolary salutation but is also serving as a standard element of an exordium utilizing a Subtle Approach. If, on the other hand, the strange expansions in 1:1–5 do not have a compositional or liturgical history, they nevertheless provide a supporting argument for Paul's cause regarding the gospel of Jesus Christ, for here Paul succinctly summarizes the gospel.

There are other signs that Paul may be incorporating elements of a rhetorical Subtle Approach in the opening of this letter-speech. For instance, the Subtle Approach was effective in conflictual situations, and the rhetorical situation of Galatians is certainly contentious. The indirect exordium was also to be used whenever the subject matter would alienate the audience or incite retaliation, when hearers are siding with the opposition, or when listeners are fatigued from their attention to previous speakers. Paul's strategic use of a letter likely circumvented the possible problem of listener fatigue. Galatians itself, though, demonstrates that the first two reasons for utilizing a Subtle Approach are integral elements of Paul's rhetorical situation.

In such difficult circumstances, trained rhetoricians could still accomplish the exordium's goals of making listeners well-disposed, attentive and receptive to the speaker and the message.[104] This was achievable by introducing and promising to discuss first the very point that one's adversaries consider their strongest argument. Ideally, then, the speaker should begin with the concluding statement made by the persuasive opponent, for it is here that the opponent would have sealed his or her argument in the minds of the hearers.

Undoubtedly, Paul's apostolic identity and authority are being challenged by the "disturbers" in Galatia, and Paul's apostleship is both the first matter

---

[104]*Rhetorica ad Herennium* 1.6.10, 4.29.40; Cicero *De Inventione* 1.17.25.

introduced in the opening of Galatians (1:1) and the first topic discussed at length in the body of the letter-speech (1:11–2:21). Scholars have well noted these dimensions of the text. Less noticeable is that the opening of Galatians also incorporates two other essential elements of a Subtle Opening—elements called Indecision and an exclamation of astonishment.[105] Epistolary critics, of course, have analyzed the θαυμάζω statement in verse 6 as an epistolary formula for letters of rebuke and request, but exclamations of astonishment in the subtle approach of rhetorical exordiums were standard enough in practice to be included among the rhetorical rules for persuasiveness. That is because exclamations of astonishment were deemed especially well-suited for intensifying emotion.[106]

Paul also uses Indecision in verses 6–7 where he seems to ask if there is such a thing as a "different gospel" and then argues that there is only one true gospel of Christ, and it is the one that the Galatians first received from Paul.[107] By using Indecision over a figure of diction, Paul gives the Galatians cause to reconsider their understanding of the gospel and re-evaluate their relation to it.

The opening of Galatians includes the standard elements of an epistolary prescript (vv. 1a, 2–3a), but it also incorporates rhetorical elements for both Subtle and Direct exordiums. Characteristic of a Direct Opening, which is appropriate when the speaker is certain of having the attention and receptivity of the hearers, Paul's beginning includes an attack on his opponents (vv. 7b–10). Such a move only makes good rhetorical sense in the beginning of an address when it is sure to draw support from many listeners and solidify their attention and receptivity. Paul's expression in v. 10, however, may acknowledge that he is purposefully flying in the face of rhetorical conventions. That is, his attack on anyone promoting the perverted gospel may be issued without an expectation of capturing goodwill or pleasing men from among the listeners who have been largely won over by the Galatian agitators. We cannot know fully Paul's intent in v. 10, but it is clear that initiating an attack upon opponents in an exordium is characteristic of a Direct Opening.

More prevalent in this letter-speech opening are rhetorical characteristics of a Subtle Approach. Whether or not Paul's opponents charged him with being a second-rate apostle whose authority was from men or through a man rather than through association with Jesus before the crucifixion and resurrection (which does in fact seem to be the charge), Paul introduces the topic of his apostleship in the first words of the address and makes it his first topic to

---

[105]*Rhetorica ad Herennium* 1.6.10, 4.29.40; Cicero *De Inventione* 1.17.25; Quintilian *Institutio* 9.2.26–27, 9.3.88.

[106]Ibid.

[107]Quintilian shows that Indecision can be used in either figures of thought or figures of diction (*Insitutio* 9.3.88). Here Paul uses it in a figure of diction.

discuss. Similarly, whether or not Paul is actually citing an early church compositional formula or liturgical confession—and, again, it seems as though he is, these curious expansions to the epistolary formulas summarize crucial points about the gospel that support Paul's entire argument (vv. 1, 3b–5). Other prominent features of the Subtle Approach that are present in the opening of Galatians include Paul's use of Indecision regarding the term "gospel" and Paul's statement of astonishment (vv. 6–7).

The opening of Galatians incorporates rhetorical elements of both a Direct Opening and a Subtle Approach. There is also a prevalence of periodic sentence movements in these opening verses of Galatians. And, as we saw in the previous chapter, the concentration of periods is a chief characteristic of exordiums and perorations, as well as of beginnings and endings of speech sections. The opening of this letter-speech also reveals Paul's wise-adaptability in fusing an epistolary prescript with various rhetorical elements to form a single, unified opening or salutation-exordium. Paul's flexibility is evident further in his combination of elements from both kinds of exordiums.[108]

Indeed, there is ample evidence of rhetorical forms and strategies at work throughout Gal 1:1–10. Here Paul has fused elements of a rhetorical exordium and epistolary prescript together into a salutation-exordium. Though the address is written and sent as a letter, it is written to be presented orally and to be heard. The opening is carefully constructed so that the listeners will be set on the tracks Paul desires them to travel as he guides them through his argument to the destination or point of view he desires them to share with him. Still, what exactly is Paul determined for them to understand? How does he utilize the rhetorical advantage of a strong and clear opening to begin establishing his most important points? When we look at 1:1–10 as a salutation-exordium, several central themes or emphases are apparent. Let us now clarify the central themes that Paul introduces in this salutation-exordium before we follow them through this letter-speech to the Galatians.

III. GALATIANS 1:1–10 AS THEMATIC OVERTURE

To be sure, an exordium is not the place for a communicator to present all the important matters of the address.[109] It is the place, however, where trained communicators strike the keynote of the discourse. This is because the

---

[108]The *Rhetorica ad Herennium* advises a speaker to use one approach or the other. Luther seems to have recognized the characteristics of both types of exordiums in Galatians and so proposed that Paul's address is both to opponents and those who stand between the opponents and Paul.

[109]Cf. Quintilian *Institutio* 4.1.24.

beginning of a communication is an especially effective location for providing a sample of the key themes to be developed in the body of the communication.

When we view Gal 1:1–10 as a salutation-exordium, the unmistakable keynote is the "gospel of Christ" (v. 7). Not only does some form of the word "gospel" occur 5 times in these opening verses, but the expansions in 1:1, 4–5 and 6 all describe and qualify this gospel in some way. Indeed, these few verses present a concise summary of the gospel of Christ. Jesus Christ gave himself on behalf of our sins in order to rescue us from the present evil age (v. 4). Jesus died and was raised from the dead by God the Father (v. 1). Moreover, all this was done in accordance with God's will (v. 4), thus a chief characteristic of the gospel as Paul presents it in the opening is grace (vv. 3, 6).

But there are some who are perverting the gospel of Christ and bringing a curse from God upon themselves and those Galatian Christians who are accepting their message. Paul, however, insists that the Galatians cannot uphold this perverted gospel (1:7) without condemning themselves (1:8–9). Thus Paul impresses upon the minds of his hearers that they are putting their lives at stake by deserting the true gospel of Jesus Christ. That is, their decisions about the gospel have eternal consequences. It now remains for Paul to develop in the body of the discourse the error of this so-called gospel and to prove the truth of the gospel he professes. What is the gospel of Christ?

Chief among the characteristics of this gospel of Christ, as highlighted in the opening and developed throughout Galatians, is not only the saving work of Jesus Christ but also the reality and significance of Jesus risen from the dead. As we noted above, the periodic arrangement of v.1 moves from a strong beginning of Παῦλος ἀπόστολος to a stronger climax of Ἰησοῦ Χριστοῦ καὶ θεοῦ πατρὸς τοῦ ἐγείραντος αὐτὸν ἐκ νεκρῶν. Paul's apostleship is stressed (1:1a, 6–10), but Paul emphasizes more the risen Jesus Christ's saving work and its significance for the present eschatological day (1:1b, 3–5). Because he stresses the source of his apostleship with eschatological claims regarding Jesus' resurrection in this opening, one may expect Paul to explain further the nature and significance of his eschatological apostleship. But while many interpreters hold that 1:1 is simply Paul's way of emphasizing the independent nature of his apostleship, the rhetorical shape and position of this verse at the beginning of the exordium calls attention to Paul's eschatological understanding of his apostleship and establishes an eschatological foundation for Paul's entire message to the Galatians. Stated another way, Paul's opening establishes an apocalyptic stasis upon which his apostleship, the gospel, and the lives of both himself and the Galatians stand. God the Father has raised Jesus Christ from the dead, and Paul's life and the lives of the Galatians are not unaffected. In the opening, then, Paul sets forth the resurrection of the crucified Christ as a keynote of his address.

A second major chord that resonates throughout Galatians is the nature and significance of Jesus the Christ's self-offering (1:4). That is, the one whom God raised from the dead is the Crucified and the Christ who has acted to rescue people from their sins. Paul's stress upon the saving work of Christ Jesus in the salutation-exordium indicates that this matter, also, will figure prominently in the following discourse.

A third major chord sounded in the opening of Galatians is the topic of God's purposes (1:4–5, 10). What exactly is God's purpose for Paul and the Galatians? According to God's plan, Jesus Christ gave himself up on behalf of sinners in order to deliver them from evil (v. 4), and Paul argues forcefully from the beginning of this communication that he has given himself up as a slave to Christ (v. 10). The opening of Galatians, then, invites the listeners to begin considering carefully to what or to whom they are giving up their lives. Whom are they trying to please? In this salutation-exordium, Paul sounds the rhetorical cord[110] of God's purposes and human activity, thus one may expect to see this theme resonate also through the remainder of the address.

Let us now investigate the text of Galatians and follow these themes along their respective trajectories to the close of Paul's address in 6:11–18. If our assessment of 1:1–10 as a salutation-exordium is correct and if Paul is, in fact, following an ancient Greco-Roman rhetorical practice of putting an argument's strongest points at the beginning and ending of an argument, then we can expect these themes to reach their climactic heights together in 6:11–18. Moreover, we will observe the crucial role of the Risen Crucified Christ for understanding and interpreting Galatians.

---

[110]By the term "rhetorical cord," I mean those thematic indicators that ought to be established in the opening and developed throughout the message. See the discussion of arrangement above.

CHAPTER FIVE

THE RHETORICAL CORD OF THE RISEN CHRIST

Though it has been called the least apocalyptic of Paul's epistles,[1] Galatians is thoroughly eschatological.[2] To be sure, Paul's slight and singular reference to Jesus' resurrection in 1:1 suggests that the Risen Christ Jesus has little to do with Paul's argument with the Galatians. Paul's emphasis on the Risen Jesus in the opening words of this letter-speech, however, calls the listener to hold the resurrection in mind as foundational for everything else that follows. That is, the interpretive importance of God's act of raising Jesus from the dead is here inversely proportional to Paul's solitary mention of it in the letter's beginning. Resurrection language is wholly apocalyptic[3] and its periodic

---

[1]Cf. J. C. Beker, *Paul the Apostle: The Triumph of God in Life and Thought* (Philadelphia: Fortress Press, 1984), 58, where he writes, "The situation also dictates the virtual absence of an otherwise central feature in Paul's letters—the future apocalyptic dimension of the gospel. Apart from Gal. 5:1, 5, 21b, and 6:7–8, this topic is completely ignored." Beker's central point, however, that Paul's world view is apocalyptic is still widely accepted. See also Käsemann, *Romans*, 1980.

[2]For the apocalyptic theology of Galatians, see especially J. Louis Martyn, *Galatians*, 97–105; idem, "Apocalyptic Antinomies in Paul's Letter to the Galatians," *NTS* 31 (1985): 401–25; C. B. Cousar, *Galatians*, 65; J.D.G. Dunn, *Galatians*, 29, 35–36, 45, 52, 252–54; Beverly Roberts Gaventa, "The Singularity of the Gospel," *Pauline Theology*, vol. 1, ed. J. M. Bassler (Minneapolis: Fortress Press, 1994), 147–59.

[3]As J. C. Beker (*Paul the Apostle*, 152) writes, "Resurrection language is end-time language and unintelligible apart from the apocalyptic thought world to which resurrection language belongs. Resurrection language properly belongs to the domain of the new age to come and is an inherent part of the transformation and the recreation of all reality in the apocalyptic age." On Paul's apocalyptic world view, see especially J.C. Beker, *Paul the Apostle* (Philadelphia: Fortress Press, 1980), 135–81; idem, *Paul's Apocalyptic Gospel: The Coming Triumph of God* (Philadelphia: Fortress Press, 1982), 29–53, 117–21; F. F. Bruce, *Paul: Apostle of the Heart Set Free* (Exeter: Paternoster Press, 1977), 141–42; E. Käsemann, "The Beginnings of Christian Theology" and "On the Subject of Primitive Christian Apocalyptic," in *New Testament Questions for Today* (Philadelphia: Fortress Press, 1969), 82–137; L. Keck, "Paul and Apocalyptic Theology," in *Interpretation* 38 (1984): 229–41; P. J. Achtemeier, *Romans*, Interpretation (Atlanta: John Knox Press, 1985), 7–15; A. Oepke, "καλύπτω, etc.," in *Theological Dictionary of the New Testament*, ed. G. Kittel, vol. 3 (Grand Rapids: Wm. B. Eerdmans Publishing Co., 1965), 556–92.

emphasis in the opening of this letter-speech stresses its centrality to Paul's message in Galatians.

In this chapter, then, we will follow the rhetorical cord of Paul's eschatological claims epitomized by Jesus' resurrection as it weaves its way from the salutation-exordium (1:1–10) to the communication's close. Consequently, we will see how key points in Paul's argument rest upon the apocalyptic stasis that God raised Jesus from the dead.[4] It is from this perspective that, for Paul, the true gospel of the crucified Christ becomes intelligible.

I. THE THEMATIC OVERTURE FOR THE RISEN CHRIST: GALATIANS 1:1

As we saw in the previous chapter, Paul opens his communication to the Galatians with the strong periodic assertion that his apostleship is a consequence of the cooperative act of God the Father and Jesus Christ whom the Father raised from the dead (1:1). That is, Paul's initial stress upon his apostleship leads to a greater emphasis upon the present eschatological day in which the Christ of God who was dead is now alive once more. The immediate implication is that both the risen Christ and God the Father initiated Paul's apostolic call and authority. Simultaneously, Paul's assertion signals the inauguration of the apocalyptic age.[5] That is, Paul views his apostleship as wholly related to God's will and apocalyptic activity revealed in and through the Risen Jesus Christ. So, while Paul's apostleship is presented as an important topic or *topos* for him to address in this communication, the periodic form of his expression subordinates this theme under that of the Risen Christ. Consequently, the recipients of Paul's communication hear from the start that Paul's apostleship is based upon the activity of God the Father and the Risen Christ. They also hear that God has inaugurated the new age by raising Jesus from the dead. Paul thus prepares his listeners to hear more about his apostleship but—even more—he sets their reflections upon the apocalyptic activity of God manifested especially in the resurrection of Jesus from the dead.

---

[4]On the generative position of the resurrection of Christ from the dead in Paul's theology, see especially P. J. Achtemeier, "Finding the Way to Paul's Theology: A Response to J. Christiaan Beker and J. Paul Sampley," *Pauline Theology*, vol. 1, ed. J. M. Bassler (Minneapolis: Fortress Press, 1991), 25–36. See also in the same volume J. Paul Sampley, "From Text to Thought World: The Route to Paul's Ways," 3–14, and J. Christiaan Beker, "Recasting Pauline Theology: The Coherence-Contingency Scheme as Interpretive Model," 15–24. See also L. Keck, "Paul as a Thinker," *Int* 47 (1993): 27–38.

[5]Cf. 1 Cor 15:12–24; 1 Thess 4:13–18. See also Dan 12:1–3.

Paul's early emphasis in the salutation-exordium upon God's eschatological movement does not stop in 1:1, however. Not only does Paul state that God raised Jesus from the dead but he also declares that "our Lord Jesus Christ . . . gave himself for our sins to rescue us from the present age of evil, according to the will of our God and Father" (1:4). The opening declaration that God raised Jesus from the dead is an immediate apocalyptic affirmation of the new age's dawning.[6] Yet in the following assertion of 1:4, Paul makes two other apocalyptic declarations. First, Paul contrasts the "present age of evil" with another age into which he and the Galatians may be delivered. Thus there are at least two ages in the concept of time expressed here. Such language is characteristic of Jewish apocalyptic, which divides history into "this age" and "the coming age."[7] Second, the Lord Jesus Christ has acted in accordance with the will of God the Father to accomplish this deliverance. All three of these opening assertions declare God's apocalypse of the new aeon. All of them are grounded in Jewish apocalyptic.

Simply put, Jewish apocalyptic—which is rooted in ancient Israel's prophetic tradition—holds that history is a creation of God and God is in control of it. The events of history are in accordance with God's will. Also central to Jewish apocalyptic is the belief that the world has become so evil that only God can save it by direct intervention. At a time of God's own choosing, God will issue a final judgment against the powers of evil. Then, following the destruction of the present evil, God will establish a new heaven and a new earth—a new creation—in which the righteousness and obedience God desires for all people will flourish. This Jewish perspective is called "apocalyptic" because it is based upon the God of Israel who has revealed himself and his purposes to Israel in the past and has promised to reveal divine judgment and blessing in the future. Until that time when God's good and incorruptible aeon comes, though, God will continue making his purposes known through revelation. When that time of rewards and punishments arrives, all people—the living and the dead—will be summoned before God's revealed judgment seat

---

[6]See J. C. Beker, *Paul the Apostle*, 152. Also, while the rich apocalyptic character of Paul's theology in Galatians has been noted recently by J. Louis Martyn (*Galatians*, 97), he locates the first apocalyptic expression in the phrase "present evil age" (1:4b).

[7]The phrase "the present age" (ὁ αἰὼν ὁ ἐνεστώς), as we noted in chapter four, is a hapax legomenon for Paul and the New Testament. It reflects, however, a common contrast in Second Temple Judaism between "this age" (ὁ αἰὼν οὗτος) and "the age to come" (ὁ αἰὼν ὁ ἐρχόμενος or ὁ αἰὼν ὁ μέλλων). Cf. 4 Ezra 5:55; 7:12–13, 50. Also, by the word "apocalyptic" I mean a theological construct rather than a literary genre. See, for instance, Paul D. Hanson, "Apocalypticism," in *The Interpreter's Dictionary of the Bible Supplementary Volume* (Nashville: Abingdon Press, 1976), 28–33.

but only the righteous will be spared from destruction and given resurrected life in God's kingdom.[8]

In the salutation-exordium of Galatians, Paul draws upon such Jewish apocalyptic thinking when he uses language pertaining to resurrection from the dead, God's rescuing activity, and two ages of history. In each case, Paul points to a new and present dimension of time. Indeed, the language of resurrection is fundamentally a word about time even as it is a word about a new kind of existence. Now, to be sure, belief in human immortality is not unique to Judaism.[9] There is, however, in the Old Testament evidence of belief in the resurrection of individuals,[10] and belief in the resurrection of the dead began to take on greater significance in intertestamental Judaism as groups like the Pharisees and Essenes advocated and the Sadducees denied such a belief. Furthermore, as the intertestamental literature shows,[11] resurrection of the dead was, for many Jews, a central component of the transformation of the age—a time in which persons who were found righteous before God would be granted an incorruptible and immortal life and become inhabitants of a newly created world.[12]

---

[8]On Jewish and early Christian apocalyptic and Paul, see especially E. Käsemann, "The Beginnings of Christian Theology" and "On the Subject of Primitive Christian Apocalyptic," in *New Testament Questions for Today*, 82–137; P. J. Achtemeier, *Romans*, 6–9; Martinus C. de Boer, "Paul and Jewish Apocalyptic Eschatology," in *Apocalyptic and the New Testament*, eds. J. Marcus and M. Soards (Sheffield: JSOT Press), 169–90; L. E. Keck, "Paul and Apocalyptic Theology," 229–41; J. L. Martyn, *Galatians*, 98–99 (Martyn notes that the contrast of ages is also evident in the Synoptic Gospels as evidenced in texts such as Matt 12:32). See also the important articles on "righteousness" by E. R. Achtemeier, A. Cronbach, and P. J. Achtemeier in *The Interpreter's Dictionary of the Bible*, vol. 4, ed. G. A. Buttrick (Nashville: Abingdon Press, 1990), 80–99.

[9]Cf. Edwin Yamauchi, "Life, Death, and the Afterlife in the Ancient Near East," and Peter G. Bolt, "Life, Death, and the Afterlife in the Greco–Roman World," in *Life in the Face of Death: The Resurrection Message of the New Testament*, ed. R. N. Longenecker (Grand Rapids: Wm. B. Eerdmans Publishing Co., 1998), 21–79. See also Longenecker's insightful introduction to this volume (1–18).

[10]See especially Isa 25:8; 26:19 and Dan 12:2.

[11]The fusion of resurrection with the time of judgment preceding the new aeon occurs throughout the intertestamental scriptures. See, for instance, WisSol. 3:1–19; 14:7; 15:15; 1 Enoch 13:6–14:7; Test. Simeon 6; Test. Levi 18; Test. Judah 25; Test. Zebulun 10; 2 Baruch 30:1–5; 50:1–4; Adam and Eve (Apoc.) 13:1–6. See also Josephus, *Antiq.* 18.1.3; *War* 2.8.14. See also Isa 25:8; 26:19; Ezek 37:1–14; Dan 12:2, 13; 2 Macc 7:9, 14; 12:44; 4 Macc 18:17. For non-canonical texts, see *The Old Testament Pseudepigrapha*, 2 vols., ed. James H. Charlesworth (Garden City, N.Y.: Doubleday, 1983–85).

[12]Richard Bauckham, "Life, Death, and the Afterlife in Second Temple Judaism," in *Life in the Face of Death: The Resurrection Message of the New Testament*, ed. R. N. Longenecker (Grand Rapids: Wm. B. Eerdmans Publishing Co., 1998), 80–95. See also E. Yamauchi, "Life, Death, and the Afterlife," 46–47. Regarding the Essenes and the Qumran community, Yamauchi calls attention to the recent important work of M. Wise, M. Abegg, Jr., and E. Cook, *The Dead Sea Scrolls: A New Translation* (San Francisco: Harper & Row,

In the opening of Galatians, then, Paul not only emphasizes from the beginning of his message that God raised Jesus from the dead (1:1)—an immediate apocalyptic declaration of the new age's dawning—but he also utilizes the distinctive apocalyptic language of "the present age of evil" (1:4b). Here, the temporal nature of Paul's communication becomes more explicit. First, Paul stresses the rescuing work of Jesus Christ.[13] Second, Paul confesses that it is by Christ's self-offering that persons may be delivered out of the "present age of evil" and into the new age that God has promised—the age signaled by the resurrection of Jesus Christ from the dead.

In the next chapter, we will examine the work of Christ more closely. Yet here it is important to note that, in the salutation-exordium, Christ's risen advent and saving work are related integrally to God's commencement of the new age. Through the Risen Christ, Paul receives the authority of apostleship. Moreover, the resurrection not only verifies Christ's identity and work but also indicates that the new time of God's eschatological deliverance has begun. Let us now see where and how Paul continues to relate the Risen Christ to his message to the Galatians.

II. THE RISEN CHRIST AND PAUL'S APOSTLESHIP: GALATIANS 1:11–2:10

Immediately after the salutation-exordium (1:1–10), Paul continues to emphasize God's apocalyptic activity, particularly as it relates to his own apostolic call and ministry (1:11–2:10). He both defends and promotes the eschatological nature of his apostleship[14] by arguing that the true gospel he preaches (1:11; cf. 1:6–9; 2:14) is a gift to him through God's apocalyptic revelation of Jesus Christ (δι' ἀποκαλύψεως 'Ιησοῦ Χριστοῦ; 1:12). Here, Paul's language calls for close attention, for 'Ιησοῦ Χριστοῦ may be interpreted as either an objective or subjective genitive. As a subjective genitive, it is Jesus Christ's revelation to Paul that is the source of Paul's gospel. Nothing more is asserted about the revelation's content at this point. The clause, then, would assert that Paul's gospel was not *from* a man

---

1996). See also Emil Schürer, *A History of the Jewish People in the Time of Jesus Christ*, 2d ed. (Edinburgh: T & T Clark, 1897–98), 2.2.13, 174, 179–81 and T. H. Gaster, "Resurrection," *IDB*, vol. 4 (Nashville: Abingdon Press, 1990), 39–43.

[13]Cf. Rom 12:2; 1 Cor 1:20; 2:6, 8; 3:18–19; 10:11; 2 Cor 4:4. See also Betz, *Galatians*, 42, n. 58; Longenecker, *Galatians*, 8–9.

[14]See especially George Lyons, *Pauline Autobiography*, 136, and B. R. Gaventa, "Galatians 1 and 2: Autobiography as Paradigm," *Novum Testamentum* 28 (1986): 309–26, who show that Paul's autobiographical narrative in Galatians 1–2 serves as a paradigm for the Galatians' own faithfulness.

(παρὰ ἀνθρώπου) or human teaching (οὔτε ἐδιδάχθην) but was "by (διά) a revelation *from* Jesus Christ."[15]

Rendering Ἰησοῦ Χριστοῦ as a subjective genitive makes sense logically by furnishing the fitting antitheses to the preceding clauses. But if Paul intended such a precise contrast regarding the source and means of his gospel here, one must wonder why Paul did not make the comparison more explicit with prepositions such as παρά or ἀπό. Furthermore, as we will see below, God is characteristically the source of an "apocalypse." The context of Paul's statement also suggests that interpreting Ἰησοῦ Χριστοῦ as an objective genitive is equally—if not more—persuasive,[16] for in a following verse Paul states plainly that God was pleased "to apocalypse (reveal) his son to me (or in me), in order that I might preach him among the Gentiles" (1:16). With an objective genitive in 1:12, then, Paul is asserting that Jesus Christ is the content of God's apocalyptic revelation to him. Thus God is both the source and revealer of Paul's gospel, and Jesus Christ is the content of this revelation and the gospel itself.

Either way, Paul states that Christ was revealed to him (or in him) and this revelation was in accordance with God's will. Moreover, the one who is revealed (or who is the revealer)—Jesus Christ—is none other than God's Son (1:16; 4:4), the Messiah of God whom God raised from the dead (1:1). This affirmation has far-reaching implications and consequences for Paul and his hearers, some of which are immediately apparent.

Regarding the origin and character of Paul's apostleship described in Gal 1:1, 11–16, for instance, Paul declares boldly that his gospel originates in God's revelation to him of the risen Christ. It is significant that Paul uses the word "apocalypse" twice in this opening portion of his argument dealing specifically with the source and nature of his apostleship. It occurs in close succession, first as a noun in 1:12 (ἀποκαλύψεως) and then as a verb in 1:16 (ἀποκαλύψαι).[17] The repetition indicates that Paul's word selection is not accidental. Furthermore, had he wanted to express simply the idea of a revelation, sign, or new understanding, he could have used other common Greek words such as ἐπίδειξις or σημαίνειν.[18] These terms were commonly used in the Hellenistic world to express a revelation from a god.[19] Instead, Paul chose to use noun and verb forms of ἀποκαλύπτειν which, while not foreign to the Hellenistic world, is used frequently and richly in the Greek translation of the Old Testament. The

---

[15]Cf. Longenecker, *Galatians*, 24; Oepke, "ἀποκαλύπτω," 583; and Heinrich Schlier, *Der Brief an die Galater*, KEK 7 (Göttingen: Vandenhoeck & Ruprecht, 1962), 47.

[16]See especially Burton, *Galatians*, 39–43; Betz, *Galatians*, 62–63; and Bruce, *Galatians*, 89.

[17]See also 2:2 and 3:23 and the discussion below.

[18]Oepke, "ἀποκαλύπτω," 566.

[19]Ibid., 570.

use of this theologically significant term would not have escaped the attention of Greek-speaking listeners who knew the Jewish scriptures.

One common use of ἀποκαλύπτειν in the Septuagint refers to the removal of a physical covering from a tangible object[20] or person.[21] However, the word is also used often in reference to particular acts and uncoverings of God. It is used to describe God's self-revelation during Israel's deliverance from Egypt[22] and God's establishment of a new covenant with David.[23] Also, according to the Septuagint, God revealed himself when calling Samuel[24] and revealed his will visibly to Balaam.[25] God also revealed his word (ῥῆμα and λόγος) to his servants (δοῦλος) Samuel, David, and Daniel.[26] Moreover, through his prophets Amos, Isaiah, Jeremiah, Ezekiel, Daniel, Micah, and Nahum, God revealed instruction (παιδεία)[27] and times of judgment—past, present, and future.[28] In the Old Testament (LXX), God is recurrently the subject of the verb ἀποκαλύπτειν.

When Paul declares to the Galatian Christians that the gospel proclaimed by him is utterly dependent upon God's revelation to (or in) him of God's own son Jesus Christ, he brings to mind other key moments in Israel's history when God made himself and his will known. Thus God's revelatory intervention in Paul's life is solidly within the scriptural testimony of God's character and activity. Paul's declaration also asserts that God is active in the world and in the lives of individuals in the present. Thus any analysis and judgment regarding Paul's apostleship depends finally upon one's understanding and belief in the God of whom the scriptures speak. Could God invade Paul's life in the way Paul describes? The thunderous answer from the Old Testament is, "Yes, God could." The testimony of Paul is, "The Living God did." Paul asserts that his

---

[20]Cf. Gen 8:13 where Noah removes the ark's covering.

[21]Cf. Exod 20:26; Lev 18:6–19; 20:11, 17–21; Deut 27:20; Ruth 3:4–7; 2 Sam 6:20.

[22]Cf. 1 Sam (1 Kgs) 2:27; 2 Sam (2 Kgs) 22:16; Isa 52:10; 53:1.

[23]2 Sam (2 Kgs) 7:27.

[24]1 Sam 3:21 in the Septuagint reads: καὶ προσέθετο κύριος δηλωθῆναι ἐν Σηλωμ ὅτι ἀπεκαλύφθη κύριος πρὸς Σαμουηλ καὶ ἐπιστεύθη Σαμουηλ προφήτης γενέσθαι τῷ κυρίῳ εἰς πάντα Ισραηλ ἀπ᾽ ἄκρων τῆς γῆς καὶ ἕως ἄκρων. In the Masoretic text we find: וַיֹּסֶף יְהוָה לְהֵרָאֹה בְשִׁלֹה כִּי־נִגְלָה יְהוָה אֶל־שְׁמוּאֵל בְּשִׁלוֹ בִּדְבַר יְהוָה. Whereas Samuel's revelation comes "by the word of the Lord" in the Masoretic text, the Septuagint asserts that "the Lord was "apocalypsed" to Samuel" and this is, in part, the basis for Samuel's acceptance and popularity as a prophet for the Lord.

[25]See Num 22:31; 24:4, 16.

[26]Cf. 1 Sam (1 Kgs) 3:7–10; 2 Sam (2 Kgs) 7:27; and Dan 10:1. See also 1 Sam (1 Kgs) 9:15; 20:2; 20:13; 22:8; 22:17.

[27]Cf. Amos 3:7; Dan 2:19, 22, 28–29, 30, 47. See also Pss 118:18; 97:2; 28:9.

[28]Cf. Isa 3:17; 47:2; Jer 11:20; 13:26; 20:12; Lam 2:14; 4:22; Ezek 13:14; 16:36–37, 57; 21:29; 22:10; 23:18, 29; Dan 11:35 (see also Zech 13:9); Hos 2:12; 7:1; Mic 1:6; Nah 2:8; 3:5.

apostleship is a direct consequence of God's self-revealing activity through which the living Christ becomes known.

God's unveiling of Jesus Christ to Paul—in whatever manner it occurred—is the genesis of Paul's gospel (1:12) and the impetus behind Paul's preaching (1:16).[29] It is the basis of Paul's apostolic commissioning and authority. Paul also states, however, that since God's initial revelation of Jesus Christ to him, God has continued to direct Paul's way by revelation (2:2).[30] Because of a disclosure of God, Paul went to Jerusalem after 14 years of preaching the gospel in order to meet with other apostles. There, Paul and Barnabas received the right hand of fellowship and a commission to preach the gospel to the Gentiles and remember the poor (2:9–10).

The foundational importance to Paul of God's revelation of the risen Jesus Christ and God's ongoing unveiling activity is evident in this early portion of Paul's epistle. Yet Paul's reliance upon this central tenet of God's apocalyptic activity continues throughout the remainder of his message to the Galatians. In the same way that Paul's autobiography in Galatians stands upon God's revelation of the Risen Christ, Paul continues to set other points of his argument upon the stasis that God has revealed Jesus the Christ who is risen from the dead and so has inaugurated God's apocalyptic age.

III. THE RISEN CHRIST AND THE TRUTH OF THE GOSPEL: GALATIANS 2:11–21

In the summation of his controversy with Peter in Antioch (2:11–21), Paul gives a brief exposition of his gospel (2:15–21) which is intelligible only in light of Jesus' resurrection and the dawning of God's eschatological age. To begin with, Paul appeals to the common beginning and earlier agreement that he and Peter had shared. In light of Jesus Christ, they had come to believe that it was impossible to be made righteous (or justified; δικαιοῦται) through the Jewish law (2:15–16). Righteousness was possible only by means of faith in Jesus Christ (2:16b).[31] But, Paul reasons, since he and Peter came to hold this

---

[29]In 1:15, the implied subject is God, which is indicated by the strong textual support where scribes undoubtedly sought to make the subject explicit.

[30]As we will see below, Paul also stresses God's present revealing activity of directing the faithful by means of the Spirit.

[31]For discussions on the old and still debated question as to whether or not Ἰησοῦ Χριστοῦ is best interpreted as an objective or subjective genitive, see especially Richard B. Hays, *The Faith of Jesus Christ*; George E. Howard, "On the Faith of Christ," *Harvard Theological Review* 60 (1967): 459–65; Sam K. Williams, "Again pistis Christou," *CBQ* 49 (1987): 431–47; Morna D. Hooker, "Pistis Christou," *NTS* 35 (1989): 321–42; Arland J. Hultgren, "The pistis Christou Formulation in Paul," *Novum Testamentum*, 22 (1980): 248–63; J.D.G. Dunn, *Galatians*, 138–39. See also Ian G. Wallis, *The Faith of Jesus Christ in Early Christian Traditions*, SNTSMS 84 (Cambridge: Cambridge University Press,

tenet, they must now be sinners under the law, for they have rejected the law's authority. Consequently, Jesus must be an agent of sin (2:17). But to this premise and conclusion Paul issues a resounding, "No!" Paul's point, in fact, is just the opposite. One becomes a transgressor of God's will by insisting on obedience to the law (2:18), and this is the basis for Paul's declaration that through the law he died to the law in order to live for God (2:19). Paul maintains further that in dying to the law he has become a sharer in Christ's death and a participant in Christ's ongoing life (2:19–20). Paul writes, "it is no longer I who live, but Christ who lives in me" (2:20). Such an assertion makes sense only if Jesus the Crucified lives (ζῇ is present tense), which is the point Paul made in the communication's opening statement (1:1) and has reasserted since (cf. 1:1, 3, 10, 16; 2:17).

Paul's use of the perfect tense verb form of σταυρόω is also revealing at this point. We will examine Paul's emphasis on the Crucified Christ and the gospel in the next chapter, but here it is significant to observe that Christ's ongoing life is as the Crucified One. The resurrection has not obliterated Jesus' identity as the Crucified. That is, even though Jesus' crucifixion is in the past, it is still in force. This would be true whether or not Jesus was risen from the dead, given the perfect passive verb συνεσταύρωμαι (2:19). But Paul has already declared that Jesus is risen (1:1), that he himself is a servant of this crucified Christ who lives (1:10), and that this crucified and risen Son of God was revealed to him (1:16). Paul has also used the apocalyptic concept of living for God (2:19) to describe this new life he now experiences in Christ.[32] For Paul, then, the truth of the gospel is that the risen One is forever the Crucified and that righteousness is available only through trust in him. Moreover, faithfulness requires a vital, participatory relationship with the Risen Crucified Christ through the sharing of Christ's suffering. These components lie at the heart of Paul's gospel truth and they are reiterated and developed further in his communication, as we will see.[33] First, however, Paul elaborates upon God's eschatological revelation of the Risen Christ by turning to the Galatians' own experiences of the Spirit of Christ.

1995), 124–25, and Brian Dodd, "Romans 1:17—A *Crux Interpretum* for the Πίστις Χριστοῦ Debate?," *JBL* 114 (1995): 470–73.

[32]See Martyn, *Galatians*, 257, 570–72.

[33]Some scholars contend that 2:15–21 fulfills the requirements of a propositio. Cf. Betz, *Galatians*, 114. But see Kennedy, *New Testament Interpretation*, 148.

IV. THE RISEN CHRIST AND THE ADVENT OF THE SPIRIT:
GALATIANS 3:1–5

In 3:1–5, Paul reminds the Galatians of their shared faith in the crucified and risen Christ.[34] He also calls to mind the gift of the Spirit that ensued from their faith in Christ, a faith that came through Paul's proclamation of the gospel (3:1–5). Paul's preaching, then, was not about a Christ whose death had no significance (2:21). Neither was his proclamation about a Christ that no longer lived (1:1, 3, 10, 16; 2:20). Rather, Paul's clear public pronouncement—which the Galatians accepted—was of the living Jesus Christ who had been crucified (again, in 3:1 Paul uses the perfect tense of the verb σταυρόω)[35] and who now lives as the Crucified Christ. Moreover, it was through their faith in Jesus Christ that God supplied to them the Spirit and worked miracles among them. That is, the Galatians experienced the miraculous life-changing power of God not through the law but through faith in the Crucified Christ. This is the true gospel which Paul contrasts with those who want to pervert the gospel of Christ (1:7) and who are leading the Galatians astray (βασκαίνω; 3:1) through Torah legalism (3:2–5). Not surprisingly, Paul proceeds to discuss the significance of the law in light of the Risen Crucified Christ.

V. THE RISEN CHRIST AND THE LAW:
GALATIANS 3:6–4:7

In the careful argument regarding the superiority of faith over the temporary and inferior status of the law (3:1–29), Paul's position continues to stand upon the premise that God raised Jesus from the dead (1:1). More than simply refer to Christ in the present tense (3:16), Paul contends that it is through faith in Jesus—the risen Christ and Son of God—that believers gain fellowship with Jesus the Christ and God the Father (3:26). Moreover, it is through this trust that believers obtain a new and right way of relating to one another (3:28) and to God as Abraham's true offspring and heirs of God's promise (3:29).[36]

---

[34]Paul's account of his conflict with Peter in 2:11–14 parallels this portion of address to the Galatians. Paul encourages the Galatians, as he did even Peter before them, to remember and reclaim the truth of the gospel.

[35]See also 1 Cor 1:23 and 2:2 where Paul again uses perfect passive participles of σταυρόω with the clear implication that Jesus Christ lives.

[36]Although Paul uses the phrase ἐν Χριστῷ six times in Galatians (1:22; 2:4, 17; 3:14, 26, 28; 5:6), 3:26 is the only occurrence in Galatians—or in Paul's seven undisputed letters—where the phrase follows πίστις. Elsewhere in Galatians, Paul uses the genitive Ἰησοῦ Χριστοῦ with πίστις (2:16; 3:22). Here in 3:26, Paul is not qualifying or limiting faith. Rather, he is asserting that through faith and baptism believers enter into the sphere of

It is also evident in his discussion of the role of the law in 3:15–29 that Paul has in mind here a temporal perspective that includes three periods of time, the last of which stands as an apocalyptic climax. There is the time before the law from Abraham (Adam) to Moses (i.e., 3:17), the time of the law from Moses to Christ (i.e., 3:24), and the time of Christ after the law (i.e., 3:25–26). Paul also makes the startling declaration that the people of God "were held under the law, kept under restraint for the destined faithfulness to be revealed" (εἰς τὴν μέλλουσαν πίστιν ἀποκαλυφθῆναι; 3:23).[37] As in 1:12–16, Paul uses the language of "apocalypse" and asserts that it is God who has revealed the faithfulness God desires. We will examine more thoroughly what Paul means by God's revelation of faithfulness in the next chapter. Here it is sufficient to observe that Paul relates it to the time of Christ's coming. It is also important to observe that the faithfulness that is both revealed and made possible in Christ is contrasted with the faithfulness that is guided by the law.[38] To make these points unmistakable, Paul declares in the following verse (3:24a) that "the law was our tutor (παιδαγωγὸς) until Christ came" (or "for the purpose of Christ's coming").[39] In this way, Paul contends that the availability of trusting faithfulness has now come fully and that God's people are no longer under the custodianship of the law (3:25).[40] That is, the faithfulness of which Paul speaks is that which Christ exhibited and which is accessible for God's people through a relationship with Christ by means of faith in him. Thus Paul avers that now "*in* Christ Jesus you are all sons of God" (3:26). In this way, Paul argues that the law has served its purpose as a tutor and custodian for the people of God until the coming of the Messiah. With the Christ's advent, though, the law's essential function and authority have ended.[41] The coming of Christ marks the dawning of a radically new age.[42]

Christ. Christians are believers who live in the realm of Christ's dominion and have close fellowship with the living Jesus and one another (3:27–28).

[37]While this prepositional phrase may be interpreted as temporal (cf. NRSV), I take it to be purposive (Cf. Rom 8:18; πρὸς τὴν μέλλουσαν δόξαν ἀποκαλυφθῆναι).

[38]Paul makes an extended contrast between faithfulness directed by the law (1:13–14) and faithfulness directed by Christ (1:15–2:21) through his autobiography.

[39]I take εἰς Χριστόν (3:24) to be both temporal and purposive.

[40]Paul's use of the temporal adverb οὐκέτι also highlights his emphasis upon two periods of time: the time of the law and the time of the Christ.

[41]Note, also, that Paul's more positive view of the law here (as in Rom 7:12, 23) is contrasted with his earlier negative assessment where he compares the law to a jailor holding prisoners (3:22–23). On Paul's view of the law in Galatians, see J. D. G. Dunn, "The Theology of Galatians: The Issue of Covenantal Nomism," *Pauline Theology*, vol. 1, J. M. Bassler, ed. (Minneapolis: Fortress, 1991), 125–46; J. L. Martyn, "Events in Galatia: Modified Covenantal Nomism versus God's Invasion of the Cosmos in the Singular Gospel: A Response to J. D. G. Dunn and B. R. Gaventa," ibid, 160–79. On Paul's view of the law more generally, see especially Douglas Moo, "Paul and the Law in the Last Ten Years,"

In 4:1–7, Paul again stresses a time of change when he turns to the matters of adoption and freedom in Christ. Here, building upon the earlier figures regarding the predicament of God's people under the law as jailer (3:22) and tutor (3:24), Paul compares people under the law to fatherless heirs awaiting the designated time of maturity when they may receive their inheritance (4:1–2). The time of God's choosing has now come in the revelation of Jesus the Christ. As Paul puts it, "when the fullness of time (τὸ πλήρωμα τοῦ χρόνου) came, God sent forth his son, born of woman, born under the law, in order that he might ransom those who were under the law" (4:4–5a). That is, the followers of Christ have received their inheritance of freedom from their guardian, the law (cf. 1:4). Furthermore, as heirs, they have received from God the Spirit of his Son Jesus (4:6–7). Through the Spirit—not the law—believers are in direct communication with God (4:6) and this is a clear indication that a new time has begun.

Paul's emphasis on the ages in this discussion of a Christian's relation to God builds upon his early premise that God has revealed the new age, the inauguration of which is signaled by the resurrection of Jesus from the dead. Thus the "fullness of time" (4:4) corresponds to the present time (1:4) and highlights Paul's view of a transition in the ages. Moreover, God's gift of "the Spirit of his Son" (4:6) relates to Paul's foregoing emphasis on the Galatians' reception and experience of the Spirit (3:2) even as it points ahead to Paul's forthcoming emphasis on the life of faithfulness lived in the Spirit (5:5–6:10) in this eschatological day.[43] Paul not only means that it is through trust in the living Christ that the gift of the Spirit comes, but he also means that Christ and the Spirit are indicators that the eschatological age has arrived. Both the "fullness of time" and God's gift of the Spirit are apocalyptic concepts.[44] Moreover, they are based on Paul's decisive affirmations that the living Christ has appeared (1:1; 1:4, 12, 16; 4:4) and that Christ's advent signals the arrival of a new dimension of time (4:4). In the present day, God's people are to relate to God through the Spirit of his Son rather than through the law. Now is the age of liberation for the people of God.

Scottish Journal of Theology 40 (1987): 287–307; E. P. Sanders, *Paul, the Law, and the Jewish People* (Minneapolis: Fortress, 1983), 70–76.

[42]On Jewish Messianism and the apocalyptic age, see Henning Reventlow, ed., *Eschatology in the Bible and in Jewish and Christian Tradition* (Sheffield: Sheffield Academic Press, 1997); Craig A. Evans and Peter W. Flint, eds., *Eschatology, Messianism, and the Dead Sea Scrolls* (Grand Rapids: Wm. B. Eerdmans Publishing Co., 1997).

[43]On Paul and the Spirit, see especially Gordon D. Fee, *God's Empowering Presence: The Holy Spirit in the Letters of Paul* (Peabody, Mass.: Hendrickson, 1994).

[44]Cf. J. C. Beker, *Paul the Apostle*, 145–46, 245. See also Gal 3:2 and Ezek 11:14–21; 36:22–32; Rom 8:15; and 1 Cor 2:12.

VI. THE RISEN CHRIST AND THE LIBERATION OF FAITH: GALATIANS 4:8–5:12

In an expression of personal concern for the Galatians (4:8–20), Paul reminds them of their earlier expectancy and hope for receiving the living Christ in person (4:14)! He also reminds them of their first encounter with one another. Although Paul's physical condition tempted (πειρασμὸν) them to reject him and his message, they received him as an angel or messenger of God (ἄγγελον θεοῦ)—as Christ Jesus himself. That is, they treated Paul with the respect and honor that they would have given to God's personal envoy or God's own living Christ, Jesus.

Now, it is possible that the Galatians' initial hospitality was motivated by their pagan beliefs in the consequences of welcoming or rejecting gods or their messengers who visited the earth incognito.[45] Nevertheless, when Paul brings to his listeners' remembrance their early desire to please God and to welcome God's emissaries, he also reminds them again (cf. 3:1–5) of their earlier trust in God's presence and activity through faith in Jesus Christ. Moreover, he reminds them that, along with their acceptance of Paul and his gospel, they had fully embraced the necessity of self-sacrificing service in the manner of Jesus Christ. They would have even given Paul their own eyes (4:14–15)! In these ways, Paul tactfully implies that they were more in line with the true gospel of Christ in the infancy of their faith than in their new-found legalistic religion that resembles their old pagan rituals and bondage (4:8–11). Thus their turning away from the true gospel perplexes Paul (4:20). Still, he continues to hope that they will again become faithful to Jesus Christ and be liberated in Christ as Paul is now (4:12) and as they were earlier apart from Torah observance (4:14–15). Here, too, Paul expresses a deep desire that Christ be formed in them (4:19)—a desire that assumes a Christ who lives and who may live within them (cf. 2:20).[46] Paul also points to the heavenly Jerusalem of apocalyptic hope and the freedom promised to its inhabitants (4:26).[47]

---

[45]See, for instance, Heb 13:2. On the popularity of this code of hospitality in Phrygia in the province of Galatia, see especially Ben Witherington, *Grace in Galatia: A Commentary on St. Paul's Letter to the Galatians* (Grand Rapids: Wm. B. Eerdmans Publishing Co., 1998), 311–12. See also Dunn, *Galatians*, 234–35.

[46]The word μορφωθῇ occurs nowhere else in the NT or LXX, thus its precise meaning is not entirely clear. In other writings, the verb often means "to take on form" (especially as an embryo in a womb). Paul's passive use of the verb stresses both that Christ's form is received and that Christ will be formed in the faithful to the extent that Christ lives in them. Paul also uses the noun μορφός in the Christ Hymn (Phil 2:6–7), which emphasizes Christ's self-sacrificing act of taking the form of a δοῦλος to serve as Redeemer. For a thorough discussion of this matter, see Burton, *Galatians*, 248–49.

[47]J. L. Martyn, *Galatians*, 440–41.

Here, then, in this portion of his address to the Galatians, before exhorting the Galatians to embrace the benefits that only a trusting relationship with the living Christ can bring through the power of the Spirit (5:16, 22–26), Paul discusses the freedom that the Galatians have in Christ (5:1–15). Again, Paul builds his case upon the foundational premise that Jesus Christ lives, for God raised him from the dead. For instance, of what use is it for Paul to speak of advantages coming from a Christ who does not live (5:2)? Or what reason is there for Paul's confidence in the Lord, if the Lord Jesus who was crucified is not risen (5:10)?[48] Again, why would Paul warn the Galatians that seeking righteousness through the law would annul or make ineffective (καταργέω) their relationship with Christ (5:4) if Christ was not alive?

Christ's resurrection confirms Paul's central point in this portion of his communication that it is Christ who liberates persons from legalism's "yoke of slavery" (5:1). This becomes particularly clear when Paul responds rhetorically to a real or hypothesized charge that he is preaching a gospel of circumcision (5:11). If that is the case, Paul wonders what motivation his opponents (who evidently preach such a gospel) could possibly have for their continued persecution of him, for he would be their ally, not an adversary. The mere thought of yielding his gospel in this way (cf. 2:4–5), however, elicits from Paul the immediate counterpoint that such a surrender would remove the "scandal of the cross" (5:6; τὸ σκάνδαλον τοῦ σταυροῦ). In short, the scandal is that the Messiah of God could be crucified (3:13) and die under the judgment of God's law (cf. Deut 21:23). From the Jewish perspective, if Jesus was crucified then he could not be the Messiah. Thus Jesus' death alone does nothing to alter the verdict of the law and religious leaders who condemned Jesus and his message. God's reversal of that verdict, however, through the resurrection of Jesus Christ from the dead not only overturns the authority of the law and religious leaders but also verifies the scandal of the cross.[49] That is, the crucified and risen Jesus is the Christ (1:1). Moreover, if the law condemned the Christ of God to be crucified, then God's resurrection of Jesus from the dead means that something is quite wrong with the law and with those who trust in it as the basis for being in a right relationship with God. We will examine further in the next chapter the significance of the cross and the law for Paul, but here it is important to note that Jesus' resurrection confirms and clarifies the scandal of the cross and the centrality of the cross to the Christian gospel. Through the Crucified Christ, Christians are freed from the yoke of the law. But they are freed for a new kind of existence. On this note, Paul focuses on the significance of the Risen Crucified Christ for living the Christian life.

---

[48]Paul's frequent use of the term κύριος indicates that Jesus Christ is typically in mind (cf. Gal 1:3, 19; 6:14, 18).

[49]Cousar, *Galatians*, 118.

VII. THE RISEN CHRIST AND THE CHRISTIAN LIFE:
GALATIANS 5:13–6:10

Prior to this point in his argument, Paul has asserted that the two ages are not wholly separate (4:8–20), thus evil and righteousness are both possible during this time between the ages. The first indication of what Beker calls elsewhere in Paul's epistles "the proleptic presence of the new in the old"[50] comes in the salutation-exordium of Galatians at 1:4. Regardless of whether or not this phrase is drawn from an early confession or whether or not Paul has altered any part of the statement,[51] Paul presents the verse using the subjunctive mood of the verb ἐξαιρέω (ἐξέληται)—not the indicative—to describe Christ's rescuing act. That is, in its present form Paul is declaring that Christ gave himself for our sins "in order that he might rescue us out of the present age of evil." In this way, Paul indicates that the deliverance effected by Christ is not yet complete. Paul also leaves open the possibility that persons might not be so delivered. Thus, in Paul's view, the new age of God's complete rule which is characteristic of Jewish apocalyptic must not yet be totally in place. This is evident also where Paul uses the subjunctive εὐαγγελίζηται in 1:8 to warn of impending condemnation upon anyone who might yet preach a gospel contrary to the true gospel Paul proclaims (2:5). Such rebelliousness would not be possible in the Jewish apocalyptic age to come.

Later in Galatians, Paul adds that there was a time before God sent Christ and Christ's Spirit when persons were "in bondage to beings that by nature are not gods" (4:8). There is also a time after God's apocalyptic activity of revealing Christ (1:1, 4, 12, 16), the Spirit (3:2; 4:6), and faithfulness (3:23) in which God may be known (4:9) and in which self-sacrificing service in the manner of Jesus Christ is a reality (4:9–19).[52] It is now possible to be in relation with God as a son or daughter (4:7), but God's revealing acts have not yet precluded the possibility of "turning back again to the weak and beggarly elemental spirits" or being enslaved to them (4:9). It is still possible for persons to use other persons for their own advantage or purpose (4:17).

---

[50]J. C. Beker, *Paul the Apostle*, 146. For an insightful and succinct summary of this in-between time in Paul's apocalyptic perspective, see P. J. Achtemeier, *Romans*, 6–9. See also his article "An Apocalyptic Shift in Early Christian Tradition: Reflections on Some Canonical Evidence," *CBQ* 45 (1983): 234–37.

[51]There is no way to know whether or not Paul has altered what appears to be a received confessional statement in 1:4, as Paul has evidently done in Phil 2:8b. If Paul is combating a type of Christian triumphalism in Galatia that does not recognize the cross's significance, however, the use of the subjunctive mood, rather than the indicative, would be instructive.

[52]See also 5:13–15.

Thus, whereas the new age in Jewish apocalyptic excludes the possibility of evil's continuance—a time for which Paul also hopes (cf. 5:5; 6:15), Paul views the present evil age as still current and interrelated with it. Thus there is now a new and present time in which the righteousness God desires for God's people is possible in and through Christ and the Spirit of Christ (cf. 2:16, 21; 3:11, 24; 5:4–5, 22–25; 6:14–18). But it is also possible to live life in opposition to God and God's purposes, to persist in unrighteousness and evil (cf. 3:10; 4:8–11; 5:1–4, 7, 13, 15–21, 26; 6:8, 13).[53]

In Galatians, the present time of evil is a time of conflict and struggle, which is a component of Jewish apocalyptic thought.[54] But the present time is also an age of deliverance. Paul identifies this clash of the ages in the opening of his communication when he refers to Christ's rescuing act (1:4). It is significant to observe, however, that Paul does not mention "the present age of evil" (1:4b) until after he has asserted God's invasive act of raising Jesus from the dead (1:1) and affirmed the rescuing work of Jesus Christ (1:4a).

For Paul in Galatians, God has broken into "the present age of evil" so that it is now possible to receive grace and peace from God the Father (1:3). God has dealt with "our sins" through the self-sacrifice of the Lord Jesus Christ, thus deliverance is now receivable (1:4). All this is cause for celebration (1:5). It is also cause, however, for carefully considering one's relation to the gospel of what "God the Father and our Lord Jesus Christ" have done through this assault on the present time of evil (1:7–9). Now is a time of apocalyptic warfare, and the followers of Jesus are engaged in combat.[55] It is in the context of this temporal framework, then, that Paul discusses the Christian life (5:13–6:10).

Paul emphasizes this cosmic struggle and its significance for discipleship at various points in his message to the Galatians. First, Paul continues this concept by underscoring his personal struggles with antagonistic human powers that are set against him and the true gospel (1:6–10; 2:4–5, 11–14; 3:1; 6:17) and by relating human activity directly to the governance of certain cosmic powers—either the elemental spirits of the universe (4:3, 8–9) and Flesh (5:17–21) or the Spirit of God's Son (4:6; 5:5, 16, 18, 22–6:10).

As elsewhere in Paul's undisputed epistles, "flesh" (σάρξ) in Galatians often signifies either a present material existence that is in a right relation with God through Jesus Christ (cf. 1:16; 2:20; 4:13) or an orientation bent against

---

[53]Martyn, *Galatians*, 99.

[54]See M. C. de Boer, "Paul and Jewish Apocalyptic Eschatology," 174–75; Klaus Koch, *The Rediscovery of Apocalyptic: A Polemical Work on a Neglected Area of Biblical Studies and Its Damaging Effects on Theology and Philosophy*, Studies in Biblical Theology 2/22 (London: SCM Press, 1972), 28–33; J. C. Beker, *Paul the Apostle*, 135–36.

[55]Martyn, *Galatians*, 100–01.

God and God's purposes (cf. 3:3; 4:23, 29; 5:13, 16–17, 19–20, 24; 6:8, 12–13). The "Spirit," on the other hand, is Christ's Spirit (4:6) and it is opposed to the self-interested ways and works of the flesh (5:19–21). In this way, Paul frequently uses the terms Spirit and flesh to describe opposing forces at work in the cosmos. The terms also bear, however, a temporal connotation so that life governed by self–interest—the flesh—is characteristic of the "old age" and life ruled by the Spirit of Christ is characteristic of the "new age." The Christian life is the latter, and it is possible because of God's act in Christ.

This leads us to the second and most significant way that Paul stresses this cosmic struggle in Galatians. Paul locates God's decisive victory in this struggle as Jesus' self-offering and resurrection from the dead. From the beginning of his message, Paul declares that, in Christ, God has begun the conflict with the "present age of evil." God has done this through Christ's self-giving on behalf of our sins. Moreover, God has launched a new time of deliverance by raising the self-sacrificing Jesus from the dead. In the salutation-exordium, then, Christ's self-offering is organically related to Jesus' resurrection from the dead and his saving activity.[56]

The present struggle described in Galatians is the consequence of God's act in Christ to combat rebellious flesh and its ways. As Paul puts it, the Lord Jesus Christ "gave himself for our sins to deliver us from the present age of evil" (1:4). The Lord's act of deliverance, then, is an event (τοῦ δόντος is aorist) that was initiated in accordance with God's will and constitutes an assault against the present evil age. It is also a saving event for Christ's true followers who trust in him, have received his Spirit, and who bear the Spirit's fruit (5:22f). The righteousness that God desires is possible through faith in the Risen Christ.

VIII. THE RISEN CHRIST AND GOD'S NEW CREATION: GALATIANS 6:11–18

Finally, in the closing of Galatians (6:14–15), Paul focuses his hearers' attention once more upon the Risen crucified Christ. First, he does this by stressing that it is the living Christ who has rescued Paul from a life lived under the dominion of a world that is pitted against the ways of Christ (6:14; cf. 1:4). Here, as in 2:20 and 3:1, Paul's use of the perfect tense of "crucify" is most intelligible by means of Jesus' resurrection. Second, Paul declares that "neither circumcision counts for anything, nor uncircumcision, but a new act of

---

[56]See also R. B. Hays, *The Faith of Jesus Christ*, 256, where he writes that "in Galatians the kerygma of the cross (3:1, 13) is united in an organic fashion with the motifs of pre-existence and incarnation (4:4–5)." We would add that the message of the cross is also bound inseparably with the resurrected Christ.

creation" (6:15). On one hand, Paul leaves it to his hearers to draw their own conclusions about what he means by καινὴ κτίσις. But, given his early and continued apocalyptic affirmations epitomized in the declaration that God raised Jesus from the dead, there can be no doubt that the resurrection of Jesus Christ and its significance as the harbinger of the apocalyptic age are solidly congruent with Paul's terminology here.[57] With this declaration, Paul's emphasis on the emergence of God's apocalyptic age comes into sharp focus. Here in 6:15, Paul presents in striking terms the antithesis of "the present age of evil" (1:4).[58] Now is the time of the "καινὴ κτίσις," which may mean "new creation" or the "new creative activity (of God)" (6:15).[59] Either way, the phrase "καινὴ κτίσις" is solidly apocalyptic.[60] Moreover, it is a climactic recapitulation of his apocalyptic perspective, for here at the end of Galatians he makes the first explicit contrast between the old "world" (6:14) and the "καινὴ κτίσις" (6:15). In this way, Paul reemphasizes once again that a new apocalyptic era has dawned and the Risen Christ signals its beginning (1:1). The expression "καινὴ κτίσις" forms the fitting and memorable capstone to Paul's message to the Galatian Christians regarding the significance of the Risen Christ.

IX. THE RISEN CHRIST IN GALATIANS

Throughout Galatians, Paul states explicitly and affirms implicitly that Jesus Christ is risen and lives. His message to the Galatians depends upon God's revelation or apocalypse of the Risen Christ to him, a point that Paul stresses in the opening period of his communication and carries throughout this letter-speech. God's apocalypse of the risen Jesus Christ is foundational in Paul's arguments for the legitimacy of his apostleship (1:11–2:10) and the necessity of justification by faith (2:11–21). So, too, when he appeals to the

---

[57]From a rhetorical perspective, it is also of interest to note that, in the same way that an enthymeme is preferred to a straight syllogism for its ability to engage the mind of the listener in providing the missing premise, so, too, Paul's argument throughout Galatians gains persuasive force by allowing the listeners to provide the premise necessary for Paul's conclusion. In this particular case, the law (typified by circumcision) is inadequate because God has overturned the law's verdict (3:13) by God's new act in creation of raising Jesus Christ from the dead.

[58]J. L. Martyn, *Galatians*, 98; idem, "Apocalyptic Antinomies," 412.

[59]There is some discussion over whether κτίσις is best interpreted as a verbal noun or a concrete noun. I am peruaded by Burton's argument that the term's use in 2 Cor 5:17 is clearly as a concrete noun; however, the antithetical context of περιτομή and ἀκροβυστία here in Gal 6:15 is parallel to 1 Cor 7:19 and Gal 5:6 where the second component of this antithesis is an active or verbal noun. See Burton, *Galatians*, 356. See also Betz, *Galatians*, 319–20, n. 79; Dunn, *Galatians*, 342–43.

[60]Cf. Isa 42:9; 43:18–19; 65:17; 66:22; Rom 5:17–21; etc. See also J. C. Beker, *Paul the Apostle*, 101–102, 151–52; and Betz, *Galatians*, 319, n. 79.

Galatians' own experience of receiving the Spirit (3:1–5) and expresses hope for their return to faith (4:8–20) and practice of faithfulness (5:13–6:10), Paul affirms that Christ lives. Again, in his critical arguments for the superiority of trust in Jesus Christ over trust in the law (3:6–4:7) and regarding the nature of Christian freedom (5:1–26), Paul's case depends on God's act of raising Christ from the dead. This has become evident through attention to the rhetorical cord that Paul identified at the message's beginning and climaxed forcefully at its end.

Clearly, Paul's assertion that God raised Jesus Christ from the dead continues to impact his argument well beyond his singular, explicit reference to it in 1:1. Still, there is more to Paul's resurrection gospel than his confidence in the risen Christ. As Paul also stresses in the opening of his communication and maintains throughout his discourse, God has inaugurated the apocalyptic age in this act of raising Jesus from the dead, and the people of God are invited to participate in it (6:15–16). That participation, though, bears a certain character, for it is as the Crucified that Jesus lives. Let us, then, examine what Paul has to say in Galatians about the significance of Jesus Christ who has been crucified.

CHAPTER SIX

THE RHETORICAL CORD OF THE
CRUCIFIED CHRIST

Students of Galatians may differ on many points regarding this letter-speech—such as the epistle's place of origin, date of composition, and rhetorical and epistolary characteristics—but few deny the centrality of Jesus' crucifixion. Perhaps nowhere else does Paul present such a comprehensive view of Jesus' death and its significance. Not surprisingly, this dimension of Galatians has received much attention over the years.[1] The aim of this chapter, however, is not so much to review the wealth of scholarship on this matter as it is to trace the way in which Paul introduces and develops in Galatians the theme of Jesus' crucifixion. We will also consider Paul's view of how Jesus' death effects Christian faithfulness.

In the previous chapter, we saw that God's revelation of the risen Jesus forms the stasis for Paul's argument regarding his apostleship (1:11–2:10). It is the one point upon which everything else depends. We also considered some ways in which the rhetorical cord of Jesus' resurrection is present in Galatians as a continuous sub-structural theme. In this chapter, we will examine the more

---

[1]Along with the many good commentaries on Galatians cited above, see also C. Andresen and G. Klein, eds., *Theologia Crucis – Signum Crucis: Festschrift für Erich Dinkler zum 70 Geburtstag* (Tübingen: J.C.B. Mohr, 1979), especially "Sundenverstandnis und theologia crucis bei Paulus" by G. Klein (249–82), and "The Crucified World: The Enigma of Galatians 6:14," by P. S. Minear (395–407); C. H. Cosgrove, *The Cross and the Spirit: A Study in the Argument and Theology of Galatians* (Macon: Mercer University, 1988); C. B. Cousar, *A Theology of the Cross: The Death of Jesus in the Pauline Letters* (Minneapolis: Fortress, 1990); J. D. G. Dunn, "Paul's Understanding of the Death of Jesus as Sacrifice," *Sacrifice and Redemption: Durham Essays in Theology*, ed. S. W. Sykes (Cambridge: Cambridge University Press, 1991), 35–56; idem, *The Theology of Paul's Letter to the Galatians*, New Testament Theology (Cambridge: Cambridge University, 1993), 29–33; R. B. Hays, *The Faith of Jesus Christ*; idem, "Crucified With Christ: A Synthesis of the Theology of 1 and 2 Thessalonians, Philemon, Philippians, and Galatians," *Pauline Theology, Volume 1*, ed. J. M. Bassler (Minneapolis: Fortress Press, 1991), 227–46; E. Käsemann, "The Pauline Theology of the Cross," *Int* 24 (1970): 151–77; idem, "The Saving Significance of the Death of Jesus in Paul," *Perspectives on Paul*, trans. M. Kohl (Philadelphia: Fortress Press, 1971), 32–59.

openly pervasive topic of Jesus' crucifixion. By the end of this chapter, we will see how the rhetorical cord of Jesus' crucifixion begins in the salutation-exordium, continues to be developed in a logical progression through the discourse, and reaches its memorable climax in the conclusion of this letter-speech. For Paul, Jesus' substitutionary and saving death on the cross is an eschatological revelation of faithfulness that makes possible the faithfulness and righteousness of Jesus' followers.

Of course, in the scope of this study it is not possible to elaborate fully upon all the sub-themes and texts to which the prominent strand of Jesus' crucifixion is related in Galatians. Fortunately, there are numerous good commentaries and monographs on many of these matters already. Instead, we will address supporting issues only as much as they are helpful for delineating more clearly the direct role that the crucified Christ plays for Paul throughout this communication. Let us now examine how Paul presents the topic of the crucified Jesus Christ to the Galatians.

I. A THEMATIC OVERTURE FOR THE CRUCIFIED CHRIST: GALATIANS 1:3–5

After his opening affirmation in the salutation-exordium that his apostleship is from the risen Jesus Christ and God the Father (1:1)—evidence that Paul views his apostleship and the present day as wholly apocalyptic, Paul sets forth a carefully composed statement that summarizes the saving work of Christ Jesus. In this way, Paul identifies for his listeners and readers a second central theme to be developed in the remainder of the communication. Jesus whom God raised from the dead and through whom God called Paul to apostleship is the Christ "who gave himself for our sins to deliver us from the present evil age, according to the will of our God and Father" (1:4). Moreover, the Lord Jesus Christ, along with God the Father, gives blessings of grace and peace (1:3), and all of this elicits praise to God (1:5).

To be sure, there are many components to this complex expression. Earlier we considered some of the literary and rhetorical aspects of these verses. Now it remains for us to highlight the theological claims made here. To begin with, the phrase "who gave himself" (τοῦ δόντος ἑαυτὸν; 1:4a) is a direct allusion to Christ's death (cf. 2:20; Rom 5:6, 8; 1 Cor 15:3). The first thing to note regarding the work of Christ, then, is that his death was voluntary. It was an act of willful self-sacrifice. Christ's self-offering, though, was also in accordance with the will of God the Father. Thus Paul can write elsewhere that God gave Jesus over (cf. Rom 4:25; 8:32). The phrase κατὰ τὸ θέλημα τοῦ θεοῦ καὶ πατρὸς ἡμῶν (Gal 1:4c), however, also refers to Christ's rescuing activity (ὅπως ἐξέληται ἡμᾶς; 1:4b). Thus a second christological affirmation made in this opening declaration is that Jesus' self-offering and work of deliverance are consequences of God's will.

But why did Jesus give himself up to death? The text asserts in a third christological claim that Jesus' self-sacrificial death was "for our sins." The plural noun "sins" may be uncharacteristic of Paul's vocabulary, yet Paul uses the word here and elsewhere in the letter.[2] So, also, Paul characteristically speaks of Christ's death on our behalf.[3] Thus even as he stresses the rescuing work of Christ "for us" according to God's will as a point to develop in the body of the communication, Paul also prepares his listeners to hear more about the "sins" for which Christ gave himself. Similarly, Paul prepares his audience to appraise the consequence of Christ's death for our sins.

A fourth christological assertion made in v. 4 is that Jesus' death on behalf of our sins was for the purpose of rescuing us from the present age of evil. Here, as we have seen, the apocalyptic character of the phrase "present age of evil" is striking. But the question remains; in what way does Jesus' death effect an apocalyptic rescue?

Finally, in v. 4 Paul asserts that Jesus' self-offering is integrally related to the grace and peace which are available from God our Father and the Lord Jesus Christ (1:3). Moreover, glory and praise are the appropriate responses to God's rescuing work through Jesus Christ (1:5). The concepts of grace and peace, then, are not only characteristic of Paul's usual epistolary greetings,[4] but here they are presented as particular benefits from Christ's saving work. Consequently, we may expect Paul to elaborate on the grace and peace that come from God the Father and the Lord Jesus Christ who gave himself up on behalf of others. We may also anticipate that the remainder of the letter-speech will give causes for praising God.

With these points in mind, let us proceed to the body of Paul's address to the Galatians in order to see further where and to what extent Paul develops the event and the consequences of Jesus' self-sacrificial death.

---

[2]In Galatians, Paul uses the noun ἁμαρτία three times in different ways (1:4; 2:17; 3:22) and does not use the verb ἁμαρτάνω at all. In 1:4, the emphasis is on Christ's salvific death on our behalf which plays a major role throughout Galatians.

[3]Paul customarily speaks of Christ's death for us. Cf. Rom 5:6–8; 8:3; 14:15; 1 Cor 1:13; 15:3; 2 Cor 5:14–15; Gal 2:20; 3:13.

[4]All 13 letters attributed to Paul include the common epistolary opening greeting of "grace" and "peace" (cf. Rom 1:7; 1 Cor 1:3; 2 Cor 1:2; etc.). The "grace" and "peace" components of the opening greeting are also repeated, though separately and with some modification, at the end of the Pauline letters (cf. Rom 16:20; 1 Cor 16:23–24; 2 Cor 13:14; etc.).

II. THE CRUCIFIED CHRIST AND THE GIFT
OF RIGHTEOUSNESS: GALATIANS 2:11–21

Paul returns to the rhetorical cord of Jesus' self-offering in 2:11–21.[5] By this point in his discourse, he has made his case that his apostolic call and work are rooted in the apocalyptic activity of God and that the "pillars" of the church confirmed his commission to serve in this way (1:1; 1:11–2:10). Beginning at 2:11 he expands his address to include more directly his second major concern—the saving work of Jesus Christ and its significance. The revealed crucified Christ has not only effected Paul's life (cf. 1:13–16); he has also changed forever the way in which Jews and Gentiles are to be related to one another and to God through their relationship with him.

Paul moves seamlessly to this topic with an account of a critical confrontation with Peter and some other Christians in Antioch (2:11–14).[6] As the text shows and scholars have long noted there was considerable controversy over Jewish-Christian and Gentile-Christian relations in the early church.[7] According to Acts 15:6–29, this issue was resolved by a council in Jerusalem. By testing their experiences against the witness of scripture, the council concluded that Christians of Jewish and Gentile lineage belonged together.

---

[5]Paul presents 2:11–14 and 15–21 as an account of his speech to Peter, but it is clear that he is now employing particular points from it to address a different and perhaps broader audience. Some rhetorical critics identify 2:15–21 as the *propositio* of Paul's entire argument which summarizes Paul's preceding material and foreshadows the remainder of his address to the Galatians (cf. Betz, Brinsmead, Howard, Longenecker, Standaert, and Vouga). One scholar expands the *propositio* to 2:14–3:5 (Mack). Others, however, follow G. A. Kennedy and locate the *propositio* in the letter–speech's opening within 1:6–12 (cf. Hall, Jegher-Bucher, Hester, Pitta). As Kennedy puts it, "The central idea of the proem, that there is no other gospel, is a general statement of the proposition of the letter, which will be taken up and given specific meaning in the headings which follow" (*New Testament Interpretation*, 148). As I have argued above, the strong periodic form of 1:6–7 and the common Greco-Roman rhetorical practice of placing at the beginning of a communication the central idea to develop throughout the communication supports this latter position. Paul's message to the Galatians is foremost a matter of presenting the essential character of the "gospel."

[6]For an insightful discussion of Paul's portrayal of Peter in Galatians, see Raymond E. Brown, Karl P. Donfried, and John Reumann, eds., *Peter in the New Testament: A Collaborative Assessment by Protestant and Roman Catholic Scholars* (Minneapolis: Augsburg, 1973), 24–32.

[7]Cf. Ferdinand Christian Baur, *Paul, the Apostle of Jesus Christ*, 2 vols, trans. E. Zeller, Rev. A. Menzies (Edinburgh: Williams and Norgate, 1876); C. K. Barrett, *Paul: An Introduction to His Thought* (Louisville: Westminster/John Knox, 1994), 22–54; Terence V. Smith, *Petrine Controversies in Early Christianity*, WUNT 2, Reihe 15 (Tübingen: J.C.B. Mohr [Paul Siebeck], 1985); Nicholas Taylor, *Paul, Antioch and Jerusalem. A Study in Relationships and Authority in Earliest Christianity* (Sheffield: Sheffield Academic, 1992), especially 13–59. See also the historical interpretations of this particular text surveyed by F. Mussner, *Der Galaterbrief*, 146–67.

According to Paul in Gal 2:11–14, the controversy reached another critical moment in Antioch when—as Paul describes it—he and Peter had a public showdown over this matter because Peter and some other Christians—including Barnabas—had withdrawn from table fellowship with Gentile Christians there (2:11–14).[8] In doing this, Peter and the others had contradicted the earlier verdict of the Jerusalem council and the promise sealed with "the right hand of fellowship" (2:9). Thus Peter "stood condemned," in part because he himself had participated in the earlier resolution of this problem and had pledged to uphold it but had broken his promise and returned to a lifestyle characteristic of the old age. So even as Paul prepares to give an account of this tragic event, he alternates between Peter's Greek name Petros and Aramaic name Cephas—a not too subtle way of rhetorically highlighting Peter's oscillation (2:7–9, 11, 14). Peter also stood condemned with the others because he was not living in accord with the gospel (οὐκ ὀρθοποδοῦσιν πρὸς τὴν ἀλήθειαν τοῦ εὐαγγελίου; 2:14) which he had fully embraced (2:16).

The logic of Paul's argument in 2:11–21 runs like this. Peter and the others are acting hypocritically (αὐτῶν τῇ ὑποκρίσει; v. 13) by withdrawing from table fellowship with the faithful Gentiles on the basis of the law (v. 12). In so doing, they are rejecting the validity of the Gentiles' full participation in Christ. That is, they are restricting the extent of God's grace demonstrated through Christ's life and declared by the true gospel (v. 14). Moreover, Christ's death has proven the law's inability to put a person in a right relationship with God (vv. 15–16).[9] So accepting the law as a requirement for both fellowship with God and the reception of God's blessing is a denial of the Christian faith (v. 16) and of any purpose in Christ's death (v. 21). The law opposed God's

---

[8]On the difficult relation between Acts and Galatians, see especially P. J. Achtemeier, *Quest for Unity*. Achtemeier argues persuasively that the dispute of Gal 2:11–14 followed, rather than preceded, the council in Jerusalem recorded in Acts 15:6–29. Toward this end, he relates Gal 1:18–21 with Acts 9:26 and Gal 2:1–10 with Acts 11:1–18 (cf. 2, 44–55). For an opposing view, see N. Taylor, *Paul, Antioch and Jerusalem*, 51–9, 222–26. On this issue, see also J. D. G. Dunn, "The Incident at Antioch," *JSNT* 18 (1983): 3–57; C. K. Barrett, *Freedom and Obligation: A Study of the Epistle to the Galatians* (Philadelphia: Westminster, 1985), 91–108.

[9]Paul's first use of the verb δικαιόω occurs here in 2:16. So important is the concept that he uses the verb three times in this verse. It also occurs in Gal 2:17; 3:8, 11, 24; 5:4. In Paul's undisputed letters, the verb is also used 15 times in Rom 1–8 and twice in 1 Cor. Much traditional scholarship translates δικαιόω as "to justify" and interprets the word as to do or show justice to someone or to treat someone as just or vindicated. The verb also means, however, to make or pronounce as righteous, pure, or free. The former translation stresses the forensic aspect of δικαιόω while the latter emphasizes the relational and even holy dimensions of the word. The relational dimension of δικαιόω is the best interpretation of the word in the majority of uses throughout the Old and New Testaments and is most appropriate for Paul's use of the word in Galatians and Romans. See E. Achtemeier, "Righteousness," 80–5 and P. Achtemeier, "Righteousness," 91–9.

Christ and led others to oppose him, thus it was torn down (v. 18a). So if one returns to the law, one becomes a transgressor of the law[10] because a return acknowledges that becoming a Christian in the first place apart from the law was a sin (v. 18b). But if in following Christ and placing one's trust in him for establishing a right relationship with God one abandons the law or never places one's trust in it, one is in accord with God's will (v. 19). Following God's will is not a sin. Following the law, however, sets one against God's will as revealed in the life, death, and resurrection of Jesus and so makes one a transgressor (παραβάτην).[11] According to Paul, it is impossible to be in a right relationship with God or to gain God's favor by means of obedience to the law. These are the consequences of trust (πίστις) alone, and this is the "truth of the gospel" (2:14) which Paul courageously defends.

The tragedy of this event for Paul is that Peter and the others were contradicting what Paul calls "the truth of the gospel" of God's grace—that God accepts persons solely on the basis of their faithfulness in Jesus Christ. Thus Paul's account of this confrontation serves as a preface to his central argument that righteousness does not come through obedience to the law but comes through faith in the crucified and risen Christ Jesus (2:16). So crucial is this tenet of the gospel that Paul asserts three times in a single sentence (v. 16) that the law cannot make a person righteous. His rhetorical emphasis on this point is unmistakable. Still, to make sure that the Galatians hold this aspect of the gospel firmly in mind, especially for the next major part of his message (chaps. 3–4), Paul restates the point of v. 16 antithetically at the conclusion of this portion of his message. "If righteousness comes through the law, then Christ died in vain" (v. 21). With this condition of reality, Paul sets forth a false presupposition, the acceptance of which would result in a false conclusion regarding the significance of Christ's death.[12] But Christ did not die in vain, and righteousness does not come through the law.

In vv. 11–21, Paul argues for the total sufficiency of trust in Christ over against reliance on the law and Jewish heritage for being in a right relation with God and receiving God's blessings of grace and righteousness. Central to this argument is Christ's death, which is stressed emphatically in the periodic climax of v. 21 (εἰ γὰρ διὰ νόμου δικαιοσύνη, ἄρα Χριστὸς δωρεὰν

---

[10]Though Paul does not say exactly what one transgresses, most scholars agree that Paul is referring to the law (cf. Gal 3:19; Rom 2:23; 4:15; 5:14).

[11]While παράβασις and ἁμαρτία are related, the former pertains more specifically to breaking a law. In the NT, the word παραβάτης also occurs in Rom 2:25–27 and Jas 2:9–11. Paul's argument here in Galatians—not unlike Rom 5:20 and 7:7f—is that the law, in part, formalizes sin and so "increases" it by revealing sin for what it is. For Paul, the law now demonstrates the need for redemption. See Johannes Schneider, "παραβάτης," *TDNT*, vol. 5, 740–41.

[12]Betz, *Galatians*, 126.

ἀπέθανεν).[13] Paul will need to say more about the relation between "works of the law" (ἔργων νόμου) and "faith" (πίστις) in what follows, and he does (3:1–4:7), but here in 2:11–21 Paul presents the death of Christ as the foundation for understanding the relation between the two. Paul also presents the death of Christ as fundamental to Paul's own faith and new life (vv. 19–20). Consonant with the autobiographical material presented in 1:11–2:10, then, Paul once more appeals to his own experience of God's activity and grace manifested in his own life through Christ. Remarkably, though, he epitomizes this experience with the curious expression "crucified with Christ" (v. 20).

Paul's striking expression "crucified with Christ" sets before his listeners' eyes the point he wants to make here. The context reveals that he is not referring to a physical reality or fact. Rather, he is describing how a person who is not properly related with God comes to be in a right relationship with God. To begin with, Paul "died to the law." That is, Paul abandoned the law when God revealed through the crucifixion of the Messiah—God's own Son— sin's corrupting influence upon the law. As Paul stated earlier (1:13–14), he thought he was in a right relationship with God during his former life as a Jew when he scrupulously obeyed the law. But, after God's revelation of Jesus Christ to him (1:15–16), Paul abandoned the law and gave up the life that it directed against the church and the will of God. Now, in 2:19–21, Paul returns to this point regarding God's transforming impact upon his life through Jesus Christ. In this way, Paul has been crucified with Christ, for, through trust in the Christ whom God revealed, sin's power to distort the law and to misdirect those who trust in it has been broken. Paul is not under the distorted law's power or influence any more than is the crucified Jesus. Instead of living a life directed against God and God's will under the law's direction, Paul is living a new life of trust in the Son of God.[14]

---

[13]This periodic expression's climactic word ἀπέθανεν (2:21) echoes the climactic word νεκρῶν at the end of 1:1 and calls to mind the corresponding concept of Christ's resurrection. Together they form a type of aural inclusio. Only in 1:1 and 2:19, 21 does Paul speak directly of death in Galatians and in both places he stresses, instead, life. In 1:1, the focus is on the Lord Jesus Christ whom God the Father raised from the dead (νεκρῶν). In 2:19, the focus is on Paul who declares "I through the law died (ἀπέθανεν) to the law, that I might live to God." In 2:20, Paul states negatively his positive affirmation that Christ died (ἀπέθανεν) to show that righteousness does not come through works of the law. Thus Paul's present apostolic life and work (1:1a, 11f) are in line with God's grace, which Paul also stresses in this first portion of his argument (1:3, 6, 15; 2:9, 21). The only other occurrences of χάρις are 5:4, where Paul warns the Galatians that they are in danger of falling away from God's grace, and in the closing benediction of 6:18.

[14]The idea of being crucified with Christ is common in Paul's writings (cf. Rom 6:1– 10, 8:17; 2 Cor 5:15 Phil 3:10; Col 2:12–14, 3:1–4). Like other Pauline terms, though, there are nuances of meaning which are shaped by the contexts in which the concept is used. Paul often employs the term to describe the believer's participation in the benefits of Christ, close fellowship with Christ, and the follower's similar journey of self-sacrificing service and love.

Placing one's trust in Christ aligns one properly with God's will, so that one might live according to God's will and for God's glory. By faith in Jesus, the unrighteous person becomes righteous according to God's will. This is not only because faith in Jesus puts one in a right relation with God. It is due particularly to Christ's own living presence and work in the believer. For Paul, "it is no longer I who live, but Christ who lives in me" (v. 20). Christ is the source of this righteousness and life that Paul now bears. As we stressed in the previous chapter, Paul assumes the resurrection of Christ here (v. 20). Paul, however, does not live in a resurrected body, for he quickly adds that "the life I now live in the flesh (i.e., human body) I live by trust in the Son of God who loved me and gave himself for me" (v. 20). Although Paul and other believers may share in the new life Christ gives, it is not yet a resurrected life for them as it is for Christ.

In this passage, then, Paul grounds his position on the risen crucified Christ as he addresses how an unrighteous person becomes counted as righteous on the basis of faith in Christ and not by obedience to the law. Through Christ's death on the cross, Paul sees that his old law-centered-self stands condemned. For Paul, Christ's death is purposive for it exposes sin's corrupting influence upon the law and reveals that the grace of God is accessible apart from the law. So, because of God's revelation of the risen Christ to Paul and the accompanying experience of God's grace, Paul abandons his trust in the law as the basis for being in a right relation with God. Instead, he trusts in Jesus' love and self-sacrifice for him. Moreover, by faith in the Son of God, Paul asserts that Christ's own life and righteousness are manifested in him. That is, the righteous manner of life God desires is now increasingly possible for Paul through the Son "who loved me and gave himself for me." This is God's doing, though; not Paul's nor the law's. Thus righteousness, for Paul, is finally a gift of a merciful God who accepts sinners on the basis of faith in Jesus Christ the Crucified.[15] Now let us see how Paul continues to develop the significance of Jesus' crucifixion beyond the experience and example of his own life.

III. THE CRUCIFIED CHRIST AND THE ADVENT OF THE SPIRIT: GALATIANS 3:1–5

Following the account of his crisis with Peter in Antioch, Paul utters a declaration of astonished indignation at the Galatians' reported abandonment of the gospel of grace (3:1). News that the Galatians are returning to the law, after

---

The context here, however, shows that Paul has in mind death to the law along the lines of Rom 10:4 and Col 2:14. See, for instance, Betz, *Galatians*, 120–21; Burton, *Galatians*, 135–36; Longenecker, *Galatians*, 90–1.

[15]Burton, *Galatians*, 140–42, 472; Cousar, *Galatians*, 53–6, 74–5.

having received by faith the gospel and the Holy Spirit, can only be described as foolishness (ἀνόητος; 3:1; 3) or the result of bewitchment by a deceiver (βασκαίνω; 3:1).[16] Paul suggests that an evil incantation must have been cast over them, so he speaks forcefully here as one who might break the spell they are under (3:1–5).

Why do the Galatians not see that the gospel of grace plus the law is a distortion of the true gospel? According to Paul, it is because they have lost sight of the Crucified. Therefore Paul reminds the Galatians of his active preaching among them when "Jesus Christ was publicly portrayed as crucified" (Ἰησοῦς Χριστὸς προεγράφη ἐσταυρωμένος) for them (cf. 1:4; 2:20; 3:13). The verb προγράφω means literally "to write, display, proclaim in front of, or exhibit,"[17] and with this verb Paul describes his preaching as a public and visible depiction—even a painting[18]—of Jesus Christ as the Crucified. Unlike other places where Paul downplays his rhetorical talent (cf. 1 Cor 2:1, 4; 2 Cor 10:10), here he celebrates his rhetorical skills, for rhetoric at its best is always a matter of turning ears into eyes so that the audience can see what the speaker is saying. The text is clear, however, that Paul subordinates his effective preaching under the message he proclaims.

When Paul first told the Galatians about Jesus Christ the crucified, he had evidently set before them the nature and significance of the person of Jesus and the event of his crucifixion. Now once more, Paul points to the crucified Christ who is the center of his preaching and the core of his message to the Galatians. The good news (εὐαγγέλιον) that Paul proclaims is that Christ has been crucified. In announcing this, Paul uses the perfect form of σταυρόω (ἐσταυρωμένος), not the aorist (σταυρωθείς), which means that Paul preaches about the Christ who has suffered and died on a cross. Thus Jesus who is risen from the dead (1:1) has an ongoing existence and authority as the Crucified One even as the event of Jesus' crucifixion has a continuing power

---

[16]On Paul's use of βασκαίνω which occurs only here in the NT, see the insightful article by Jerome H. Neyrey, "Bewitched in Galatia: Paul and Cultural Anthropology," *CBQ* 50 (1998): 72–100.

[17]The prefix of this compound verb, προ, means "before" as in "in front of," though it could also mean "first." The root verb γράφω means "to write" but it may also mean to "describe" or to "draw or paint." See H. G. Liddell and R. Scott, *Greek-English Lexicon* (New York: Oxford University Press, 1996), 1473b and 360a. But see also Eph 3:3 where the verb is also translated as "to write briefly before" (cf. NIV, RSV, NRSV).

[18]Calvin writes that *"painted* is less ambiguous, and in my opinion, the most appropriate. To show how forceful his preaching had been, Paul first compares it with a picture which showed them the portrait of Christ . . . By this he suggests that the actual sight of Christ's death could not have affected them more than his preaching" (John Calvin, *The Epistles of Paul the Apostle to the Galatians, Ephesians, Philippians and Colossians*, trans. T.H.L. Parker, Calvin's Commentaries, eds. D. W. Torrance and T. F. Torrance [Grand Rapids: Wm. B. Eerdmans, 1965], 47.).

and significance. The resurrection of Jesus—as we saw in the previous chapter—is integrally related to Jesus' death on the cross (1:1; 2:19–20), but this Risen One is forever the Crucified One whose death is purposive.

Little wonder Paul is surprised by the Galatians' folly of returning to works of the law. How can they possibly believe that obedience to the law can improve their relations with God when God has established the way to be in a right relation with God through the work of the risen and crucified Christ and trust in him? The Galatians' addition of the law to this faith is a contradiction of God's revealed purpose in Christ, for Christ "gave himself for our sins to deliver us from the present age of evil, according to the will of our God and Father" (1:4). Moreover, any reliance on the law to assure their relation with God is a contradiction of their early trust in Christ and their own experience of God's grace apart from the law.[19] Thus, in reminding the Galatians of his effective preaching of the Christ who has been crucified (3:1), Paul calls them to remember also their acceptance of his message, their own awakening to faith in Christ, and their entrance into the new age of God—an apocalyptic age signaled by the presence and work of the Spirit in their midst (3:2, 3, 5).

Here in 3:2, Paul uses for the first time in Galatians the word "Spirit" (τὸ πνεῦμα), which as we saw in the previous chapter is a chief characteristic of God's promised apocalyptic age.[20] That Paul repeats the term in vv. 3 and 5 indicates that the Spirit is important to his message to the Galatians and that he intends to say more about the Spirit in the message-body.[21] To be sure, the term "Spirit" is common in Paul's writings and Paul employs it in several ways.[22] Here, though, Paul simply means by the term "Spirit" God's active presence at work in the world.

In this passage Paul makes some important assertions regarding the Spirit through the artful use of questions.[23] To begin with, Paul states that the Spirit

---

[19]The phrase ἐξ ἀκοῆς πίστεως could be translated as either "a faithful hearing" or "a hearing about faith." The context indicates, however, that Paul has in mind the Galatians' belief in what was proclaimed. Cf. E. P. Sanders, *Paul and Palestinian Judaism* (Minneapolis: Fortress Press, 1977), 482. See also S. Williams, "The Hearing of Faith;" Betz, *Galatians*, 133, n. 50; and a summary of interpretations in Hays, *Faith of Jesus Christ*, 143–49.

[20]Cf. Isa 4:4; 26:18; 30:28; 34:16; 42:1; 44:3; Joel 2:28–29; Zech 12:10; 13:2. See also Fee, *God's Empowering Presence*, 896–99, and E. Schweizer, "πνεῦμα," *TDNT*, vol. 6, 415–37. It is interesting, as Hays observes (*Echoes of Scripture in the Letters of Paul*, 214, n. 70), that Paul does not use the citation from Joel 2:28 here, since it would have strengthened his argument considerably. He does show an awareness of Joel later, however, in his correspondence to the Romans where he cites Joel 3:5 (LXX) at 10:13.

[21]See especially Gal 3:14; 4:6; 4:29; 5:5; 5:16–25; 6:8.

[22]See Fee, *God's Empowering Presence*, 14–36.

[23]Ibid., 380–89. See also Betz, *Galatians*, 28–33; Burton, *Galatians*, 486–95; Cousar, *Galatians*, 66–70; Dunn, *Galatians*, 145–46, 151–58.

came upon the Galatians through their acceptance and trust (ἐξ ἀκοῆς πίστεως) in the Crucified Christ whom Paul proclaimed (3:1–2). Observances of the law had played no part in their coming to faith in Christ or in their experience of the Spirit. Secondly, Paul avers that trying to perfect this faith and relation to God through the Spirit by means of attention to the flesh is sheer foolishness (3:3). As we have seen, Paul often relates the flesh antithetically to the Spirit, and here Paul evidently links the flesh to the law, for the agitators in Galatia were promoting circumcision and other requirements of the law as necessary for faithfulness.[24] Paul's third assertion regarding the Spirit is that along with the Spirit there were other signs of God's unveiling of the new age. There were miracles or divine works of power (ἐνεργῶν δυνάμεις; 3:5).[25] Finally, Paul's use of the plural pronoun "you" (ὑμῖν; 3:5) stresses that the Spirit was present and active throughout the community of believers.[26]

In short, Paul attests in this passage that the gift of the Spirit came apart from the law and that miracles were experienced throughout the Galatian community of faith during and following the Galatians' acceptance of Paul's gospel of the Christ who has been crucified. Jesus' death on the cross, then, is not only central to Paul's faith and life (2:15–21), it is also foundational to the Galatians' own awakening to faith in Christ and entrance into the new age of God (3:1–5). Moreover, the advent of the Spirit among the Galatians is rooted in their assent to Paul's preaching of the Christ who has been crucified. Of course, the Galatians' acceptance of Jesus as the Christ through the proclamation of the gospel differs from Paul's coming to faith through God's revelation of Jesus (1:16). But there can be no doubt, according to Paul, that the Galatians had shared Paul's faith in the crucified Lord and had experienced the power of faith—the Spirit—who was at work in and among them.[27] Paul will have more to say about the Spirit later (cf. 5:1–25), but first he continues to develop his prior point (2:19–20) regarding the relation between Christ's death, the law, and faith.

---

[24]Cf. 2:12; 3:10, 18; 4:5, 21; 5:2–6, 18; 6:13–15.

[25]Various interpretations of the kind of miracles are suggested in Betz, *Galatians*, 135, n. 78. See also the literature cited there.

[26]Betz, *Galatians*, 135, n. 80; Cousar, *Galatians*, 69–70. Note also that the present participle ἐπιχορηγῶν in 3:5 suggests a continuous supply of the Spirit among them.

[27]The periodic forms of 3:3 and 3:5 stress πίστεως. Also, on the shared experience among believers of Christ's Spirit in relation to faith in Christ, see Gal 4:6. Gordon Fee writes, "this appeal to 'reception of the spirit' as evidence of entry into Christian life demonstrates the crucial role the Spirit plays not only in Christian conversion but also as the singular 'identity mark' of those who belong to Christ" (*God's Empowering Presence*, 383).

IV. THE CRUCIFIED CHRIST AND THE
PRIORITY OF FAITH: GALATIANS 3:6–14

In order to demonstrate further to the Galatians the priority of faith and the sufficiency of Christ's rescuing work, Paul moves swiftly into a discussion of Abraham's faith (3:6–9), the problem of the law (3:10–12), and the substitutionary nature of Christ's death on the cross (3:13–14). To be sure, each of these examples or proofs is integrally related to 3:1–5, but they are separated here for the sake of analysis.[28]

Regarding faith's primacy, Paul introduces Abraham as a scriptural proof for the Galatians' own experience of receiving the Spirit through faith. Paul demonstrates from scripture (Gen 15:6; 12:3; 18:18) that God judged Abraham to be righteous on the basis of his faith (3:6),[29] a point highlighted by the periodic shape of 3:6 which moves from Abraham's trust in God to God's acceptance of Abraham's faith as righteousness (Ἀβραὰμ ἐπίστευσεν τῷ θεῷ, καὶ ἐλογίσθη αὐτῷ εἰς δικαιοσύνην). With this assertion, Paul relates the Galatians' early trust in God to that of Abraham.

Paul goes on to argue that all true descendants of Abraham are those who share Abraham's trust in God (3:7).[30] Indeed, on the basis of scripture, Paul argues that God promised long ago to bless the Gentiles by counting them as righteous on the basis of faith (3:8).[31] Even more, as Paul's periodic

---

[28]The adverb καθώς in 3:6 shows the close relation between 3:1–5 and what follows. The content of 3:1–14 also stresses the close relationship between the verses of this passage. Paul uses the word πίστις nine times in 3:1–14 (3:2, 5, 6, 7, 8, 9, 11, 12, 14) and so leaves no doubt that πίστις lies at the core of 3:1–14. In vv. 1–5, however, Paul stresses the consequence of faith as reception of the Spirit—the point to which he returns in v. 14. The examples of 3:6–13 center more precisely on the priority of faith over the law. Among commentators on Galatians, Bruce and Matera view 3:6 as belonging more closely to 3:1–5 and translate καθώς as "in the same way" (Bruce, *Galatians*, 147–53; Matera, *Galatians*, 111–16). Others view v. 6 as the beginning of 3:6–14. On the notoriously complicated nature of Paul's argument in this portion of Galatians, see especially Betz, *Galatians*, 137–53, and Longenecker, *Galatians*, 107–25.

[29]On the tradition of Abraham in Galatians and in Jewish literature, see G. W. Hansen, *Abraham in Galatians*, especially Appendix 2, 175–99. See also the helpful excursus in Betz, *Galatians*, 139–40, and Longenecker, *Galatians*, 110–12.

[30]Cf. Cousar, *Galatians*, 71; Martyn, *Galatians*, 294–96.

[31]For a thorough examination of Paul's reasoning and interpretation of the blessing of Abraham in 3:8, see Burton, *Galatians*, 160–62, and Betz, *Galatians*, 142–43. Also, Paul's reference to Gen 12:3 ("ἐνευλογηθήσονται ἐν σοὶ πᾶσαι αἱ φυλαὶ τῆς γῆς") and 18:18 ("ἐνευλογηθήσονται ἐν αὐτῷ πάντα τὰ ἔθνη τῆς γῆς") in the LXX may not be a precise quote of either text ("ἐνευλογηθήσονται ἐν σοὶ πάντα τὰ ἔθνη"), but his use of σοί rather than αὐτῷ does not alter the meaning expressed in the Gen 18:18 citation anymore than his use of πάντα τὰ ἔθνη alters the meaning of πᾶσαι αἱ φυλαι in Gen 12:3. In all three texts, blessing from God will come to all the tribes, nations, or Gentiles of the earth through Abraham. See Hays, *Echoes of Scripture*, 108–11.

arrangement of 3:8a emphatically shows, it is God who makes the Gentiles righteous through their faith (προϊδοῦσα δὲ ἡ γραφὴ ὅτι ἐκ πίστεως δικαιοῖ τὰ ἔθνη ὁ θεός). Therefore, whoever joins the faithful Abraham in placing one's trust in God—whether Jew or Gentile—is an heir of Abraham's blessing (3:9; ὥστε οἱ ἐκ πίστεως εὐλογοῦνται σὺν τῷ πιστῷ Ἀβραάμ). Faith, then, is the basis for being included in God's blessing to Abraham.[32]

The relation of this argument (3:6–9) with the preceding one (3:1–5) is clear. Paul first appeals to the Galatians' experience of receiving the Spirit. They accepted the gospel of the Crucified Christ and received the Spirit. So Paul asks twice whether they received the Spirit by "works of the law, or by hearing with faith" (3:2, 5). In this way, Paul frames the question rhetorically as mutually exclusive possibilities so that the Galatians must answer one way or the other. They cannot choose both faith in the Christ who has been crucified and works of the law.

With the priority of faith established by their own experience and by scripture, Paul strikes the antithesis of Abrahamic trust—reliance on works of the law (3:10–12).[33] Up to this point, Paul has been arguing that faith or trust in God is the common denominator between Abraham and Abraham's heirs and that the blessing that God promised to Abraham has now come to the Gentiles. In 3:10–12, Paul shifts to the counter point and addresses the problem of trusting in the law. As Paul sees it, the predicament facing those who want to base their relationship with God upon the law is that they are "under a curse" (3:10). The law itself asserts in Deut 27:26 that "Cursed is everyone who does not keep abiding by all the things written in the book of the law, and do them" (3:10).[34] The stark contrast between Paul's claims here and in v. 9 mirrors the earlier polarity struck in vv. 2–5—that the blessing of faith and the curse of the law are mutually exclusive choices. Moreover, to accept any part of the law—such as dietary restrictions or circumcision—is to become bound to "all the things written in the book of the law" (see also 5:3).

The law's requirement to keep the whole law is part of the law's curse, but Paul's appeal in 3:10 to Deut 27:26, 28:58, and 30:10 goes beyond that.[35] In order to see more clearly Paul's intentions, it is helpful to revisit the phrase and

---

[32]Paul presents a more thorough argument of this same point in Romans 4.

[33]The close relation between 3:10 and 3:9 is evident by Paul's use of the causal or inferential conjunction γάρ. Here, Paul is echoing and developing the contrast between faith and works of the law presented earlier in 2:15–21.

[34]The present tense verb ἐμμένει expresses continuation, thus the text Paul draws from Deut 27:26 means "Cursed is everyone *who does not remain continuously in* (or *does not continue to do*) all the things written in the book of the law."

[35]Paul's use and adaptations of these proof texts are well-noted. Cf. Betz, *Galatians*, 140–53; Bruce, *Galatians*, 153–68; Longenecker, *Galatians*, 116–23. See also Hays, *Echoes of Scripture*, 107–11.

concept "ἐξ ἔργων νόμου" ("from works of the law"), which Paul introduced in 2:16 and reemphasized in 3:2–5. Much traditional scholarship interprets the phrase as equivalent to "works righteousness" or salvation by works.[36] That is, the only way to be in a right relation with God is to obey all of the law. But since no one can keep the law completely, no one can be set into a right relationship with God by means of the law. The logic of this argument is this: the life God desires for humans is possible by means of the law (3:12), but no one can keep the law completely; therefore God's people are cursed by the law from the law's beginning and cannot put themselves in a right relationship with God. Salvation cannot come through the law, for the law curses and condemns law-breakers.

Paul, however, asserts nothing here about setting oneself in a right relation with God on the basis of one's personal achievement in fulfilling the whole Jewish law. When Paul first uses the term in 2:16 regarding his confrontation with Peter and the others in Antioch who were not associating with Gentile Christians there, at issue is the necessary reception of the Gentiles into the community of faith's total life. Similarly, when Paul uses the term in 3:2–5 and here in 3:10, he does not describe the agitators as promoters of works righteousness by means of the law. In fact, he later states clearly that the agitators do not keep the law (6:13). They do promote part of the law, however, especially the necessity of circumcision. The problem, then, is that the agitators' use of the law is no different from the way that Peter and others in Antioch used dietary laws as a basis for distinguishing the true community or Israel of God. In both cases, the law is used as the boundary to distinguish the faithful of God from the unfaithful. Paul's point in 2:15–21 and here again in 3:1–14, though, is that the faithful of God—the true children of Abraham—are those who exhibit Abraham's trust in God.

It now remains for Paul to explain why the law is a dead end and cannot make a person righteous before God (3:11a). Drawing support from Lev 18:5 and Hab 2:4, Paul answers that it is because "the righteous person shall live by means of faith" (3:11b).[37] The law, however, did not originate out of trust nor is it founded upon faith.[38] There is no organic union between them. Therefore, the

---

[36]This is the view set forth by Martin Luther and maintained more recently by Betz, *Galatians*, 116–17; Burton, *Galatians*, 164; Longenecker, *Galatians*, 118; Mussner, *Galaterbrief*, 170–71, 226.

[37]Hays interprets ὁ δίκαιος to mean Jesus Christ and does not take it generically as I have interpreted it here (Hays, *Faith of Jesus Christ*, 150–57). If Hays is correct, however, then the christological force of this passage would be stronger and would emphasize Paul's stress on the crucified Christ here.

[38]Cf. Exod 19:5–6 and 32:7–9. Moses brings the law down to a "corrupt" and "stiff-necked" people. See also A. A. Das, "Would a Covenantal Nomist Recognize the "(Old) Covenant" in Paul," Union Theological Seminary in Virginia Biblical Colloquy Paper

legalist who keeps the law—even if he or she keeps all of it—cannot obtain faith, for faith is not the basis upon which the law was founded nor is it the outcome that it produces. That is, a person who observes the law will live only in the realm of the law and not in the realm of faith (3:12). So rather than lead one to trust God in the manner of Abraham, the law leads one to trust in the law. As Paul sees it, the problem with the law is not that its statutes are impossible to fulfill. They can be done.[39] Rather, he affirms here that "The one who does them shall live in them" (3:12). The problem is that the way of the law and the way of faith are mutually exclusive paths—they are unrelated spheres of existence.[40] For Paul, the blessing of Abraham comes by living in the realm of faith. In the realm of the law, there is life only under the law and the law's judgment.

Having demonstrated the priority of trust in God over observance of the law in this tightly composed argument, Paul is ready to advance the theme of the cross by stating explicitly and succinctly how Jesus "gave himself for our sins to deliver us" (1:4a; 3:13–14). The groundwork is now laid for Paul to make his climactic point regarding the work of Christ on the cross.

In vv. 13–14, Paul contends that God has broken the realm of the law through the crucifixion of Jesus the Christ. Paul begins by affirming that Jesus "redeemed us from the curse of the law by becoming a curse on our behalf" (3:13). That Jesus the Christ became a "curse" (κατάρα) is a shocking and offensive proclamation.[41] How could the Christ of God be cursed? Paul's

---

[March 11, 1997], 18–25, who makes this point largely following the works of Scott Hafemann, *Paul, Moses, and the History of Israel* (Tübingen: J.C.B. Mohr [Paul Siebeck], 1995), 243–48; R. W. L. Moberly, *The Mountain of God: Story and Theology in Exodus 32–34* (Sheffield: JSOT Press, 1983), 49–50; and George A. F. Knight, *Theology as Narration: A Commentary on the Book of Exodus* (Grand Rapids: Eerdmans, 1976), 186–7.

[39]This is the position taken by Cousar, *Galatians*, 74–5; Dunn, *Galatians*, 135–41; Matera, *Galatians*, 32, 197–98; Sanders, *Paul and Palestinian Judaism*, 550–52; Schlier, *Der Brief*, 92. See also Phil 3:6; Gal 4:8–10; Rom 3:9, 7:12.

[40]See E. P. Sanders, *Paul and Palestinian Judaism* (Minneapolis: Fortress Press, 1977), 482–84; Hays, *The Faith of Jesus Christ*, 198–207; T. L. Donaldson, "'The Curse of the Law' and the Inclusion of the Gentiles: Galatians 3:13–14," *NTS* 32 (1986): 101. In short, Sanders uses the term "covenantal nomism" to describe the function of the law in Judaism and to help describe Paul's new perspective of the law, particularly as it is expressed here (cf. 482–84). According to Sanders, Jews were members of God's covenant community and heirs of God's promises to Israel by the nature of their membership in the Jewish community. The law was understood as the means for remaining in this covenant and community. One's relation to the law, then, determined the realm of life in which one lives. The realm of the law is the arena of God's covenant promises and community. The realm outside of the law is the arena of God's judgment and condemnation. Obedience to the law, then, was seen as the means for continuing to live in the realm of God's blessings.

[41]On the practice of crucifixion and Jewish and Gentile assessments of it, see especially Martin Hengel, *Crucifixion in the Ancient World and the Folly of the Message of the Cross* (Philadelphia: Fortress, 1977), especially 69–90; J. A. Fitzmyer, "Crucifixion in

adaptation of Deut 21:23 is informative at this point. He omits the phrase "by God," thus it is the written law that cursed Jesus.[42]

Paul goes on to emphasize Christ's work and the believers' benefit (cf. 1:4). The act of redemption is entirely Christ's and the consequence of that act is "for us."[43] But how did Christ become a curse for us? By receiving the law's severest penalty—death on a cross (Deut 21:23). There is no stronger contrast than the way of faith, exhibited by God's anointed who accepted the curse of the law for us, and the way of the law, exhibited by its curse even upon the Christ of God. Moreover, the people's use of the law to condemn the Messiah of God exposes another problem with the law—it can be used to oppose God's will. Yet the Messiah's acceptance of the law's curse on our behalf and the exposure of sin's power to misdirect the law now render the law ineffective and ends its curse. So, Christ received the punishment of the law—which, according to the law, the unfaithful deserve[44]—as a substitution for us. Paul makes the same point in the Corinthian Correspondences where he writes that God made Jesus to be "our righteousness and sanctification and redemption" (1 Cor 1:30) and "The one who did not know sin was made sin for our sake, in order that we might become the righteousness of God (2 Cor 5:21). Jesus' death on the cross also shows that the curse of the law for the Jews is that their trust in the law pits them against God and God's purposes. Furthermore, the curse of the law for the Gentiles is that it excludes them from the covenant community of God, although God has promised to include them.[45] Christ, then, has acted on behalf of all believers—Jew and Gentile—to redeem them from the curse of the law.

Christ's act of redemption through his crucifixion on behalf of both Jew and Gentile is attested in 3:14. Because of Christ's death on the cross,[46] God's covenant promise to Abraham in Gen 12:3 is now fulfilled (3:8). The blessing of Abraham is extended to Jew and Gentile alike. Moreover, a significant part

---

Ancient Palestine, Qumran Literature, and the NT," *CBQ* 40 (1978): 493–513; Y. Yadin, "Pesher Nahum (4QpNahum) Reconsidered," *IEJ* 21 (1971): 1–12.

[42]Cf. Betz, *Galatians*, 148–52; Bruce, *Galatians*, 165–67; Longenecker, *Galatians*, 121–23.

[43]On the controversial issue of whether "us" refers only to Jewish Christians or includes also Gentile Christians, see the comprehensive summary and related notes in T. L. Donaldson, "The 'Curse of the Law,'" 95–9. It seems more in line with Paul's argument at this point that he has in mind both Jewish and Gentile Christians, for the parallel ἵνα clauses in 3:14 are dependent on the main clause Χριστὸς ἡμᾶς ἐξηγόρασεν ("Christ redeemed us") in 3:13. This is supported further by Paul's climactic statements for this portion of his message in 3:26–28. See for instance Sam K. Williams, "Justification and the Spirit in Galatians," *JSNT* 29 (1987): 91–92, and Hays, *The Faith of Jesus Christ*, 113. For a contrary interpretation of the clauses as sequential, see Betz, *Galatians*, 132–33.

[44]Cf. Deut 27:26; 28:15, 47, 58b.

[45]Dunn, "Works of the Law and Curse of the Law," 536; Williams, "Justification and the Spirit in Galatians," 91–2.

[46]Though the crucifixion is not specifically mentioned, it is no doubt implied.

of that blessing is this: through faith in Christ Jesus both Jew and Gentile may receive the promise of the Spirit. That—according to Paul—is precisely the reality that the Galatians already experienced (3:1–5). In this way, the gift of the Spirit is the proof that God accepted the Galatians by their faith in the crucified Christ and not by their obedience to the law.[47] Similarly, the resurrection of Jesus from the dead proves that God favors the Son over the law.

Throughout this tightly woven argument, Paul's message of the crucified Christ is central. He begins this portion of his address by recalling his proclamation of the crucified Christ to the Galatians (3:1). He ends this portion of his communication by asserting the substitutionary or atoning nature of Christ's death on a cross (3:13). Together with his proofs of the Galatians' own experience of the Spirit apart from obedience to the law (3:2–5), the scripture's witness to Abraham (3:6–9), and the law's judgments upon the Torah observant and the Messiah (3:10–13), Paul builds steadily to his climactic point in 3:14: Jesus Christ's death is significant because it reveals that the blessing of being counted by God as righteous and receiving the eschatological Spirit comes only through faith in the Crucified One who bore "for us" the curse of the law. Moreover, now that the blessing of Abraham is available to Jew and Gentile alike, it is clear that a new time has begun. The age of faith has arrived.

V. THE CRUCIFIED CHRIST AND THE
REVELATION OF FAITHFULNESS: GALATIANS 3:15–4:7

Immediately following Paul's conclusion that the eschatological promise of the Spirit comes through faith in the Crucified Christ Jesus, Paul lays the foundation for a more elaborate treatment of the believer's relationship with God through faith in Christ and through participation in Christ's life and faithfulness. That foundation is the faithfulness of God the Father and the faithfulness of Christ the Son.

In 3:15–29, Paul begins elaborating upon the new eschatological era that has begun with the crucifixion of Christ Jesus. Christ has accomplished atonement for the people of God and has ended the age and authority of the law. The true heirs of Abraham are not those who keep the law but are those who belong to Christ, the "seed" of Abraham.[48] They are not under the law's

---

[47]Fee, *God's Empowering Presence*, 387.

[48]Here in his confrontation with the agitators in Galatia, Paul clearly draws considerable rhetorical advantage from his own attention to the letter of the law by stressing the singular aspect of the noun "seed." Paul and his opponents have in mind passages such as Gen 13:15–17 (LXX); 15:18; 17:8; and 24:7. Paul, however, rejects the collective sense of the singular noun, which his opponents probably stressed to number themselves as Abraham's descendents. Paul interprets the noun singularly as Christ. For an overview of

dominion. Thus, regarding the relation between the law and God's promise of blessing, Paul insists that the promise precedes the law and is better, therefore, on the basis of historical priority alone (3:15–18). Paul then addresses the difficult matter of why God gave the law in the first place (3:19–25). Paul answers that God gave the law because of the people's transgressions. The law made wrongdoing a legal offense. That is, it exposed and condemned self-righteousness and pride. Stated more positively, the law had the power to demonstrate where and how God's people erred from God's will, but it did not have the power to make the people righteous or free. It did not have the power to instill within one's heart a love and reverence for the Lord.[49] Thus the law served as a tutor (παιδαγωγός) assigned to the children of Israel until the children came of age to receive their full inheritance when Christ came. The law was to prepare Israel for Christ's coming (3:23).[50]

In Christ's coming, God's faithfulness in keeping the promise to Abraham is revealed (3:22–23). Up to this point, as Richard Hays has shown, Paul has built his case upon a christological substructure, but here Paul makes this infrastructure explicit, for the "seed" (σπέρμα) of Abraham (3:16) is the Faithful One through whom the promise is now given to all who believe in him (3:22).[51] Jesus is the promised one of God through whom God's pledged inheritance comes. Jesus reveals the faithfulness of God. Yet the faithfulness of Christ is also revealed for Christ faithfully accepted the curse of the cross in order to rescue humankind from the law's curse. Thus Christ's faithfulness makes the blessing of Abraham and the eschatological Spirit available to the Gentiles and Jews alike.

Now, Paul does not specifically state the nature of Christ's faithfulness here, but Paul has already established the faithfulness of Christ in redeeming us from the curse of the law by means of his death upon the cross (3:13–14; 4:4–5).[52] Christ's faithfulness to God the Father upon the cross is the means by which God's faithfulness to Abraham is revealed. Moreover, Christ's faithfulness is the means by which the promise is received by all who trust in him. So as Paul concludes this portion of his argument, he asserts that if one

---

Paul's interpretive technique here, see especially Dunn, *Galatians*, 183–85, and the references cited there.

[49]See, for instance, Isa 54:13; Jer 24:6–7; 31:31–34; 32:38–41.

[50]The clause εἰς Χριστόν in v. 24 is often interpreted as temporal but may also be interpreted as purposive, not unlike the preceding clause εἰς τὴν μέλλουσαν πίστιν ἀποκαλυφθῆναι in v. 23.

[51]Hays, *Faith of Jesus Christ*, 157–67. Also, Hays shows why Ἰησοῦ Χριστοῦ in 3:22 is best interpreted as a subjective genitive.

[52]Ibid., 110–15. On this point, Hays concludes: "Gal 3:13 picks up the thread of the gospel story precisely at its climactic point, alluding to and summarizing Christ's completion of his mission" (115).

belongs to Christ, then one must be a "seed" (σπέρμα) of Abraham (3:29). The faithful Crucified Christ thus marks the end of the law's service and reveals the faithfulness of God in fulfilling the promise to Abraham. The faithful God ends the former distinctions and reveals the nature of faithfulness through the Crucified Christ.

There is more at the end of chapter three, however, regarding the centrality of Jesus' crucifixion, for the Christ who revealed faithfulness upon the cross is also the one with whom the people of God now have fellowship. Believers are baptized into Christ and have put on Christ (3:27). They belong to Christ (3:29). By faith in Christ Jesus, they are all children of God (υἱοὶ θεοῦ; 3:26). Indeed, through their participation in the life of the Crucified Christ, the divisions of Jew and Greek, slave and free, male and female no longer have any bearing on their relationship with God or with one another (3:28). They are all "one in Christ Jesus" (3:28). Through trust in the crucified Christ Jesus, believers are the true offspring of God regardless of former distinctions (3:26, 28). They are united. In these ways, Paul asserts that believers now participate in the life of Christ.

In 3:15–29, Paul presents the cross of Christ as crucial for understanding the faithfulness of God and the faithfulness of Christ. With the revelation of Christ comes the revelation of faithfulness. Having established these points, Paul is now prepared to say more about living the Christian life as a child of God, as Abraham's offspring (4:1–7). Paul thus discusses further the points he raises in 3:26–29.[53] As Paul·sees it, now that the fullness of time has come through Christ's arrival (4:4) and his rescue of those who were under the law (4:5)—another reference to Christ's saving work on the cross (1:4; 2:20–21; 3:1; 3:13)—there should be no return to life lived under the "elemental spirits" of the old age (4:3). Rather, the new age of the Spirit has begun for all who by faith in Christ are adopted into God's family (4:5–7). In and among these heirs of Abraham, the Spirit is at work, and the proof of this adoption and God's activity in one's life through "the Spirit of his Son" is the believer's ability to address God in the manner of Jesus himself.[54]

---

[53]Betz, *Galatians*, 202.

[54]Paul also uses the phrase Αββα ὁ πατήρ ("Abba,! that is, Father!) in Rom 8:15 where, again, he is discussing the believer's status as a child of God and life in the Spirit. The phrase is also found in Mark 14:36 (compare with Matt 26:39 and Luke 22:42 which use only πατήρ). Betz is probably right in his observation that this duplication of the word "father" in Aramaic and Greek "seems to reflect the bilingual character of the early church" (211). It is interesting to note further, however, that in Mark's Gospel Jesus utters this phrase while expressing submission to the will of God the Father, even if it involves suffering and dying. Moreover, Paul explains the significance of the phrase in Rom 8:15–17. For Paul, to pray "Αββα ὁ πατήρ" is to have the power of the Spirit to face suffering as Christ faced the cross but also to face it with the assurance that Christ's followers are "heirs of God and fellow heirs with Christ" who "will also share his glory." There may be, then, a correlation

Throughout this portion of Paul's argument, the foundational importance of Christ's crucifixion is clear. In Christ's death on the cross, the promised age of faithfulness has dawned. Paul now picks up the theme introduced in 1:6 and turns to the matter of how one is to live in light of God's rescuing act through Jesus Christ (4:8–6:10). Let us then review some important elements in this portion of Paul's communication that continue the development of Paul's emphasis on the Crucified Christ.

VI. THE CRUCIFIED CHRIST AND THE CHALLENGE TO FAITHFULNESS: GALATIANS 5:1–12

After expressing his personal concern for the Galatians over their apparent abandonment of the true gospel (4:8–20; cf. 1:6), Paul uses a scriptural allegory of Hagar and Sarah to make his point that the Galatians belong to the family of Sarah and are the children of the promise (4:21–5:1).[55] Throughout this portion of his communication, Paul's stress on the grace of God is evident. At 5:1, Paul concludes his appeal to the Galatians that they see themselves as children of the free woman—that is, children of the promise—who need no rites such as circumcision to be in a right relationship with God.[56] Yet at 5:1, Paul also begins a forceful appeal to his listeners to hold fast to the freedom they have in Christ and to resist the temptation to be enslaved by the law.

---

between the phrase Ἀββα ὁ πατήρ and the corporate prayer and worship life of the early church. This is the case made by Ben Witherington in *Christology of Jesus*, 216–21. What is striking here for our purposes, however, is that the liturgical line Ἀββα ὁ πατήρ—with its accompanying implication of worshiping and praising God—makes a fitting corollary to Paul's earlier liturgical refrain in 1:4–5 which concludes with a doxology and incorporates the corresponding emphases on: the Galatians' fellowship with God the Father and the Lord Jesus Christ, Christ's self-offering which brought about their deliverance from "the present evil age" and "the elemental spirits of the universe," a new dimension of time, and the accomplishment of God's will. In 4:8–9, Paul turns to the Galatians' dangerous movement away from God, which corresponds to Paul's introduction of this topic in 1:6, and occupies much of Paul's attention in 4:8–6:10.

[55]The complexity of Paul's exegetical analysis of Gen 21:9–12 is well-noted and need not be rehearsed (cf. Betz, *Galatians*, 238–52, and Longenecker, *Galatians*, 200–06. It is important to observe here, however, that while Paul draws conclusions from this text that may be foreign to the intentions of the writer of Gen 21, Paul's midrash of this text uncovers an unexpected relevancy for the Galatian Christians. As Cousar comments (*Galatians*, 105–106), "Isaac and Ishmael were both circumcised (Gen 17:25–26; 21:4), but what gives Isaac a place as Abraham's free heir is the fact that he was a child of the promise."

[56]Within Judaism, circumcision is a sign of membership in the covenant community of Israel and marks those who submit to the authority of the Torah. Paul's opponents in Galatia promoted the rite of circumcision (2:12; 5:2–6; 6:12–13) and certain other observances, such as particular calendar celebrations (4:10), but they did not observe the entire law. Paul insists, however, that the law cannot be accepted in part. As Paul has already argued, a right relationship with God is established by faith alone.

Indeed, as Paul puts it, it is "for the purpose of freedom" that "Christ set us free" (τῇ ἐλευθερίᾳ ἡμᾶς Χριστὸς ἠλευθέρωσεν).[57]

The grammatical abruptness of 5:1a highlights the significance of this expression for Paul. Reader and speaker alike must pause at the beginning of this strong rhetorical period. This periodic expression begins and ends with the concept of "freedom" (τῇ ἐλευθερίᾳ and ἠλευθέρωσεν). In the word "freedom," Paul summarizes the point of his argument from 3:1 to 4:31. Freedom is the goal of Christ's rescuing act (1:4; 4:4–5) and God's saving grace and call (1:6; 5:13). There is, however, another possible outcome. So, with the corresponding period that follows in 5:1b (στήκετε οὖν καὶ μὴ πάλιν ζυγῷ δουλείας ἐνέχεσθε), Paul exhorts the Galatians to reject the law–entangled gospel. Perhaps we can see better the force of Paul's strong warning if our translation preserves the Greek word order so that the second period reads, "Stand fast, therefore, and never again in a yoke of slavery be entangled."[58] Paul is warning the Galatians of impending enslavement.[59] It now remains for Paul to explain further the threat that endangers the Galatians' Christian freedom (5:2–12) and to explicate the nature of Christian freedom (5:13–26) and responsibility (6:1–10). Once more, Paul appeals to the reality and significance of the Crucified Christ to make his case.

In 5:2–12, Paul warns the Galatians about the life-threatening challenge to their faith. The forcefulness of his expression shows the severity of the danger. With a series of tight rhetorical periods that come one after another,

---

[57]Whether 5:1 is more closely associated with 4:31 or 5:2 has been long debated. If it is aligned with the preceding context (cf. Bruce, Lightfoot, Moffat et al), it would form the conclusion of the Hagar-Sarah allegory, but it lacks a connecting particle or phrase to make that relation explicit. If it introduces the following context, it is an unusual way to begin a sentence, but it is not without precedence (cf. Betz, Longenecker, et al). The textual apparatus of the Nestle-Aland Greek Text shows additions of the relative pronoun ᾗ, which suggests an inclination to read τῇ ἐλευθερίᾳ as an instrumental dative ("by means of freedom," cf. Bruce, *Galatians*, 226; Burton, *Galatians*, 271). As the text stands, however, it could also be a dative of purpose, as I take it ("for freedom,"cf. Betz, *Galatians*, 255; Cousar, *Galatians*, 111; Dunn, *Galatians*, 261–62; Ebeling, *Truth*, 241; Longenecker, *Galatians*, 224; Matera, *Galatians*, 180), or a locative dative of place (i.e., "into freedom," Martyn, *Galatians*, 447).

[58]The "yoke of slavery" probably refers to the "yoke of the law," which was a common expression in the Judaism of Paul's day. See, for instance, Matt 11:29–30; 1 Tim 6:1; Sir 51:26; 1 Clem 16:17. These and other references are noted thoroughly by Bruce, *Galatians*, 226–27.

[59]The verb ἐνέχω occurs in the NT only here and in Mark 6:19 and Luke 11:53. It is also used in 2 Thess 1:4 in Codex Vaticanus in place of ἀνέχεσθε. In the active form, it means to "have a grudge" or "be very hostile toward someone or something." In the passive form, as it is in our text, it means to "be subject to someone else's grudge or hostility" or to "be loaded down with a burden"—a common type of existence for slaves and prisoners of war. See W. Bauer, et al, eds., *A Greek-English Lexicon of the New Testament* (Chicago: University of Chicago Press, 1979), 265, and references there.

Paul insists that accepting circumcision—or any other rite or requirement of the law—will sever one's relationship with Christ and remove one from the realm of God's grace.[60] Again, Paul frames the choice for faith in terms of "either-or." Either they accept the truth that righteousness and the Spirit come through faith alone, and so live in the domain of God's grace (5:5), or they add circumcision to the gospel of grace, and remove themselves to the realm of the law apart from Christ, God's grace, the Spirit, and the hope of righteousness (5:4).

The threat or challenge to their faith is the temptation to perfect what God has already completely accomplished by grace on their behalf through the Crucified Christ. By faith, they already have a relationship with Christ. By faith, the Spirit of Christ is at work in their lives and relationships moving them toward the eschatological righteousness for which they hope. By faith, the power of love is already active in their midst.[61] No wonder Paul has such strong words for whoever is confusing and troubling the Galatians with their "gospel plus." He not only assails them as obstacles to the truth (5:7) but also wishes that they would have themselves castrated (5:12).[62] Hard words against his opponents, however, are insufficient for breaking their spell over the Galatians (3:1). So to persuade the Galatians to uphold the freedom and gifts they already possess by faith, Paul refocuses their attention upon the "scandal of the cross" (5:11; τὸ σκάνδαλον τοῦ σταυροῦ).[63]

Crucifixion is offensive.[64] Josephus called it "the most wretched of deaths."[65] The Stoic philosopher Seneca wrote that it is better to commit suicide

---

[60]Paul's expression in 5:4 warrants comment. Here, "falling away from grace" is a result not of sin but of seeking to become acceptable to God through obedience of the law (κατηργήθητε ἀπὸ Χριστοῦ, οἵτινες ἐν νόμῳ δικαιοῦσθε, τῆς χάριτος ἐξεπέσατε).

[61]Paul's phrase at the end of 5:6 is "faith working through love" (πίστις δι᾽ ἀγάπης ἐνεργουμένη). By "faith," he means in Jesus Christ (cf. 1:23; 2:16, 20; 3:22, 26). With the word "love," Paul returns to a topic first mentioned in 2:20. In 5:22, he identifies love as a fruit of the Spirit. By being a believer, then, a Christian becomes a channel for God's love (cf. Rom 12:9; 13:8–10; 14:1–5; 15:30; 1 Cor 8:1; 13; 14:1; 16:14; 2 Cor 2:4, 8; 6:6; 8:7–8, 24; Phil 1:9, 16; 2:1–2; etc.).

[62]In De Elocutione, Demetrius notes that "orators will always employ, as they always have employed, the weapon of sarcasm" (262). Demetrius also quips that "there is some indication of a man's character in his jokes" (171). Here, Paul's strong personality is certainly apparent. On the use of sarcasm, see also De Elocutione 135 and 227.

[63]The word "σκάνδαλον" is often translated as "stumbling block," but I am using the English cognate "scandal" for the cross as something that gives offense and causes revulsion and opposition.

[64]For a thorough treatment of crucifixion in the ancient world and a rich bibliography, see Martin Hengel, Crucifixion. See also J. Schneider, "σταυρός, etc.," TDNT, vol. 7, 572–84; J. F. Strange, "Crucifixion," The Interpreter's Dictionary of the Bible Supplementary Volume, ed. Keith Crim (Nashville: Abingdon, 1976), 199–200; and Gerald G. O'Collins, "Crucifixion," The Anchor Bible Dictionary: Volume 1 (New York: Doubleday, 1992),

than allow oneself to be crucified.[66] For the Romans, crucifixion was a slave's punishment. For the Jews, as we saw above (3:13), it was a sign of God's curse upon the crucified (Deut 21:22–23). The crucifixion of the Christ, then, is precisely as Paul puts it in 1 Cor 1:23—a stumbling block to Jews and folly to Gentiles. That is because Jews would have understood the term "messiah" in some way as a designation for a political or priestly ruler sent by God who signaled the triumph of God on behalf of God's people.[67] No one could have anticipated, from existing Jewish sources, that an anointed one sent by God could suffer the shameful death and condemnation of crucifixion. The law guaranteed the impossibility of such a fate for the Christ (Deut 21:22–23).

Gentiles who understood the Judeo-Christian use of the word Christ would have also viewed a crucified Christ as an oxymoron, but for different reasons.[68] For the Greco-Roman Gentiles, it was not the collision of messianic claims with Jesus' crucifixion that proved so troubling. Rather, it was that Jesus died and yet was exalted as Lord and even Son of God. Little in the Greek or Roman philosophical spheres could have prepared Greco-Roman Gentiles for a divine being who would willingly suffer and die.[69] From either perspective, a Crucified Christ is a scandal that elicits offense, even revulsion. To both Jews and Greeks, it appears to be a failure. But as Paul has argued so persistently up to this point, the crucifixion of Jesus is God's act of salvation. It is the event by which God rescues his people from their sin and makes a new kind of life and freedom possible.

In sum, regardless of whether or not charges of promoting circumcision were made against him,[70] Paul insists that preaching circumcision masks the offensiveness of the cross. For Paul, promoting circumcision also detracts from the gospel's power (cf. 1 Cor 1:17). Paul sees the cross of Jesus, then, as central to the conflict between himself and those who would avoid persecution by

---

1207–10. See also E. Dinkler, *Signum Crucis* (Tübingen, 1967) and H. F. Hitzig, "crux," in *Paulys Realencyclopoadie der classischen Altertumswissenschaft*, vol. 4, ed. A. F. von Pauly (München: A. Druckenmüller, 1903), 1728–31.

[65]Josephus, *Jewish Wars* 7.203 (θανάτων τὸν οἴκτιστον). See also *Antiquities of the Jews* 19:94.

[66]M. Hengel, *Crucifixion*, 30–31, citing Seneca, Epistle 101 to Lucilius.

[67]See E. Schürer, *History of the Jewish People*, vol. 2, 488–554.

[68]The Greek term "χριστός" meant "ointment" or "cosmetic." In some compound uses, it can even mean "newly plastered" (W. Grundmann, et al, "χρίω," *TDNT*, vol. 9, 493–96). Some confusion was inevitable on the basis of the term itself.

[69]See, for instance, B. A. G. Fuller, *A History of Philosophy*, v. 1 (New York: Henry Holt & Co., 1951), 18.

[70]Paul could be reflecting an accusation from his opponents that he advocated circumcision, or he could be employing a rhetorical technique for the purpose of contrasting the "circumcision gospel" with his gospel of the Crucified Christ. Later, in 6:12, Paul contrasts this component of his gospel with opponents who are promoting circumcision in order to avoid persecution from proclaiming Christ's death on the cross.

promoting a form of legalism rather than proclaim Christ crucified (6:12). Paul contends, however, that trusting in the possibility of human achievement by keeping the law or any part of it minimizes what God has done through Christ's death on the cross. So by emphasizing circumcision over the cross, the agitators in Galatia are denying the sufficiency of God's grace, the reality of salvation by faith, and their status as heirs of the promise. Paul, on the other hand, preaches Christ crucified and so denies the presence of any saving power in the law. It is a proclamation that offends human pride, for it prohibits any possibility of humans saving themselves. The great hazard to faith, then, as Paul sees it, is to lose sight of the scandal of the cross, a scandal confirmed by Jesus' resurrection from the dead.

Now that he has issued this strong warning, both to the Galatians who are considering circumcision and to his opponents who are promoting it,[71] Paul proceeds to describe more fully the nature of Christian freedom.

VII. THE CRUCIFIED CHRIST AND THE CHRISTIAN LIFE: GALATIANS 5:13–6:10

In 5:13, Paul returns to the theme that he struck so forcefully in 5:1—Christian freedom. Paul hit upon the topic of freedom earlier, however. In 2:4, Paul uses the term "freedom" (ἡ ἐλευθερία) when he mentions those "false brothers who were brought in surreptitiously, who slipped in to spy out our freedom which we have in Christ Jesus." He uses the term again in the important summary statement of 3:28 (ὁ ἐλεύθερος) that "there is neither slave nor free" in Christ Jesus. Again, in chapter four, Paul uses the term when he describes Sarah as the "free woman" (4:22, 23) and Hagar as the "slave." So, also, Paul affiliates the Jerusalem located on Mt. Sinai with Hagar and slavery (4:24–25) while the Jerusalem above is aligned with Sarah. It is this heavenly Jerusalem—another apocalyptic motif—that is called "free" and "our mother" (4:26).[72] Paul also argues that the members of Sarah's family who are children of the promise are those who trust in Christ (4:30–5:1). In short, Paul wants the Galatians to resist the temptation to be enslaved to the law or to any former pagan practices (4:5, 8–10). He wants them to live freely in the freedom that is theirs in Christ Jesus.[73]

---

[71] Paul warns the Galatians that this contrary gospel is against the truth (5:7), is not from God (5:8), and threatens to effect the whole community (5:9). Moreover, its proponent(s) will receive judgment from God (5:10).

[72] On the relationship between Jewish apocalyptic expectations and the heavenly Jerusalem, see J. L. Martyn, *Galatians*, 457–66.

[73] As is well known, Paul uses the imperative frequently throughout this final section of the communication's body (5:13–6:10).

The freedom of which Paul speaks, however, is not unbridled permission to do whatever one pleases. Paul reminds the Galatians that God called them (1:6; 5:13) to freedom, but Paul adds "do not use your freedom as an opportunity for the flesh, but through love be servants of one another" (5:13). Here, Paul presents the corollary of "faith working through love" (5:6). In Christ Jesus, faith expresses itself through love and love is demonstrated through serving one another. Freedom, however, is intimately related to love and service, in Paul's mind, for freedom in Christ is what makes this loving service possible.

Freedom is a gift from God. But Paul indicates with graphic language that freedom can be misused and even cause calamity (5:15). "If you bite and devour one another," he says, "take heed that you are not consumed by one another." Thus Paul warns against the "works of the flesh" which are reflected in such practices as "fornication, impurity, licentiousness, idolatry" and the like (5:19–21). This is the negative side of freedom. Instead, Paul exhorts the Galatians to rely on the Spirit's power for experiencing the positive life of freedom. Love, joy, peace, patience, kindness, goodness, faithfulness, gentleness and self-control are chief examples of the Spirit's fruit which are manifested in and through believers (5:22–23).

For Paul, the Christian life involves loving your neighbor as yourself (5:14).[74] It is a matter of being servants of one another through love (5:13). Love is the way in which freedom in Christ expresses itself. Love is manifested in the lives of believers as a fruit of the Spirit. Servanthood, freedom, love and the Spirit are all interrelated in the closing portion of Paul's communication to the Galatians regarding the Christian life and its responsibilities (5:13–6:10). And here in this text (5:13–26), Paul appeals to the Crucified Christ as the basis for understanding these terms and their relationships for the Christian.

The significance of the Jesus' crucifixion for the believers' ethics and behavior is set in sharp relief at the end of chapter five (5:24–25) where Paul writes, "those who belong to Christ Jesus have crucified the flesh with its passions and desires" (5:24). That is, the followers of Christ are those who have died to the life-controlling, self-indulgent powers of the flesh. Instead, Christians live under the power of the Spirit and are able to exercise self-control and exhibit loving, self-sacrificing service in the manner of the Crucified Jesus Christ (cf. 5:13). Servanthood, then, is exemplified in Jesus Christ's act of exchanging places with sinful humanity in order to take the curse it deserved and to make the blessing of God available (2:20; 3:13–15). So, too, Paul has argued that the faithfulness of God the Father and Jesus Christ the Son in Christ's rescuing act on the cross brings about freedom from the law and

---

[74]Paul quotes Lev 19:18 to show that the law itself supports Paul's point. Loving one's neighbor fulfills the law.

freedom from the realm of the flesh—arenas characteristic of the old age (3:13; 4:5, 23, 29). Through Christ's crucifixion, the Spirit of the Son is now at work among the children of the promise who have been transferred into the realm of God's eschatological age (3:14, 25–29; 4:4–7, 31). Moreover, the basis for this divine faithfulness is love, which is also a fruit of the Spirit and a characteristic of those who are in Christ (5:6, 13–14).

Paul's emphasis on the Crucified Christ in 5:24 forms a fitting capstone to this portion of his argument for it brings to mind Paul's earlier appeals to the Crucified Christ under the topic of faithful discipleship. Notice, though, that again there is no middle ground for the followers of Jesus. They are either under the power of flesh (5:17) and exhibit the characteristics of unrighteousness (5:19–21) or under the power of the Spirit (5:18) and display the fruits of righteousness (5:22–23). They are either under the law (5:18) or free in Christ and empowered by his Spirit. Thus Paul strongly encourages the Galatians to "walk by the Spirit" (5:16, 25), "be led by the Spirit" (5:18), and "live by the Spirit" (5:25).

Certainly, the proof of one's relationship with God through faith in Christ is demonstrated by the fruits of the Spirit in one's life. That is, the fruits of the Spirit are gifts. The presence of the Spirit's fruit in one's life, though, depends to some extent on one's participation in crucifying the flesh. It is noteworthy that Paul uses the active form of the verb "to crucify" (ἐσταύρωσαν) in 5:24, and its meaning is to be distinguished from Paul's earlier use of the verb in the passive form in 2:19 (συνεσταύρωμαι). In Paul's earlier point regarding the significance of Jesus' death on the cross, Paul stresses that one characteristic of a believer's union with Christ is that the believer has been crucified with him. There, Paul means that the believer's faith in Jesus results in being freed from the law's control and condemnation. Here in 5:24, Paul indicates that believers are also responsible for their own active participation in crucifying the flesh with its passions and desires.[75] In light of what Paul has said earlier, the believer's death to the desires and passions of the flesh is made possible through association with the Crucified Christ. But believers gain freedom from the flesh also by actively participating in the flesh's crucifixion. By participating in putting to death the power of the flesh over their lives, believers are empowered with new life and are transferred into the "realm" of the Spirit.

Paul views the Christian life, then, both as a lifestyle that is received as a gift through faith in Christ and as active involvement in which the believer participates. In this way, Paul clearly and forcefully advances his discussion of

---

[75]Matera, *Galatians*, 211. Interestingly, this point regarding Paul's view of the believer's responsibility for "crucifying the flesh" has received little comment from interpreters of Paul. Here we see that, for Paul, "belief" and "action" correspond with one another. Indeed, by πίστις, Paul often has in mind "faithfulness."

the believer's relationship with the Crucified Christ. In 1:4, Paul mentions only Christ's self-giving to deliver sinners from the present evil age. In 2:20, Paul mentions Christ's crucifixion for the first time, but here it is in terms of Paul's co-crucifixion with Christ in a passive sense. Being crucified with Christ has happened to him, and he sees it as the basis of the new life he lives in the flesh. In 3:1, Paul describes the Christian proclamation as fundamentally a message about the Crucified Christ, the acceptance of which results in the presence and work of the Holy Spirit (3:5). Paul goes on to emphasize the significance of Christ's self-offering through his crucifixion. Jesus' death on the cross was the means by which God delivered sinners from the curse of the law—a characteristic of the present evil age (3:10–13). Now in 5:24, Paul describes the believer's life with the Crucified Christ as one in which the believer actively opposes in his or her own life the "desires of the flesh" that are opposed to God's will.[76] The Christian life, then, is a matter of active participation in Christ's death and life; it is a matter of faithfulness—belief and action together. The Christian participates in God's activity of perfecting—or making righteous—the Christian's life.

In the last movement in the body of Paul's communication to the Galatians (6:1–10), Paul elaborates on the Christian responsibility to fulfill the law of Christ by bearing one another's burdens. He then moves swiftly into his conclusion (6:11–18), and here—as we have been prepared to expect—Paul has some final words and impressions to impart upon the hearts and minds of the Galatians regarding the Crucified Christ.

VIII. THE CRUCIFIED CHRIST AND THE BOAST OF FAITH: GALATIANS 6:11–18

At the end of Galatians (6:11–18), Paul recapitulates the central points that he has presented and developed throughout this communication. The summarizing character of the closing of Galatians has long been recognized,[77] and we will see more fully in a succeeding chapter that the closing of Galatians

---

[76]The law of love and this verse's context, however, prohibit any legitimate use of this text to promote or justify violence in the name of Christ.

[77]Scholars who recognize the summarizing character of 6:11–18 include G. J. Bahr, "Subsciptions in the Pauline Letters," 32; Betz, *Galatians*, 313; Bruce, *Galatians*, 268; Burton, *Galatians*, 347–49; Cousar, *Galatians*, 148; idem, *A Theology of the Cross*, 137; Dunn, *Galatians*, 334–35; Ebeling, *Truth*, 263; Hanson, *Abraham in Galatians*, 53; Kennedy, *New Testament Interpretation*, 151; S. J. Kraftchick, "Ethos and Pathos Appeals, 260–65; Longenecker, *Galatians*, 288–89; J. L. Martyn, *Galatians*, 559–60; Matera, *Galatians*, 228–29; Mussner, *Der Galaterbrief*, 410; Jeffrey A. D. Weima, "Gal. 6:11–18: A Hermeneutical Key to the Galatian Letter," *CTJ* 28 (1993): 90–107 (see especially the extensive references here); Witherington, *Grace in Galatia*, 444. For an opposing view, see Cosgrove, *The Cross and the Spirit*, 30–31.

is as remarkable as the letter-speech's opening in summarizing Paul's major thrusts. Here, however, in drawing this chapter to a close, we will restrict ourselves to a few observations regarding the radical presence of crucifixion language in the closing of this message. Paul speaks specifically about the cross in 6:12 and 14, and in 6:17 he refers to Jesus' crucifixion by making a startling declaration that he bears on his body the marks of Jesus.

Paul's first direct statement in the closing of Galatians regarding the Crucified Christ and his cross comes in 6:12. Here, in a neatly shaped period that focuses on his opponents' desire to avoid being persecuted, Paul identifies the basis of their evangelistic work. They are more concerned with the outward appearances of the flesh, typified by their promotion of circumcision, than with promoting the gospel of the Crucified Christ, which will result in their persecution. That is, their motives have more to do with the appearance of proselytizing than with serving the needs of the proselytized.[78]

In this charge against his opponents—the first of two in the closing (cf. 6:13)[79]—Paul's use of the verb διώκωνται ("to be persecuted") calls to mind the question Paul raised in 5:11: if he is still preaching circumcision, why is he still being persecuted? There, in an aside to his audience that is difficult for us to understand, Paul seems to refer to his opponents' misrepresentation of his view of circumcision.[80] In any event, Paul is referring to his own present circumstances in which his gospel of the Crucified Christ and abandonment of the law has resulted in his persecution.[81] Here in 6:12, Paul makes a similar point in accusing his opponents. It seems they may be persecuted by Jewish Christians for not promoting circumcision among the Gentiles in Galatia.[82]

The crucial point to observe in 6:12 for now is that here, as elsewhere (3:1; 5:11), Paul identifies the watershed between himself and his opponents as the cross of Christ.[83] The cross represents the faithfulness of Christ and what God has done on behalf of sinners to rescue them (cf. 1:4). Circumcision

---

[78]Cousar, *Galatians*, 149.

[79]As we will see below, 6:12 and 13 are closely related and constitute Paul's most elaborate statement regarding the character and purposes of his opponents. Cf. 1:7; 4:17; 5:10, 12.

[80]According to Acts 16:3, Paul circumcised Timothy because his father was a Gentile. So it is possible that there was a period after Paul's call in which he assented to a relationship between circumcision and the gospel. Paul insists in 1 Cor 7:18–19, however, that circumcision was not to be sought if one was not circumcised at the time of one's call. Here in Galatians, Paul leaves no doubt that circumcision has no bearing on faithfulness to God through Christ.

[81]Cf. Gal 1:13, 23; 4:29; 2 Cor 11:23–29.

[82]Regarding persecution from Jewish Christians, see especially R. Jewett, "The Agitators," 205.

[83]Cf. Phil 3:18 where Paul calls persons who are disturbing the church "enemies of the cross of Christ."

epitomizes human faithfulness to the law and what humans do to mark themselves as heirs of God's covenant promises. According to Paul, the cross of Christ is central to his conflict with his opponents.

In 6:14, Paul champions his alignment with the gospel of the Crucified Christ. He declares "Far be it from me to boast except in the cross of our Lord Jesus Christ." The contrast between himself and his opponents could hardly be more striking. In 6:13, Paul asserts that they are boasting in the circumcised flesh of the Galatians. In v. 14, Paul proclaims emphatically that his ground for boasting is the cross of Christ. The cross of Christ lies at the heart of his gospel (cf. 1 Cor 1:17–18, 23; 2:1–2) and Paul now presents it as the antithesis of his opponents' gospel of circumcision.

The concept of boasting figures prominently in Paul's writings.[84] This is due in part to Paul's view of humanity's inclination toward self-idolatry and the corresponding boast in human achievement. For Paul, though, humans can boast of nothing before the Lord (1 Cor 1:29; 3:21), for the source of every good gift is the Lord (Rom 11:35; 1 Cor 1:7; 2:12; 4:7). The only legitimate boast, then, is in the Lord (1 Cor 1:21; 2:2; 2 Cor 10:17; Phil 3:3) or in one's weakness through which God's power is revealed (2 Cor 11:30; 12:5, 9).[85] Thus Paul boasts in the cross of the Lord Jesus Christ, for it shows the severity of Paul's need and the grace of God's power.

Paul also asserts in this verse that the cross forms the dividing wall between the present evil age that is opposed to God and God's purposes and the emerging apocalyptic age which is aligned with God and God's will. As Paul puts it in the second clause of 6:14, he will boast only in the cross of our Lord Jesus Christ "through which (or "whom"[86]) the world has been crucified to me, and I to the world" (6:14). It is still possible for one to be enslaved to "the weak and beggarly elemental spirits" (τὰ ἀσθενῆ καὶ πτωχὰ στοιχεῖα; 4:9) and so be enslaved to sin in the present age of evil (1:4).[87] But Christ died to free Jew and Gentile alike from this age and the curse that is upon it (3:13) so that in Christ Jesus one may be delivered into the realm that is aligned with God's will (3:14). Thus, in the same way that Paul described his new life earlier in terms of being crucified with Christ (2:19–20), Paul now describes his present life as one

---

[84]See C. K. Barrett, "Boasting (καυχᾶσθαι, κτλ.) in the Pauline Epistles," *L'Apôtre Paul: Personnalité, Style et Conception du Ministère*, ed. A. Vanhoye (Leuven: Leuven University Press, 1986), 363–68.

[85]Matera, *Galatians*, 226, 231.

[86]The antecedent of δι᾽ οὗ in 6:14 is not altogether clear. Since the relative pronoun οὗ could be masculine or neuter, it could refer το τοῦ κυρίου ἡμῶν Ἰησοῦ Χριστοῦ (masculine), in which case it would be translated as "through whom." It could just as well refer to τῷ σταυρῷ (neuter), however, and would be translated as "through which." I prefer the latter.

[87]See also 4:3; 1 Cor 2:12; 3:19.

that is delivered from the present age of evil. He has died to the world. That is, the world no longer controls him.

In 6:14, then, Paul claims the cross of the Lord Jesus Christ as his solitary boast. The cross of Christ is presented as the central contention between himself and his opponents in Galatia. Crucifixion is also the decisive factor in Paul's understanding of his new relationship to the present age of evil. In the opening four verses of this letter-speech's closing (6:11–14), Paul has mentioned the cross of Christ twice (vv. 12, 14), bringing to mind twice the crucifixion of Christ. He has also highlighted two other crucifixions—his and the world's (κόσμος). Here, Paul is not asserting that he no longer has any relation to the physical world and its inhabitants or that the world as ceased to exist. Rather, he is declaring that he has died to a world that is rebelling against God. He has died to the world's values and the temptation to secure his own advantage over others.[88]

With these points in place, Paul moves closer to the end of his communication in 6:17 by graphically emphasizing his intimate relation with the Crucified Christ: Paul bears on his body the scars of Christian service.[89] In this way, Paul aligns his apostolic ministry with the sufferings of Christ (cf. 2 Cor 11:23–28) and reasserts his co-crucifixion with the Lord Jesus. Moreover, he appeals to his suffering on behalf of the crucified Lord to prove his identity as a true slave of Christ (1:10).

IX. THE CRUCIFIED CHRIST IN GALATIANS

Without doubt, the Crucified Christ is a central and persistent theme throughout Galatians. Moreover, as the section headings of this chapter indicate, there is a logical progression throughout Galatians in Paul's presentation of the Crucified Christ. First, he provides a summary statement in the salutation-exordium to serve as a thematic overture for the topic (1:3–5). Here, Paul highlights the self-giving nature and the saving work of Jesus Christ (1:4). He also avers that Jesus' self-offering constitutes God's deliverance of the faithful from the present age of evil.

---

[88]Longenecker, *Galatians*, 295. See also Betz, *Galatians*, 317–19; Matera, *Galatians*, 226.

[89]Much has been made over Paul's curious phrase τὰ στίγματα τοῦ Ἰησου. Some interpreters hold that Paul has been branded or marked with a tatoo (cf. the NRSV, NEB, REB, and NJB). Such a practice was common in the ancient world for distinguishing slaves (cf. Bruce, *Galatians*, 275) or devoted followers of religious sects (cf. O. Betz, "στίγμα," *TDNT*, vol. 7, 657–64). Most interpreters, however, view Paul's reference to "the marks of Jesus" in terms of Paul's many sufferings in proclaiming the gospel (cf. Betz, *Galatians*, 323–24; Cousar, *Galatians*, 149; Dunn, *Galatians*, 346–47; Longenecker, *Galatians*, 300).

Paul then describes the self-offering of Jesus more specifically by stressing Christ's death on the cross (2:20). For Paul, a right relation with God and one's neighbor is only possible through trusting faith in Jesus Christ; righteousness does not come through works of the law. As an example of this kind of faith, Paul points to himself and stresses for the first time the believer's participation in the life of the Christ who has been crucified. Christ's death on the cross is the basis for Paul's new life (2:11–21).

Paul then turns to the Galatians' own lives of faith. He reminds them how he presented Jesus' death on the cross, for Paul sees this as central to his faithful proclamation of the gospel (3:1). He also reminds them that their acceptance of the gospel of the Crucified Christ was the foundation of their faith and experience of the Spirit (3:2–5).

Next, Paul argues for the priority of faith over the law (3:6–14). Jesus' death on the cross is the act by which persons are rescued from the curse of the law and its misdirected values (3:13). But how are the faithful of God to behave without the law to guide them (3:15–20)? First, Paul points to the faithfulness of God the Father and of the Son Jesus Christ who in Christ's crucifixion have fulfilled the promise and made righteousness available to all through faith in Jesus Christ. In the Crucified Christ, it is apparent that the new age of eschatological faithfulness has dawned (3:21–4:7).

Not everyone, however, acknowledges these truths and so they are not entering into God's eschatological realm. Indeed, the Galatians are in danger of severing their relation with God (4:8–20). Thus, secondly, Paul argues from scripture that the Galatians are already heirs of the promise by faith (4:21–31) and warns them that the great danger to their faith is the temptation to believe that any human act can improve the effect of Christ's saving work on the cross. As Paul sees it, the Galatians are in their present predicament because they have lost sight of the scandal of the Crucified Christ who died for them, a scandal confirmed by Jesus' resurrection from the dead (5:1–12).

To trust in the Christ who has been crucified, though, is to live as an heir of the promise in the realm of God's grace and to walk by Christ's Spirit, bearing the Spirit's fruit in the world. It is this trust that makes possible the law's intention that one should love one's neighbor as oneself and serve others in the manner of Christ himself. Such is the nature and responsibility of Christian freedom (5:13–6:10).

In the end, then, the Christian life and boast depend on trust in the Crucified Christ and his saving work on the cross. Christian discipleship is a matter of participating in the self-sacrificing life of the Crucified Christ on behalf of others. For Paul, the Crucified Christ is the basis for understanding the Christian faith and life (6:11–18).

Throughout Galatians, then, Paul presents the Crucified Christ as the evidence of God's apocalyptic activity and the paradigm for Christian faithfulness and discipleship. Jesus Christ who has been crucified reveals the purposes of God and makes possible the faithfulness and right relationships that God desires. This, of course, Paul affirms on the basis of God's revelation to him of Jesus the Crucified Christ whom God raised from the dead. Let us now examine in the next chapter the third major aspect of the gospel that Paul introduces in the salutation-exordium and carries throughout Galatians—the theme of God's grace-filled call and human responses to it (1:6–10).

CHAPTER SEVEN

THE RHETORICAL CORD OF THE ONE WHO CALLS IN THE GRACE OF CHRIST

The salutation-exordium of Galatians (1:1–10) shows that, although he is presenting a defense for himself, Paul frames his concern for asserting his apostolic identity and authority within his larger concern for re-presenting to the Galatians the essential character of the gospel. We have seen how Paul opens this communication by asserting his apostolic status and by rooting it in the will and calling activity of the Lord Jesus Christ and God the Father who raised Jesus from the dead (1:1). From the beginning, Paul claims his apostolic standing and identifies his apostleship as a matter to address in his letter-speech. His greater emphasis, however, lies on the apocalyptic activity of God the Father and the Lord Jesus Christ through whom Paul's apocalyptic apostleship has come.

We have also seen above that Paul employs portions of a confessional statement regarding the saving work of Jesus Christ according to the will of God (1:4). These affirmations summarize crucial theological elements of the gospel which Paul then develops in the remainder of the communication to support his position regarding the gospel (1:6–7). Paul moves from a celebration of Christ's saving work to an emphasis upon participation in the Crucified Christ's life.

In the opening of Galatians, then, the gospel declaration of God's apocalyptic activity in and through Jesus Christ, on behalf of Paul and all believers, emerges immediately as a central concern for Paul to address in this letter-speech. But it is not only his apostleship and the good news of the Risen Crucified Christ that Paul identifies here as major thrusts to amplify. In the salutation-exordium, Paul also emphasizes the One to whom all glory is due for ever and ever, the One who calls in the grace of Christ and to whom Paul, the Galatians, and Paul's opponents are all finally responsible (1:5–10). The opening of Galatians exhorts listeners and readers alike to consider carefully whom they are trying to please—to what or to whom they are offering their lives. Are they glorifying God, seeking God's favor, and acting as Christ's

195

servant? Or are they deserting God, seeking the favor of humans, and abandoning the grace of Christ?

In this chapter, we will examine the rhetorical cord of the One who calls in the grace of Christ and the significance of this call as presented in Galatians. That is, we will now consider Paul's opening assertion that the content of the gospel is not only about the Risen Crucified Christ who has accomplished the work of salvation. The gospel is also about God the Father who willed this to be so and who has called in the grace of his Son Jesus to bestow the promise upon everyone who believes the gospel of Christ. For Paul, the gospel of the Risen Crucified Christ is God's eschatological call and one's response to this gospel is a matter of life and death.

I. A THEMATIC OVERTURE FOR THE ONE WHO CALLS IN THE GRACE OF CHRIST: GALATIANS 1:6–10

The style and content of this portion of the salutation-exordium leave no doubt that Paul believes the present situation in Galatia is an affair of grave importance. As we saw above in the rhetorical and literary study of this text,[1] Paul's amazement over the Galatians' behavior is not that they are turning to different apostles but that they are turning to a different gospel, which is not the gospel of Christ. Paul's charge and warning to the Galatians, then, is that they are abandoning essential tenets of the Christian faith. They are deserting not Paul but God himself.

This is the third major concern that Paul identifies in the salutation-exordium. In fact, the periodic form of 1:6–7 suggests that this is Paul's primary concern for writing to the Galatians. Paul writes to assert his own apostolic authority and to re-present to the Galatians the Risen Crucified Christ and the significance of his death on the cross. But Paul establishes from the beginning, also, his intention to demonstrate how the Galatians are deserting the One who called them in the grace of Christ as well as why they ought to return to God as servants of Christ, following the example of Paul himself (1:6–10).

By the time Paul introduces this topic in the opening of his communication, he has already drawn his listeners and readers into a doxological refrain praising God the Father who through Jesus Christ accomplished his purpose of saving his people from the present evil age (1:4–5). It is in this light of Jesus' self-offering on "our" behalf, then, that Paul first expresses astonishment that anyone would respond to God's grace so perversely as to desert God or distort the gospel of Christ (1:6).

---

[1]See especially chapter 4 above.

Paul's use of the word μετατίθημι ("to turn away") is especially revealing at this point. Although uncharacteristic of Paul's vocabulary,[2] the word was used commonly in the Greco-Roman world to describe the act of "changing one's mind, turning oneself away, deserting, or turning apostate."[3] Within the realm of Greco-Roman philosophical schools, it designated a defector who leaves one school for another. Within the realm of Judaism—at least since the second century BC and the Syrian oppression under Antiochus IV Epiphanes—the term was applied to Jews who committed apostasy (cf. 2 Macc 4:46; 7:24). In some instances, the law prescribed death for such turncoats[4] (cf. Lev 24:16; Deut 17:1–7) and many Jews would rather die than defect from God and God's people.[5]

Both Gentile and Jewish Christians in Galatia, then, likely understood Paul when he harshly compared them to turncoats and apostates. Indeed, Paul's comparison undoubtedly shocked those who were accepting the "other gospel"

---

[2]This is the only occurrence of this word in the letters attributed to Paul. It occurs elsewhere in the NT only in Acts 7:16; Heb 7:12; 11:5; and Jude 4. It is fairly common, however, in Greek literature and usage. See Bauer, et al, *A Greek-English Lexicon*, 513, and Liddell and Scott, *Greek-English Lexicon*, 1117. Jude 4b reflects a perspective similar to that of Paul here in Galatians. It reads, ἀσεβεῖς τὴν τοῦ θεοῦ ἡμῶν χάριτα μετατιθέντες εἰς ἀσέλγειαν καὶ τὸν μόνον δεσπότην καὶ κύριον ἡμῶν Ἰησοῦν Χριστὸν ἀρνούμενοι ("ungodly persons who pervert the grace of our God into licentiousness and deny our only Master and Lord Jesus Christ").

[3]Bauer, et al, *A Greek-English Lexicon*, 513, 2b.

[4]The Temple Scroll (11Qtemple) of Qumran gives the startling warrant within Judaism for hanging a living person upon a tree (crucifixion) as the just penalty for treasonous behavior and flight from a crime punishable by death. Any Jew who betrays his people before a foreign power or flees to escape punishment for a capital offense is to be hanged on a tree. This was not the custom throughout Judaism, but the Temple Scroll indicates that such a sentence was prescribed at the time of this scroll's writing for the Jews affiliated with the Qumran community. See Y. Yadin, "Pesher Nahum," 1–12.

[5]See, for instance, the appearance of this term in the heroic account of seven brothers and their mother who accepted death from Antiochus rather than abandon their Jewish customs and faith (2 Macc 7:1–41). The significance and use of this passage and others like it in Hellenistic Judaism might well repay further study for understanding better the situation in Galatia. Particularly striking in this text is the correlation between suffering for one's own sins, the Lord's reconciling act, and the brothers' righteous suffering on behalf of all Jews. There are also some interesting correlations between this story and Paul's argument in Galatians. For instance, the story reaches its climactic conclusion with the speeches of the mother and the seventh son (2 Macc 7:24–38). First, the mother admonishes the seventh son to accept death and to trust in the merciful God who creates out of nothing and who alone gives life (2 Macc 7:28–29). Second, the seventh son pledges before Antiochus his undying devotion to "the command of the law given by Moses to our ancestors" (2 Macc 7:30), and he holds fast to God's covenant with confidence that "brief pain" in the service of God "leads to eternal life" (2 Macc 7:36). This last brother also curses his opponent Antiochus and warns of God's inescapable penalty (7:35–36) upon those "who lay hands on the heavenly children" (7:34) who are God's "servants" (δούλοις; 7:33).

because they thought it was in line with God's will.[6] The shock would have been greater still, though, for those who knew the scriptures and realized that Paul might be comparing them also to the Israelites who were deserting God even as God was sealing the covenant with Moses (cf. Exod 32:8 and Deut 9:16).[7] Paul recognizes, however, that the Galatians' abandonment of the true gospel is not complete, for Paul uses the present tense, middle voice verb form μετατίθεσθε ("are deserting"). The Galatians are in the process of turning themselves away from God, and in this turning they are already violating the first commandment and endangering their relation with God.[8] There is a real danger of becoming severed from Christ and his benefits (5:4), but there is still an opportunity for correction, and Paul is writing toward that end (cf. 4:12, 19).

From the beginning of this letter-speech, then, Paul wants his listeners and readers to hold firmly in mind the larger issue before them—their relationship with God. They are not just rejecting Paul's apostolic authority and his gospel of the Risen Crucified Christ. They are repudiating the "one who called [them] in the grace of Christ" (1:6). Grammatically, of course, the phrase "from the one who called you" (1:6) may refer either to God or Christ.[9] But Paul everywhere else refers to God as the One who calls,[10] and here, too, Paul has in mind God's activity of choosing—even commissioning—the Galatians for life and work according to God's will.[11] In turning to a different gospel, though, the Galatians are showing that their trust in the One who called in the grace of Christ is waning. Indeed, as Paul will soon argue, by accepting this other "gospel," they are denying their own experience of God's powerful life-and-community-changing presence through the Spirit (cf. 3:1–5; 4:8–9).

As Paul puts it in the opening of this letter-speech (1:1–10), the cause and power of salvation are rooted in the God who calls, and the chief expression of this call—which Paul identifies here—is "the grace of Christ."

---

[6]Dunn, *Galatians*, 40.

[7]Cited by Betz, *Galatians*, 47; Dunn, *Galatians*, 40; and Witherington, *Grace*, 82, who credit this insight to Mussner, *Der Galaterbrief*, 53, n. 54.

[8]Ebeling, *Truth of the Gospel*, 47. So also Dunn, *Galatians*, 40.

[9]Some of the older commentaries translate this phrase as "from Christ who called you in grace." Cf. Betz, *Galatians*, 48, n. 46, and the references there. Among the Reformers, Calvin, like others, translated the verse in this way (cf. Calvin, *The Epistles of Paul the Apostle to the Galatians, Ephesians, Philippians and Colossians*, 12–13) while Luther interpreted the implied subject as God (cf. M. Luther, *Lectures on Galatians – 1519*, Luther's Works, vol. 27, eds. J. Pelikan and W. A. Hansen [Saint Louis: Concordia Publishing House, 1964], 175).

[10]See Gal 1:15; 5:8, 13; Rom 4:17; 8:30; 9:12, 24, 25; 11:29; 1 Cor 1:9, 26; 7:15, 17–24; Phil 3:14; 1 Thess 2:12; 4:7; 5:24. See also K. L. Schmidt, "καλέω," *TDNT*, vol. 3, 487–89.

[11]Cf. Isa 41:8–9; 42:6; 43:1; 45:3–4; 48:12; 49:1; 51:2 as noted by K. L. Schmidt, "καλέω," *TDNT*, vol. 3, 487–91.

That is, God has made his call known in raising Jesus from the dead (1:1), in sending the self-sacrificing Jesus Christ to rescue people from both their sins and the present evil age (1:4), and in bestowing the eschatological gifts of grace and peace (1:3). God is the One who calls in the grace of Christ (1:6a). Yet it is also this calling God whom Paul contrasts with a "different gospel" (1:6). God's calling activity in the grace of Christ, then, is presented effectively as shorthand for the gospel itself. This is the good news from God that Paul neatly summarized before making his subsequent point regarding the Galatians' present circumstances. As Paul sees it, Jesus Christ is the gospel through whom God calls.[12]

One of the chief characteristics of this summons from God is "grace."[13] But there are some in Galatia who are abandoning the One who calls them in grace. So Paul alerts the Galatians from the beginning of this communication that some are calling their teaching "gospel" but are opposing God and God's purposes (1:7). The grace of Christ is not the basis or the means of their message. Thus against these opponents Paul hurls his curses (1:8–9). Their misrepresentation of the Christian gospel is a grievous offense to God, for to pervert the gospel of Christ is to desert the One whom the Christ represents and to lead others away from God. Paul wants the Galatians to know that their lives are at stake—that deserting the true gospel of Jesus Christ has eternal consequences.[14]

In 1:6–10, then, Paul not only elaborates on God's role and significance in relation to the gospel (cf. 1:4b–5) but also stresses the problem of conflicting

---

[12]B. Witherington contends that "Paul speaks here of leaving some*one* behind (the one who called you) in exchange for some*thing* (a different Gospel)," and from this draws the conclusion that "the agitators were not offering a different God or Christ or Spirit . . . but they were offering a different message" (*Grace*, 82). It seems to me, rather, that Paul does mean that the different missionary gospel of his opponents misrepresents God, Christ, the Spirit, and one's right relation with God and one's neighbor. Thus Paul admonishes the Galatians later, "Do not be deceived; God is not mocked" (6:7). Indeed, the consequence of preaching this different gospel, as Paul sees it, is God's own curse (1:8–9), for it is a perversion of the gospel of Christ, which means also that it is necessarily a perverted presentation of God, Christ, the Spirit, and living the Christian life.

[13]See above, p. 117.

[14]On Paul's curses here (1:8–9), see especially Morland, *The Rhetoric of Curse in Galatians*, and Ebeling, *Truth of the Gospel*, 43, 56–60. Ebeling writes, "This section is no more dominated than the rest of the letter by the monotony of a judgment of wrath staged by Paul himself. Instead we find here at the very beginning the polyphony growing out of the fact that the gospel, because it is a message of joyous good news, is a matter of the utmost gravity. And precisely because the gospel is the ground of freedom it does not permit arbitrary deviation. Paradoxically, the gospel must be intolerant on behalf of freedom. Therefore we can already see in vv. 6–9 the intensity of Paul's struggle on behalf of the Galatians, which will later find expression in the moving words that imply an equally intense solidarity with them (cf. especially 4:12ff)" (43).

responses to this gospel that impact one's relation with God. Indeed, the contrasting responses to God's summons in Christ could hardly be cast more antithetically in 1:7–10. On one hand, some are troubling the Galatians and wishing to promote a perverted gospel. They know the gospel, in part, then, but Paul accuses them of distorting it and being motivated by "the favor of men" (1:10). On the other hand, Paul presents himself as one who is holding fast to God the Father who calls in the grace of Christ. It is alignment with God's purposes that Paul seeks, and it is as Christ's slave that Paul acts. Here, then, in the salutation-exordium, Paul prepares the readers and listeners of this letter-speech to hear more in the body of the communication about the One who calls in the grace of Christ and the significance of this call for all to whom it is given. Let us now see how Paul develops this matter throughout Galatians.

II. THE ONE WHO CALLS FORTH GRACE: GALATIANS 1:11–2:10

In 1:11–12, Paul introduces in periodic form the first major theme of his message, which he proceeds to elaborate in the first portion of the body of the communication (1:13–2:10).[15] As the salutation-exordium shows, Paul's central concern for the entire letter-speech is the gospel of Christ. But the opening also stresses that there are particular aspects of that gospel which Paul intends to develop. The first dimension of the gospel that Paul presents is its origin (1:11–12). The gospel Paul preaches "is not according to man" (οὐκ ἔστιν κατὰ ἄνθρωπον). It is not a humanly devised construct or tradition.[16] Rather, its origin is entirely from God. The gospel of Christ was a gift to Paul from God who revealed Christ Jesus to him.

Earlier, we saw something of the apocalyptic significance of this assertion. Now, it is important to observe further that Paul presents the gospel not only as that which is synonymous with the revelation of the Risen Jesus Christ to him but also as that which came to him by God's authority and

---

[15]The form of 1:11–12 has been described as chiastic by J. Jeremias ("Chiasmus in den Paulusbriefen," 145–56) followed by Mussner (*Der Galaterbrief*, 77), Beker (*Paul the Apostle*, 44–45), and Bruce (*Galatians*, 89). Some have also followed Jeremias in positing this chiasm as the basis for describing all of Galatians as a chiasm of παρὰ ἀνθρώπου "not from a human being" (1:13–2:21) and κατὰ ἄνθρωπον "not in a human manner" (3:1–6:10) (cf. Mussner and Beker). Longenecker, however, has exposed the problems of this chiastic imposition upon the text. He contends that 1:11–2:21 are better understood on the basis of epistolary formulas and the rhetorical characteristics of narratio (1:11–2:14) and propositio (2:15–21) (Longenecker, *Galatians*, 21–22). It should be noted regarding the form of 1:11–12, however, that it is better described as periodic rather than chiastic. It bears the characteristic signature of balanced antithetical clauses but moves steadily to the climactic expression ἀποκαλύψεως Ἰησοῦ Χριστοῦ.

[16]Bauer, et al, *A Greek-English Lexicon*, 68, 1c.

revealing power. For Paul, Jesus Christ is the content of God's eschatological revelation.[17] As such, Paul is asserting that Jesus Christ is God's own expression of God's purpose for the world.

The revelation of Jesus Christ to Paul was a startling and life-changing event.[18] Indeed, Paul immediately explains that before his encounter with the Risen Crucified Christ, he was conducting his life in the manner of a faithful and zealous Jew. He was progressing in Judaism,[19] surpassing many of his Jewish contemporaries in observing the law and the traditions surrounding it.[20] He confesses that he was even an ardent and violent persecutor of those who opposed the law.[21] Paul's pre-Christian faith and conduct, then, brought him into direct conflict with the followers of Jesus Christ, whom Paul designates here as the "church of God" which Paul was seeking to destroy.[22] How astonishing, then, that God should voluntarily come to this virulent opponent of God's purposes and God's faithful people and reveal the Risen Crucified Christ to him. Yet God revealed Jesus Christ to him and the persecutor became the promoter.

Paul also wants his listeners and readers to understand that the transformation in Paul's way of life and perspective regarding the "church of God" was entirely God's doing (1:12, 16). Paul proclaims confidently that "he (God) considered it appropriate—that is, he who set me apart from my mother's womb and had called me through his grace—to reveal his Son to me" (1:15–16a).[23] The placement of the verb εὐδόκησεν at the beginning of this Greek sentence, followed by a lengthy clause describing God as the One who sets

---

[17]The phrase ἀποκαλύψεως Ἰησοῦ Χριστοῦ is best taken as an objective genitive here. See above, chapter 5.

[18]Dunn (*Galatians*, 53) and Bruce (*Galatians*, 88–89) contend that Paul must mean here the event described in Acts of Jesus' appearance to Paul along the road to Damascus. Ebeling argues, however, that the "peculiar textual witness in Acts itself precludes any attempt to interpret Paul's words on the basis of these accounts with their legendary elaborations, in order to identify particular details" (*Truth of the Gospel*, 68).

[19]Paul uses the imperfect verb προέκοπτον.

[20]Zealousness for the law and the traditions of Israel are a recurrent theme in the OT (cf. Gen 34; Num 25; 1 Kgs 18–19; 1 Macc 2; 2 Macc 4). See T. L. Donaldson, "Zealot and Convert: The Origin of Paul's Christ–Torah Antithesis," *CBQ* 51 (1989): 655–82.

[21]See also 1 Cor 15:9 and Phil 3:6. On the violent action associated with the verb πορθέω, see especially Dunn, *Galatians*, 58, along with the references there.

[22]The conative sense of the imperfect verb ἐπόρθουν is well-noted. Cf. J. A. Brooks and C. L. Winbery, *Syntax of New Testament Greek* (Lanham, Md.: University Press of America, Inc., 1979), 91.

[23]Compare the close parallel of Jeremiah's call and commissioning in Jer 1:5f. See also Isa 49:5.

apart[24] and calls through his grace, emphasizes God's initiative in rescuing Paul from a life bent against God's will.

It is also significant here that the revelation of Jesus Christ is Paul's key for understanding his own life within the will and purposes of God. Following his encounter with Christ, Paul sees and affirms that God's earliest and constant design for Paul's life has been to make him a bearer of God's eschatological good news to the Gentiles (1:16). Paul's new way of life as an apostle is the result of God's appointment for the work of evangelizing the Gentiles. The content of this good news, again, is the revealed Christ, Jesus—crucified and risen.[25]

So crucial are these dimensions to the origin of Paul's gospel and the change in Paul's life that he swears an oath of truthfulness before God when he recounts his first trip to Jerusalem as a believer (1:20).[26] In this way, he emphasizes again that he did not receive the gospel through human means. No one but God can receive credit as the source of Paul's gospel and the transformer of his life. On this truth, Paul stakes not only his apostleship but his entire relationship with God, for God is not mocked without just punishment (1:8–9; 6:7). With this pledge, then, Paul also brings to mind once more God's role as the Judge before whom all people must answer regarding the conduct of their lives.[27]

Paul gives further support regarding the truth of his testimony and legitimacy of his God-commissioned apostolic work in the churches of Christ when he states succinctly the consequence of his ministry. The people to whom he preached glorified God because of him (1:24).[28] Paul's apostolic service as a slave of Christ (1:1, 10, 16–23) did not generate praise and honor for Paul. Rather, the consequence of God's gracious call and Paul's faithful conduct in

---

[24]God's activity of setting persons and things apart (ἀφορίζειν and ἀφόρισμα, -μός) for a particular service to God is deeply rooted within the OT (cf. Exod 13:12; 19:12, 23; Lev 14:12; 20:26; 27:21; Num 15:19; 18:24; Isa 56:3; Ezek 44:29; 45:1, 4; 48:9).

[25]Paul consistently notes that Jesus Christ is the core content of the gospel. See, for instance, Gal 3:1 as well as Rom 1:3–4, 9; 15:19; 1 Cor 1:23; 2:2; 2 Cor 1:19; Phil 1:15, 27.

[26]See H. Conzelmann, "ψεύδομαι," TDNT, vol. 9, 594–603; Bauer, et al, A Greek-English Lexicon, 891; J. P. Sampley, "'Before God, I Do Not Lie' (Gal 1:20)," 477–82. On the rhetorical use of oaths, see Quintilian, Institutio, 5.6.1; 9.2.98.

[27]On the prevalence in the OT and NT of God's role as judge, see F. Büchsel, "κρίνω," TDNT, vol. 3, 921–38. In Galatians, see 1:8–9; 1:20; 2:11; 5:10; 6:7. For Paul's view more generally, see especially Rom 1:18–32; 2:1f; 5:9–10; 8:31f; 1 Cor 3:15; 2 Cor 5:10. Note, too, that Paul consistently views God's judgment within the realm of God's love and mercy.

[28]The phrase ἐν ἐμοὶ may be translated in as "in me," "to me," "for me," or "because of me." The causal force of the preposition and dative personal pronoun in the last example is best here, however, for Paul is asserting that the people are praising God because of his apostolic call and work. Also, Paul's climactic emphasis on glorifying God is evident in the order of Paul's words (ἐδόξαζον ἐν ἐμοὶ τὸν θεόν).

proclaiming the Risen Crucified Christ was the glorification of God among the people—including Gentiles. It is to this end that Israel's faith and history have pointed.[29] Moreover, giving glory to God forever is appropriate (1:5) because of God's gracious initiative in Christ's rescue of sinners. This is the chief consequence of Paul's preaching (cf. Gal 6:13; Rom 15:6–7; 1 Cor 10:31; 2 Cor 4:15; 8:19; 1 Thess 2:6).[30]

Throughout this portion of his address to the Galatians, then, Paul establishes his claim that his gospel is not of human origin (1:1, 11–12). He was not commissioned to be an apostle by others who were apostles before him nor was he taught the gospel (1:18–20). Rather, the good news came to him through God's eschatological revelation of Jesus Christ (1:12, 15–16). Paul also stresses the surprising grace of God through whom Paul's call came (1:15). Because of God's gracious intervention, a new person has been created out of an obedient Jew who was persecuting God's own church and opposing God's will. Paul is now fulfilling God's purpose for his life and people are glorifying God because of him. All of this stands on the initiating and sustaining grace of God.

God's grace is central to Paul's call and new life. It is also a distinguishing characteristic of the chief leadership of the early church (2:6–10). According to Paul, the leaders of the church in Jerusalem recognized and accepted the fact that God had entrusted him with the work of evangelizing the Gentiles even as Peter was entrusted with the work of evangelizing the Jews (2:7–8).[31] Of course, it is not clear whether they accepted the validity of Paul's apostleship more on the basis of his commission (1:11–16), his work (1:21–23), reports about his work (1:23–24), or his own presentation to them of the gospel that he preached (2:2).[32] What is clear is that the church leaders in Jerusalem recognized that Paul was bearing God's grace to the Gentiles in his ministry just as Peter was conveying God's grace in his ministry among the Jews (2:7–9).[33] God's grace, then, is not only foundational to Paul's new apostolic life but

---

[29]Cf. Exod 15:2; Lev 10:3; 1 Sam 2:30; 1 Esdras 8:25; 2 Esdras 8:36; Pss 22:23; 50:15, 23; 86:9, 12; Isa 5:16; 25:1; 33:10; 42:10; 44:23; 49:3; 59:19; 60:4–7; 66:5, 18–19; Hab 2:14. Also, the glorification of God among the Gentiles is an eschatological sign.

[30]Giving glory to God is an important theme throughout the Pauline letters. In addition to the references cited above, see also such texts as Rom 4:20; 11:36; 16:27; 2 Cor 8:23; Phil 2:11; 4:20; Eph 3:16–17, 21; 1 Tim 1:17.

[31]The perfect passive verb πεπίστευμαι ("I had been entrusted") indicates that the Jerusalem apostles came to recognize Paul's apostolic authority that had already been in effect. The unexpressed subject of ὁ ἐνεργήσας ("the One who was at work") is God; Paul and Peter are the objects. The two gospels in 2:7 refer not to different content but to different audiences. This is Paul's point of clarification in 2:8.

[32]Longenecker, *Galatians*, 55.

[33]Paul's use of the article with the word "grace" (τὴν χάριν) indicates that he is not referring to grace in general but has in mind specifically the grace of God. This is also the view of Betz, *Galatians*, 99; Burton, *Galatians*, 95; and Longenecker, *Galatians*, 56. Others,

it is also a distinguishing element of the gospel proclaimed by both Paul and Peter. This grace of God made evident in the preaching of Paul and Peter, then, has recognizable characteristics. One distinguishing trait stressed here is that divine grace was a distinctive mark of the church when it was united in Jerusalem. Jewish and Gentile Christians shared the "right hand of fellowship" with one another, and they committed themselves to the proclamation of the gospel of Christ and to the service of the poor (2:6–10). Now it is not certain what Paul means by the phrase "only they would have us remember the poor."[34] It may be, though, that Paul is not only referring to the needs of Jewish Christians in Jerusalem but is also calling attention here to the ethical dimension of the gospel that they are proclaiming (cf. 5:13–6:10). Serving the poor is always an act of grace, and here it is tied to the proclamation of the One who calls through his grace. God's grace through Christ brings forth grace from Christ's followers.

III. THE ONE WHO CALLS FORTH TRUST:
GALATIANS 2:11–21

Beginning at 2:11, Paul signals for his listeners a transition in his argument by disrupting the narrative flow of his argument regarding the origin and character of his apostleship and the gospel. The narrative cadence that he marked most audibly by the repetition of ἔπειτα ("then," 1:18; 1:21; 2:1) is broken by the insertion of ὅτε δέ ("but when"). The transition becomes more pronounced in 2:14–16 where the personal pronouns also shift from the singular "you" of 2:14 (σύ) to the plural "we" (ἡμεῖς) in 2:15–16. Moreover, Paul uses direct discourse for the first time, which heightens the significance of this account for his present purposes. In these ways, Paul now focuses the attention of his listeners and readers on the chief matter that concerns them both.

As we observed in the previous chapter, Paul asserts that he and Peter had a showdown in Antioch (2:11–14). The issue was the inclusion of Gentile Christians into the full fellowship of the church.[35] At stake was the "truth of the gospel" (2:14). And while the truth of the gospel had been preserved from earlier attacks (2:5), now even church leaders like Peter and Barnabas were surrendering the truth of the gospel for fear of those who were attacking it and

---

such as Bruce, *Galatians*, 121; Mussner, *Galaterbrief*, 118; Schlier, *Der Brief an die Galater*, 78, have proposed that Paul is referring to apostolic grace.

[34]On this complicated issue, see E. Bammel, "πτωχός," *TDNT*, vol. 6, 888–915; Betz, *Galatians*, 101–03; Longenecker, *Galatians*, 59–61; Martyn, *Galatians*, 222–28.

[35]See the discussion in chapter 6 above. Also, while the historical concerns of this incident are not an issue in this study, this brief account continues to draw the attention of many able scholars, as well it should. See especially Betz, *Galatians*, 101–112, and Longenecker, *Galatians*, 62–80, and the many sources cited there.

its supporters (2:12). But Paul seems to reason that if the truth of the gospel is being abandoned out of fear—even in part—then the gospel's truth must not yet be sufficiently grasped. So drawing a parallel between this earlier conflict in Antioch and the Galatians' own present situation, Paul turns to the matter of explaining more fully here the truth of what God has accomplished in Jesus Christ (2:15–21). Again, using himself as an example, Paul contends that the righteousness and the kind of life that God desires for his people come only through faith in Christ and not by works of the law (2:16). Indeed, "living for God"—an eschatological goal and status for God's faithful,[36] is not possible through the law. Rather, if one desires to live for God now and in the day to come, then one must be dead to the law and the trust it fosters (2:19). The law has run its course. Thus one must be willing to die to the law and to the lifestyle it shapes in order to receive the new life God gives through his Christ who gave himself for sinners and resides in them on the basis of trust (2:20). One cannot become justified with God on the basis of works of the law. Being counted as righteous and becoming righteous depend wholly on one's trust in the saving grace of God.

In these ways, God's grace is central to the gospel Paul proclaims. It is by God's grace that Paul's call is received (1:12, 15–16). It is God's grace that stands at the center of the church's ministry and unity (2:9; 3:27–28).[37] It is God's grace that Paul's message and life declare (1:3–4, 6; 2:4–5, 10, 16–20; 6:18). In no way does Paul's apostolic life and work nullify the grace of God (2:21).

This is the climactic point to which Paul has steadily moved.[38] Throughout 1:11–2:21, Paul has shown that any actual or hypothetical charge that he has nullified God's grace must be unfounded.[39] As Paul sees it, the "grace of God" (ἡ χάρις τοῦ θεοῦ) is not demonstrated through God's gift of the law. Rather, it is exemplified in the salvation that Christ brings through his

---

[36]Matera, *Galatians*, 96. See also Dan (DanTh) 6:21; 4 Macc 7:19 (πιστεύοντες ὅτι θεῷ οὐκ ἀποθνήσκουσιν ὥσπερ οὐδὲ οἱ πατριάρχαι ἡμῶν Αβρααμ καὶ Ισαακ καὶ Ιακωβ ἀλλὰ ζῶσιν τῷ θεῷ); 4 Macc 16:25 (ἔτι δὲ καὶ ταῦτα εἰδότες ὅτι οἱ διὰ τὸν θεὸν ἀποθνήσκοντες ζῶσιν τῷ θεῷ ὥσπερ Αβρααμ καὶ Ισαακ καὶ Ιακωβ καὶ πάντες οἱ πατριάρχαι); Rom 7:1–6.

[37]Paul's dual emphasis on grace and its accompanying unity runs from 2:11 to 3:28.

[38]Paul refrains from using the phrase "the grace of God" (τὴν χάριν τοῦ θεοῦ) until the climactic conclusion of this pericope (2:15–21). A sentence of refutation is a common way to end a *propositio*. Cf. Betz, *Galatians*, 126–27, and Longenecker, *Galatians*, 94. A *refutatio*, however, may also be part of a proof. See Quintilian, *Insitutio*, 3.9.1–5.

[39]As Betz observes (*Galatians*, 126), "The implication is that the denial rejects a charge actually made by Paul's opponents. They could make such a charge if their concept of divine redemption ('grace of God') would include Torah covenant. But it could also be Paul himself who draws the conclusion from whatever his opponents say against him, and denies it."

death on the cross (2:20; 3:1). Thus Paul declares that if God is not behind
Christ's death for the purpose of salvation, then Christ died in vain.
Furthermore, it is through the grace of the "Son of God who loved me and gave
himself for me" that Paul now experiences a new kind of life in the flesh. This
new life is not held in bondage to a Law (2:4–5) that would restrict the
extension of God's grace in Christ from those whom God has called (2:6, 11–
14; 3:1–14). Neither does this new life sever one from Christ, divine grace, and
the hope of righteousness (5:2–5). Rather, Paul sets his whole new life in Christ
within the realm of God's grace (1:1, 15–16; 2:9, 19–20). For Paul, one is made
righteous and will live for God in the eschatological day not through trust in the
law's standards (2:18) but through trust in the saving death and the continuing
presence of the Risen Crucified Jesus Christ. It is only Christ who saves, who
makes possible the life and service God desires for the new era which has
already begun in the present day. This, for Paul, is the purpose of God's call in
Christ's grace. It is Paul's witness regarding the gospel. It is a gospel that can
be trusted.

IV. THE ONE WHO CALLS FORTH A NEW PEOPLE:
GALATIANS 3:1–14

Now that Paul has brought to a close his preliminary testimony regarding
his apocalyptic apostleship (1:1; 1:11–2:10) and re-introduced his concern for
the truth of the gospel (1:4; 2:11–21), he is ready to develop the particular
aspects of the gospel's truth (2:14) which he believes are most pertinent to the
Galatians and their situation. To mark this turn in his address, he reprimands the
Galatians with an expression of rebuke (3:1) and asks them to recall how they
first experienced the truth of the gospel through the eschatological gift of the
Spirit (3:2). If they will but answer this one question in truth, the problem that
exists between them regarding their trust in the gospel will be resolved.[40]
Before they became Christians, were they Gentiles apart from the law or were
they law-abiding Jews? In honesty, they were neither Jews nor obedient to the
Law (4:8–9), thus their experience of God's grace and power came through
their acceptance of the true gospel quite apart from trust in the law and
adherence to its demands. It was by accepting Paul's message regarding the
significance of Jesus' death on the cross and by faith in the Risen Crucified
Christ that the Galatians turned to the One who calls in the grace of Christ and
received the divine Spirit.

Although the Galatians were Gentiles who "were in bondage to beings
that by nature are no gods" (4:8), God called the Galatians in the grace of Christ

---

[40]Paul begins this sentence by declaring, "This only do I wish to learn from you"
(τοῦτο μόνον θέλω μαθεῖν ἀφ ὑμῶν).

(1:6) through Paul's proclamation of the Crucified Christ (2:8; 3:1; 4:13). And because the Galatians placed their trust in God as Abraham did before them, God gave the Spirit continuously and worked mighty acts among them (3:5; 4:6). That is, the Spirit manifested itself in the believers in a powerful, miraculous way.[41] This is because the Spirit that God sent is the Spirit of God's own Son (4:6) who empowers the believer to live the Christian life (5:18, 25) and bear the fruit of the Spirit (5:22).

Such was evidently the Galatians' own experience of God's presence and work among them. Thus, as Paul argues throughout chapter three, God does not show partiality on the basis of race, gender, or social status (3:27–28). The blessing promised to Abraham is now available to all who trust God as Abraham trusted (3:6–7, 9, 14). By God's grace, the promised blessing to Abraham is now coming to fulfillment in Christ Jesus. As God planned and scripture itself foresaw,[42] the good news of the gospel was proclaimed long ago: in Abraham all the nations shall be blessed (3:8).[43] Indeed, Christ died on the cross, in part, for the very purpose of extending the blessing of Abraham to the Gentiles (3:14a).[44] Thus, by Christ's death, Gentiles of faith are now included with Jews of faith as Abraham's heirs. Moreover, Christ died on the cross in order that all who believe might receive the promised Spirit (3:14b). Thus, the sign of a person's inclusion among the heirs of Abraham, Paul argues, is one's trust in God through Jesus Christ and the presence and activity of the Spirit in one's life (3:14).

Throughout this portion of his address (3:1–14), Paul stresses that, in the Crucified Christ, God acted mercifully on behalf of all the peoples of the earth. Jew and Gentile alike have been rescued from the curse of the law (3:10–13),[45] and this is entirely God's doing through Christ Jesus. By Christ's death, it is now possible for all who are in Christ to be heirs of Abraham (3:7, 16).

---

[41]This is also the sense in which Paul uses the word δυνάμεις in Rom 15:19; 1 Cor 12:10, 28, 29.

[42]Paul's attribution of foresight to scripture is similar to the rabbinic practice of personifying scripture (cf. Longenecker, *Galatians*, 115). Paul views scripture similarly in 3:22 and 4:30 as well as in Rom 4:3; 9:17; 10:11; and 11:2. See also 1 Tim 5:18.

[43]Cf. Gen 12:1–3; 13:14–17; 15:5–6; 17:4–8; 18:18; 22:17–18; 28:4.

[44]This verse (3:14) is comprised of two purpose clauses (ἵνα) that modify 3:13 by explaining Christ's redemptive work of becoming a curse for us upon the cross.

[45]For the Jews, the curse of the law is that it leads them to trust in the law rather than in God. One does not have to trust God in the manner of Abraham in order to do the law (3:12a). Paul contends, however, that one must trust God in the manner of Abraham if one is to receive the blessing of Abraham and receive the promise of the Spirit through faith. For the Gentiles, the law excludes them from the covenant community even though God promised to include them in the blessing of Abraham. Paul's use of the first person plural "we might receive" (λάβωμεν) in 3:14b indicates that the promised eschatological gift of the Spirit is now available to Jew and Gentile through Christ's redemptive act on the cross.

Through Christ's redemptive act on the cross, God extends the blessing of Abraham to all who trust in Christ—including Gentiles. In Christ, God is calling forth the countless descendants of Abraham as God had promised to do and as scripture foretold (Gen. 22:17–18; 28:4). In Christ, God has given the gift of the Spirit to the Jews and Gentiles alike and made them descendants of Abraham and heirs of God's blessing. As Paul sees it and presents it here, the grace of God is everywhere apparent. God has called forth a new people from among both Jews and Gentiles—a people of faith. But how exactly are all these heirs to relate to one another, and how are they to relate to God? To these matters Paul now turns.

V. THE ONE WHO CALLS FORTH NEW RELATIONSHIPS: GALATIANS 3:19–29

By faith in Christ, a new people is formed (1:13–16, 23; 2:16, 19–20; 3:2–5, 8, 14). God is now adopting both Jews and Gentiles into the household of faith on the basis of their trust in Christ. As Paul presents it in 3:15–18, God's gift of sonship[46] is now being offered to Jew and Gentile on the basis of God's promise to Abraham's seed who is Christ. The law, then, which God gave to the Jews centuries after God's promise to Abraham, does not change or nullify God's earlier promise. Still, Paul must explain for the benefit of the Galatians who are being tempted to yoke themselves to the law, as well as for Paul's opponents who are promoting such a union, the relationship between sonship in Christ and the law (3:19–22). That is, if being in Christ by faith is the basis for receiving the blessing of Abraham, then what is the purpose of the Law (3:19)?

In 3:19, Paul asserts that the law was added for the purpose of making transgressions known.[47] The law made it possible for the Jews to identify

---

[46]Paul uses the phrase "sons of Abraham" (υἱοὶ Ἀβραάμ) in 3:7 and throughout his argument in chapter four (3:26; 4:4, 6, 7, 22, 30). The use of this phrase in 3:26, however, demonstrates that Paul has both men and women in mind. It is also important to note that Paul is using a metaphor that reflects the social custom of his time. Male children typically received the inheritance.

[47]The difficult phrase τῶν παραβάσεων χάριν προσετέθη in 3:19 may be translated in several ways. This is due largely to the preposition χάριν which may indicate either cause ("because of transgressions") or goal ("for the purpose of transgressions"). Some interpreters take it to mean the former, thus they interpret the law as something God gave to increase transgressions (cf. Betz, *Galatians*, 165–67; Martyn, *Galatians*, 354–55). Others take it to mean the latter, thus they interpret the law as that which God gave for making transgressions known (cf. Dunn, *Galatians*, 188–89; Longenecker, *Galatians*, 138; Matera, *Galatians*, 128). This latter view is better supported by other statements Paul made regarding the law's function of making sin known (cf. Rom 3:20; 4:15; 5:13; 5:20; 7:7–8, 13) and is the

transgressions against God's will, and that was a distinctive advantage for the Jews while the law was serving its purpose. Unlike Gentiles, the Jews were able to discern when they committed sin. The law, then, served as a guide for the Jews, a tutor assigned by God to help prepare the people of God for the coming of Christ (3:24). It was not given as a remedy for sin; its purpose was for sin's diagnosis.

God's prescribed remedy for sin is the crucifixion of Christ and the believer's participation in Christ's life through faith. Since God has acted in Jesus Christ and graciously gives the Spirit of his Son to those who are in Christ, the law's purpose has come to an end (3:19b; 4:4).[48] According to Paul in Galatians, the law is a merciful gift of God to the people of Israel. But it had a beginning at a particular time 430 years after God's promise to Abraham and it has an end now in the coming of Christ, the promised seed of Abraham (3:19). For this reason Paul can argue that the law is not opposed to the promises of God (3:21). Rather, the problem of the law is that it does not make one alive to God or make one righteous before God.[49] These are only possible by faith in Jesus Christ. Faith is now the basis upon which God's blessing is given and received. Thus anyone who grounds his or her relationship with God on the law must now abandon the law, for it is a thing of the past, part of the old age that is passing away. God has now fulfilled the promise given to Abraham so that righteousness is available to Jew and Gentile by faith in Christ (3:7–8, 9, 18, 21–22, 24–26). "In Christ Jesus," Paul says, "you are all sons of God, through faith" (3:26).

What Paul argued primarily on a personal dimension in chapters one and two, he asserts on a corporate dimension in chapters three and four. In Christ, a new people is formed. For instance, here Paul contends that anyone who is in Christ is not under the law. The law that once divided Jews and Gentiles has come to an end in Christ (3:24; cf. Rom 10:4). Furthermore, believers cannot be under the law's jurisdiction because they are already "children of God" (3:26;

---

position adopted here. See also Gal 5:14 and 6:2 where Paul uses the word "law" in a positive light.

[48]Paul's reference to angels in 3:19 and cryptic comment in 3:20 are given as support for his view that the tradition of angelic mediation in the giving of the law at Sinai (cf. Deut 33:2, LXX; and Ps 68:17 [67:18, LXX]) proves not the law's superiority but its inferiority to the promise. See the discussion and references in Longenecker, *Galatians*, 138–43.

[49]It has been argued that this view of the law is "not how the Old Testament presents the Law," that it is a "Christological interpretation developed in light of the revelation of Jesus Christ" (Matera, *Galatians*, 140). While this is certainly true in large measure, there are hints in the Old Testament of the Mosaic law's inability to bestow righteousness. That is, Paul's christological interpretation has support in the OT. For instance, the prophet Jeremiah certainly understood that something more was needed regarding the Mosaic Law, particularly God's own activity within the believer (Jer 31:31–34; 32:38–41). Again, the relationship between Paul and Jeremiah might repay further study.

υἱοὶ θεοῦ). This is the result of God's gift of the Spirit (4:6–7). God's redeeming act in Jesus Christ, then, means that Jews and Gentiles must now relate to God and to one another in a new way.

In 3:26–29, Paul brings this portion of his argument to a forceful climax.[50] This new people comprised of Jews and Gentiles is to relate to God and to one another "in Christ Jesus" (3:26). This, in fact, is the same point Paul made earlier in presenting his own life in Christ (2:19–20) and its significance for relating to others who are also in Christ (2:11–14). Being in Christ is the way to be properly related to God (2:16; 3:7, 9, 14). Moreover, in Christ there is a new order of equality among believers. "There is neither Jew nor Greek, there is neither slave nor free, there is neither male nor female" (3:28). By God's act of grace through Christ, the divisions of race, social position, and gender—partitions that customarily promote and maintain inequality between persons and communities—are obliterated for all who "through faith" have been "baptized into Christ" and have "put on Christ" (3:27).[51] In Christ there is a new order of unity shared among believers which pays no heed to the social and cultural boundaries that are characteristic of the old age.

Paul's central affirmation here is that God has done an entirely new thing in Christ Jesus. The blessing of Abraham has now come to the Gentiles as God promised through Abraham's seed, who is Christ (3:9, 15–16, 29). God is now supplying the Spirit in and among those who believe (3:2, 5, 14; 4:6). God is now making Gentiles righteous by faith in Christ (3:6, 8, 11, 21, 24). God has ended the law's work as παιδαγωγός for the age of faith has now come (3:13–14, 24–25; 4:2–6).

Throughout this portion of his communication (3:1–29), Paul has stressed that God—who raised Jesus Christ from the dead (1:1), who radically altered Paul's life on behalf of the gospel (1:12–16), and who commissioned evangelists for calling in Christ both Jews and Gentiles (2:8)—has already created in Christ a new order for relating to God and to others. That is, the gospel of God's grace in Christ that Paul has received and proclaims is not just

---

[50]Witherington (*Grace in Galatia*, 193) agrees with Hansen's view ("Paul's Three-Dimensional Application of Genesis 15:6 in Galatians," *Trinity Theological Journal* [1989]: 73) that, "The unity and equality of all believers in Christ is the foundational principle and overarching aim of Paul's entire argument." For Witherington, "Galatians is one large deliberative act of persuasion for the unity of the body of Christ in Galatia" (193). To be sure, these matters are important to Paul in his address to the Galatians, but it is the contention of this study that more foundational still is Paul's understanding and presentation of the gospel of the Risen Crucified Christ.

[51]Betz's proposal, following Schlier (*Der Brief an die Galater*, 174–75), that "Paul has lifted Gal 3:26–28, in part or as a whole, from a pre-Pauline liturgical context" (*Galatians*, 184) is generally supported. See Hansen (*Abraham in Galatians*, 137) and Longenecker (*Galatians*, 154–55).

a summons to a new type of personal religious experience (3:1–5). It is also a community-changing force through which all the nations shall be blessed (3:8).

In Christ, God has called into being a new family, one family comprised of Jews and Gentiles.[52] Thus the family of Abraham, which was once divided (cf. 4:22–23; Gen. 16:1–16; 20:1–34), is now united in Christ, and the distinguishing characteristic of this unique family is faith in the Risen Crucified Christ.[53] By God's gracious will and initiative (1:4), the promise of God (3:29) is given to all who entrust their lives to Jesus Christ the Lord (1:3). To be in Christ and to be a member of this new family, then, means that one's life and relationships cannot go on as before. Consequently, Paul must now clarify the decision before the Galatians and address the radical consequences that come from accepting the gospel of Jesus Christ and living in this new fellowship.

VI. THE ONE WHO CALLS FORTH A DECISION: GALATIANS 4:8–5:12

Paul wants to impress upon his hearers the seriousness of their situation. But before pleading with the Galatians to examine the consequences of accepting the alien gospel of the agitators who are in Galatia, and before strongly urging them to return to the true gospel of Jesus Christ, Paul recapitulates certain highpoints of his preceding discussion regarding the truth of the gospel. He signals this move toward summation aurally in 4:1 with the phrase λέγω δέ ("but I say").[54] In 4:1–7, Paul notes that, prior to God's act in Christ, Jews and Gentiles alike were enslaved to lords other than God (cf. 4:8).[55] But when the time of God's choosing came, God sent forth his Son to redeem those who were estranged from God, and God sent the Spirit of his Son into the hearts of both Jewish and Gentiles believers who were in Christ.

---

[52]Cousar, *Galatians*, 89, writes that here "the redefinition of the people of God is now complete."

[53]N. T. Wright, "Gospel and Theology in Galatians," *Gospel in Paul: Studies on Corinthians, Galatians and Romans for Richard N. Longenecker*, JSNTSup 108, eds. L. A. Jervis and P. Richardson (Sheffield: Sheffield Academic Press, 1994), 235–36.

[54]Paul also uses the phrase in a summary fashion in 3:17 and 5:16.

[55]On the difficult matter and longstanding controversy over the precise meaning here of the phrase τὰ στοιχεῖα τοῦ κόσμου ("elemental substance of the world"), see Betz, *Galatians*, 204–05 (especially the literature cited in n. 30); Burton, *Galatians*, 510–18; G. Delling, "στοιχέω, συστοιχέω, στοιχεῖον," *TDNT*, vol. 7, 670–87; and Dunn, *Galatians*, 212–13. Dunn summarizes the matter precisely when he writes that Paul is likely "referring to the common understanding of the time that human beings lived their lives under the influence or sway of primal and cosmic forces, however they were conceptualized" (213). This is also Paul's perspective in Rom 1:14–23 where he argues that human beings are creatures whose fundamental question is what sort of lord will rule over us. See P. J. Achtemeier, *Romans*, 35–39.

Here, Paul emphasizes the intimate relationship that believers have with God through Christ Jesus—God's Son—apart from the law. As heirs of the promise who are already receiving their inheritance by faith, they now have free and continuous access to God the Father through the Spirit. Moreover, the Spirit's presence in their hearts and the Spirit's activity within them of crying out loudly and urgently (κράζω) to God is proof of their sonship. The cause of all this is not a human accomplishment, however. The heirs of the promise had to wait to receive their inheritance until the time appointed by the father (4:1–2). That is, the cause of this new relationship with God through Christ is God. God is the explicit subject of the main verbs in 4:4–6, and so important is this to Paul that he repeats the phrase ἐξαπέστειλεν ὁ θεός ("God sent") to impress this point upon the minds of his hearers. The status of their sonship is accomplished entirely by God's mercy. This is the climactic point that Paul strikes solidly in 4:7 with the concluding phrase διὰ θεοῦ ("through God").[56]

Paul has been addressing the particular issues that he believes are necessary in light of the situation, but he has been emphasizing from the beginning of his communication also the graciousness of God. God the Father: raised Jesus Christ from the dead (1:1), willed Christ's saving work (1:4), called the Galatians in the grace of Christ (1:6), revealed Jesus Christ to Paul (1:12), brought Paul's life into harmony with God's purposes for it (1:15–16), directed the work of Paul, Peter, and the early church (2:2, 7–9), bestowed freedom (2:4) and grace (2:9) in Christ, made righteousness accessible through faith in Christ Jesus (2:16), made it possible for one to live for God (2:19–20), manifested grace through his Son (2:20), gave the Spirit to the Galatian believers and worked miracles among them (3:1–5; 4:6), ended the jurisdiction of the law (3:10–13), fulfilled the promise to Abraham (3:6–9, 29), united Jews and Gentiles into one family as the heirs of Abraham (3:6–9, 27–28), and inaugurated the eschatological age of faithfulness in Christ (3:23–24; 4:4).

Now in 4:8–9, Paul once again emphasizes the graciousness of God. Here he reminds the Galatians that before they heard and accepted the gospel of the Risen Crucified Christ they were being "enslaved by gods that by nature are not

---

[56]This phrase has caused considerable difficulty for both scribes and interpreters of Galatians and Paul since God is often presented as the source and Christ as the mediator. There are eight variant readings of διὰ θεοῦ in existent manuscripts. The "heir" is portrayed as διὰ θεόν ("on account of God"), διὰ Χριστοῦ ("through Christ"), διὰ Ἰησοῦ Χριστοῦ ("through Jesus Christ"), θεοῦ ("of God"), θεοῦ διὰ Χριστοῦ ("of God through Christ"), θεοῦ διὰ Ἰησοῦ Χριστοῦ ("of God through Jesus Christ"), διὰ θεοῦ ἐν Χριστῷ Ἰησοῦ ("through God in Christ Jesus"), and μὲν θεοῦ συγκληρονόμους δὲ Χριστοῦ ("of God, and fellow heir with Christ"). The best reading, however, is διὰ θεοῦ (see Metzger, *A Textual Commentary*, 595–96), for it is strongly supported by early and diversified manuscripts and the expression fits precisely within Paul's argument in Galatians regarding the gracious activity of God.

(gods)" (ἐδουλεύσατε τοῖς φύσει μὴ οὖσιν θεοῖς; 4:8). Since their conversion in Christ, however, they have come to "know God," the one true God, the God of Israel. They have experienced close fellowship with God through the Spirit of the Son whom God the Father sent (4:9a; 4:6–7). But, again, to keep his listeners from drawing the false conclusion that their new relation with God was based on their own initiative, Paul makes the critical correction that they have become "known by God" (4:9b). In this way, Paul emphasizes once more his persistent point that their relation with God and knowledge of God in Christ is foremost a matter of God's initiative.[57] Because it is a relationship that God has established with Jews and Gentiles in Christ Jesus, recognition and commitment run both ways. But this relationship is only possible because of God's knowledge of persons on whose behalf God has acted through Jesus Christ.[58]

God's merciful activity is everywhere apparent throughout Galatians 1:1–4:11. As Paul addresses specific topics of his discourse, he shows that God is due "glory for ever and ever" (1:5). In Christ Jesus, God the Father gives Jews and Gentiles a new life and a new status for a new age. So why would the Galatians want to turn back again to the old life and old status in the old age (4:9)? Now that they have come to know God and be known by God,[59] why would they want to return to a lifestyle that alienates them from God and one another? Why choose enslavement to weak and beggarly elemental forces when they can be free from such tyrannical forces by accepting the sufficiency of God's grace in Christ and so become heirs of God's promise?

Such is Paul's central concern for the next portion of his address in 4:8–5:12. It is the point he first raised in the salutation-exordium in 1:6–9, mentioned briefly in 3:2–5 to keep the issue in his listeners' minds, addresses directly with passion beginning at 4:8, and recapitulates in 5:1–12.[60] The

---

[57]Dunn, *Galatians*, 225; Longenecker, *Galatians*, 180; Matera, *Galatians*, 152.

[58]Dunn, *Galatians*, 225.

[59]The concept of knowing God and being known by God (4:8–9) is deeply rooted in the scriptures and traditions of Judaism. Israel was encountered by God (cf. Gen 12:1–3; 32:22–32; 3:1f; Exod 19:16f; etc.) and pledged itself to honor and obey God (cf. Exod 19:8; 24:3–7; Josh 24:16–18; etc.). Gentiles were viewed as those who did not know God and so did not stand within God's covenant and the realm of its blessing (cf. Ps 79:6; Jer 10:25; etc.).

[60]Some interpreters designate 5:1–12 as the beginning of the exhortatio or start of a new section (cf. Betz, *Galatians*, 253–55; Burton, *Galatians*, 269; Bruce, *Galatians*, 228). Others include this pericope more closely with the preceding context rather than the following and so find the beginning of the last major portion of this letter-speech at 5:13 where Paul issues a more general exhortation (cf. Cousar, *Galatians*, 121–25; Dunn, *Galatians*, 260–84; Longenecker, *Galatians*, 221–22; O. Merk, "Der Beginn der Paränese im Galaterbrief," *ZNW* 60 [1969]: 83–104; Matera, *Galatians*, 185–86; Mussner, *Der Galaterbrief*, 342, 364–74; Schlier, *Der Brief an die Galater*, 241–42). The latter view is

Galatians have a fundamental decision to make regarding their relationship with the God who knows them and who makes possible their knowledge of him through Jesus Christ and the Spirit. How they come out on this matter will be determined in large measure by the decisions they make regarding Paul and the agitators (4:12–20), the law (4:21–5:1), and their freedom in Christ (5:1–6). So, to move them to make faithful responses[61] that will help them remain in the realm of God's grace, Paul appeals to their personal bonds with him,[62] to the

---

supported for the reasons they state: (1) Paul shifts from using mainly first person plural personal pronouns in 4:31–5:5 to second person plural personal pronouns in 5:13f thus indicating a more general type of discussion in 5:13f; (2) Paul's use of the phrase "yoke of slavery" (ζυγῷ δουλείας) in 5:1 and the summary statement regarding the problem of the law correspond to his preceding discussion regarding the law and slavery (cf. 3:21–26; 4:1–3, 8–9, 22–31); (3) Paul uses the word "grace" (χάρις) in 5:4 which he has highlighted earlier (1:3, 6, 15; 2:9, 21) but does not use again until the closing of the communication at 6:18; (4) the phrase "fallen away from grace"(τῆς χάριτος ἐξεπέσατε) in 5:4 corresponds to the phrase "the grace of Christ" (χάριτι Χριστοῦ) in 1:6; (5) Paul uses the noun "righteousness" (δικαιοσύνη) in 5:5 and the verb "to make righteous" (δικαιόω) in 5:4 which are used frequently in the foregoing discussion (2:16 [3 times], 17, 21; 3:6, 8, 11, 21, 24) and do not appear again in Galatians after this passage; (6) Paul again stresses in 5:5–6 the priority of faith over the law for determining a right relation with God (cf. 1:23; 2:16; 2:20; 3:2, 5, 7–9, 11–12, 14, 22–26), whereas in the following text Paul simply lists faith as a spiritual fruit (5:22) and characterizes the church as "the household of faith" (6:10); (7) the statements of judgment (5:10–12) parallel earlier threats and warnings in 1:7–9 and 4:8–11; (8) In 5:7–12, Paul returns directly to the Galatians and their situation (cf. 1:7; 3:1–5; 4:8–31), expressing confidence that they will make the right decision regarding the truth of the gospel and referring to the agitators (cf. 1:7: 4:17); and, perhaps most importantly, (9) Paul uses the phrase "the One who calls you" (τοῦ καλοῦντος ὑμᾶς) in 5:8 and "the One who called you" (τοῦ καλέσαντος ὑμᾶς) 1:6. In these ways, it is evident that in 5:1–12 Paul recapitulates critical high points from the preceding discussion before issuing his paranesis and conclusion. Indeed, as Longenecker contends (*Galatians*, 221–22), there is a striking relationship between 5:1–12 and 1:6–10. He identifies these two units of text as marking an *inclusio* on the basis of their: "sustained severity"; use of "again" (πάλιν) in 1:9 and 5:3; parallel between the "repeated anathema" in 1:8–9 and the "threat of divine judgment of 5:12;" and points 4 and 8 noted above.

[61]Longenecker (*Galatians*, 184–87) and Hansen (*Abraham*, 16, 59) have identified a major rhetorical shift at 4:12 from forensic to deliberative rhetoric. They base this shift primarily on the basis of epistolary formulas that they find in 4:12–20 and so miss the rhetorical quality of 4:1–11 as summary (4:1–7) and introduction (4:8–11). N. T. Wright contends, however, that 4:1–11 comes "at a fairly climactic moment in the whole letter, drawing together the argument of the preceding chapter . . . and laying the foundations for what is to come" ("Gospel and Theology in Galatians," 230). Such is the position also of this study.

[62]S. J. Kraftchick writes of 4:12–20 that Paul's "rehearsal of feelings and memories of their prior warm relations is an attempt to reestablish the relationship so that the argument can continue" (*Ethos and Pathos Appeals*, 225). Betz contends that here Paul offers a "string of topoi belonging to the theme of friendship" (*Galatians*, 221). Dunn, however, is more to the point on the significance of this text within Paul's argument when he points out that Paul is not as concerned with reestablishing mutual sincerity or highlighting their friendship (cf.

scripture's own foreshadowing of the eschatological fulfillment of God's new Jerusalem that will be comprised only of "children of promise,"[63] and to their own experience of Christian freedom by means of the Spirit through faith, not by means of obedience through the law. Then, after he asks the Galatians to consider how their trust in the truth of the gospel of Christ has been weakened (5:7), and before he forcefully assails the agitators again (5:10–12), Paul asserts that the persuasion of the agitators is "not from the One who calls" them (5:8).[64]

Again, Paul emphasizes that the Galatians' situation is fundamentally a matter of their relationship with God. Moreover, this relationship with God involves a human response. On one hand, Paul stresses the inaugurating activity of God who first makes a proper relationship with God possible through Jesus Christ. On the other hand, Paul also stresses here the role of human decision regarding God and the truth of God's activity in the Risen Crucified Christ. The Galatians were clearly drawn into close fellowship with God through their acceptance of Paul's proclamation of the gospel (3:1–5). In Christ, they have known the One who "supplies the Spirit" and "works miracles" (3:5; 4:6). Through faith, they have also experienced a new way of relating to one another (3:26–28). But their earlier responses of faithfulness have not precluded the possibility that they might turn away from God and accept the leaven-like persuasion of the agitators typified by circumcision and its requirements. So, while Paul expresses his hopeful confidence that the Galatians will embrace once more the truth of the gospel that God's grace is through faith in Christ (5:10a), he also warns them of the grave threat to their faithfulness presented by the agitators and their message (5:9) and expresses confidence that whoever is troubling the Galatians will receive a severe judgment from God (5:10b). Paul himself suggests castration as a suitable punishment (5:12).

In 5:1–12, Paul brings the matter of the Galatians' impending decision to a forceful climax, and, again, he presents Galatians with an "either/or" choice (cf. 3:1–5; 4:8–9). The Galatians must decide whether they will remain in

---

4:12–15) as he is with revealing his "emotional intensity" over the danger they are in and "heighten[ing] the emotional impact of the whole" (*Galatians*, 231).

[63]Barrett ("The Allegory of Abraham, Sarah, and Hagar in the Argument of Galatians," *Essays on Paul* [Philadelphia: Westminster Press, 1982], 118–31) and Longenecker (*Galatians*, 200–06) propose that Paul had to address the scriptural material presented in 4:21–31 because it was employed by Paul's opponents. Whether or not this was actually the case is disputable, though such a position does help explain Paul's use of the allegory here (cf. Dunn, *Galatians*, 243). More important is Paul's use of this allegory to emphasize that those who are in Christ are the "children of the promise" who belong to the new Jerusalem of the eschatological age (cf. 3:8–9, 16, 18).

[64]While Paul uses the present participle τοῦ καλοῦντος ("the one who calls"), he uses it not in a durative ("the one who keeps calling") or iterative ("the one who [repeatedly] calls") sense here but in a descriptive way describing God's character. Cf. Rom 4:17; 9:11; 1 Thess 2:12; 5:24.

Christ and accept the Risen Crucified Christ's gift of freedom or whether they will accept circumcision and the yoke of the law and so forfeit the eschatological gifts of the Spirit and the hope of righteousness.[65] This is the critical decision before them. It now remains for Paul to set forth some specific consequences that come from accepting the gospel of the Crucified Christ and living in this new fellowship by faith in Christ.

VII. THE ONE WHO CALLS FORTH RESPONSIBLE FREEDOM: GALATIANS 5:13–6:10

At 5:13, Paul begins amplifying the gospel's effect on individual believers and the community of faith that God has called into being. Now that he has presented his case regarding his apocalyptic apostleship (1:1; 1:11–2:10) and the truth of the gospel—that justification or being made righteous comes by faith and life in the Risen Crucified Christ and that the people of God find their identity and unity in Christ (1:3–4; 2:11–5:12)—Paul is ready to encourage the Galatians to use properly their freedom from the law. God has called them to a newfound freedom (5:13), a freedom that comes from God as a gift in the grace of Christ (1:6; 5:1) and with the supply of the Spirit (3:5; 4:6). It is, however, a gift that may be misused (5:13b) and lost (5:4, 15). So Paul offers the Galatians instruction—positively and negatively—on the proper use of Christian freedom. Paul also lays out the practical consequences of rejecting (5:19–21) or accepting (5:22–25) God's call in the grace of Christ, for he wants them to understand why they ought to remain in the "household of faith" (6:10) as "servants of one another" (5:13).

To begin with, Paul again takes up the matter of freedom in 5:13 but presents another dimension of it. To be in Christ is to be free from the yoke of the law (5:1) but it is also to be free for serving one another through love (5:13; cf. 5:6).[66] That is, Christ has already given the gift of freedom by taking the law's curse upon himself and bestowing the blessing of Abraham (3:13–14). Now, in 5:13–15, Paul describes more fully the purpose of living freely in Christ. First, Paul warns that freedom can be used either negatively in the selfish service of one's own desires or positively in the loving service of one's neighbors (5:13). Paul then asserts that it is the love of one's neighbor that fulfills the law (5:14; Lev 19:18). Finally, Paul cautions that their failing to serve one another lovingly will breed their mutual destruction (5:15).

Regarding the One who calls in the grace of Christ, it is the second matter that most concerns us here. Being in Christ and accepting the freedom God offers in Christ means serving one another through love (5:13–14). This,

---

[65]Mussner, *Der Galaterbrief*, 342.

[66]The phrase ἐπ’ ἐλευθερίᾳ ("for freedom") expresses the purpose of their call.

for Paul, is the aim of the whole law, that "you shall love your neighbor as yourself." And even though Paul expresses the consequence of the believer's freedom as a command—"through love serve one another"—his subsequent discussion of walking in the Spirit (5:16–26) reveals that—in Christ—this "law" of love is not a burden or curse, like the old law. Rather it is a gift of the Spirit that is manifested in the believer's life (5:22). Paul presents love, then, as the chief activity of faithful obedience to God's will (5:6, 13–14), and this love of which he speaks is expressed by serving one's neighbors (5:13) and bearing one another's burdens (6:2). Furthermore, it is God who makes this kind of love possible. God does this through the supply of the Spirit for those who belong to Christ Jesus and walk by the Spirit (5:22–25). The Spirit is the means through which God empowers the life of freedom—the life to which God has called the Galatians and in which those who belong to Christ will experience such benefits as "love, joy, peace, patience, kindness, goodness, faithfulness, gentleness, [and] self-control" (5:22), all of which are examples of fruit of the Spirit. Also significant is Paul's implication that those through whom such fruit of the Spirit is manifested will inherit the kingdom of God (5:21–26), for, certainly, those who do the "works of the flesh" (5:19–21, 26) will not inherit the kingdom. In this way, the eschatological dimensions of Paul's discussion of the fulfillment of the law and life by the Spirit become explicit. How each individual uses his or her freedom will impact his or her eternal relation with God and God's kingdom. How an individual responds to God's call in the grace of Christ is a matter of everlasting significance.

In 6:1–10, Paul stresses another critical aspect of Christian freedom that he believes is pertinent to the Galatians' situation. Living by the Spirit involves being responsible for one another. Thus there is also a corporate aspect of belonging to Jesus Christ (6:1a, 2, 6, 9–10).[67] So to the Galatians Paul gives an example of bearing the burdens of others (6:1–5), an admonition to support faithful teachers (6:6), and some encouragement to persevere in doing good to all people (6:7–10). Here, again, Paul makes some important theological claims regarding the One who calls them in the grace of Christ.

First, in 6:1–5, Paul notes that members of the Christian community may not be free from sin. It is possible for a member of the Christian community[68] to transgress God's will by walking according to the flesh (5:16, 18; 6:1). It is also possible for such a person to be detected in the process of sinning (6:1). Should

---

[67]Matera, *Galatians*, 218.

[68]Though the text simply states ἄνθρωπος ("a person") in 6:1, Paul is addressing a Christian community. The textual variants of ἄνθρωπος ἐξ ὑμῶν ("a person from among you") and τὶς ἐξ ὑμῶν ("someone from among you") in the apparatus, though later additions, are correct clarifications.

such a circumstance occur,[69] Paul states that the whole community—all the spiritual ones (οἱ πνευματικοί)—has a shared responsibility to correct the one who sinned. This correction is to be done in a spirit of gentleness, however, for gentleness is a fruit of the Spirit (5:23). Moreover, apart from such gentleness, those who assist in restoring the sinful member may themselves fall into sin by becoming conceited and by provoking the one who sinned (5:26). Then, immediately after this general example, Paul gives instructions to bear one another's burdens, for in this they "will fulfill the law of Christ" (6:2).

It is not exactly clear what Paul means by the difficult phrase "the law of the Christ" (τὸν νόμον τοῦ Χριστοῦ). It has been argued that it refers to a Messianic law of the eschatological age, the love commandment, self-sacrificing service in the manner of Christ, and the Mosaic law redefined by Christ.[70] It may also be a combination of these, or all of these. In any event, the important point here is that Paul roots "the law of the Christ" in the will of God by describing this law as the Christ's. Furthermore, Paul summarizes the content of this law as the activity of "bearing one another's burdens." Living by the Spirit, then, is not without its own peculiar costs or indications of faithfulness. Indeed, living by the Spirit through faith in Christ in response to God's call makes one able to respond appropriately to the neighbor in order to alleviate the neighbor's burdens. Why? Because Christ "gave himself for our sins to deliver us" (1:4) and he "redeemed us from the curse of the law" (3:13; 4:5). Christ himself demonstrates how to bear the burdens of others. Moreover, because it is Christ who lives in the believer (2:20) and the Spirit of Christ who guides the believer (5:18), the same fruit of the Spirit evident in the Crucified Jesus' life of burden-bearing becomes manifested in the life of the believer (2:19–20) who has "crucified the flesh with its passions and desires" (5:22–25).

Secondly, in 6:7, Paul reminds his listeners once more that God is the One before whom they are ultimately accountable.[71] God will judge the Galatians' decisions and actions. God has called in the grace of Christ and salvation is by faith, not works. But a person's actions are not inconsequential. One's behavior bears certain consequences in personal relationships (6:1–6) and in relationship with God (6:7–8).[72] Believers and non-believers "sow" their actions throughout their lives, for good or bad, and in the day of God's final

---

[69]Paul's use of a third class condition (ἐάν with the subjunctive in the protasis and nearly any verb form in the apodosis) indicates that Paul may not have a particular instance in mind but offers this example hypothetically.

[70]For a helpful discussion of these positions and the scholars who support them, see Matera, *Galatians*, 219–21.

[71]As in 1:8–9; 1:20; 2:11; 5:4, 10, 21 and 6:5, Paul refers to God's role as Judge. Clearly, Paul views the final judgment as important to his communication and it is likely important also to the recipients of Paul's letter-speech.

[72]Cf. 1 Cor 12:25–26; 2 Cor 5:10; Phil 2:12–13.

judgment "will reap" (θερίσει) accordingly either "corruption," as the fruit of the flesh, or "eternal life," as the fruit of the Spirit.[73] So, there is no room for complacency in serving one another through love and bearing one another's burdens, for faith expresses itself as faithfulness—as "doing good to all people, especially to those of the household of faith"—in the manner of the Crucified Christ. In short, God's grace and call in Christ are not to be taken for granted. The followers of Christ must not presume upon God's mercy toward them as though God is unconcerned about their actions. In Christ, God called them to freedom so that through love they may be servants of one another. This is the responsible use of freedom that God expects and makes possible through faith in Jesus Christ.

Finally, the freedom to which the faithful are called (5:13) and in which they presently stand (5:1) is an eschatological freedom. Not only has Paul emphasized here the eschatological presence and work of the Spirit and the impending final judgment of God, but in 6:9–10 Paul concludes his discussion on living by the Spirit by stressing that "well-doing" is the work of faithfulness for the present eschatological age. Twice, Paul uses here the word "καιρός" ("time"), which means "a decisive point in time."[74] In each instance, Paul points ahead to the Day of Judgment and confirmation for those who will enter the kingdom of God. In 6:9, Paul refers to God's appointed time for reaping the faithful. In 6:10, Paul indicates that this present eschatological time is the appropriate period for accomplishing the work of love (cf. Rom 13:11), for the day is coming when the hope of righteousness will be fulfilled for the faithful who have walked by the Spirit and loved their neighbors as themselves. On this note, Paul moves swiftly to bring his communication to a close. There, he sets before the Galatians his climactic point regarding God and God's purposes.

VIII. THE ONE WHO CALLS FORTH THE ISRAEL OF GOD: GALATIANS 6:14–16

Throughout his communication to the Galatians, Paul has been arguing that one's response to the gospel of the Risen Crucified Christ affects one's relation with God who calls in the grace of Christ. In chapter five, we saw that Paul repeatedly points the Galatians to God's new eschatological age and, in 6:15, uses the striking phrase "new creation" (καινὴ κτίσις) as the fitting capstone to this thread of his discourse. In chapter six, we observed that Paul

---

[73]Cf. Isa 2:4; 3:13; Joel 4:12–16; Matt 13:24–30, 41–43; Rev 14:14–20.

[74]Betz, *Galatians*, 309. Betz calls this use of καιρός an "eschatological topos." English translations tend to hide this eschatological aspect. See also in the Septuagint: Num 23:23; Job 39:18; Eccl 3:11; Lam 1:21; Dan 2:21. In the NT, see Matt 26:18; Mark 1:15; Luke 12:56; John 7:6–8; Rom 5:6. See also G. Delling, *TDNT*, vol. 3, 455–64.

establishes the eschatological revelation of Jesus Christ as the basis for the gospel's authority and continues to appeal to the Crucified Christ until, in 6:14, Paul asserts climactically that the Lord Jesus Christ Crucified is the basis for understanding the Christian faith and life—for glorying in the cross of Christ. Now, once more in the conclusion of his message, Paul brings to a climax yet another central cord of his discourse—the calling activity of God and the appropriate response to it. On this point, Paul states succinctly and memorably: "Peace and mercy be upon those who keep in line with this rule, upon the Israel of God" (6:16; καὶ ὅσοι τῷ κανόνι τούτῳ στοιχήσουσιν, εἰρήνη ἐπ' αὐτοὺς καὶ ἔλεος καὶ ἐπὶ τὸν Ἰσραὴλ τοῦ θεοῦ).

Though Paul expresses this wish with remarkable brevity, scholars have long recognized that there are certain difficulties in interpreting it. To be sure, part of the expression's meaning is evident. For instance, it is clear that by the phrase τῷ κανόνι τούτῳ, which means "this rule" or "this standard," Paul is emphasizing the point he just made in 6:15. "Neither circumcision counts for anything nor uncircumcision, but a new creation." That is, the standard for all who would be in Christ, according to Paul, is trust in the New Creation Jesus Christ Crucified whom God raised from the dead and the Spirit's new-creation presence and activity in the believer. The verb στοιχήσουσιν means "to keep in line" or "agree with," and Paul used the same verb στοιχέω in 5:25 where he states, "If we live by the Spirit, let us indeed keep in line with the Spirit." Thus Paul's closing wish for peace and mercy is issued for all those who conduct themselves in a manner appropriate for the followers of Jesus Christ.[75]

It is the second portion of 6:16 that proves to be problematic. Is Paul referring to two groups of people, or to one? And whom does Paul have in mind with the unusual expression "the Israel of God"? What is the significance of this clause in the conclusion of his address? In the first case, Paul's expression εἰρήνη ἐπ' αὐτοὺς καὶ ἔλεος καὶ ἐπὶ τὸν Ἰσραὴλ τοῦ θεοῦ could be translated along the lines of "peace upon them, and mercy also upon the Israel of God" or "peace and mercy be upon them, indeed upon the Israel of God." The problem of interpretation lies in Paul's duplications of the preposition ἐπί and the conjunction καί, for the way in which one resolves the syntactical relationships here determines whether or not Paul is understood to be addressing two groups or one.[76]

It is possible that Paul first wishes peace to the Gentile Christians in Galatia who exhibit the standard of new creation in Christ—so that

---

[75]Throughout the NT where εἰρήνη and ἔλεος are joined in benedictions, the order is reversed. Paul's arrangement of the words in this order here, however, is not necessarily a sign of non-Pauline language. Cf. Burton, *Galatians*, 357–58; Longenecker, *Galatians*, 297.

[76]For thorough summaries of the various positions on this matter, see Betz, *Galatians*, 322–23; Hansen, *Abraham in Galatians*, 160–61; Longenecker, *Galatians*, 298–99.

circumcision and the law are inconsequential—and then wishes for mercy also upon the Jewish Christians or even pious Jews moving toward Christianity.[77] It is also grammatically possible, and more likely, however, that Paul is referring to one group. Indeed, the thrust of this entire communication has focused on the One who calls in the grace of Christ and the corresponding problem of distinguishing the ones who are faithfully responding to God's call—an issue that was first expressed in the strong rhetorical period of 1:6–7 and continued throughout this communication. Who is deserting God (1:6), and who belongs to the household of faith (6:10)? Who is enslaved in the present evil age (1:4; 2:4; 3:11, 23; 4:8–10, 21; 5:3–4, 17–21), and who is free in the eschatological age of Christ (1:1, 10; 2:19–20; 3:2, 5; 4:1–7; 5:1–6:10)? Who are the true heirs of Abraham and the recipients of the blessing of Abraham (3:6–29; 4:21–31), and who will not inherit the kingdom of God (5:21)? The context of Galatians indicates that Paul has in mind all those who belong to Christ and live by the Spirit, whether Jew or Greek, slave or free, male or female.[78] The clause is best interpreted, then, by reading the second καί as introducing a clarification of the first phrase in the clause. Thus Paul means, "peace and mercy be upon them, indeed upon the Israel of God."

What, then, is the significance here of the phrase "the Israel of God"? Paul does not use it anywhere else and it does not occur in any Jewish literature of the time.[79] Why, then, does Paul use the term here? Paul probably uses the phrase "the Israel of God" because his Jewish-Christian opponents in Galatia used it to describe themselves and their followers.[80] That is, the agitators in Galatia were evidently asserting that acceptance of their message secured one's inclusion in the true Israel of God. Paul, on the other hand, has argued throughout his address that the ones who belong to God's household are those who have accepted God's call in the grace of the Christ, who have received the Spirit of Christ, and who are living and united by the Spirit. In this way, Paul

---

[77]Longenecker, *Galatians*, 297, calls attention to Burton, *Galatians*, 358, and Richardson, *Israel in the Apostolic Church*, 80–81, as chief proponents of this line of interpretation. See also Hansen's summary in *Abraham in Galatians*, 161.

[78]As for the arguments that "the Israel of God" is a designation for Gentile Christians alone or is a reference to a separate group of nonjudaizing Jewish Christians or to all Jews who will be saved, such a position must depend on the grammatical possibility of 6:16b coupled with Paul's wider use of the term "Israel" outside of Galatians. To be sure, Paul does distinguish between Israel and Gentile Christians elsewhere (cf. Rom 11), but the context of Galatians supports the view that Paul uses the term to describe all believers in Christ in the Galatian church. For a contrary position, see Dunn, *Galatians*, 343–46.

[79]Betz, *Galatians*, 322–23; Longenecker, *Galatians*, 299; Burton, *Galatians*, 358.

[80]Longenecker, *Galatians*, 298, and Hansen, *Abraham in Galatians*, 161, which is also hinted at by Betz, *Galatians*, 323.

has likely issued here a consummate rhetorical rebuttal, if—as it seems—he has used and redefined one of his opponents' chief terms.[81]

IX. THE GOD WHO CALLS IN THE GRACE OF CHRIST IN GALATIANS

For Paul, God—who called forth Israel long ago—is now fulfilling through Christ the promise to extend the blessing of Abraham to all the nations of the earth. God is doing this by calling forth uncircumcised Gentiles to be included in God's Israel for the new-age creation. Thus the Israel of God is comprised of those who have been crucified with Christ and who, by the Spirit, are living as a new creation. These are the defining characteristics of God's people—not circumcision or obedience to the law. It is trusting faithfulness in the Risen Crucified Jesus Christ that establishes one's inclusion in the household of faith. Those who belong to Christ are God's people, and whether or not one belongs to Christ is a matter of how one responds to the truth of the gospel.

From this point, Paul hastily closes his communication by ending the postscript-peroratio (6:17–18) as he ended the salutation-exordium (1:10). Paul stresses emphatically his own relation with God through Jesus Christ and so answers the questions he raised at the beginning. Is Paul seeking the favor of God? Is Paul a slave of Christ? The answer to both questions is "yes." Paul cannot be seeking the favor of men (1:10a) or he would not be involved in the conflict caused by agitators in the Galatian churches. Indeed, his declaration, "From now on let no one cause me trouble" (6:17a), indicates that Paul perceives the disturbance of the churches in Galatia as a personal—even physical—assault against himself.[82] But this is only the preliminary basis for Paul's stronger, more emphatic point that he is bearing on his body the marks of Jesus (6:17b). Both of the clauses in v. 17 are expressed as forceful rhetorical periods, but Paul's emphatic use of the first person personal pronoun and the conjunction γάρ in 17b indicate that Paul's greater emphasis is here. That is, the second periodic clause explains the basis for the first and it is not until the final word βαστάζω ("I am bearing or carrying") that the whole expression may be fully understood. Whatever Paul may mean by the τὰ στίγματα τοῦ Ἰησοῦ ("the marks of Jesus"), there can be no doubt that Paul has in mind Christ's self-sacrificing death upon the cross and his own self-sacrificing

---

[81]Cf. Aristotle *Art of Rhetoric* 2.25; Cicero *De Inventione* 1.42–90; Quintilian *Institutio Oratoria* 2.4.18.

[82]The noun κόπος ("trouble") reflects the state of extreme weariness from hardship or struggle, even to the point of feeling beaten. See Bauer, et al, *A Greek-English Lexicon*, 443b, and *TDNT*, vol. 3, 827.

alignment with Jesus (cf. 2:20). In this way, Paul asserts that he is a "slave of Christ" (1:10b) who has responded faithfully to God's call in the grace of Christ.

In closing his address to the Galatians, Paul extends a brief benediction that is similar to those he uses elsewhere (cf. Rom 16:20; 1 Cor 16:23; 2 Cor 13:13; Phil 4:23; 1 Thess 5:28; Phlm 25). Paul makes it more than a customary epistolary convention, though, for his wish for them for "grace" is wholly fitting as a concluding statement in a communication where God's initiative in granting grace is so persistent and prominent. That the grace of which Paul speaks is more particularly that of "our Lord Jesus Christ" highlights once more Christ's saving work according to the will of God the Father. Moreover, Paul's wish or prayer for his Galatian brothers and sisters (ἀδελφοί) is that this divine grace might be the distinguishing mark of their lives and relationships.

CHAPTER EIGHT

DRAWING THE RHETORICAL CORDS TOGETHER

In the three preceding chapters, we have seen how Paul develops and climactically concludes each of the principal themes that he establishes in the opening of his communication (1:1–10). We have pursued this path of study on the basis of our recovery of an ancient Greco-Roman principle for communicating appropriately and persuasively. That is, ideal communication ought to progress in a tight linear fashion and the most central points ought to be placed as early and late in the message as possible, regardless of the communication's medium. Beginnings and endings of effective communications were not to be drawn from some extraneous matter but were to be taken from the very heart of the message.

Appealing, then, to epistolary and rhetorical terms and categories, we identified 1:1–10 as the "salutation-exordium" of the letter-speech of Galatians and examined it closely. There we delineated three principal themes that Paul emphasizes for development in the body of the letter-speech: the apocalyptic activity of God epitomized by the resurrection of Jesus Christ from the dead; the saving work of the Risen Crucified Christ; and the One who is calling forth the new Israel of God in the grace of Christ.

We then examined the text of Galatians and found that Paul does indeed amplify each of these themes throughout his communication to the Galatians and brings them to their memorable climaxes at the message's end. It now remains for us to consider how Paul relates these central themes to one another in the conclusion of this letter-speech to the Galatians, for here (6:11–18), as in the salutation-exordium (1:1–10), Paul stresses his central points in juxtaposition. Following this, we will bring this study to a close by summarizing our findings and stating our conclusion. That is, we will consider how the recognition of Paul's adherence in Galatians to the ancient Greco-Roman practice of placing an argument's central points at the opening and closing of a communication aids in the interpretation of this letter-speech.

I. A STRIKING ENDING: GALATIANS 6:11–18

Paul begins his address to the Galatian Christians in a startling way and he concludes his message in a manner that is no less dramatic and memorable.

225

Here at the end he impresses his points upon his listeners' minds with vivid language to help his listeners "see" what he means. He declares, "See with what large letters I am writing to you with my own hand." With these words, he departs from his discussion of Christian discipleship and turns the focus of his address back upon himself, which is where his message to the Galatians began (1:1a). Here Paul indicates that a scribe or amanuensis—likely "one of the brothers" who were with him (1:2)—has transcribed Paul's spoken message to the Galatians up to this point and that Paul himself is now writing in his own hand. This emphatic declaration, however, does more than call attention to Paul. As several studies have shown, the statement also highlights the climactic character of the expressions that follow.[1] That is, Paul's declaration prepares his listeners for the ensuing recapitulation and summation of his message's main points. Paul's emphasis on his large letters is also significant in that it establishes the tone for the closure of his letter. In the Greco-Roman world of Paul's time, writing in large characters was a means of instructing children. In *The Life of Cato the Elder* (20.3–6), for instance, Plutarch celebrates how Cato himself took responsibility for his son's full education. Cato even "wrote his History in large characters with his own hand, that his son might thus have at home the means to acquaint himself with his country's ancient traditions."[2] That Paul viewed the Galatian Christians as his children is evident (4:19; see also 3:23–4:7), thus here he appears to be reiterating their essential relationship with one another. Paul, the Galatians' parent in the faith, is their teacher who is now imparting in simple direct fashion the final instructions of this particular lesson.

What, exactly, are Paul's parting instructions? First, as he did in the opening of his address, he warns the Galatians about the agitators at work in

---

[1] On the role of autographic postscripts and the function of this passage as *peroratio*, see especially Betz, *Galatians*, 312–14, and the references cited there. Betz calls attention to the significance of 6:11–18 for interpreting Galatians where he writes that "it contains the interpretive clues to the understanding of Paul's major concerns in the letter as a whole and should be employed as the hermeneutical key to the intentions of the Apostle"(313). Of late, Weima has examined this text's role of summation in relation to the preceding portion of the letter. See "Gal. 6:11–18: A Hermeneutical Key." See also Dunn, *Galatians*, 334–35; Longenecker, *Galatians*, 286–89; and Martyn, *Galatians*, 559–60. There is a hermeneutical "key" here at the end of Galatians, but Paul has not held the "key" until the end so that his letter-speech is to be understood and interpreted backwards. The argument of this study is that Paul has set his key points at the beginning to open the way of understanding for his listeners and readers and then positions the same key points in a climactic fashion at the end of his communication so that they may hold these essential points in mind.

[2] Plutarch *Marcus Cato* 20.3. Arguments that Paul's large letters were the result of a hand injury or weak eyes are unconvincing (cf. Theodor Zahn, *Der Brief des Paulus an die Galater*, KNT 9 [Leipzig: Deichert, 1922], 278). So, also, it seems unlikely that Paul wrote large letters here so that a listening assembly could read this portion of the letter from a distance (cf. Bruce, *Galatians*, 268).

their midst (6:12–13; cf. 1:7–9). Not every response to God's call in the grace of Christ is faithful, even if it is promoted as such. For instance, in addition to reliance on Christ's saving work for establishing and maintaining a right relationship with God, some would add the works of the law—exemplified especially in the rite of circumcision. But Paul has argued that faithfulness in Christ cannot be improved through circumcision or obedience to the law (2:15–21; 3:10–14, 21–29), so he warns the Galatians not to be circumcised (5:2–6) and to reconsider the significance of the law in the light of Jesus Christ (3:10–4:7). Moreover, Paul asserts that these circumcising agitators (6:12; cf. 2:12) are driven by their desire for prestige among other Jewish Christians and perhaps the Jews themselves (cf. 4:17; 6:13). They "want to make a good showing in the flesh" (θέλουσιν εὐπροσωπῆσαι ἐν σαρκί). Self-interest is their chief concern (6:13).[3] Paul, on the other hand, has declared at the beginning of his address (1:10) and maintained (cf. 2:1–7, 11–21; 3:1; 4:8–20) that he is not "seeking the favor of men" or "trying to please men." Rather, he is seeking only the favor of God as a slave of Christ (1:10). He is an authentic servant apostle (1:10) commissioned by God (1:1, 16) and the gospel he proclaims is true; there is no other (1:6–7). Indeed, Paul is willing to be persecuted on behalf of the Risen Crucified Christ (cf. 2:4–6, 12–14; 4:16; 5:10–11), something which he claims his opponents are unwilling to do (6:12). In the postscript-peroratio (6:11–18), then, Paul seals his personal defense by emphasizing his close relationship with Jesus—he glories only in the cross of Jesus, has been crucified to the world, and bears on his body the marks of Christ.

Simply put, responses to the One who calls in the grace of Christ may be faithful or unfaithful and, regarding the present situation, Paul asserts that the agitators in Galatia are responding unfaithfully while he is answering faithfully the One who calls in the grace of Christ. He is writing in part, then, to defend his apostleship. But Paul's own apostolic call is a direct consequence of the apocalyptic activity of God the Father who inaugurated the apocalyptic age through the resurrection of Jesus Christ from the dead. Paul is also writing, therefore, to encourage the Galatians to respond faithfully to God's call in Christ, for God is actively working in their midst and is now establishing the end-time community for the new creation that is dawning. To these matters he returns at the end of his postscript-peroratio (6:16–18), but first he proceeds to reassert some essential tenets of the true gospel regarding Christ's saving work on the cross. The tension between Paul, his opponents and the Galatians over such matters as his apostleship, the law, becoming righteous, and membership in the church are all symptomatic of a deeper issue.

---

[3] Paul's use of a purpose clause makes this assertion explicit.

One problem with the agitators' promotion of circumcision and the law, according to Paul, is that it is not according to God's will (5:8; 1:6–9). Indeed, the opponents' insistence that the Galatians accept circumcision and obey the law is hypocritical, for the agitators themselves evidently do not keep the law that they promote (6:13; 3:10–14).[4] Still, they want to "compel" (ἀγαγκάζουσιν) the Galatians to be circumcised (6:12; cf. 2:3, 14). The fundamental reason for this, as Paul contends in Galatians, is that they do not recognize the significance of Jesus' death on the cross (3:10–14). They do not yet perceive the full glory of God's rescuing act through Jesus' crucifixion and Jesus' on-going life as the Risen Crucified Christ and Lord. Thus, while the agitators are glorying and boasting in circumcised flesh, Paul highlights again in his closing comments the centrality of Jesus' cross and resurrection for the Christian faith and life.

The cross of Christ is the second major point Paul seeks to impress upon the minds of the Galatian Christians. As we saw above, the cross looms large throughout Paul's letter-speech to the Galatians. In fact, here it is evident that Paul views the cross of Christ as the watershed between himself and his opponents. Whereas the agitators boast in what they may do to mark themselves as heirs of God's covenant promises (i.e., receive circumcision and obey the law), Paul boasts only in Christ's saving work on the cross. The contrasts of their gospels and boasts could hardly be sharper. For Paul, trust in the Risen Crucified Christ is sufficient for salvation (cf. 2:11–21). Over against any boast in human achievement, Paul insists that humans can boast only in the Son of God who loves them and who has given himself for them (cf. 1:4; 2:20).

Paul also insists that Christ's work on the cross forms the dividing wall between the present evil age opposed to God and God's purposes and the new apocalyptic age which is aligned with God and God's will (1:4; 4:1–11; 6:14). Because Paul has been "crucified with Christ" (2:20), he has died to the influences of a world that is rebelling against God. The present evil age no longer exercises authority or power over him. Instead, the life Paul now lives, he lives through Christ (2:20). Paul contends further that people of faith share and participate in this same Spirit (3:1–5; 4:6; 5:5f), freedom (5:1; 13) and life (2:16–20; 3:1–14, 22–27; 4:5–7; 5:5, 13–14, 16, 18, 22–26; 6:2, 8). They, too,

---

[4]Interpreters have long struggled with how best to translate περιτεμνόμενοι, whether it should be taken as a middle or passive present participle. In the middle voice, it would indicate the Galatians who are receiving circumcision. In the passive voice, it would refer more broadly to anyone who trusts in circumcision as the basis for being rightly related to God, such as the agitators and their converts. The perfect participle περιτετμημένοι is used in some texts (P46, B, F, G, L, et al.) and would point more narrowly to the Jews. Here, however, the context (ἵνα ἐν τῇ ὑμετέρα σαρκὶ καυχήσωνται) supports the present passive participle option.

may be rescued from the present evil age by Christ's work on the cross (1:4; 6:15–16, 18).

For Paul in Galatians, the Christian life and boast are based on trust in the Crucified Christ's saving work on the cross. Furthermore, Christian discipleship is a matter of participating in the self-sacrificing life of the Crucified Christ on behalf of others. As Paul sees it here, the faithful people of God are equipped by the Spirit to fulfill the law of Christ (6:2; 5:14, 22–26). Christ frees them to love their neighbors as themselves. In this way they exhibit the "new creation" standard, and so it is to them that the peace and mercy of God comes (6:16).

Still, on what basis can Christians confidently love their neighbors as themselves (5:5, 14), even to the point of being persecuted for the cross of Christ (6:12)? How can Christians trust in the sufficiency of Christ's death on the cross to seal their covenantal relationship with God? This kind of faith and action is possible, says Paul, because God raised Jesus from the dead and the people of God may now walk by the Spirit (4:6; 5:16, 18, 5:22–6:10). God has now made possible to all who trust in Jesus the kind of faithfulness God desires (5:22–6:10). As Paul sees it, those who are in Christ are free from the world's dominion; they have died to its powers and authorities (6:14–15). But the Christian gospel and life do not end there. Paul has yet another critical point to make.

Paul's third central theme is that God has inaugurated the apocalyptic age of the new creation through the resurrection of Jesus Christ from the dead. Indeed, the Crucified Christ and the Christian life lived in response to God's call in Christ only make sense if the Crucified Christ is risen from the dead (1:1). Paul declares, "Neither circumcision counts for anything, nor uncircumcision, but a new creation" (6:15). In the utterance of the phrase "new creation," Paul summarizes climactically the apocalyptic activity of God epitomized by the resurrection of Jesus Christ from the dead. He also points to a new kind of existence for Christ's followers. Deliverance from the present evil age and participation in God's new apocalyptic age come through faith in the crucified and risen Christ. Moreover, the present life of faithfulness has a future consequence (cf. 4:26–31; 6:7–8).

As with his other central themes, Paul has moved steadily to this point from the beginning of his communication. He began by asserting that his apostleship is the result of a cooperative act of the Risen Jesus Christ and God the Father who raised him from the dead (1:1, 12, 16). Paul also emphasized that his encounter with the Risen Crucified Christ radically changed his life. He was transformed from a persecutor of the church of God to a faithful proponent of it (1:13–2:14). Moreover, following the revelation of the Risen Crucified Christ to him, Paul died to the law, for in Christ he was freed to live for God (cf. 2:19–20). Similarly, the Galatians themselves experienced new creation existence when, by faith in the Risen Crucified Christ, they received the Spirit (3:1–5). Clearly, the promised eschatological Spirit of the new age has now come upon the Gentiles (3:14). By trust in Christ, God sends the Spirit of his Son into the hearts of all believers (4:6). Furthermore, the new creation inaugurated by God's activity in Christ has become evident through a new kind of unity among people in which the usual barriers of race, social class, and gender no longer cause divisions (3:26–29). In Christ, a new community has come into existence. Through the Spirit, members of this community find that, by faith, the hope of righteousness is realistic (5:5). Indeed, by the Spirit's power, believers are able to exhibit even now such righteous fruit of the Spirit as "love, joy, peace, patience, kindness, goodness, faithfulness, gentleness," and "self-control" (5:22–23). Finally, the Risen Crucified Christ makes possible a new kind of community in which "trespassers" and troublemakers may be restored to wholesome, right relations with God and their neighbor (6:1). Members of this community may also "do good to all people, especially those who are of the household of faith" (6:10). Throughout Galatians, then, Paul emphasizes the presence of God's new creation that has come to individuals and communities through the crucifixion and resurrection of Jesus Christ.

How one responds to God's activity in Christ is of grave importance. It should come as no surprise, then, that, as he makes his final statements, Paul issues a wish for peace and mercy upon the "Israel of God" (6:16)—those whom God has called and who are responding to God appropriately. With the expression, "Israel of God," however, Paul not only highlights the community established by God for accomplishing God's purposes (cf. Gen. 12: 3), but he also brings to a climax his rhetorical emphasis upon the One to whom he, the Galatians, and the agitators are all responsible—the God who calls in the grace of Christ. They are all accountable to God for their decisions and actions in light of the gospel of the Risen Crucified Christ.[5] Paul has also indicated that it is possible to identify the Israel which God has called into being and which is now faithfully responding to God's call in Christ. How? By the kind of life it leads as a part of God's new creation. Circumcision is no longer relevant for identifying the Israel of God (6:15). Rather, through faith in the Risen Crucified Christ, God is now extending the blessing of Abraham to the Gentiles (3:6–29; 4:21–31). Thus the Israel of God is comprised of everyone who belongs to Christ and lives by the Spirit, whether Jew or Greek, slave or free, male or female. The Israel of God and the members of it are new creations who are able to live in the world in a new way—the self-sacrificing way of Jesus Christ.

---

[5]In this way, Paul sounds very much like the prophets Jeremiah (cf. 31:29–30) and Ezekiel (cf. 18:1–20).

They are defined not by circumcision or obedience to the law but by faithfulness through trust in the Risen Crucified Christ.

On this note, Paul completes the task of binding the rhetorical cords of his address together and issues a final pathos appeal that corresponds to the questions he raised at the conclusion of the salutation-exordium (1:10). He is not seeking the favor of men, for, if he were, he would be untroubled by the agitators in Galatia (6:17). As it is, however, he is deeply troubled and perplexed over the spread of the agitators' perverted gospel (4:11–20). Moreover, to set his relationship with Jesus and his own example of faithfulness firmly within the mind's eye of his hearers, Paul declares that he bears on his body the marks of Jesus. Paul identifies himself as a servant of Christ who will not avoid persecution when the truth of the gospel is at stake. Jesus is the risen Christ who lives as the Crucified, and it is through trust alone in him that one is counted as an heir of God's covenant promises. The implication of this for Paul in Galatians is clear. But Paul is also calling the Galatians themselves to choose faithfulness to Christ, even if it brings suffering on Christ's behalf, rather than choose unfaithfulness through the misguided assurances of the agitators in order to avoid some persecution that faithfulness to God's purposes in Christ might bring. Paul is calling the Galatians back to the truth of the gospel.

So what exactly is the truth of the gospel according to Paul in Galatians? It is that the Christ of God was crucified but God raised Jesus from the dead, thus Jesus Christ now lives as the Crucified. Consequently, deliverance from the present evil age is the work of Christ alone. In Christ alone is there hope for righteousness. Through the Risen Crucified Christ, God has begun forming the new creation, which includes a new humanity for the new age. Moreover, inclusion in this new humanity—the Israel of God—is based entirely upon one's trust in the love and rescuing work of the Risen Crucified Christ Jesus. In these ways, Paul stresses in the conclusion of Galatians the very points he raises at the beginning of this address and develops throughout his communication.

Now that we have seen how Paul draws his rhetorical cords together in the closing of his address to the Galatians, let us summarize our findings and state our conclusion.

II. CONCLUSION

Throughout this study, we have built upon the contributions of many scholars who have shown that attention to epistolary and rhetorical practices and theory is helpful for understanding Paul's letter-speeches and their content. We surveyed the modern developments of rhetorical and epistolary criticism of Paul's letters, especially critiques of Galatians (chapter one). There we found a wide range of interpretations of Galatians' genre classification and textual divisions—an immediate indication of confusion over this communication's order and purpose. Clearly, the diverse conclusions on these matters drawn by so many capable scholars demonstrate that Paul's letter to the Galatians cannot be wholly contained within a single rhetorical or epistolary pattern. Galatians presents a masterful mixture of Greco-Roman communication forms and techniques.

From these observations, several questions emerged. For instance, what other important clues are there in Galatians and in other ancient Greco-Roman communications that might help us understand better both Galatians and its author Paul? Another question raised in this preliminary study is this: what is one to make of the unusual opening of Galatians (1:1–10) where the epistolary salutation is curiously expanded and the customary εὐχαριστῶ thanksgiving is absent?

Questions such as these led to further investigation of the relationship between letter and speech in the Greco-Roman world (chapter two). To begin with, we focused on the arena of rhetorical theory and then we considered epistolary theory. In this portion of our study, we found first that the ancients prized eloquence. Described in a variety of ways, common aspects of eloquence included clarity, orderliness, rhythm, vividness, timeliness and appropriateness of expression. We saw also that eloquence was the celebrated goal of orators, and they sought this prize through the development of their natural abilities, the acquisition and perfection of linguistic skills, ample practice, and attentiveness to propriety. We adopted Quintilian's terminology of "wise adaptability" to describe this latter component of eloquent communication. Secondly, we found that rhetoric and writing are not as separate in the Greco-Roman world as some modern scholars have argued. In fact, we observed that the rhetorical handbooks themselves may stress oral communication in the three main areas of civic discourse, but they never lose sight of the whole communication process, which includes writing. Moreover, speakers and writers alike stressed the importance of observing certain rules and principles in order to express themselves eloquently—regardless of the medium or genre of expression. Then, after considering the medium of letters in the Greco-Roman world, we noted that many other letters besides Paul's are rich in rhetorical artistry. Also, the variety of letter types indicates further the ancient stress upon communicating appropriately in many different situations. In writing as in speech, the ancients were deeply concerned with propriety.

In the third chapter, we sought to identify some of the fundamental Greco-Roman principles and resources for persuasive communication. We sought to identify the common resources that speakers and writers could draw from in their formation and delivery of a communication that would be appropriate in content, arrangement, style of expression, and delivery. We

examined the areas of invention, arrangement and expression, and there we
discovered a recurrent emphasis upon the beginnings and endings of units of
expression that ranged from periodic clauses and sentences to entire
communications. Regarding the latter, the ancient teachers of communication
show evidence of preferring the linear development of ideas and the placement
of a message's most central points at the beginning and ending of the
communication. The body of the message between the opening and closing was
in no way inconsequential. Still, beginnings and endings were deemed
especially important for effective communication.

From this point, we returned in chapter four to Paul's communication to
the Galatians and concentrated on its beginning (1:1–10). Here we observed
that one way in which Paul demonstrates the prized practice of "wise
adaptability" is through the combination of epistolary and rhetorical forms and
functions in the opening of his message to the Galatians. That is to say that the
unusual expansions to the epistolary prescript, the presence of Paul's θαυμάζω
statement, and the absence of the customary εὐχαριστῶ thanksgiving are all
understandable in light of rhetorical theory and practice. This means that Paul's
"unusual" opening in Galatians is not an accidental ordering of epistolary and
rhetorical forms but is an intentional merger of the two. It also means that the
so-called "epistolary prescript" (1:1–5) is intimately related to the whole
message of Galatians, for it is bound together with 1:6–10 to form the opening
salutation-exordium. Furthermore—in light of chapter three—we suggested that
the location of central themes in the customary opening εὐχαριστῶ thanksgiving periods that follow the prescripts in Paul's other letters might be due
more to the position of the thanksgiving at the *beginning* of a letter than with
the particular expression of εὐχαριστῶ.

Recognizing that his letter will be received and heard as a speech, even
though it is written and delivered as a letter, Paul gains a well-known rhetorical
advantage by clarifying the goal and purpose of his communication as early in
the address as possible. Evidently, the issues at stake in Galatia regarding the
gospel were too important for Paul to withhold these matters until after an
epistolary salutation. Instead, Paul fused elements of a rhetorical exordium with
components of an epistolary salutation to constitute a single opening that strikes
the keynote of his letter-speech and makes his main points conspicuous. In this,
Paul is following a common Greco-Roman communication principle of placing
an argument's key points at the beginning of the address. The advantage of
such a strategy is to establish in the minds of his hearers as early as possible the
main themes that he wants them to follow throughout the discourse.

Our identification of 1:1–10 as a salutation-exordium then led us to
examine the text for thematic indicators. Here we determined that the
unmistakable keynote of the address, as indicated by the salutation-exordium, is

the gospel of Christ. The main components of this gospel, which Paul artfully presents for further elaboration, include: the apocalyptic activity of Jesus Christ and God the Father who raised him from the dead, the nature and significance of Jesus Christ's self-offering, and the intentions of God who is calling in the grace of Christ. In chapters five, six, and seven of this study, then, we followed each of these themes through the letter-speech to the communication's end (6:11–18) where we found each of them recapitulated in vivid climactic expressions. Here, we also found them bound together as in the salutation-exordium.

With the opening statements (1:1–10), then, Paul sets his listeners on the paths of his central themes and so minimizes the potential for confusion over the meaning of his message. He then guides his listeners through the supporting developments of these themes in the body of his address (1:11–2:10; 2:11–4:7; 4:8–6:10). Finally, he reiterates these essential points in a forceful and memorable conclusion (6:11–18).

In the course of following these themes through the letter, it became evident that the opening of his communication functions not only as an indicator of the message's central themes but also as a general indicator of the communication's order. That is, Paul opens with a statement regarding his *apocalyptic* apostleship (1:1a) and then makes this the first issue to develop (1:11–2:10). He does this, however, by relating his apostolic authority directly to the apocalyptic activity of God who revealed Christ to him. Indeed, the periodic form of Paul's opening expression indicates that his greater emphasis is upon the significance of Christ's resurrection from the dead. A second keynote in the opening pertains to the work and significance of the Crucified Christ (1:4) and it is this matter that Paul addresses most directly in 2:11–4:7. Then in 1:6–9, Paul expresses concern for the Galatians who are unwittingly walking away from the One who is purposively calling in the grace of Christ— the very One whom they are seeking to obey and follow—and Paul addresses this problem and its solution in 4:8–6:10. Paul then closes the salutation-exordium by sharpening his focus on the issue of true discipleship (1:10) and it is upon this note that Paul's message to the Galatians ends (6:11–18).

These are broad strokes, to be sure, and further study along this line may be useful, but 1:1–10 can be applied to the whole of Paul's letter-speech to the Galatians as an ideal exordium in the manner described by Quintilian and Cicero. That is, the whole "speech" of Galatians can be unpacked—both thematically and organizationally—from the points that Paul introduces at its beginning. Moreover, these same points stand climactically at the communication's end.

An examination of these thematic movements in Galatians has also shown that fundamental to the main issues raised in this letter-speech is the point raised at the end of the opening periodic declaration that God the Father raised Jesus Christ from the dead (1:1b). Though issues surrounding the matters of Paul's apostleship, the law, justification by faith, life in the Spirit, and the inclusion of Gentiles into the church are all important in Galatians, this study indicates that Paul viewed them as topoi that are secondary to the more fundamental matter regarding the truth of the gospel: Jesus is the Risen Crucified Christ through whom God is calling forth a new creation. Upon this point stand all the other main elements in Paul's message to the Galatians. The Risen Crucified Christ is Paul's stasis. It is understandable, then, that Paul would place this component of the gospel so prominently at the beginning of his message to the Galatians, something unique among Paul's letters. How his listeners respond to this assertion—more than any other—will affect their considerations and decisions regarding all of Paul's other claims. It also appears that, given Paul's early emphasis on the Risen Christ, especially in conjunction with his contested apostleship, the resurrection of Jesus Christ from the dead was one point held in common between himself and the recipients of his letter-speech in Galatia. Upon this tenet of the gospel, Paul had a basis for addressing the Galatians and their situation. That Christ is risen was not at issue. Problematic was the truth of the gospel that the Risen Christ lives as the Crucified and that God's rescuing activity in Christ is wholly sufficient for being reckoned as righteous and included among the heirs of Abraham. Thus Paul argues that one's relationship with God and one's inclusion in God's covenant family through Christ cannot be improved by obedience to the law. Rather, one's relationship with God and one's inclusion in the covenant promises of God are based upon one's utter trust in the Christ who is risen as the crucified.

APPENDIX

PERIODIC OVERTURES

As we saw above, periods received attention from orators not only as a matter of stylistic arrangement for sentences but also as an especially appropriate stylistic form for exordiums and perorations. While a thorough investigation of these practical relationships would be useful, it is sufficient for the purposes of this study to show simply the common practice of striking important themes in a composition's opening lines and the stylistic clues of the periodic form that are often present there.

One common and important function of the period in Greco-Roman communication was its use for stating clearly and memorably at a composition's beginning central elements of the message which followed. For instance, in the opening periodic lines of the *Odyssey* (1.1–2), which are arranged in hexameter rhythm, Homer launches central themes of the story in this way:[1]

Ἄνδρα μοι ἔννεπε, μοῦσα, πολύτροπον, ὃς μάλα πολλὰ
πλάγχθη, ἐπεὶ Τροίης ἱερὸν πτολίεθρον ἔπερσεν·
πολλῶν δ᾽ ἀνθρώπων ἴδεν ἄστεα καὶ νόον ἔγνω,
πολλὰ δ᾽ ὅ γ᾽ ἐν πόντῳ πάθεν ἄλγεα ὃν κατὰ θυμόν,
ἀρνύμενος ἥν τε ψυχὴν καὶ νόστον ἑταίρων.

Speak to me of the man, O Muse, the one much-traveled,
    who very many times
was thrown sideways, after Troy's city temple he sacked;
and many were the cities of men he saw and whose mind he knew,
and many pains he suffered against his spirit upon the open sea,
while striving for his life and the return of his comrades.

---

[1] Homer *Odyssey,* trans. A. T. Murray, The Loeb Classical Library (Cambridge: Harvard University Press, 1995). On the language of Homer, see especially Bernard Knox, *Homer: The Odyssey,* trans. Robert Fagles (New York: Viking Penquin, 1996), 12–22. Regarding Homer's hexameter lines, Knox notes that they may consist of "dactyls (one long plus two shorts) or spondees (two longs) in the first four places but must be dactyl and spondee in that order in the last two (rarely spondee and spondee, never spondee followed by dactyl). The syllables are literally long and short; the meter is based on pronunciation time, not, as in our language, on stress" (12).

The *Odyssey* is chiefly about a man, Odysseus, who, after the Greek conquest of the Trojans, traveled for ten years to return home to Ithaca, enduring considerable dangers and struggles. The periodic force of these opening lines is difficult to convey in English, but the Greek lines show the importance of the first and last members. Other core components of this great epic poem are quickly added with the accompanying periodic members in lines 3–10. Homer emphasizes from the story's beginning that the central character is exceptionally wise in the ways and thoughts of humankind (3) yet suffers to the core of his being in the voyage home (4) while striving to preserve his life and the lives of his comrades (5). Odysseus survives but, despite his best efforts, (6) cannot save his foolish companions who perish on account of their own wickedness, for they fail to offer appropriate sacrifices to the gods (7–8). Moreover, divine vengeance also figures prominently in their demise (9). The poem's opening then concludes with a period that rounds out all ten lines as an aural unit by echoing the first line while expanding it to include the whole audience as the hearers of the composition that follows (10).[2]

Undoubtedly, this periodic opening does not make the remainder of the story superfluous. In fact, everything between this opening and the poem's dramatic conclusion builds toward the climax and is essential for understanding the entire work.[3] Thus the audience is fully satisfied at the end of the story when Odysseus, with the strengthened hand of his father Laertes, succeeds in defeating Eupithes and peace for Odysseus and his family is established at the goddess Athena's command.[4] Nevertheless, Homer uses carefully constructed periods in the opening of his work that stand as sign-posts identifying important

---

[2]The accompanying periods in lines 6–10 are: ἀλλ οὐδ ὣς ἑτάρους ἐρρύσατο, ἱέμενός περ· / αὐτῶν γὰρ σφετέρῃσιν ἀτασθαλίῃσιν ὄλοντο, / νήπιοι, οἳ κατὰ βοῦς Ὑπερίονος Ἠελίοιο / ἤσθιον · αὐτὰρ ὁ τοῖσιν ἀφείλετο νόστιμον ἦμαρ. / τῶν ἁμόθεν γε, θεά, θύγατερ Διός, εἰπὲ καὶ ἡμῖν. // *But he could not save his comrades, although working on their behalf; / for through their own wickedness they perished, / childish ones, those who devoured the ox of Hyperion's son Helios; / moreover, this one was taking away the day of their return. / Of all these things, goddess, daughter of Zeus, speak also unto us.*

[3]For instance, in the middle of the story—as in the middle of a well-formed period— there is crucial information that shapes how the audience understands the future of Odysseus beyond what Homer tells. Odysseus may possess divine wisdom, but he is not immortal, for, near the middle of the story, Tiresias of the underworld foretells the death of Odysseus (Homer *Odyssey* 11.100–137). According to this prophecy, after his victory over the suitors for his wife Penelope, Odysseus must make peace with Poseidon by travelling inland to make a sacrifice to Poseidon and then return home to sacrifice to all the gods of Mt. Olympus. Once this mission is completed, Odysseus will soon die peacefully, surrounded by his family.

[4]Homer *Odyssey* 24.513–548; on the matter of whether book 24 was a later addition, see Bernard Knox, ed., *Homer: The Odyssey*, 59.

movements of the story that follows. This was the model exordium which, according to Quintilian, established the standard for well-formed openings.

A similarly strong period stands at the beginning of Homer's *Iliad* (1.1–7).[5] As with the *Odyssey*, these opening lines strike the core of the story that follows. Indeed, here the very first word in Greek is "wrath" or "rage" which is bound quickly to the character Achilles whose name is the last word of the first line. Other important elements of the story are added through the rounding of the period, and together they constitute the chief subject matter of this work. From here the entire work moves swiftly to render an account of Achilles' rage—its origin, its development, and its fatal outcome. In a sense, then, the very beginning of this epic poem highlights this story's stirring content.[6] It provides an immediate framework for receiving and understanding all that follows.

The practice of periodic overtures was not limited to the epic poetry of Homer. For instance, Plato opens the *Republic* with periods that create a vivid image for the entire work and begin forecasting the work's conclusion.[7] They are less dramatic and not as rounded as Homer's opening periods in the *Iliad* and *Odyssey*, but they, too, are periods. Demetrius, in fact, used the first period of the *Republic* (327a) as an example of the subtle conversational periodic style,

---

[5]Homer, *The Iliad*. Μῆνιν ἄειδε, θεά, Πηληϊάδεω Ἀχιλῆος / οὐλομένην, ἣ μυρί Ἀχαιοῖς ἄλγε ἔθηκε, /πολλὰς δ ἰφθίμους ψυχὰς Ἄιδι προΐαψεν / ἡρώων, αὐτοὺς δὲ ἑλώρια τεῦχε κύνεσσιν / οἰωνοῖσί τε πᾶσι, Διὸς δ ἐτελείετο Βουλή, / ἐξ οὗ δὴ τὰ πρῶτα διαστήτην ἐρίσαντε / Ἀτρείδης τε ἄναξ ἀνδρῶν καὶ δῖος Ἀχιλλεύς. // The wrath do thou sing, O goddess, of Peleus' son, Achilles, / that baneful wrath which brought countless woes upon the Achaeans, / and sent forth to Hades many valiant souls of / warriors, and made themselves to be a spoil for dogs / and all manner of birds; and thus the will of Zeus was brought to fulfillment; / sing thou thereof from the time when at the first there parted in strife / Atreus' son, king of men, and goodly Achilles.

[6]As in the *Odyssey*, Homer achieves a strong climax in the *Iliad* when Achilles succeeds in killing Hector (24.804). Unfortunately for Achilles, though, the success of rage signals his own inevitable self-destruction, for, earlier in the body of the poem (18.94–96), the prophetic fulfillment of Hector's death at Achilles' hands seals the reciprocating prophecy of his own demise. See for instance, Homer, *The Iliad*, trans. Robert Fagles, ed. Bernard Knox (New York: Viking Penquin, 1990), 3–5.

[7]Cf. Plato *Republic* 327a–b. With these lines, Plato depicts the righteous man Socrates coming down to a new festival honoring a foreign Thracian goddess and with this signals the startling transformation from the old age of the righteous or just man to the new age of the republic and the problem of relating justice to the state. In the remaining lines of this lengthy introduction (327–331), Plato's main characters define and describe justice in a way contrary to the conventional standard. For them, a just or righteous person cannot harm others or do evil (330–336). Rather, a righteous citizen must always do good even if it means standing against one's countrymen. Throughout the remainder of the *Republic*, then, Plato demonstrates some critical challenges to living justly and proves that the just life is better and more fulfilling than the unjust life. The righteousness, reason, and self-control of individual citizens is the basis of a just republic. Cf. vii–xlv.

which is simpler and looser than either the historical or rhetorical arrangements.[8]

A periodic overture also appears in a Hebrew composition of the Old Testament, though Hebrew more often uses the continuous or narrative style of sentence formation and movement. The prophetic books, however, frequently use the periodic style[9] and there is in the book of Amos a hymnic period that succinctly portrays the central theme of the book.[10] Immediately after the title (1:1), the Masoretic Text reads:

וַיֹּאמַר יְהוָה מִצִּיּוֹן יִשְׁאָג וּמִירוּשָׁלַ͏ִם יִתֵּן קוֹלוֹ
וְאָבְלוּ נְאוֹת הָרֹעִים וְיָבֵשׁ רֹאשׁ הַכַּרְמֶל

And he said, 'Yahweh roars from Zion, and from Jerusalem
gives his voice,
the pastures of shepherds dry up,[11] and the top withers,
namely that of Carmel.'

The poetic characteristics of this verse are best described as two bi-cola arranged as synonymous parallelisms.[12] The overall arrangement, however, is periodic. It has a strong beginning and moves clearly and swiftly to a climactic end. In this way, it resembles the rhetorical period. It vividly describes the awesome power of God's voice that can scorch the fertile fields around Jerusalem, even the lush slopes and peak of distant Mount Carmel in the north. This overture aptly summarizes the oracles of destruction that follow in Amos's prophetic utterances.[13]

---

[8]Demetrius *De Elocutione* 21. This model was widely known. Demetrius cites only its beginning and ending. The whole period is: κετέβην χθὲς εἰς Πειραιᾶ μετὰ Γλαύκωνος τοῦ Ἀρίστωνος προσευξόμενός τε τῇ θεῷ καὶ ἅμα τὴν ἑορτὴν βουλόμενος θεάσασθαι τίνα τρόπον ποιήσουσιν ἅτε νῦν πρῶτον ἄγοντες. The festival (τὴν ἑορτὴν) is the object of θεάσασθαι, ποιήσουσιν and ἄγοντες. Also, tradition holds that Plato lavished considerable attention upon it. Beside his deathbed were found wax tablets upon which he had been testing words and their various arrangements to perfect the opening of the *Republic*. The end of Plato's life, then, highlighted his own maxim that "the beginning is the most important part in every work" (*Republic* 2.377b). See also Demetrius *De Elocutione* 25; Dionysius of Halicarnassus *De Compositione Verbum* 25; and Quintilian *Institutio Oratoria* 8.6.64.

[9]Cf. A. T. Robertson, *A Grammar of the Greek New Testament*, 467.

[10]The thematic significance of Amos 1:2 is noted by J. L. Mays in *Amos*, Old Testament Library (Philadelphia: Westminster Press, 1969), 21. Mays views this verse as a later editorial insertion that is accurate in its summary of the book's content.

[11]An alternative meaning of אבל is "mourn" but the context supports the meaning of "dry up."

[12]Mays, 21.

[13]Regarding the significance of Carmel, it is worth noting further that Amos was a prophet from Judah in the south who uttered God's judgment against Israel in the north. On

The opening lines of the book of Proverbs may also be understood as a periodic overture or sign-post for the whole work. These verses move in a clear progressive manner from the superscription (1:1) to the climactic assertion that "The fear of the Lord is the beginning of knowledge; fools despise wisdom and instruction" (1:7). Again, though, the middle portions are critically important. Between the beginning and ending of this progressive purpose statement are positioned the core communal virtues of "righteousness, justice, and equity" (3b)—virtues that characterize the community of God's faithful which is comprised of both students and teachers of wisdom who fear God.[14]

There are other examples of periodic openings in Greco-Roman communication, particularly in the works of Isocrates, Aristotle, Sophocles, and Cicero. Their opening periods vary in length and forcefulness from work to work but nevertheless often identify fundamental elements of the communication that follows. In each case, the diction and the word arrangements show careful composition to emphasize important topics that are then discussed. Perhaps, though, the most prominent and persistent use of the periodic overtures is found in the literary epistles of Seneca and the discourses of Dio Chrysostom, both of whom were contemporaries of Paul.

It should come as no surprise that educated writers would use periods advantageously as thematic sign-posts and signals for transitions in their letters or discourses. This is very often the case for Seneca as evidenced by the collection of his letters to Lucilius. In the opening of *Epistle* 1, for instance, the orator Seneca marks the course for the letter with a strong rhetorical period. He writes:[15]

Seneca Lucilio suo salutem. Ita fac, mi Lucili; vindica te tibi, et tempus, quod adhuc aut auferebatur aut subripiebatur aut excidebat, collige et serva.

From Seneca to Lucilius with greetings. Continue to act thus, my dear Lucilius, setting yourself free for your own sake, and time—which until lately has been forced from you, or stolen, or has slipped away—gather and watch over!

Here, immediately after the brief conventional epistolary salutation, Seneca states the essence of his entire message with a concise and eloquent period. He is writing to encourage Lucilius to manage his time wisely. He does

---

Amos's rhetorical characteristics, see especially Yehoshua Gitay, "A Study of Amos's Art of Speech: A Rhetorical Analysis of Amos 3:1–15," *CBQ* 42 (1980): 293–309.

[14]See especially W. P. Brown, *Character in Crisis: A Fresh Approach to the Wisdom Literature of the Old Testament* (Grand Rapids, Mich.: Wm. B. Eerdmans Publishing Co., 1996), 22–30.

[15]Seneca, *Epistulae Morales.*

this by offering several proofs to support his opening position. First, there is no escape from the reality that everyone loses time for a variety of reasons, the only inexcusable loss, however, is that due to one's own carelessness. Moreover, it is senseless to lose more time by fretting over time which has passed. "Whatever years lie behind us," he writes, "are in death's hands"(2). Secondly, in the same way that time is lost irresponsibly by looking too far back, time is also lost to negligence by looking too far forward, by postponing life as it rushes past; thus Seneca's admonition to Lucilius to embrace every present hour (omnes horas complectere). The present time, fleeting though it may be, is a precious commodity which "even a grateful recipient cannot repay" (3).

At this point in his letter, Seneca highlights the example of his own present conditions regarding time and emphasizes that he, too, struggles with the problems of minimizing wasteful expenditures of time and managing the remnants of time left to him.[16] He then moves to the letter's closing with a rhetorical question that calls attention to the common property of time. Regarding his own poor condition in this respect, Seneca answers, "I do not regard a man as poor, if the little which remains is enough for him"(5). As for Lucilius, Seneca encourages him to pay closest attention to the time he has, which is the present.[17] In these words and sentiments, Seneca has come full circle so that the letter itself forms a neat period driving to a strong and vivid ending. Seneca closes the letter swiftly with a well-known saying from Hesiod which needs no explanation to Lucilius.[18] Time—like wine and any other good commodity one might possess—is a poor saving if one waits too long to enjoy it or lets everyone else drink from the cask first so that nothing remains but the dregs. With this vivid image, Seneca strikes his central point which he had marked from the beginning and then closes the letter quickly with a single word—"farewell" (Vale).

To a large extent, Seneca maintains this same pattern throughout his epistles.[19] Where he varies it, he nevertheless uses the first position most often for stating his theme, and his conclusions ordinarily bring his point to a vivid

---

[16]Seneca does not mention his precise situation, but this letter was probably written sometime during the last three years of his life (ca. A.D. 63–65). After years of prominent civil service, a change of power in Rome in A.D. 62 resulted in a drastic reversal in Seneca's fortunes. He spent the next 2–3 years traveling around southern Italy and finally committed suicide in A.D. 65 in the face of impending violence against him under the direction of the Emperor. See R. M. Gummere, *Seneca ad Lucilium Epistulae Morales*, vii–ix.

[17]"Tu tamen malo serves tua, et bono tempore incipies," or "You, however, choose rather to keep watch over what is yours, and an advantageous time you are beginning" (5).

[18]See Hesiod *Works and Days* 369 in *Hesiod: The Homeric Hymns and Homerica*, trans. Hugh G. Evelyn-White, The Loeb Classical Library (Cambridge, Mass.: Harvard University Press, 1936).

[19]Cf. Seneca *Epistles* 2, 3, 4, 5, 6, 7, 9, 10, 12, 15, 17.

climax. Regarding exceptions to his customary openings, Seneca may postpone his periodic overtures, but not for long. For instance, in *Epistle* 8 he begins by quoting certain questions raised in a letter that he received from Lucilius and the questions identify the topic, but it is Seneca's periodic expression which immediately follows that sets the course for what remains, even as it gives his own position by answering the questions. Seneca wanted Lucilius to know from the start his basic stance on the issue. The importance of beginnings in correspondences is shown further by Seneca's comment to Lucilius in *Epistle* 16 where he writes, "If I know you well, you have already been trying to find out, from the very beginning of my letter, what little contribution it brings to you"(7). What sense would there be in such a comment, if it were not a common practice for them to prefigure in the very beginnings of their letters their central points to be developed in the letter-body?

Dio Chrysostom was another prominent Greco-Roman orator and writer during the first century A.D., and he, too, frequently opened his compositions with periodic overtures. Dio's existant discourses often use Koine Greek and reveal a consistent style marked by simplicity, rhythm, and stateliness. His writings show, furthermore, a clear interest in making his messages as accessible as possible to the common Roman citizen.[20] Not surprisingly, toward that end he opens several discourses with clearly defined periods that emphasize the works' central components.[21]

In his *Second Discourse on Kingship* (περὶ βασιλείας β), for instance, Dio presents a possible dialogue or *prosopopoeia* between Philip of Macedon and his son Alexander. In this supposed conversation, Alexander gives voice to some of Dio's views regarding the chief characteristics of a true king. Drawing his ideals primarily from Homer, Dio argues through Alexander that Homer not only provides guidelines for practical living, but, more importantly, provides sound instruction for developing a king's necessary powers for correct thinking and persuasive communication. The opening period marks this central theme:

Λέγεταί ποτε ᾿Αλέξανδρον τῷ πατρὶ Φιλίππῳ μειράκιον ὄντα
διαλεχθῆναι περὶ῾ Ομήρου μάλα ἀνδρείως καὶ μεγαλοφρόνως·
οἱ δὲ αὐτοὶ λόγοι οὗτοι σχεδόν τι καὶ περὶ βασιλείας ἦσαν.
It is said that at one time Alexander, while still a boy, was conversing
very manly and wisely with his father Philip about Homer,
and these were almost the same words also concerning kingship.

---

[20]Cf. Dio Chrysostom *Discourses*, vol. 1, trans. J. W. Cohoon, LCL (New York: G. P. Putnam's Sons, 1932), vii–xi.

[21]See especially Dio Chrysostom *Discourses* 2, 4, 13, 14, 18, 23, 26, 27.

The dual emphasis here on kingship and the powerful use of language is stressed repeatedly, and, not surprisingly, it is precisely these two themes that are held tightly together and figure prominently throughout the entire discourse.[22] Through the elaborate depiction of Alexander's accurate thinking and eloquent speech, Dio proves that a king will find the diligent study of rhetoric and philosophy a proper and necessary pursuit.[23]

Chrysostom's periodic overture in the Fourth Discourse on Kingship is similarly clear. Here, Dio stresses from the opening period his topic on the use of leisure time. He writes (1):

Φασί ποτε Ἀλέξανδρον Διογένει συμβαλεῖν οὐ πάνυ τι σχολάζοντα πολλὴν ἄγοντι σχολήν.
It is said that once Alexander, while not quite being at leisure, met Diogenes, who was taking much leisure.

Following this opening sentence, Dio gives some brief introductory remarks about both Alexander the Great and the Cynic philosopher Diogenes. He then states humorously that he wants to render this likely account of their conversation because he and his readers also have nothing better to do at the moment (3). Dio proceeds with a reported description of Alexander as "the most ambitious of men and the greatest lover of glory" (4) and one who "looked down upon all other men . . . For he perceived that they had all been well-nigh ruined in soul by luxury and idleness and were slaves of money and pleasure"(5–6). Diogenes, however, created a problem for Alexander in that he was poor and lived simply yet was admired and celebrated by the Greeks in a way that rivaled or even surpassed Alexander's own fame (6–12). Thus Alexander tells his attendants that he wanted some leisure time and he goes to visit Diogenes (12).

Dio then presents a vigorous conversation between the two men throughout the remainder of the discourse, and he proves that Diogenes is the better and stronger of the two. Diogenes desired that Alexander "might be moved from his pride and thirst for glory and be able to sober up a little"(77–78). He aims to achieve this end by arguing that the love of honor and glory—pride—is worse than the love of money and pleasure (83–84). Diogenes then

---

[22]See especially 2.3, 6, 7–19, 24–25, 44, 65, 77–79.

[23]Dio is obviously set on portraying rhetoric and philosophy favorably throughout this discourse. Historically, this is significant for it was during the first century A.D. that rhetoric was eclipsing philosophy with the rise of the New Sophistic movement. Advocates of this perspective esteemed oratory over all other disciplines and believed that rhetorical prowess was more important than the speech's content. This shallow view of rhetoric and rejection of philosophy drew increasing criticism. Dio contends in this discourse, however, that good moral character and persuasive speech belong together.

addresses each of the three forms of "wickedness" which are identifiable by a person's habits and acts (88). Avarice (91–100), hedonism (101–115), and the love of honor (116–132) are taken up in turn, and, in each case, they affect a person's use of time. The point is that how one uses leisure time is often a fair measure of one's character. Thus Dio ends the discourse by having Diogenes invite Alexander to join him in using leisure time in the pursuit of harmony with the "good and wise guardian spirit or god" and in gaining a sound education (139).

In many of Dio Chrysostom's discourses, as in Seneca's epistles and elsewhere, opening sentences in periodic form—simple or compounded—often signal the principal theme(s) of the work that follows. This is because the very beginning of a work—regardless of its form—was valued highly as the place to establish the topic to which the subsequent subject matter would relate.

In sum, the opening words of a communication—regardless of its genre and other characteristics—often struck the heart of the communicator's message. Periods were an effective way to make the opening memorable and persuasive. The same is also often true regarding the use of periods in closings where, once again, a communicator often wanted to reiterate and stress a central point of the argument. In few places is the Greco-Roman emphasis on beginnings and endings more apparent than in the development and use of the periodic style. Beginnings and endings were highly esteemed in Greco-Roman communication. This is because the ancients recognized that the opening and the closing of a speech, like the opening and closing words of a period itself, are often the easiest parts of a communication to remember. A well-formed exordium also helped minimize the listeners' confusion by identifying from the very start the topic(s) to which everything that followed would relate. Sometimes they even established the course that lay ahead. Moreover, by knowing from the start the message's fundamental theme(s), the receiver of the message—listener or reader—could better understand and interpret the communication.

BIBLIOGRAPHY

Achtemeier, Elizabeth. "Righteousness in the OT." In *The Interpreter's Dictionary of the Bible*, ed. George Arthur Buttrick, vol. 4, 80–85. Nashville: Abingdon Press, 1990.

Achtemeier, Paul J. "An Apocalyptic Shift in Early Christian Tradition: Reflections on Some Canonical Evidence." *Catholic Biblical Quarterly* 45 (1983): 231–45.

————. "Finding the Way to Paul's Theology: A Response to J. Christiaan Beker and J. Paul Sampley." In *Pauline Theology*, ed. Jouette M. Bassler, vol. 1, 25–36. Minneapolis: Fortress Press, 1991.

————. "Omne Verbum Sonat: The New Testament and the Oral Environment of Late Western Antiquity." *Journal of Biblical Literature* 109 (1990): 3–27.

————. "Righteousness in the NT." In *The Interpreter's Dictionary of the Bible*, ed. George Arthur Buttrick, vol. 4, 91–99. Nashville: Abingdon Press, 1990.

————. *Romans*. Interpretation. Atlanta: John Knox Press, 1985.

————. *The Quest for Unity in the New Testament Church: A Study in Paul and Acts*. Philadelphia: Fortress Press, 1987.

Aland, Kurt, et al. *Novum Testamentum Graece*. 27th rev. ed. Stuttgart: Deutsche Bibelgesellschaft, 1993.

Aletti, Jean Noël. *Comment Dieu est-il juste? Clefs pour interpréter l'épître aux Romains*. Paris: Editions du Seuil, 1991.

————. "La présence d'un modèle rhétorique en Romains: Son rôle et son importance." *Biblica* 71 (1990): 1–24.

————. Review of *Galatians: A Commentary on Paul's Letter to the Churches in Galatia*, by H. D. Betz. In *Recherches de Science Religieuse* 69 (1981): 601–2.

Alfsvag, Knut. "Language and Reality: Luther's relation to classical rhetoric in Rationis Lattomianae confutatio (1521)." *Studia Theologica* 41 (1987): 85–126.

Andresen, Carl and Günter Klein, eds. *Theologia Crucis – Signum Crucis: Festschrift für Erich Dinkler zum 70 Geburtstag*. Tübingen: J. C. B. Mohr, 1979.

Aristotle. *The Art of Rhetoric*. Translated by John Henry Freese. The Loeb Classical Library. Cambridge, Mass.: Harvard University Press, 1926.

————. *The Nicomachean Ethics*. Translated by H. Rackham. The Loeb Classical Library. Cambridge, Mass.: Harvard University Press, 1926; reprint 1990.

————. *Poetics*. Translated by Stephen Halliwell. The Loeb Classical Library. Cambridge, Mass.: Harvard University Press, 1995.

————. *Politics*. Translated by H. Rackham. The Loeb Classical Library. Cambridge, Mass.: Harvard University Press, 1932; reprint 1990.

————. *Rhetorica ad Alexandrum*. Translated by H. Rackham. The Loeb Classical Library. Cambridge, Mass.: Harvard University Press, 1937.

————. *Topica*. Translated by E. S. Forster. The Loeb Classical Library. Cambridge, Mass.: Harvard University Press, 1960; reprint 1989.

Augustine. *On Christian Doctrine*. Translated by D. W. Robertson, Jr. The Library of Liberal Arts. Indianapolis: Bobbs-Merrill Educational Publishing, 1958.

Aune, David E. *The New Testament in Its Literary Environment*. Library of Early Christianity, ed. Wayne A. Meeks, vol. 8. Philadelphia: Westminster Press, 1987.

————. W. D. Davies, and P. W. Meyer. Reviews of *Galatians: A Commentary on Paul's Letter to the Churches in Galatia*, by H. D. Betz. In *Religious Studies Review* 7 (1981): 304–18.

————. Review of *Galatians—Dialogical Response to Opponents*, by B. H. Brinsmead. In *Catholic Biblical Quarterly* 46 (1984): 145–47.

Bahr, Gordon J. Bahr. "The Subscriptions in the Pauline Letters." *Journal of Biblical Literature* 87 (1968): 27–41.

Bammel, Ernst. "πτωχός." In *Theological Dictionary of the New Testament*, ed. Gerhard Friedrich, vol. 6, 888–915. Translated by G. W. Bromiley. Grand Rapids: Wm. B. Eerdmans Publishing Co., 1968.

Barclay, John M. G. "Mirror-Reading a Polemical Letter: Galatians as a Test Case." *Journal for the Study of the New Testament* 31 (1987): 73–93.

Barclay, William. *Educational Ideals in the Ancient World*. Grand Rapids: Baker Book House, 1959.

Barrett, Charles Kingsley. "Boasting (καυχᾶσθαι, κτλ.) in the Pauline Epistles." In *L'Apôtre Paul: Personnalité, Style et Conception du Ministère*, ed. A. Vanhoye, 363–68. Bibliotheca Ephemeridum Theologicarum Lovaniensium 73. Leuven: Leuven University Press, 1986.

————. *Essays on Paul*. Philadelphia: Westminster Press, 1982.

———. Review of *Galatians: A Commentary on Paul's Letter to the Churches in Galatia*, by H. D. Betz. In *Interpretation* 34 (1980): 414–17.

———. *Freedom and Obligation: A Study of the Epistle to the Galatians*. Philadelphia: Westminster Press, 1985.

———. *Paul: An Introduction to His Thought*. Louisville: Westminster/John Knox Press, 1994.

Bassler, Jouette M., ed. *Pauline Theology I: Thessalonians, Philippians, Galatians, Philemon*. Minneapolis: Fortress Press, 1991.

Bauckham, Richard. "Life, Death, and the Afterlife in Second Temple Judaism." In *Life in the Face of Death: The Resurrection Message of the New Testament*, ed. R. N. Longenecker, 80–99. Grand Rapids: Wm. B. Eerdmans Publishing Co., 1998.

Bauer, Walter, William F. Arndt, F. Wilbur Gingrich, and Frederick W. Danker, eds. *A Greek-English Lexicon of the New Testament and Other Early Christian Literature*. Chicago: The University of Chicago Press, 1979.

Baur, Ferdinand Christian. *Paul, the Apostle of Jesus Christ*. Translated by Allar Menzies, 2 vols. Edinburgh: Williams and Norgate, 1876.

Beker, J. Christiaan. *Paul the Apostle: The Triumph of God in Life and Thought*. Philadelphia: Fortress Press, 1980.

———. *Paul's Apocalyptic Gospel: The Coming Triumph of God*. Philadelphia: Fortress Press, 1982.

———. "Recasting Pauline Theology: The Coherence-Contingency Scheme as Interpretive Model." In *Pauline Theology*, ed. Jouette M. Bassler, vol. 1, 15–24. Minneapolis: Fortress Press, 1991.

———. *The Triumph of God: The Essence of Paul's Thought*. Translated by Loren T. Stuckenbruck. Minneapolis: Fortress Press, 1990.

Bentley, Jerry H. *Humanists and Holy Writ: New Testament Scholarship in the Renaissance*. Princeton: Princeton University Press, 1983.

Berger, Klaus. "Apostelbrief und apostolische Rede: Zum Formular frühchristlicher Briefe." *Zeitschrift für die neutestamentliche Wissenschaft und die Kunde der älteren Kirche* 65 (1974): 190–231.

Betz, Hans Dieter. *2 Corinthians 8 and 9: A Commentary on Two Administrative Letters of the Apostle Paul*. Philadelphia: Fortress Press, 1985.

———. *Galatians: A Commentary on Paul's Letter to the Churches in Galatia*. Hermeneia. Philadelphia: Fortress Press, 1979.

————. "Galatians, Epistle to the." In *The Anchor Bible Dictionary*, vol. 2, ed. David Noel Freedman, 872–75. New York: Doubleday & Co., 1992.

————. "The Literary Composition and Function of Paul's Letter to the Galatians." *New Testament Studies* 21 (1975): 353–79.

————. "The Problem of Rhetoric and Theology According to the Apostle Paul." In *L'Apôtre Paul: Personalité, Style et Conception du Ministère*, ed. A. Vanhoye, 16–48. Bibliotheca Ephemeridum Theologicarum Lovaniensium 73. Leuven: Leuven University Press, 1986.

Betz, Otto. "στίγμα." In *Theological Dictionary of the New Testament*, ed. Gerhard Friedrich, vol. 7, 657–64. Translated by G. W. Bromiley. Grand Rapids: Wm. B. Eerdmans Publishing Co., 1968.

Bible Windows. Silver Mountain Software, Cedar Hill, Tex.

Bjerkelund, Carl J. *Parakalo: Form, Funktion und Sinn der Parakalo–Sätze in den paulinischen Briefen*. Bibliotheca Theologica Norvegica. Oslo: Universitetsforlaget, 1967.

Black, C. Clifton. "Rhetorical Criticism and Biblical Interpretation." *Expository Times* 100 (1989): 252–58.

Bligh, John. *Galatians in Greek: A Structural Analysis of St. Paul's Epistle to the Galatians, With Notes on the Greek*. Detroit: University of Detroit Press, 1966.

————. *Galatians: A Discussion of St. Paul's Epistle*. Householder Commentaries, no. 1. London: St. Paul Publications, 1969.

Bolt, Peter G. "Life, Death, and the Afterlife in the Greco-Roman World." In *Life in the Face of Death: The Resurrection Message of the New Testament,* ed. R. N. Longenecker, 51–79. Grand Rapids: Wm. B. Eerdmans Publishing Co., 1998.

Bonhöffer, Adolf. *Epiktet und das Neue Testament*. Religionsgeschichtliche Versuche und Vorarbeiten, x. bd. Giessen: A. Töpelmann (vormals J. Ricker), 1911.

Bonner, Stanley F. *Education in Ancient Rome*. Berkeley: University of California Press, 1977.

————. *Roman Declamation in the Late Republic and Early Empire*. Berkeley: University of California Press, 1949.

Bonsirven, Joseph. *Exégèse rabbinique et exégèse paulienne*. Paris: Beauchesne, 1939.

Booth, Wayne C. *The Rhetoric of Fiction*. 2d ed. Chicago: University of Chicago Press, 1982.

Bornkamm, Günther. *Paul*. Translated by D. M. G. Stalker. New York: Harper & Row, Publishers, 1971.

Bovon, François. "Une Formule Prépaulinienne dans L'Épître aux Galates." In *Paganisme, Judaïsme, Christianisme: Influences et affrontements dans le monde antique: Mélanges offerts à Marcel Simon*, 91–107. Paris: Éditions E. De Boccard, 1978.

Bower, E. W. "Epodos and *insinuatio* in Greek and Latin Rhetoric." *Classical Quarterly* 52 (1958): 224–30.

Brandis, C. G. "Ἐκκλησία." In *Paulys Realencyclopädie der klassischen Altertumswissenschaft*, ed. August Friedrich von Pauly, vol. 2, 2163–2200. München: A. Druckenmüller, 1905.

Brinsmead, Bernard Hunderford. *Galatians—Dialogical Response to Opponents*. Society of Biblical Literature Dissertation Series, vol. 65. Chico, Calif.: Scholars Press, 1982.

Brooks, James A., Carlton L. Winbery. *Syntax of New Testament Greek*. Lanham, Md.: University Press of America, Inc., 1979.

Brown, Francis, S. R. Driver, and Charles A. Briggs, eds. *The New Brown—Driver—Briggs—Gesenius Hebrew and English Lexicon*. Peabody, Mass.: Hendrickson Publishers, 1979.

Brown, Raymond E., Karl P. Donfried, and John Reumann, eds. *Peter in the New Testament: A Collaborative Assessment by Protestant and Roman Catholic Scholars*. Minneapolis: Augsburg, 1973.

Brown, William P. *Character in Crisis: A Fresh Approach to the Wisdom Literature of the Old Testament*. Grand Rapids: Wm. B. Eerdmans Publishing Co., 1996.

Bruce, F. F. *The Epistle to the Galatians: A Commentary on the Greek Text*. New International Greek Testament Commentary. Exeter: The Paternoster Press, 1982; reprint, Grand Rapids: Wm. B. Eerdmans Publishing Co., 1982.

―――. *Paul: Apostle of the Heart Set Free*. Exeter: The Paternoster Press, 1977.

Bultmann, Rudolf. *The History of the Synoptic Tradition*. Revised edition. Translated by John Marsh. Peabody, Mass.: Hendrickson Publishers, 1994.

―――. *Der Stil der paulinischen Predigt und die kynisch-stoische Diatribe*. Forschungen zur Religion und Literatur des Alten und Neuen Testaments 13. Göttingen: Vandenhoeck & Ruprecht, 1910; reprint 1984.

Burke, Kenneth. *A Rhetoric of Motives*. Berkeley: University of California Press, 1970.

Burton, Ernest De Witt. *A Critical and Exegetical Commentary on the Epistle to the Galatians*. International Critical Commentary, vol. 39. New York: Charles Scribner's Sons, 1920.

Büchsel, Friedrich. "κρίνω." In *Theological Dictionary of the New Testament*, ed. Gerhard Kittel, vol. 3, 921–38. Translated by G. W. Bromiley. Grand Rapids: Wm. B. Eerdmans Publishing Co., 1965.

Calvin, John. *The Epistles of Paul the Apostle to the Galatians, Ephesians, Philippians and Colossians*. Translated by T. H. L. Parker. Calvin's New Testament Commentaries, vol. 11. Grand Rapids: Wm. B. Eerdmans Publishing Co., 1965.

Campbell, William S. "The Contribution of Traditions to Paul's Theology." In *Pauline Theology II: 1 & 2 Corinthians*, ed. David M. Hay, 234–54. Minneapolis: Augsburg Fortress, 1993.

Charlesworth, James H., ed. *The Old Testament Pseudepigrapha*. 2 vols. Garden City, N.Y.: Doubleday, 1983–85.

Church, F. Forrester. "Rhetorical Structure and Design in Paul's Letter to Philemon." *Harvard Theological Review* 71 (1978): 17–33.

Cicero. *Brutus*. Translated by G. L. Hendrickson. The Loeb Classical Library. Cambridge, Mass.: Harvard University Press, 1939; reprint 1997.

_____. *De Inventione*. Translated by H. M. Hubbell. The Loeb Classical Library. Cambridge, Mass.: Harvard University Press, 1949.

_____. *De Optimo Genere Oratorum*. Translated by H. M. Hubbell. The Loeb Classical Library. Cambridge, Mass.: Harvard University Press, 1949; reprint 1993.

_____. *De Oratore*. Translated by E. W. Sutton. The Loeb Classical Library. Cambridge, Mass.: Harvard University Press, 1942; reprint 1996.

_____. *Letters*. 7 vols. Translated by G. L. Hendrickson, H. M. Hubbell, et al. The Loeb Classical Library. Cambridge, Mass.: Harvard University Press, 1912–72.

_____. *Orator*. Translated by H. M. Hubbell. The Loeb Classical Library. Cambridge, Mass.: Harvard University Press, 1939; reprint 1997.

_____. *De Partitione Oratoria*. Translated by H. Rackham. The Loeb Classical Library. Cambridge, Mass.: Harvard University Press, 1942; reprint 1997.

[____]. *Rhetorica ad Herennium*. Translated by Harry Caplan. The Loeb Classical Library. Cambridge, Mass.: Harvard University Press, 1954; reprint 1989.

_____. *Topica*. Translated by H. M. Hubbell. The Loeb Classical Library. Cambridge, Mass.: Harvard University Press, 1949; reprint 1993.

Clark, Donald L. *Rhetoric in Greco-Roman Education*. New York: Columbia University Press, 1967.

Classen, C. Joachim. "Paulus und die antike Rhetorik." *Zeitschrift für die neutestamentliche Wissenschaft und die Kunde der älteren Kirche* 82 (1991): 1–33.

_____. "St. Paul's Epistles and Ancient Greek and Roman Rhetoric." In *Rhetoric and the New Testament*, eds. S. E. Porter and T. H. Olbricht, 265–91. Sheffield: Sheffield Academic Press, 1993.

Conzelmann, Hans. "χάρις." In *Theological Dictionary of the New Testament*, ed. Gerhard Friedrich, vol. 9, 387–415. Translated by G. W. Bromiley. Grand Rapids: Wm. B. Eerdmans Publishing Co., 1974.

———. "ψεύδομαι." In *Theological Dictionary of the New Testament*, ed. Gerhard Friedrich, vol. 9, 594–603. Translated by G. W. Bromiley. Grand Rapids: Wm. B. Eerdmans Publishing Co., 1965.

Cook, David. "The Prescript as Programme in Galatians." *Journal of Theological Studies* 43 (1992): 511–19.

Cosgrove, Charles H. "Arguing Like a Mere Human Being: Galatians 3.15–18 in Rhetorical Perspective." *New Testament Studies* 34 (1988): 536–49.

———. *The Cross and the Spirit*. Macon: Mercer University Press, 1988.

Cousar, Charles B. *Galatians*. Interpretation. Atlanta: John Knox Press, 1982.

———. *The Letters of Paul*. Nashville: Abingdon Press, 1996.

———. *A Theology of the Cross: The Death of Jesus in the Pauline Letters*. Minneapolis: Fortress Press, 1990.

Dahl, Nils Alstrup. "Paul's Letter to the Galatians: Epistolary Genre, Content, and Structure." Unpublished paper for the Society of Biblical Literature Paul Seminar, 1973.

———. *Studies in Paul: Theology for the Early Christian Mission*. Minneapolis: Augsburg Publishing House, 1977.

Dana, H. E., and Julius R. Mantey. *A Manual Grammar of the Greek New Testament*. New York: Macmillan Publishing Co., 1957.

Danker, Frederick. "Paul's Debt to the De Corona of Demosthenes: A Study of Rhetorical Techniques in Second Corinthians." In *Persuasive Artistry: Studies in New Testament Rhetoric in Honor of George A. Kennedy*, ed. Duane F. Watson, 262–80. Journal for the Study of the New Testament, Supplement Series 50. Sheffield: Sheffield Academic Press, 1991.

Das, A. Andrew. "Would a Covenantal Nomist Recognize the "(Old) Covenant" in Paul." Union Theological Seminary in Virginia Biblical Colloquy Paper, March 11, 1997.

Daube, David. "Rabbinic Methods of Interpretation and Hellenistic Rhetoric." *Hebrew Union College Annual* 22 (1949): 239–64.

Davison, M. E. "New Testament Greek Word Order." *Literary and Linguistic Computing* 4 (1989): 19–28.

De Boer, Martinus C. "Paul and Jewish Apocalyptic Eschatology." In *Apocalyptic and the New Testament*, eds. Joel Marcus and Marion L. Soards, 169–90. Sheffield: JSOT Press, 1989.

Deissmann, Adolf. *Bible Studies: Contributions Chiefly from Papyri and Inscriptions to the History of the Language, the Literature, and the Religion of Hellenistic Judaism and Primitive Christianity.* Translated by A. Grieve. Edinburgh: T & T Clark, 1901.

———. *Light From the Ancient East: The New Testament Illustrated by Recently Discovered Texts of the Graeco-Roman World.* Translated by Lionel R. M. Strachan. New York: Hodder and Stoughton, 1910; 2d ed. 1927.

———. *Paul: A Study in Social and Religious History.* London: Hodder and Stoughton, 1912.

Delling, Gerhard. "καιρός." In *Theological Dictionary of the New Testament*, ed. Gerhard Kittel, vol. 3, 455–64. Translated by G. W. Bromiley. Grand Rapids: Wm. B. Eerdmans Publishing Co., 1965.

———. "στοιχέω, συστοιχέω, στοιχεῖον." In *Theological Dictionary of the New Testament*, ed. Gerhard Friedrich, vol. 7, 670–87. Translated by G. W. Bromiley. Grand Rapids: Wm. B. Eerdmans Publishing Co., 1974.

Demetrius. *On Style* (De Elocutione). Translated by W. Rhys Roberts. The Loeb Classical Library. In Aristotle, *The Poetics*. Cambridge, Mass.: Cambridge University Press, 1927. Second edition translated by Doreen C. Innes based on W. R. Roberts, 1995.

Dibelius, Martin. *From Tradition to Gospel.* Translated from the revised second edition of *Die Formgeschichte des Evangeliums* by Bertram Lee Woolf. New York: Charles Scribner's Sons, 1935.

———. *Paul*, ed. W. G. Kümmel. Translated by F. Clark. London: Longmans, 1953.

Dio Chrysostom. *Discourses.* 5 vols. Translated by J. W. Cohoon and H. L. Crosby. The Loeb Classical Library. Cambridge, Mass.: Harvard University Press, 1932–51.

Diodorus Siculus. *Diodorus of Sicily.* 12 vols. Translated by C. H. Oldfather, C. L. Sherman, et al. The Loeb Classical Library. Cambridge, Mass.: Harvard University Press, 1933–67.

Dionysius of Halicarnassus. *The Critical Essays.* 2 vols. Translated by Stephen Usher. The Loeb Classical Library. Cambridge, Mass.: Harvard University Press, 1974–1985.

Dodd, Brian. "Romans 1:17—A *Crux Interpretum* for the Πίστις Χριστοῦ Debate?" *Journal of Biblical Literature* 114 (1995): 470–73.

Donaldson, Terence L. "'The Curse of the Law' and the Inclusion of the Gentiles: Galatians 3:13–14." *New Testament Studies* 32 (1986): 94–112.

———. "Zealot and Convert: The Origin of Paul's Christ-Torah Antithesis." *Catholic Biblical Quarterly* 51 (1989): 655–82.

Doty, William G. "The Classification of Epistolary Literature." *Catholic Biblical Quarterly* 31 (1969): 183–99.

———. *Letters in Primitive Christianity.* Guides to Biblical Scholarship. Philadelphia: Fortress Press, 1973.

Dover, K. J. *Greek Word Order.* Cambridge: Cambridge University Press, 1960.

Dunn, J. D. G. *The Epistle to the Galatians.* Black's New Testament Commentaries. Peabody, Mass.: Hendrickson Publishers, 1993.

———. "The Incident at Antioch." *Journal for the Study of the New Testament* 18 (1983): 3–57.

———. "Paul's Understanding of the Death of Jesus as Sacrifice." In *Sacrifice and Redemption: Durham Essays in Theology*, ed. S. W. Sykes, 35–56. Cambridge: Cambridge University Press, 1991.

———. "The Theology of Galatians: The Issue of Covenantal Nomism." In *Pauline Theology*, ed. Jouette M. Bassler, vol. 1, 125–46. Minneapolis: Fortress Press, 1991.

———. *The Theology of Paul's Letter to the Galatians.* New Testament Theology. Cambridge: Cambridge University Press, 1993.

———. "Works of the Law and Curse of the Law (Galatians 3:10–14)." *New Testament Studies* 31 (1985): 523–42.

Ebeling, Gerhard. *The Truth of the Gospel: An Exposition of Galatians.* Translated by David Green. Philadelphia: Fortress Press, 1985.

Eckert, J. *Die urchristliche Verkuendigung im Streit zwischen Paulus und seinen Gegnern nach dem Galaterbrief.* Biblische Untersuchungen 6. Regensburg: Pustet, 1971.

Eisenhut, Werner. *Einführung in die Antike Rhetorik und Ihre Geschichte.* Darmstadt: Wissenschaftliche Buchgesellschaft, 1974.

Elliger, K., W. Rudolph, et al. *Biblia Hebraica Stuttgartensia.* Stuttgart: Deutsche Bibelgesellschaft, 1983.

Ellis, E. Earle. "Paul and His Co-Workers." *New Testament Studies* 17 (1971): 437–52.

Erasmus, Desiderius. "The Ciceronian: A Dialogue on the Ideal Latin Style / Dialogus Ciceronianus." In *Collected Works of Erasmus: Literary and Educational Writings*, vol. 28, ed. A. H. T. Levi. Translated by B. I. Knott. Toronto: University of Toronto Press, 1986.

Euripides. *Euripides*. 4 vols. Translated by Arthur S. Way. The Loeb Classical Library. Cambridge, Mass.: Harvard University Press, 1912–1994.

Evans, Craig A., and Peter W. Flint, eds. *Eschatology, Messianism, and the Dead Sea Scrolls*. Grand Rapids: Wm. B. Eerdmans Publishing Co., 1997.

Exler, F. X. J. *The Form of the Ancient Greek Letter: A Study in Greek Epistolography*. Washington: Catholic University Press, 1923.

Fee, Gordon D. *God's Empowering Presence: The Holy Spirit in the Letters of Paul*. Peabody, Mass.: Hendrickson Publishers, 1994.

———. "Freedom and the Life of Obedience (Galatians 5:1–6:18)." *Review and Expositor* 91 (1994): 201–17.

Fitzmyer, Joseph A. "The Letter to the Galatians." In *The Jerome Biblical Commentary*, eds. R. E. Brown, et al., vol. 2, 236–46. Englewood, N.J.: Prentice Hall, 1968.

———. "Crucifixion in Ancient Palestine, Qumran Literature, and the NT." *Catholic Biblical Quarterly* 40 (1978): 493–513.

———. *Paul and His Theology: A Brief Sketch*. 2d ed. Englewood Cliffs, N.J.: Prentice Hall, 1989.

———. "Some Notes on Aramaic Epistolography." *Journal of Biblical Literature* 93 (1974): 201–25.

Forbes, Christopher. "Comparison, Self-Praise, and Irony: Paul's Boasting and the Conventions of Hellenistic Rhetoric." *New Testament Studies* 32 (1986): 1–30.

Fowler, R. A. "Aristotle on the Period." *Classical Quarterly* 32 (1982): 89–99.

Fuller, B. A. G. *A History of Philosophy*. Volume 1. New York: Henry Holt & Company, 1951.

Fung, Ronald Y. K. *The Epistle to the Galatians*. New International Commentary on the New Testament. Grand Rapids: Wm. B. Eerdmans Publishing Co., 1988.

Funk, Robert W. "The Apostolic Parousia: Form and Function." In *Christian History and Interpretation: Studies Presented to John Knox*, ed. W. R. Farmer, et al., 249–68. Cambridge: Cambridge University Press, 1967.

———. *Language, Hermeneutic, and Word of God: The Problem of Language in the New Testament and Contemporary Theology*. New York: Harper & Row, 1966.

Furnish, Victor Paul. "He Gave Himself [Was Given] Up . . . .": Paul's Use of a Christological Assertion." In *The Future of Christology: Essays in Honor of Leander E. Keck*. Abraham J. Malherbe and Wayne A. Meeks, eds. Minneapolis: Fortress Press, 1993.

————. *Theology and Ethics in Paul*. Nashville: Abingdon Press, 1968.

Gamble, Harry Y. *The Textual History of the Letter to the Romans: A Study in Textual and Literary Criticism*. SD 42. Grand Rapids: Wm. B. Eerdmans Publishing Co., 1977.

Gaster, T. H. "Resurrection." In *The Interpreter's Dictionary of the Bible*, ed. George Arthur Buttrick, vol. 4, 39–43. Nashville: Abingdon Press, 1962.

Gaventa, Beverly Roberts. "Galatians 1 and 2: Autobiography as Paradigm." *Novum Testamentum* 28 (1986): 309–26.

————. "The Singularity of the Gospel: A Reading of Galatians." In *Pauline Theology*, ed. Jouette M. Bassler, vol. 1, 147–59. Minneapolis: Fortress Press, 1991.

George, Timothy. *Galatians*. New American Commentary. Nashville: Broadman and Holman Press, 1994.

Girardin, Benoit. *Rhétorique et Théologique: Calvin, le commentaire de l'Épître aux Romains*. Théologie Historique 54. Paris: Editions Beauchesne, 1979.

Gitay, Yehoshua. "A Study of Amos's Art of Speech: A Rhetorical Analysis of Amos 3:1–15." *Catholic Biblical Quarterly* 42 (1980): 293–309.

Gordon, T. David. "The Problem at Galatia." *Interpretation* 41 (1987): 32–43.

Grant, Robert M. *Early Christianity and Society*. New York: Harper and Row, 1977.

Greenwood, David. "Rhetorical Criticism and Formgeschichte: Some Methodological Considerations." *Journal of Biblical Literature* 89 (1970): 418–26.

Grundmann, Walter. "χρίω." In *Theological Dictionary of the New Testament*, ed. Gerhard Friedrich, vol. 9, 493–96. Translated by G. W. Bromiley. Grand Rapids: Wm. B. Eerdmans Publishing Co., 1973.

Gunkel, Hermann. "Fundamental Problems of Hebrew Literary History." In *What Remains of the Old Testament*. London: George Allen & Unwin, 1928.

Hagen, Kenneth. *Luther's Approach to Scripture as seen in his "Commentaries" on Galatians: 1519–1538*. Tübingen: J. C. B. Mohr (Paul Siebeck), 1993.

Hall, Robert G. "Arguing Like An Apocalypse: Galatians and An Ancient Topos Outside the Greco-Roman Rhetorical Tradition." *New Testament Studies* 42 (1996): 434–53.

————. "Historical Inference and Rhetorical Effect: Another Look at Galatians 1 and 2." In *Persuasive Artistry: Studies in New Testament Rhetoric in Honor of George A. Kennedy*, ed. Duane F. Watson, 308–20. Journal for the Study of the New Testament, Supplement Series 50. Sheffield: Sheffield Academic Press, 1991.

————. "The Rhetorical Outline for Galatians: A Reconsideration." *Journal of Biblical Literature* 106 (1987): 277–87.

Hansen, G. Walter. *Abraham in Galatians: Epistolary and Rhetorical Contexts.* Journal for the Study of the New Testament, Supplement Series 29. Sheffield: Sheffield University Press, 1989.

———. *Galatians.* The IVP New Testament Commentary Series. Downers Grove, Ill.: InterVarsity Press, 1994.

———. "A Paradigm of the Apocalypse: The Gospel in the Light of Epistolary Analysis." In *Gospel in Paul: Studies on Corinthians, Galatians and Romans for Richard N. Longenecker.* Journal for the Study of the New Testament, Supplement Series 108. Sheffield: Sheffield Academic Press, 1994.

———. "Paul's Three-Dimensional Application of Genesis 15:6 in Galatians." *Trinity Theological Journal* 1 (1989): 59–77.

Hanson, Paul D. "Apocalypticism." In *The Interpreter's Dictionary of the Bible Supplementary Volume*, 28–33. Nashville: Abingdon Press, 1976.

Harnisch, Wolfgang. "Einübung des neuen Seins: Paulinische Paränese am Beispiel des Galaterbriefs." *Zeitschrift für Theologie und Kirche* 84 (1987): 279–96.

Hatch, Edwin and Henry A. Redpath. *A Concordance to the Septuagint and the Other Greek Versions of the Old Testament.* Oxford: Clarendon Press, 1897; reprint, Grand Rapids, Mich.: Baker Book House, 1987.

Hays, Richard B. "Christology and Ethics in Galatians: The Law of Christ." *Catholic Biblical Quarterly* 49 (1987): 268–90.

———. "Crucified with Christ." In *Pauline Theology*, ed. Jouette M. Bassler, vol. 1, 227–46. Minneapolis: Fortress Press, 1991.

———. *Echoes of Scripture in the Letters of Paul.* New Haven, Conn.: Yale University Press, 1989.

———. *The Faith of Jesus Christ: An Investigation of the Narrative Substructure of Galatians 3:1–4:11.* Society of Biblical Literature Dissertation Series 56. Chico, Calif.: Scholars Press, 1982.

Heinrici, C. F. Georg. *Der zweite Brief an die Korinther, mit einem Anhang: Zum Hellenismus des Paulus.* 8th ed. Kritisch-exegetischer Kommentar über das Neue Testament 6. Göttingen: Vandenhoeck & Ruprecht, 1900.

Hengel, Martin. *Crucifixion in the Ancient World and the Folly of the Message of the Cross.* Translated by John Bowden. Philadelphia: Fortress Press, 1977.

———. *Judaism and Hellenism.* 2 vols. Translated by John Bowden. Philadelphia: Fortress Press, 1975.

Hesiod. *Hesiod: The Homeric Hymns and Homerica.* Translated by Hugh G. Evelyn-White. The Loeb Classical Library. Cambridge, Mass.: Harvard University Press, 1936.

Hester, James D. "Placing the Blame: The Presence of Epideictic in Galatians 1 and 2." In *Persuasive Artistry: Studies in New Testament Rhetoric in Honor of George A. Kennedy*, ed. D. F. Watson, 281–307. Journal for the Study of the New Testament, Supplement Series 50. Sheffield: Sheffield Academic Press, 1991.

_____. "The Rhetorical Structure of Galatians 1:11–2:14." *Journal of Biblical Literature* 103 (1984): 223–33.

_____. "The Use and Influence of Rhetoric in Galatians 2:11–14." *Theologische Zeitschrift* 42 (1986): 386–408.

Hitzig, H. F. "crux." In *Paulys Realencyclopoadie der classischen Altertumswissenschaft*, ed. August Friedrich von Pauly, vol. 4, 1728–31. München: A. Druckenmüller, 1903.

Homer. *Iliad*. 2 vols. Translated by A. T. Murray. The Loeb Classical Library. Cambridge, Mass.: Harvard University Press, 1985–1988.

———. *Odyssey*. 2 vols. Translated by A. T. Murray. The Loeb Classical Library. Cambridge, Mass.: Harvard University Press, 1980.

Hommel, Hildebrecht. "Rhetorik." In *Der Kleine Pauly*, eds. Konrat Ziegler and Walther Sontheimer, 1396–1414. München: Alfred Druckenmüller, 1972.

Hooker, Morna D. "Pistis Christou." *New Testament Studies* 35 (1989): 321–42.

Howard, George E. "On the Faith of Christ." *Harvard Theological Review* 60 (1967): 459–65

———. *Paul: Crisis in Galatia*. Society for New Testament Studies Monograph Series 35. Cambridge: Cambridge University Press, 1979.

Hübner, Hans. "Der Galaterbrief und das Verhältnis von antiker Rhetorik und Epistolo–graphie." *Theologische Literaturzeitung* 109 (1984): 241–50.

———. Review of *Galatians: A Commentary on Paul's Letter to the Churches in Galatia*, by H. D. Betz. In *Theologische Literaturzeitung* 109: 241–50.

Hughes, Frank W. *Early Christian Rhetoric and 2 Thessalonians*. Journal for the Study of the New Testament, Supplement Series 30. Sheffield: Sheffield Academic Press, 1989.

———. "The Gospel and its Rhetoric in Galatians." In *Gospel in Paul: Studies on Corinthians, Galatians and Romans for Richard N. Longenecker*. Journal for the Study of the New Testament, Supplement Series 108. Sheffield: Sheffield Academic Press, 1994.

Hultgren, Arland J. "The pistis Christou Formulation in Paul." *Novum Testamentum* 22 (1980): 248–63.

Isocrates. *Isocrates*. 3 vols. Translated by George Norlin and L. Van Hook. The Loeb Classical Library. Cambridge, Mass.: Hàrvard University Press, 1928–45.

Jegher-Bucher, Verena. *Der Galaterbrief auf dem Hintergrund antiker Epistolographie und Rhetorik: ein anderes Paulusbild*. Abhandlungen zur Theologie des Alten und Neuen Testaments 78. Zürich: Theologischer Verlag, 1991.

Jeremias, Joachim. "Chiasmus in den Paulusbriefen." *Zeitschrift für die neutestamentliche Wissenschaft und die Kunde der älteren Kirche* 49 (1958): 145–56.

———. "Paulus als Hillelit." In *Neotestamentica et Semitica: Studies in Honour of Principal Matthew Black*, eds. E. E. Ellis and M. Wilcox, 88–94. Edinburgh: T. & T. Clark, 1969.

Jewett, Robert. "The Agitators and the Galatian Congregation." *New Testament Studies* 17 (1971): 198–212.

———. *A Chronology of Paul's Life*. Philadelphia: Fortress Press, 1979.

———. "The Form and Function of the Homiletic Benediction." *Anglican Theological Review* 51 (1969): 18–34.

———. "Romans as an Ambassadorial Letter." *Interpretation* 36 (1982): 5–20.

———. *The Thessalonian Correspondence: Pauline Rhetoric and Millenarian Piety*. Foundations and Facets. Philadelphia: Fortress Press, 1986.

Johnson, E. Elizabeth and David M. Hay, eds. *Pauline Theology IV: Looking Back, Pressing On*. Society of Biblical Literature Symposium Series. Atlanta: Scholars Press, 1997.

Josephus. *The Works of Josephus*. Edited by William Whiston. Peabody, Mass.: Hendrickson Publishers, 1987.

Judge, Edwin A. "Paul's Boasting in Relation to Contemporary Professional Practice." *Australian Biblical Review* 16 (1968): 37–50.

Käsemann, Ernst. *Commentary on Romans*. Translated by G. W. Bromiley. Grand Rapids: Wm. B. Eerdmans Publishing Co., 1980.

———. *New Testament Questions for Today*. Philadelphia: Fortress Press, 1969.

———. "The Pauline Theology of the Cross." *Interpretation* 24 (1970): 151–77.

———. *Perspectives on Paul*. Translated by M. Kohl. Philadelphia: Fortress Press, 1971.

Keck, Leander. *The New Testament Experience of Faith*. St. Louis: Bethany Press, 1976.

———. "Paul and Apocalyptic Theology." *Interpretation* 38 (1984): 229–41.

———. "Paul as a Thinker." *Interpretation* 47 (1993): 27–38.

Kennedy, George A. *The Art of Persuasion in Greece*. Princeton: Princeton University Press, 1963.

———. *The Art of Rhetoric in the Roman World: 300 B. C. – A. D. 300*. Princeton: Princeton University Press, 1972.

———. *The Cambridge History of Literary Criticism, Volume 1: Classical Criticism*. Cambridge: Cambridge University Press, 1989; repr. 1995.

———. *Classical Rhetoric and Its Christian and Secular Tradition from Ancient to Modern Times*. Chapel Hill: University of North Carolina Press, 1980.

———. "The Earliest Rhetorical Handbooks." *American Journal of Philology* 80 (1959): 169–178.

———. *A New History of Classical Rhetoric*. Princeton: Princeton University Press, 1994.

———. *New Testament Interpretation through Rhetorical Criticism*. Studies in Religion. Chapel Hill: University of North Carolina Press, 1984.

Knox, Bernard, ed. *Homer: The Odyssey*. Translated by Robert Fagles. New York: Viking Penquin, 1996.

Knox, John. *Chapters in a Life of Paul*. Nashville: Abingdon Press, 1950.

Koch, Klaus. *The Rediscovery of Apocalyptic: A Polemical Work on a Neglected Area of Biblical Studies and Its Damaging Effects on Theology and Philosophy*. Studies in Biblical Theology 2/22. London: SCM Press, 1972.

Koskenniemi, Heikki. "Cicero über die Briefarten (genera epistularum)." *Arctos* (1954): 97–102.

Kraftchick, Steven J. "Ethos and Pathos Appeals in Galatians Five and Six: A Rhetorical Analysis." Ph. D. diss., Emory University, 1985.

Kroll, W. "Rhetorik." In *Paulys Realencyclopädie der classischen Altertumswissenschaft, Supplementband 8*, eds. G. Wissowa, W. Kroll, et al., 1039–1138. Munich: Druckenmüller, 1940.

Kuck, David W. "'Each Will Bear His Own Burden': Paul's Creative Use of an Apocalyptic Motif." *New Testament Studies* 40 (1994): 289–97.

Lanham, Richard A. *A Handlist of Rhetorical Terms: A Guide for Students of English Literature*. Berkeley: University of California Press, 1968.

Lategan, Bernard. "Is Paul Defending His Apostleship in Galatians?: The Function of Galatians 1.11–12 and 2.19–20 in the Development of Paul's Argument." *New Testament Studies* 34 (1988): 411–30.

Lausberg, Heinrich. *Handbuch der literarischen Rhetorik: Eine Grundlegung der Literaturwissenschaft.* München: Max Hueber Verlag, 1973.

Lemmer, Richard. "Why Should the Possibility of Rabbinic Rhetorical Elements in Pauline Writings (eg. Galatians) Be Reconsidered?" In *Rhetoric, Scripture and Theology*, eds. Stanley E. Porter and Thomas H. Olbricht, 161–79. Sheffield: Sheffield Academic Press, 1996.

Liddell, Henry George and Robert Scott. *A Greek-English Lexicon.* Revised by H. S. Jones and R. McKenzie. 9th ed. Oxford: Clarendon Press, 1996.

Longenecker, Richard N. *Galatians.* Word Biblical Commentary, vol. 41. Dallas: Word Books, 1990.

―――. "On the Form, Function, and Authority of the New Testament Letters." In *Scripture and Truth*, eds. Don A. Carson and John D. Woodbridge, 101–14. Grand Rapids, Mich.: Zondervan, 1983.

Lüdemann, Gerd. *Opposition to Paul in Jewish Christianity.* Translated by M. E. Boring. Minneapolis: Fortress Press, 1989.

Lührmann, Dieter. *Galatians.* Continental Commentaries. Translated by O. C. Dean, Jr. Minneapolis: Augsburg Fortress Press, 1992.

Lund, N. W. *Chiasmus in the New Testament: A Study in Formgeschichte.* Chapel Hill, N.C.: University of North Carolina Press, 1942.

Lütgert, Wilhelm. *Gesetz und Geist: Eine Untersuchung zur Vorgeschichte des Galaterbriefs.* Beiträge zur Förderung christlicher Theologie 22.6. Gütersloh: Bertelsmann, 1919.

Luther, Martin. *Luther's Works. Edited by Jaroslav Pelikan. Vol. 26, Lectures on Galatians 1535, Chapters 1–4.* Saint Louis: Concordia Publishing House, 1963.

―――. *Luther's Works. Edited by Jaroslav Pelikan. Vol. 27, Lectures on Galatians 1535, Chapters 5–6; Lectures on Galatians 1519, Chapters 1–6.* Saint Louis: Concordia Publishing House, 1964.

Lyons, George. *Pauline Autobiography: Towards a New Understanding.* Society of Biblical Literature Dissertation Series 73. Atlanta: Scholars Press, 1985.

Mack, Burton L. *Rhetoric and the New Testament.* Guides to Biblical Scholarship. Minneapolis: Fortress Press, 1990.

Malherbe, Abraham J. *Ancient Epistolary Theorists.* Society of Biblical Literature Sources for Biblical Study 19. Atlanta: Scholars Press, 1988.

―――. *Social Aspects of Early Christianity.* Baton Rouge, La.: Louisiana State University Press, 1977.

Marrou, Henri-Irenée. *A History of Education in Antiquity*. Translated by George Lamb. New York: Sheed and Ward, 1956.

Martin, Josef. *Antike Rhetorik: Technik und Methode*. Handbuch der Altertumswissenschaft 2, 3. München: Beck, 1974.

Martin, Ralph P. *Carmen Christi: Philippians 2:5–11 in Recent Interpretation and in the Setting of Early Christian Worship*. Society for New Testament Studies Monograph Series 4. Cambridge: Cambridge University Press, 1967.

Martyn, J. Louis. "Apocalyptic Antinomies in Paul's Letter to the Galatians." *New Testament Studies* 31 (1985): 401–24.

———. "Covenant, Christ, and Church in Galatians." *The Future of Christology: Essays in Honor of Leander E. Keck*, eds. A. J. Malherbe and W. A. Meeks, 137–51. Minneapolis: Fortress Press, 1993.

———. "Events in Galatia: Modified Covenantal Nomism versus God's Invasion of the Cosmos in the Singular Gospel: A Response to J. D. G. Dunn and B. R. Gaventa." *Pauline Theology*, ed. Jouette M. Bassler, vol. 1, 160–79. Minneapolis: Fortress Press, 1991.

———. *Galatians*. The Anchor Bible, vol. 33A. New York: Doubleday, 1997.

———. "A Law-Observant Mission to Gentiles: The Background of Galatians." *Scottish Journal of Theology* 38 (1985): 307–24.

Matera, Frank J. "The Culmination of Paul's Argument to the Galatians: Gal. 5.1–6.17." *Journal for the Study of the New Testament* 32 (1988): 79–91.

———. *Galatians*. Sacra Pagina Series, vol. 9. Collegeville, Minn.: The Liturgical Press, 1992.

Mays, James L. *Amos*. Old Testament Library. Philadelphia: Westminster Press, 1969.

Meeks, Wayne A. *The First Urban Christians: The Social World of the Apostle Paul*. New Haven, Conn.: Yale University Press, 1983.

———. Review of *Galatians: A Commentary on Paul's Letter to the Churches in Galatia*, by H. D. Betz. In *Journal of Biblical Literature* 100 (1981): 304–7.

Melanchthon, Philip. *Texte aus der Anfangszeit Melanchthons*, ed. Ernst Bizer. Neukirchener Verlag: Neukirchen-Vluyn, 1966.

Merk, Otto. "Der Beginn der Paränese im Galaterbrief." *Zeitschrift für die neutestamentliche Wissenschaft und die Kunde der älteren Kirche* 60 (1969): 83–104.

Metzger, Bruce M. *A Textual Commentary on the Greek New Testament*. Stuttgart: United Bible Societies, 1971. Corrected edition, 1975.

Meynet, Roland. "Histoire de 'l'analyse rhétorique' en exégèse biblique." *Rhetorica* 8 (1990): 291–320.

Minear, Paul Sevier. "The Crucified World: The Enigma of Galatians 6,14." *Theologia Crucis—Signum Crucis*, eds. Carl Andresen and Günter Klein, 395–407.

Mitchell, Margaret M. *Paul and the Rhetoric of Reconciliation: An Exegetical Investigation of the Language and Composition of 1 Corinthians.* Louisville: Westminster/John Knox Press, 1991.

Moffatt, James. *An Introduction to the Literature of the New Testament.* 3d ed. Edinburgh: T & T Clark, 1949.

Moo, Douglas. "Paul and the Law in the Last Ten Years." *Scottish Journal of Theology* 40 (1987): 287–307.

Morland, Kjell Arne. *The Rhetoric of Curse in Galatians: Paul Confronts Another Gospel.* Emory Studies in Early Christianity. Atlanta: Scholars Press, 1995.

Muilenburg, James. "Form Criticism and Beyond." *Journal of Biblical Literature* 88 (1969): 1–18.

Mullins, Terence Y. "Benediction as a New Testament Form." *Andrews University Seminary Studies* 15 (1977): 59–64.

———. "Disclosure, a Literary Form in the New Testament." *Novum Testamentum* 7 (1964): 44–50.

———. "Formulas in New Testament Epistles." *Journal of Biblical Literature* 91 (1972): 380–90.

———. "Visit Talk in New Testament Letters." *Catholic Biblical Quarterly* 35 (1973): 350–58.

Murphy-O'Conner, Jerome. *Paul the Letter-Writer: His World, His Options, His Skills.* Collegeville, Minn.: The Liturgical Press, 1995.

———. "Pneumatikoi and Judaizers in 2 Cor 2:14–4:6." *Australian Biblical Review* 34 (1986): 42–58.

Mussner, Franz. *Der Galaterbrief.* Herders theologischer Kommentar zum Neuen Testament, Band 9. 2d ed. Freiburg: Herder, 1974.

Neusner, Jacob. "The Use of the Later Rabbinic Evidence for the Study of First-Century Pharisaism." In *Approaches to Ancient Judaism: Theory and Practice*, ed. W. S. Green, 215–25. Missoula, Mont.: Scholars Press, 1978.

Neyrey, Jerome H. "Bewitched in Galatia: Paul and Cultural Anthropology." *Catholic Biblical Quarterly* 50 (1998): 72–100.

Norden, Eduard. *Die Antike Kunstprosa vom VI. Jahrhundert vor Christus bis in die Zeit der Renaissance.* 9th ed. Stuttgart: B. G. Teubner, 1983.

O'Brien, Peter Thomas. *Introductory Thanksgivings in the Letters of Paul.* Supplements to Novum Testamentum, vol. 49. Leiden: E. J. Brill, 1977.

O'Collins, Gerald G. "Crucifixion." In *The Anchor Bible Dictionary: Volume 1*, ed. David Noel Freedman, 1207–10. New York: Doubleday, 1992.

Oepke, D. Albrecht. *Der Brief des Paulus an die Galater.* Theologischer Handkommentar zum Neuen Testament, Band 9. Berlin: Evangelische Verlagsanstalt, 1957.

———. "καλύπτω, κάλυμμα, ἀνακαλύπτω, κατακαλύπτω, ἀποκαλύπτω, ἀποκάλυψις." In *Theological Dictionary of the New Testament*, ed. Gerhard Kittel, vol. 3, 556–92. Translated by G. W. Bromiley. Grand Rapids: Wm. B. Eerdmans Publishing Co., 1965.

Olson, Stanley N. "Epistolary Uses of Expressions of Self-Confidence." *Journal of Biblical Literature* 103 (1984): 585–97.

———. "Pauline Expressions of Confidence in His Addressees." *Catholic Biblical Quarterly* 47 (1985): 282–95.

O'Neill, J. C. *The Recovery of Paul's Letter to the Galatians.* London: SPCK, 1972.

Ong, Walter J. *Orality and Literacy: The Technologizing of the Word.* London: Methuen, 1982.

Perelman, Chaim and L. Olbrecht-Tyteca. *The New Rhetoric: A Treatise on Argumentation.* Translated by John Wilkinson and Purcell Weaver. Notre Dame: University of Notre Dame Press, 1969.

Peter, Hermann. *Der Brief in der römischen Literatur: Literargeschichtliche Untersuchungen und Zusammenfassungen.* Abhandlungen der Königlichen Sächsischen Gesellschaft der Wissenschaften, philogisch-historische Classe, 20/3. Leipzig: B. G. Teubner, 1901; reprint, Hildesheim: Georg Olms, 1965.

Philo. *The Works of Philo.* Translated by C. D. Yonge. Peabody, Mass.: Hendrickson Publishers, 1993

Pitta, Antonio. *Disposizione e Messaggio della Lettera ai Galati: Analisi retorico letteraria.* Analecta Biblica 131. Rome: Pontifical Biblical Institute, 1992.

Plato. *Laws.* 2 vols. Translated by R. G. Bury. The Loeb Classical Library. Cambridge, Mass.: Harvard University Press, 1926; reprint 1984.

———. *The Republic.* 2 vols. Translated by Paul Shorey. The Loeb Classical Library. Cambridge, Mass.: Harvard University Press, 1963.

————. *Phaedrus*. Translated by H. N. Fowler. The Loeb Classical Library. Cambridge, Mass.: Harvard University Press, 1990.

Plutarch. *De Liberis Educandis. In Plutarch's Moralia*, vol. 1, The Loeb Classical Library, trans. Frank Cole Babbitt, 3–69. Cambridge, Mass.: Harvard University Press, 1927; reprint 1986.

————. *Marcus Cato*. In *Plutarch's Lives*, vol. 2, The Loeb Classical Library, trans. Bernadotte Perrin, 302–85. Cambridge, Mass.: Harvard University Press, 1914; reprint 1985.

Porter, Stanley E. *Idioms of the Greek New Testament*. Biblical Languages 2. Sheffield: Sheffield Academic Press, 1992.

————, ed. *Rhetoric and the New Testament: Essays from the 1992 Heidelberg Conference*. Journal for the Study of the New Testament, Supplement Series 90. Sheffield: Sheffield Academic Press, 1993.

————. "The Theoretical Justification for Application of Rhetorical Categories to Pauline Epistolary Literature." In *Rhetoric and the New Testament: Essays from the 1992 Heidelberg Conference*, eds. S. E. Porter and T. H. Olbricht, 100–22. Journal for the Study of the New Testament, Supplement Series 90. Sheffield: Sheffield Academic Press, 1993.

Prestel, Peter. *Die Rezeption der ciceronischen Rhetorik durch Augustinus in de doctrina Christiana*. Studien zur klassischen Philologie 69. Frankfurt: Peter Lang, 1992.

Quintilian. *Institutio Oratoria of Quintilian*. 4 vols. Translated by H. E. Butler. The Loeb Classical Library. Cambridge, Mass.: Harvard University Press, 1995.

Rahlfs, Alfred. *Septuaginta*. Stuttgart: Deutsche Bibelgesellschaft, 1979.

Reed, Jeffrey T. "Using Ancient Rhetorical Categories to Interpret Paul's Letters: A Question of Genre." In *Rhetoric and the New Testament: Essays from the 1992 Heidelberg Conference*, eds. S. E. Porter and T. H. Olbricht, 292–324. Journal for the Study of the New Testament, Supplement Series 90. Sheffield: Sheffield Academic Press, 1993.

Rengstorf, Karl Heinrich. "ἀποστέλλω (πέμπω), ἐξαποστέλλω, ἀπόστολος." In *Theological Dictionary of the New Testament*, ed. Gerhard Kittel, vol. 1, 398–447. Translated by G. W. Bromiley. Grand Rapids: Wm. B. Eerdmans Publishing Co., 1964.

Reventlow, Henning, ed. *Eschatology in the Bible and in Jewish and Christian Tradition*. Sheffield: Sheffield Academic Press, 1997.

Rhyne, C. Thomas. *Faith Establishes the Law*. Society of Biblical Literature Dissertation Series 55. Chico, Calif.: Scholars Press, 1981.

Ridderbos, Herman N. *The Epistle of Paul to the Churches of Galatia.* Translated by Henry Zylstra. New International Commentary on the New Testament. Grand Rapids: Wm. B. Eerdmans Publishing Co., 1953.

Roberts, J. H. "Pauline Transitions to the Letter Body." In *L'apôtre Paul: Personnalité, style et conception du ministère.* Bibliotheca Ephemeridum Theologicarum Lovaniensium 73, ed. A. Vanhoye, 93–9. Leuven: Leuven University Press, 1986.

Robertson, A. T. *A Greek Grammar of the Greek New Testament in the Light of Historical Research.* 3d ed. New York: George H. Doran Company, 1919.

Roetzel, Calvin J. *The Letters of Paul: Conversations in Context.* 3d ed. Louisville: Westminster/John Knox Press, 1991.

Roller, Otto. *Das Formular der paulinischen Briefe.* Stuttgart: Kohlhammer, 1933.

Russell, D. A. *Greek Declamation.* Cambridge: Cambridge University Press, 1983.

Russell, E. A. "Convincing or Merely Curious? A Look at Some Recent Writing on Galatians." *Irish Biblical Studies* 6 (1984): 157–76.

Russell, Walter B. "Rhetorical Analysis of the Book of Galatians, Part 1." *Bibliotheca Sacra* 150 (1993): 341–58.

———. "Rhetorical Analysis of the Book of Galatians, Part 2." *Bibliotheca Sacra* 150 (1993): 416–39.

———. "Who Were Paul's Opponents in Galatians?" *Bibliotheca Sacra* 147 (1990): 329–50.

Sampley, J. Paul. "'Before God, I Do Not Lie' (Gal 1:20): Paul's Self-Defence in the Light of Roman Legal Praxis." *New Testament Studies* 23 (1977): 477–82.

———. "From Text to Thought World: The Route to Paul's Ways." In *Pauline Theology,* ed. Jouette M. Bassler, vol. 1, 3–14. Minneapolis: Fortress Press, 1991.

Sanders, E. P. *Paul, the Law, and the Jewish People.* Minneapolis: Fortress Press, 1983.

———. *Paul and Palestinian Judaism.* Minneapolis: Fortress Press, 1977.

Sanders, Jack T. "The Transition from Opening Epistolary Thanksgiving to Body in the Letters of the Pauline Corpus." *Journal of Biblical Literature* 81 (1962): 348–62.

Scheible, Heinz. *Melanchthon und die Reformation: Forchungsbeiträge.* Mainz: Verlag Philipp von Zabern, 1996.

Schlier, Heinrich. *Der Brief an die Galater.* Kritisch-exegetischer Kommentar über das Neue Testament, 7. Göttingen: Vandenhoeck & Ruprecht, 1962.

Schmidt, Karl Ludwig. "καλέω." In *Theological Dictionary of the New Testament*, ed. Gerhard Kittel, vol. 3, 487–536. Translated by G. W. Bromiley. Grand Rapids: Wm. B. Eerdmans Publishing Co., 1965.

Schmidt, Peter L. "Epistolographie." In *Der Kleine Pauly*, eds. Konrat Zieler and Walther Sontheimer, 324–327. Stuttgart: Alfred Druckenmüller, 1967.

Schmithals, W. "Judaisten in Galatien?" *Zeitschrift für die neutestamentliche Wissenschaft und die Kunde der älteren Kirche* 74 (1983): 27–58.

———. *Paul and the Gnostics*. Translated by J. E. Steely. Nashville: Abingdon Press, 1972.

Schneider, John R. *Philip Melanchthon's Rhetorical Construal of Biblical Authority: Oratio Sacra*. Lewiston, N.Y.: Edwin Mellen Press, 1990.

Schneider, Johannes. "παραβάτης." In *Theological Dictionary of the New Testament*, eds. Gerhard Kittel and Gerhard Friedrich, vol. 5, 740–2. Translated by G. W. Bromiley. Grand Rapids: Wm. B. Eerdmans Publishing Co., 1967.

———. "σταυρός, σταυρόω, ἀνασταυρόω." In *Theological Dictionary of the New Testament*, ed. Gerhard Friedrich, vol. 7, 572–84. Translated by G. W. Bromiley. Grand Rapids: Wm. B. Eerdmans Publishing Co., 1971.

Schnider, Franz and Werner Stenger. *Studien zum Neutestamentlichen Briefformular*. New Testament Tools and Studies 11. Leiden: E. J. Brill, 1987.

Schubert, Paul. *Form and Function of the Pauline Thanksgivings*. Beihefte zur Zeitschrift für die neutestamentliche Wissenschaft und die Kunde der älteren Kirche, 20. Berlin: Töpelmann, 1939.

Schürer, Emil. *A History of the Jewish People in the Time of Jesus Christ*. Edited by G. Vermes, F. Millar, and M. Black. Edinburgh: T & T Clark, 1979.

Schweizer, E. "πνεύμα." In *Theological Dictionary of the New Testament*, ed. Gerhard Friedrich, vol. 6, 415–55. Translated by G. W. Bromiley. Grand Rapids: Wm. B. Eerdmans Publishing Co., 1968.

Seneca. *Seneca Ad Lucilium Epistulae Morales*. 3 vols. Translated by R. M. Gummere. The Loeb Classical Library. New York: Putnam's Sons; Cambridge, Mass.: Harvard University Press, 1918–25; rev. ed. 1953.

———. *Seneca the Elder: Controversiae, Suasoriae*. 2 vols. Translated by M. Winterbottom. The Loeb Classical Library. Cambridge, Mass.: Harvard University Press, 1974.

Sharp, D. S. *Epictetus and the New Testament*. London: Charles L. Kelly, 1914.

Silva, Moises. "Betz and Bruce on Galatians." *Westminster Theological Jouranal* 45 (1983): 371–85.

Smit, Joop. "The Letter of Paul to the Galatians: A Deliberative Speech." *New Testament Studies* 35 (1989): 1–26.

Smith, Terence V. *Petrine Controversies in Early Christianity.* Wissenschaftliche Untersuchungen zum Neuen Testament 2, Reihe 15. Tübingen: J. C. B. Mohr (Paul Siebeck), 1985.

Staats, Reinhart. "Chrysostomus uber die Rhetorik des Apostels Paulus: Makarianische Kontexte zu De Sacerdotio IV, 5–6." *Vigiliae Christianae* 46 (1992): 225–40.

Stambaugh, John E. and David L. Balch. *The New Testament in Its Social Environment.* Philadelphia: The Westminster Press, 1986.

Standaert, Benoît. "La rhétorique antique et l'épître aux Galates." *Foi et Vie* 84 (1985): 33–40.

Stanton, Graham N. Review of *Abraham in Galatians: Epistolary and Rhetorical Contexts*, by G. W. Hansen. In *Journal of Theological Studies* 43 (1992): 614–15.

Stirewalt, M. Luther. *Studies in Ancient Greek Epistolography.* Society of Biblical Literature Resources for Biblical Study 27. Atlanta: Scholars Press, 1993.

Stowers, Stanley K. *Letter Writing in Greco-Roman Antiquity.* Library of Early Christianity, ed. Wayne A. Meeks, vol. 5. Philadelphia: The Westminster Press, 1986.

————. Review of *2 Corinthians 8 and 9: A Commentary on Two Administrative Letters of the Apostle Paul*, by H. D. Betz. In *Journal of Biblical Literature* 106 (1987): 727–30.

————. "The Social Sciences and the Study of Early Christianity." In *Approaches to Ancient Judaism*, ed. W. S. Green, vol. 5. Missoula, Mont.: Scholars Press, 1978.

Strange, James F. "Crucifixion." In *The Interpreter's Dictionary of the Bible Supplementary Volume*, ed. Keith Crim, 199–200. Nashville: Abingdon Press, 1976.

Sykutris, J. "Epistolographie." In *Paulys Realencyclopädie der klassischen Altertumswissenschaft: Supplementband 5*, ed. August Friedrich von Pauly, 185–220. München: A. Druckenmüller, 1903.

Tacitus. *Tacitus: Dialogus de Oratoribus.* Translated by William Peterson. The Loeb Classical Library. Cambridge: Cambridge University Press, 1932.

————. *The Complete Works of Tacitus.* Translated by A. J. Church and W. J. Brodribb. The Modern Library. New York: Random House, 1942.

Taylor, Nicholas. *Paul, Antioch and Jerusalem: A Study in Relationships and Authority in Earliest Christianity.* Sheffield: Sheffield Academic, 1992.

Theissen, Gerd. *Sociology of Early Palestinian Christianity.* Philadelphia: Fortress Press, 1978.

Thesaurus Linguae Graecae CD-ROM. University of California, Irvine, School of Humanities, Irvine, Calif.

Thomson, Ian H. *Chiasmus in the Pauline Letters.* Journal for the Study of the New Testament Supplement Series 111. Sheffield: Sheffield Academic Press, 1995.

Vanhoye, Albert, ed. *L'Apôtre Paul: Personalité, Style et Conception du Ministère.* Bibliotheca Ephemeridum Theologicarum Lovaniensium 73. Leuven: Leuven University Press, 1986.

Vielhauer, Philipp. *Geschichte der urchristlichen Literatur.* Berlin: de Gruyter, 1975.

Vos, Johan S. "Paul's Argumentation in Galatians 1–2." *Harvard Theological Review* 87 (1994): 1–16.

Vouga, François. "Zur rhetorischen Gattung des Galaterbriefs." *Zeitschrift für die neutestamentliche Wissenschaft und die Kunde der älteren Kirche* 79 (1988): 291–92.

Wallis, Ian G. *The Faith of Jesus Christ in Early Christian Traditions.* Society for New Testament Studies Monograph Series 84. Cambridge: Cambridge University Press, 1995.

Watson, Duane F. "1 Corinthians 10:23–11:1 in the Light of Greco-Roman Rhetoric: The Role of Rhetorical Questions." *Journal of Biblical Literature* 108 (1989): 301–18.

———. "The New Testament and Greco-Roman Rhetoric: A Bibliography." *Journal of Evangelical Theological Society* 31 (1988): 465–72.

———. "The New Testament and Greco-Roman Rhetoric: A Bibliographical Update." *Journal of Evangelical Theological Society* 33 (1990): 513–24.

———, ed. *Persuasive Artistry: Studies in New Testament Rhetoric in Honor of George A. Kennedy.* Journal for the Study of the New Testament Supplement Series 50. Sheffield: Sheffield Academic Press, 1991.

———. "A Rhetorical Analysis of Philippians and its Implications for the Unity Question." *Novum Testamentum* 30 (1988): 57–88.

———. "Rhetorical Criticism of the Pauline Epistles Since 1975." *Currents in Research: Biblical Studies* 3 (1995): 219–248.

Weima, Jeffrey A. D. "Gal. 6:11–18: A Hermeneutical Key to the Galatian Letter." *Calvin Theological Journal* 28 (1993): 90–107.

———. *Neglected Endings: The Significance of the Pauline Letter Closings.* Journal for the Study of the New Testament Supplement Series 101. Sheffield: Sheffield Academic Press, 1994

Welch, John W., ed. *Chiasmus in Antiquity: Structures, Analyses, Exegesis.* Hildesheim: Gerstenberg Verlag, 1981.

Wendland, Paul. *Die urchristlichen Literaturformen.* 3d ed. Handbuch zum Neuen Testament, Band 1. Tübingen: J. C. B. Mohr, 1912.

Wengst, Klaus. *Christologische Formeln und Leider des Urchristentums.* 2d ed. Studien zum Neuen Testament, Band 7. Gütersloh: Gütersloh Verlagshaus, 1972.

Weiss, Johannes. *Beiträge zur Paulinischen Rhetorik.* Göttingen: Vandenhoeck & Ruprecht, 1897.

Wheelock, Frederic M. *Latin: An Introductory Course Based on Ancient Authors.* 3d ed. New York: Barnes & Noble Books, 1963.

White, John L. *The Form and Function of the Body of the Greek Letter: A Study of the Letter-Body in the Non-Literary Papyri and in Paul the Apostle.* Society of Biblical Literature Dissertation Series 2. Missoula, Mont.: Society of Biblical Literature, 1972.

———. "Introductory Formulae in the Body of the Pauline Letter." *Journal of Biblical Literature* 90 (1971): 91–97.

———. *Light From Ancient Letters.* Foundations and Facets: New Testament. Philadelphia: Fortress Press, 1986.

———. "The Greek Documentary Letter Tradition Third Century B.C.E. to Third Century C.E." *Semeia* 22 (1981): 89–106.

Wilder, Amos N. *Early Christian Rhetoric: The Language of the Gospel.* New York: Harper & Row, 1964; reprint, Cambridge: Harvard University Press, 1971.

Wilke, C. G. *Die neutestamentliche Rhetorik: Ein Seitenstuck zur Grammatik des neutestamentlichen Sprachidioms.* Dresden and Leipzig: Arnold, 1843.

Williams, Sam K. "Again pistis Christou." *Catholic Biblical Quarterly* 49 (1987): 431–47.

———. *Galatians.* Abingdon New Testament Commentaries. Nashville: Abingdon Press, 1997.

———. "The Hearing of Faith: akoe pisteos in Galatians 3." *New Testament Studies* 35 (1989): 82–93.

———. "Justification and the Spirit in Galatians." *Journal for the Study of the New Testament* 29 (1987): 91–100.

Wise, Michael O., Martin G. Abegg and Edward M. Cook, translators. *The Dead Sea Scrolls: A New Translation.* San Francisco: Harper & Row, 1996.

Witherington, Ben. *The Christology of Jesus.* Minneapolis: Augsburg Fortress Press, 1990.

———. *Grace in Galatia: A Commentary on St. Paul's Letter to the Galatians.* Grand Rapids: Wm. B. Eerdmans Publishing Co., 1998.

Wright, N. T. "Gospel and Theology in Galatians." In *Gospel in Paul: Studies on Corinthians, Galatians and Romans for Richard N. Longenecker*. Journal for the Study of the New Testament Supplement Series 108. Sheffield: Sheffield Academic Press, 1994.

Wuellner, Wilhelm H. "Greek Rhetoric and Pauline Argumentation." In *Early Christian Literature and the Classical Intellectual Tradition: In honorem Robert M. Grant*, ed. W. R. Schoedel and R. L. Wilken, Théologie historique 53, 177–188. Paris: Éditions Beauchesne, 1979.

———. "Paul's Rhetoric of Argumentation in Romans: An Alternative to the Donfried-Karris Debate over Romans." *Catholic Biblical Quarterly* 38 (1976): 330–51.

———. "Paul as Pastor: The Function of Rhetorical Questions in First Corinthians." In *L'apôtre Paul: Personnalité, Style et Conception du Ministère*, ed. A. Vanhoye, 49–77. Bibliotheca Ephemeridum Theologicarum Lovaniensium 73. Leuven: Leuven University Press, 1986.

———. "Where is Rhetorical Criticism Taking Us," *Catholic Biblical Quarterly* 49 (1987): 448–463,

Yadin, Yigael. "Pesher Nahum (4QpNahum) Reconsidered." *Israel Exploration Journal* 21 (1971): 1–12.

Yamauchi, Edwin. "Life, Death, and the Afterlife in the Ancient Near East." In *Life in the Face of Death: The Resurrection Message of the New Testament*, ed. R. N. Longenecker, 21–50. Grand Rapids: Wm. B. Eerdmans Publishing Co., 1998.

Zahn, Theodor. *Der Brief des Paulus an die Galater*. 3d ed. Kommentar zum Neuen Testament 9. Leipzig: Deichertsche Verlagsbuchhandlung, 1922.

Zehetmeier, Josef. "Die Periodenlehre des Aristoteles." *Philologus* 83 (1930): 192–208

Zerwick, Maximilian. *Biblical Greek*. Adapted from the fourth Latin edition by Joseph Smith. Rome: Editrice Pontificio Istituto Biblico, 1963.

Zimmerli, W. "χάρις." In *Theological Dictionary of the New Testament*, ed. Gerhard Friedrich, vol. 9, 372–98. Translated by G. W. Bromiley. Grand Rapids: Wm. B. Eerdmans Publishing Co., 1974.